Adjectives and Adverbs

MW00805844

OXFORD STUDIES IN THEORETICAL LINGUISTICS

GENERAL EDITORS: David Adger, *Queen Mary College London*; Hagit Borer, *University of Southern California*.

ADVISORY EDITORS: Stephen Anderson, *Yale University*; Daniel Büring, *University of California, Los Angeles*; Nomi Erteschik-Shir, *Ben-Gurion University*; Donka Farkas, *University of California, Santa Cruz*; Angelika Kratzer, *University of Massachusetts, Amherst*; Andrew Nevins, *Harvard University*; Christopher Potts, *University of Massachusetts, Amherst*; Barry Schein, *University of Southern California*; Peter Svenonius, *University of Tromsø*; Moira Yip, *University College London*.

RECENT TITLES

PUBLISHED IN ASSOCIATION WITH THE SERIES

The Oxford Handbook of Linguistic Interfaces
edited by Gillian Ramchand and Charles Reiss

For a complete list of titles published and in preparation for the series, see pp 355–6.

Adjectives and Adverbs

Syntax, Semantics, and Discourse

Edited by
LOUISE McNALLY
and
CHRISTOPHER KENNEDY

OXFORD
UNIVERSITY PRESS

OXFORD
UNIVERSITY PRESS

Great Clarendon Street, Oxford OX2 6DP

Oxford University Press is a department of the University of Oxford.
It furthers the University's objective of excellence in research, scholarship,
and education by publishing worldwide in

Oxford New York

Auckland   Cape Town   Dar es Salaam   Hong Kong   Karachi
Kuala Lumpur   Madrid   Melbourne   Mexico City   Nairobi
New Delhi   Shanghai   Taipei   Toronto
With offices in
Argentina   Austria   Brazil   Chile   Czech Republic   France   Greece
Guatemala   Hungary   Italy   Japan   South Korea   Poland   Portugal
Singapore   Switzerland   Thailand   Turkey   Ukraine   Vietnam

Oxford is a registered trade mark of Oxford University Press
in the UK and in certain other countries

Published in the United States
by Oxford University Press Inc., New York

ISBN 978-0-19-921162-3

Printed in the United Kingdom by
Lightning Source UK Ltd., Milton Keynes

Contents

General Preface

The theoretical focus of this series is on the interfaces between subcomponents of the human grammatical system and the closely related area of the interfaces between the different subdisciplines of linguistics. The notion of 'interface' has become central in grammatical theory (for instance, in Chomsky's recent Minimalist Program) and in linguistic practice: work on the interfaces between syntax and semantics, syntax and morphology, phonology and phonetics, etc. has led to a deeper understanding of particular linguistic phenomena and of the architecture of the linguistic component of the mind/brain.

The series covers interfaces between core components of grammar, including syntax/morphology, syntax/semantics, syntax/phonology, syntax/pragmatics, morphology/phonology, phonology/phonetics, phonetics/speech processing, semantics/pragmatics, intonation/discourse structure as well as issues in the way that the systems of grammar involving these interface areas are acquired and deployed in use (including language acquisition, language dysfunction, and language processing). It demonstrates, we hope, that proper understandings of particular linguistic phenomena, languages, language groups, or inter-language variations all require reference to interfaces.

The series is open to work by linguists of all theoretical persuasions and schools of thought. A main requirement is that authors should write so as to be understood by colleagues in related subfields of linguistics and by scholars in cognate disciplines.

Adjectives and adverbs, whose primary functions are modificational rather than predicational, raise interesting challenges for specifying the nature of the interfaces between syntax, lexical and phrasal semantics, and discourse. The eleven chapters commissioned by Louise McNally and Chris Kennedy for the current volume explore the nature of adjectives and adverbs from the point of view of these different interfaces, while their introduction outlines the core empirical and theoretical issues. The authors use the specific properties of adverbs and adjectives to tackle questions about how the interfaces are to be structured so as to account for rigidity/flexibility of syntactic position within nominals, semantic gradability properties and interaction with verbal syntax, and the impact of discourse properties such as the grammatical encoding of the attitudes and identity of the interlocutors. Overall, the volume highlights the importance for the future development of grammatical theory of this class of expressions.

David Adger
Hagit Borer

Acknowledgments

The chapters in this volume are the result of a workshop on adjectives and adverbs that was held in March 2005 at Universitat Pompeu Fabra in Barcelona. We are grateful to the institutions whose financial and logistical support made that workshop possible, namely, the Departament de Traducció i Filologia, which hosted the event, the Catalan Agència de Gestió d'Ajuts a les Universitats i a la Recerca (2004 ARCS 2 00022), and the Spanish Ministerio de Educación y Ciencia (HUM2004-20136–E). The first editor would like to acknowledge a research grant from the Catalan government (Distinció de la Generalitat per a la Promoció de la Recerca Universitària, 2003–2007); the second editor would like to acknowledge the support of the National Science Foundation under Grants No. 0094263 and 0618917. Tom Rozario, Gemma Boleda, Stefan Bott, and Stella Puig-Waldmüller were a huge help with the organizational details. We would also like to thank our reviewers, who provided detailed comments on the contributions to this volume, as well as Tom Rozario (again) and Elena Castroviejo, who helped with the preparation of the final manuscript. Finally, we thank John Davey and Chloe Plummer, our editors at Oxford University Press, for their role in bringing the volume to press.

Figures and Tables

Figures

Tables

The Authors

Olivier Bonami is a lecturer in linguistics at the Université Paris-Sorbonne and a researcher at the Laboratoire de Linguistique Formelle (CNRS). His work deals with French grammar and focuses mostly on issues in inflectional morphology, the syntax–semantics interface, and the syntax–prosody interface.

Violeta Demonte is Professor of Spanish Linguistics at the Universidad Autónoma de Madrid. She has been a Visiting Researcher at MIT, at the University of Southern California, and at the University of Utrecht in the Netherlands. Her research is primarily centered in the areas of syntax and lexical semantics. Among her research topics are complement clauses, syntax and semantics of adjectives, NP structure, aspect and tense in secondary predication, and dialectal syntactic variation.

Jenny Doetjes is an associate professor in the French Department of Leiden University. She is a member of the Leiden University Centre for Linguistics and principal investigator of the research project Degrees across Categories, financed by the Netherlands Organization for Scientific Research (NWO). Until September 2005 she was appointed as a postdoctoral researcher at the Utrecht Institute for Linguistics, where she carried out a research project on focus in French.

Danièle Godard is a senior researcher at the Centre National de la Recherche Scientifique (also part of the University Paris 7). Her interests are syntax, lexical semantics, and the syntax–semantics interface, focusing on French and Romance languages. She works in the Phrase Structure framework HPSG. Among her publications are *La Syntaxe des relatives en français* (1989) and, as editor, *Les langues Romanes: problèmes de la phrase simple* (2003).

Graham Katz received his PhD in linguistics and cognitive science from the University of Rochester in 1995. He then held positions as a post-doctoral fellow and researcher at the University of Tübingen and the University of Stuttgart, where his research focused on temporal semantics, and as a lecturer in computational linguistics at the Institute for Cognitive Science of the University of Osnabrück. Since 2007 he has been on the faculty of the Department of Linguistics at Georgetown University.

Chris Kennedy is Associate Professor of Linguistics, University of Chicago. He is the author of *Projecting the Adjective: The Syntax and Semantics of Gradability and Comparison* (1999) and is co-general editor with Chris Barker of the *Oxford Surveys in Semantics and Pragmatics*. His publications and research investigate various aspects of scalar meaning and syntax, along with other topics pertaining to the syntax–semantics interface.

RICHARD LARSON is currently Professor of Linguistics at Stony Brook University. His research has examined a wide variety of topics in syntax and semantics, including relative and adverbial clauses, NP adverbs, disjunctions, prepositional phrases, double objects, and clausal complements. His current research is in two major areas: adjectival syntax and semantics and its relation to nominal structure, and the realization of semantic intensionality in grammar.

BETH LEVIN is the William H. Bonsall Professor in the Humanities at Stanford University. After receiving her PhD from MIT in 1983, she had major responsibility for the MIT Lexicon Project (1983–1987) and taught at Northwestern University (1987–1999). She is the author of *English Verb Classes and Alternations: A Preliminary Investigation* (1993) and the co-author with Malka Rappaport Hovav of *Argument Realization* (2005) and *Unaccusativity: At the Syntax–Lexical Semantics Interface* (1995).

LOUISE MCNALLY is Professor of Linguistics at Universitat Pompeu Fabra, Barcelona. She is the author of *A Semantics for the English Existential Construction* (1997) and co-editor, with Peter Culicover, of *Syntax and Semantics 29: The Limits of Syntax* (1998). Her publications include articles on various aspects of nominal and adjectival semantics, the compositional semantics of modifiers, and the semantics–pragmatics interface.

MARCIN MORZYCKI received his PhD from the University of Massachusetts, Amherst. He is now Assistant Professor of Linguistics at Michigan State University, and has held positions at Hampshire College and the University of Quebec. A major focus of his work is the grammar of modification, including empirical puzzles such as ad-adjectival adverbs, degree readings of size adjectives, manner anaphors, cross-categorial modifiers like *almost*, and measure phrases.

CHRISTOPHER PIÑÓN currently holds a position in English Linguistics at Université Charles-de-Gaulle Lille 3. Previously he was a researcher at the Research Institute for Linguistics at the Hungarian Academy of Sciences in Budapest. His research interests include the semantics of adverbs, agentivity, aspect, lexical semantics, modality, tense, and the semantics–pragmatics interface.

PETER SVENONIUS has a PhD in linguistics from the University of California at Santa Cruz and is a Professor and Senior Researcher at the Center for Advanced Study in Theoretical Linguistics at the University of Tromsø. He has written on various topics in syntax and its interfaces with semantics and with morphology, including work on Scandinavian and on other languages. He is co-editor, with Gillian Ramchand, of *The Oxford Handbook of Linguistic Interfaces*.

GINA TARANTO has a PhD from the University of California, San Diego. She has since joined the Professional Services Group at H5 in San Francisco, California, where she is Manager of Linguistic Technology.

ADAM ZACHARY WYNER received a PhD in linguistics from Cornell University in 1994 for a dissertation on the syntax and semantics of adverbial modification. From 1995 to 2001, he was a lecturer in linguistics at Bar Ilan University. He is currently completing a second PhD at King's College London in the Department of Computer Science on legal informatics. He is a research associate at the University of Liverpool on a European legal informatics project.

HIROKO YAMAKIDO earned her PhD in linguistics from Stony Brook University in 2005. She is currently an assistant professor in the Department of Chinese and Japanese at Lawrence University. Her research has concentrated on the historical and synchronic morphosyntax of Japanese nominals, including attributive adjective constructions and relative clauses. She is currently pursuing typological parallels in nominal structure between the Indo-Iranian languages and Japanese.

Abbreviations

1EZ	primary Ezafe
2EZ	secondary Ezafe
AGR	agreement
ANIM	animate
ART	article
AUX	auxiliary
CG	common ground
CL	classifier
COP	copula
CS	context set
D	Dutch
DA	degree achievement
DEF	definite
DELAT	delative case
DEM	demonstrative
DET	determiner
DRT	Discourse Representation Theory
E	English
EZ	Ezafe particle
F	French
FEM	feminine
GEN	genitive
HPSG	Head-Driven Phrase Structure Grammar
INAN	inanimate
INDEF	indefinite
MASC	masculine
NM	numeral classifier
NR	nonrestrictive
NUM	number
PERF	perfective

PL	plural
POSS	possessive
PRON	pronoun
QUD	questions under discussion
R	restrictive
RC	relative clause
REFL	reflexive
REL	relative clause marker
SG	singular

1

Introduction

LOUISE McNALLY AND CHRISTOPHER KENNEDY

Adjectives and adverbs are highly complex and significantly less studied than other major lexical categories such as nouns or verbs. The purpose of this volume is to devote some much needed attention to this complexity.

The editors of this volume are semanticists, and it is no accident that all of the chapters presented here touch on semantics in some way. Adjectives and adverbs (or perhaps more precisely, the analysis of modification) force the semanticist to confront three fundamental theoretical issues. The first involves semantic composition. Although early work in Montague semantics generally adopted the so-called "rule-to-rule" hypothesis, which involved associating pairs of syntactic structures or constituent structure rules with semantic composition rules (Bach 1976), since Klein and Sag (1985) it has been more common to assume the arguably simpler and more elegant hypothesis that semantic composition is type-driven, and that idiosyncratic semantic composition rules are not necessary: functors simply apply to their argument co-constituents.[1] As will become clear below, the semantics of modification is problematic for at least the simpler versions of type-driven translation when coupled with a simple theory of semantic types.

A second general issue raised by adjective and adverbial modification involves the amount and kind of semantic and discourse-related information that must be conventionally encoded in the lexicon – not only in the modifying expressions, but also in those modified – and how it should be encoded. For example, to mention just a few sorts of phenomena considered in this volume, issues of lexical representation and complexity arise when we try to capture semantic generalizations such as the relation between the gradability properties of adjectives and the Aktionsart of related verbs (see the chapter by

---

[1] Though see e.g. Miller (1992) for an early criticism of type-driven composition; note also that work such as Pustejovsky (1995), Farkas and de Swart (2003), and Chung and Ladusaw (2004) has revived interest in more complex semantic composition processes.

Kennedy and Levin), the similarities and differences between the gradability properties of adjectives, adverbs, verbs, and nouns (the contribution by Doetjes), or the differences between the ability of different classes of predicates to accept modification (that of Katz).

Finally, an account of the particular behavior of various semantic classes of adjectives and adverbs has implications for the theory of discourse structure. Notions familiar from descriptive grammars such as restrictive vs. nonrestrictive adjectival modification or speaker-oriented adverbial modification arguably require a semantic or discourse model which makes some sort of reference to the speech act or dialogue move being made; other phenomena point to the need to model separately the information states of the speaker and hearer. Recent work such as Ginzburg and Sag (2001), Gunlogson (2001), and Potts (2005) exemplify different approaches to enriching the representation of how utterances can modify the context; case studies involving adjectives and adverbs such as those presented in this volume can serve to evaluate and refine these approaches.

In the remainder of this chapter we first highlight some of the specific issues in the syntax, semantics, and pragmatics of adjectives and adverbs that are addressed in this volume; we then briefly introduce the individual contributions.

1.1 Syntax

The relation between the syntax and semantics of adjective and adverb phrases (APs and AdvPs, respectively) presents several puzzles, two of which we focus on here: the relation between word order and semantic type (including the ordering of stacked modifiers), and the restrictive/nonrestrictive modification distinction.

1.1.1 *Word order and semantic type*

In English and other languages with a productive category of adjectives, APs have perhaps the most varied distribution of any syntactic category. They can serve not only as primary or secondary predicates (the former, typically in conjunction with a copular verb; the latter, as arguments or adjuncts), as in (1), but also as modifiers of nominals, as in (2).[2] No other syntactic category manifests this degree of flexibility.

---

[2] We use the term "modifier" here as a convenient label for uses of APs inside nominal expressions, without any commitment as to how those APs or nominals should be analyzed.

(1) a. The students are responsible.

    b. The body shop considered the car too badly damaged to be worth repairing.

    c. The hikers arrived tired.

    d. The waiter served the dish cold.

(2) a. the responsible students

    b. the students responsible for organizing the meeting

Early formal semantic analyses of adjectives treated the category as ambiguous (see e.g. Siegel 1976 and the discussion in Dowty et al., 1981; note that there are differences of detail between the analyses in these works and the sketch presented here). Some adjectives were analyzed as properties of individuals (type $\langle e, t \rangle$, limiting ourselves to extensional types); this is particularly natural for those with predicative uses or strictly intersective interpretations.[3] Others, such as *former*, which lacks a predicative use (see (3b)), were taken to denote exclusively properties of properties (type $\langle \langle e, t \rangle, \langle e, t \rangle \rangle$).

(3) a. the former basketball player

    b. * The basketball player is/was former.

In fact, Siegel proposed that the vast majority of adjectives were ambiguous between these two types. One argument for doing so is the variation between intersective and non-intersective interpretations that many adjectives manifest. For example, *old job* does not denote the intersection of jobs and old things (cf. (4b) and the parallel examples involving *car*).

(4) a. my old job

    b. ??My job is old.

    c. my old car

    d. My car is old.

Another argument (see Dowty et al. 1981) for assigning as many adjectives as possible to the predicate modifier type, perhaps alongside a predicative type, is that doing so permits a uniform compositional semantic rule for AP–noun combinations – a generalization to the worst case that assimilates all adjectives to those like *former* and avoids having to postulate distinct rules

---

[3] A modifier is generally defined as intersective if the denotation of the modifier + modified is identical to the intersection of the set of individuals described by the modifier with the set described by the modified expression.

for the semantic composition of $\langle e, t \rangle$ and $\langle \langle e, t \rangle, \langle e, t \rangle \rangle$-type adjectives with nominals.[4]

However, Larson (1998) provides a series of arguments against this double type assignment for adjectives and in favor of analyzing as many adjectives as possible – even some ostensibly non-predicative ones such as *occasional* – exclusively as properties of individuals or events. It remains to be seen whether all adjectives can be profitably reanalyzed intersectively, but see Landman (2001) and McNally and Boleda (2004) for recent efforts in this direction. It may seem that Larson's effort to reduce complexity in the lexicon comes at the price of introducing greater complexity in the compositional system and syntax–semantics interface, as somewhat more elaborate compositional rules will be necessary to produce apparently non-intersective readings for most adjectives. However, that complexity might be necessary anyway: one compelling argument for positing two composition operations for AP–noun combinations is the fact that only APs that have predicative uses are systematically licensed as postnominal modifiers in English and the Romance languages (see e.g. the Spanish examples in (6)), suggesting that noun–AP structures can only be semantically composed via intersection.[5]

(5)   * the basketball player former

(6)   a.   los atracadores inteligentes
            "the intelligent robbers"

       b.   los supuestos atracadores
            "the alleged robbers"

       c.   * los atracadores supuestos

As suggested earlier, an idiosyncratic intersective composition rule seems like a rather glaring exception to the general possibility of type-driven composition in natural language. Is there anything that can be done to make sense out of this exception, or even to analyze it away? Though this question remains to

---

[4] For the former case, a special composition rule for the nominal would be needed which intersects the AP and noun denotations; for the latter, a typical functor-argument application rule.

[5] Of course, in English many APs do not function well as postnominal modifiers unless they are syntactically complex or modify a quantificational pronoun such as *everyone*:

(i)   *The kids tired can take a rest.
(ii) The kids tired of playing soccer can take a rest.
(iii) Everyone tired can take a rest.

But this simply means that being potentially predicative is only a necessary and not a sufficient condition for appearing in postnominal position. See Larson and Yamakido, this volume, and references cited there.

be answered, the beginning of an answer is suggested in the sort of proposal advocated by Richard Larson and Hiroko Yamakido in this volume.

As Larson and Yamakido point out, in the Montague semantic tradition, determiners are effectively treated as heads that take nouns or other property-type expressions as their arguments. Larson and Yamakido point to the existence of various kinds of special morphology on adjectives, including the Ezafe construction in Persian and determiner spreading in Modern Greek, which might be insightfully analyzed if we treat adjectives as Case-marked arguments of a determiner functor. Intriguingly, this sort of morphology only occurs on intersective adjectives. If not only the noun but also (at least in some cases) accompanying intersective adjectives in a noun phrase can be treated as arguments of the determiner, we might be able to recast what appears to be an idiosyncratic intersection of AP and noun denotations as the product of type-driven composition whose semantic details are a natural product of the semantics of the determiner.

If we limit our attention to just prenominal or postnominal position (depending on the language in question), a second puzzle quickly becomes evident: when a string of APs appear together, their order is not random, as the following examples show. In both cases, in the absence of any context the (a) examples sound much more natural than the (b) examples. We might call this problem the "stacking" problem.

(7) a. the painted wooden table

  b. the wooden painted table

(8) a. the long blue scarf

  b. the blue long scarf

The oddness of certain adjective orderings would not be surprising if the adjectives in question were not intersective, since in such cases different orders could yield different interpretations due to resulting differences in the relative scopes of the adjectives. Intersective adjectives such as those in (7) and (8), however, should not give rise to such scope differences, and thus there should be no a priori reason to prefer one adjective ordering to another, or to prefer any particular ordering of adjectives with respect to other intersective modifiers such as numerals within the nominal.[6]

Facts like these have led descriptive grammars such as Quirk et al. (1985) to propose ordering hierarchies on DP-internal adjectives, which works such as Cinque (1994) and Scott (2002) have attempted to formalize via a highly

---

[6] In fact, precisely the absence of scope interactions has been one of the arguments for treating adverbial phrases as intersective predicates of events.

articulated syntactic structure that makes reference to semantic categories as detailed as size and color. However, the viability of such a detailed structure is questioned by Bouchard (2005) and Svenonius (this volume). Bouchard, in a study of adjective ordering in French, suggests that the only ordering that can be imposed is one on which adjectives that serve to create sortal subcategories (e.g. *Mediterranean* in *Mediterranean diet*) appear closer to the head noun than those which simply add ancillary descriptive content. The facts discussed in the chapter by Svenonius suggest that the truth is somewhere in between: the constraints on adjective ordering might be more rigid than Bouchard would suggest, but less rigid than those fixed by the Quirk-type hierarchy or Cinque's or Scott's analyses.

Though the stacking problem does not arise with adverbs or AdvPs in the same way as it does with APs, adverbs certainly raise questions concerning the relation between word order and semantic type (see Jackendoff 1972, Wyner, this volume, and the many works cited in the latter). For example, manner adverbs have been classically treated as verb phrase modifiers and assigned a corresponding semantics (such as a property of events denotation), while so-called "speaker-oriented" adverbs like *fortunately* have been analyzed as sentence modifiers that denote properties of propositions. Such proposals account for the oddness out of context of e.g. (9b) in comparison to (9a).

(9)   a.   Fortunately, they did the work carefully.

     b.   ??Carefully, they did the work fortunately.

However, in fact adverbs do not have such a neat distribution: it is neither so restricted as analyses such as Jackendoff's would predict, though perhaps nor so free as might be expected by the kind of alternative proposed in Adam Wyner's contribution to this volume. The situation is thus reminiscent of the stacking problem for adjectives, but it remains to be explored to what extent the account for the one will extend to the other.

1.1.2 *Word order and restrictive vs. nonrestrictive modification*

When one begins to look in detail at adverb-ordering facts such as those in (9), a further issue arises concerning the interaction of adverb syntax and semantics. Even if both examples in (10) have a manner interpretation, (10a) has a reading that (10b) lacks: (10b) can only be true if the manner of dodging the question is part of what caused the annoyance, while that is not a requirement for the truth of (at least one reading of) (10a).

(10)   a.   The mayor's deftly dodging the question annoyed the press.

     b.   The mayor's dodging the question deftly annoyed the press.

Marcin Morzycki's contribution to this volume accounts for the contrast in (10) by proposing that the adverb in (10a) can function as a nonrestrictive modifier and thus does not contribute to the "at issue" content of the clause (in this he builds on Potts 2005; see below), while the adverb in (10b) serves as a restrictive modifier.

The restrictive/nonrestrictive distinction, more familiar from the adjective domain, is most easily perceived when the modified expression is known to have a unique referent (for example, when it is a proper name); however, such modification is very clearly marked syntactically in some languages, such as Spanish, where nonfocused, prenominal modification by intersective adjectives is always interpreted nonrestrictively (see Demonte, this volume). Contrast the unacceptable postnominal adjectival in cases where, as in (11b), the modification is intended to be nonrestrictive.[7]

(11)   a.   Nuestra presidente, la incansable Juana García, . . .

"Our president, the inexhaustible Juana García"

b.   ??Nuestra presidente, la Juana García incansable, . . .

The semantics and pragmatics of nonrestrictive adjectival modification remains a topic of debate. Potts (2005) argues for a multidimensional semantics which distinguishes "at issue" content from conventionally implicated content, with nonrestrictive modifiers falling into the latter category. In contrast, Macià (2002) and Schlenker (2007) defend the position that the kind of nonrestrictive modification illustrated in (11a) (so-called "expressives") is simply a special type of presuppositional phenomenon. Either way, however, the analysis involves positing a special relationship between syntactic structure and semantic interpretation.

1.2 Semantics

Let us leave the syntax–semantics interface and turn to semantics and the lexicon. Two fundamental questions, extensively explored in the typologically oriented literature on adjectives (e.g. Wetzer 1996; Dixon and Aikhenvald 2004) are what distinguishes adjectives from nouns and verbs, and what kinds of properties adjectives (as opposed to nouns or verbs) prototypically express. Though these questions have not received much attention in the formal linguistics literature, this is beginning to change, in part due to the fresh perspective the study of gradability can bring to these questions.

---

[7] (11b) is acceptable in a context where we distinguish between two Juana Garcías via restrictive modification by the adjective.

1.2.1 *Gradability and degree modification*

Kennedy and McNally (2005) present a typology of gradable predicates based on the properties of the scales along which these predicates order their arguments (or what we call their "scale structure"). Gradable predicates are classified along two parameters: whether the scale they use is open (lacks minimal or maximal values) or closed (has minimal or maximal values), and whether the standard of comparison for the predicate is relative (i.e. is fixed contextually) or absolute (a maximal or minimal value on the scale, irrespective of context). A typical example of an open-scale, relative adjective is *big*: the general size scale lacks an upper limit, as shown by the impossibility of combining the adjective with the degree-modifying *completely* (see Hay et al. 1999); the fact that it accepts degree modification by *very* shows, according to Kennedy and McNally, that the adjective has a relative standard.

(12)   a.   ??a completely big house

       b.   a very big house

In contrast, *undocumented* is a closed-scale, absolute adjective:

(13)   a.   a completely undocumented case

       b.   ??a very undocumented case

The case of the degree modifier *very* is interesting because its distribution is one of the classic diagnostics for distinguishing adjectives and adverbs from nouns and verbs: the former accept modification by *very* (when they meet an additional condition that Kennedy and McNally identify); the latter never do. This raises the question as to whether the distribution of *very* must make reference to both syntax and semantics, or whether the semantic condition is sufficient, with the failure of nouns and verbs to meet that condition being explainable on independent grounds. Jenny Doetjes' contribution to this volume explores precisely this kind of question.

1.2.2 *Adjective/adverb semantics and verb semantics*

Note that a strictly semantic account of the distribution of degree modifiers presupposes that not only adjectives and adverbs but also verbs and nouns must have gradability properties, since degree morphemes can occur with all grammatical categories. Though Kennedy and McNally mainly discuss adjectival predicates, they show that indeed there is a relationship between the scales with respect to which adjectives are interpreted and the semantics of the modified nominal in some cases. Doetjes (this volume) examines nominal predicates in greater detail and shows that they vary in gradability properties depending in part on whether they are count or non-count.

The relation between part structure and gradability is also observable with respect to verbs. Hay et al. (1999) and Kennedy and Levin (this volume) show how deadjectival verbs inherit the scalar properties of the adjectives from which they are derived. These scalar properties, in turn, largely determine the aspectual properties of the verb. As a general rule, adjectives with closed scales yield telic verbs, while adjectives with open scales yield atelic verbs. However, the task of establishing the precise relationship of scale structure to telicity is complicated in the case of verbs of variable telicity, as the different views expressed in Kearns (2007), Kennedy and Levin (this volume), and Piñón (this volume) show.

A careful consideration of the gradability properties of verbs can lead to other kinds of insights into verb semantics. Katz (this volume) maintains that stative verbs differ from non-stative verbs in not allowing true manner modification, and uses this observation to support a classical Davidsonian treatment of stative verbs on which they contrast with non-stative verbs in lacking an eventuality argument. However, this claim faces a number of apparent counterexamples in which stative verbs do appear with what appear to be manner adverbials, such as *to know well*. Katz argues that most such counterexamples in fact involve not manner modification but rather a special kind of degree modification. In addition to its implications for verb semantics, this work points to the need to explore further the lexical semantics of a whole family of adverbs such as *well* which manifest characteristics of both manner and degree modifiers.

1.3 Discourse

As the body of descriptive work on the lexical semantics of adjectives and adverbs grows, we learn more about how these expressions interact with the discourse context. Adjectives and adverbs differ substantially from nouns and verbs in their sensitivity to the speaker and in their ability to carry out metalinguistic or metadiscoursal functions. This difference is immediately evident in descriptive grammatical classifications of adverbs such as "connective," "evaluation," or "speech-act related" (Huddleston and Pullum 2002). However, there are less obvious manifestions of discourse sensitivity as well. For example, Barker (2002) argues that one of the main effects of the use of a gradable adjective is to clarify what constitutes the standard for truthful application of that adjective in a given context. That is, asserting that someone is tall can tell us something not only about the individual's height but also about what counts as tall. Moreover, Barker argues that adjectives such as *stupid* when accompanied by an infinitival complement, as in (14), have only this function.

(14)   Feynman is stupid to dance like that.

Taranto (this volume) makes a similar claim about adjectives such as *clear*, namely that their contribution to the discourse is fundamentally that of helping to synchronize the common ground by establishing which propositions are or should be evident to the conversation participants versus subject to differences of opinion.

Adverbs manifest much more heterogeneous interactions with discourse. Perhaps the best studied of these is the behavior of focus adverbs (e.g. Rooth 1985). However, the recent development of interest in incorporating speech act theory and the theory of implicature into formal semantics (e.g. Ginzburg and Sag 2001, Gunlogson 2001, Potts 2005) has turned attention particularly to those adverbs which contribute information about the speaker's attitude towards the proposition expressed; the contribution by Olivier Bonami and Danièle Godard is an example of such work.

The special behavior of adjectives and adverbs in discourse is still a very new area of study which promises to contribute significantly to our understanding of how to model discourse and how language (and speakers) exploit discourse structure.

1.4 The chapters in this volume

The first four chapters in the volume address the general question of how the syntax of adjectives and adverbs is related to their semantics.

Peter Svenonius' contribution, "The position of adjectives and other phrasal modifiers in the decomposition of DP," examines within-language and cross-linguistic generalizations concerning word order in DP. The work situates adjectives within a general theory of the structure of DP which accounts for the range of typological variation in the distribution of articles, numerals, plural marking, demonstratives, and adjectives. Svenonius then assesses the utility of a highly articulated syntactic structure in accounting for attested restrictions on adjective ordering and argues that such structure is only useful insofar as it reflects semantic properties consistently associated with APs in certain positions, and eschews it when it is made to reflect highly idiosyncratic lexical semantic facts. For example, he postulates functional projections for APs which are focused or which serve to subclassify (as opposed to simply describe) the individuals denoted by the modified noun, but rejects the use of functional projections to account for generalizations (insofar as they exist) such as the preference in English to order adjectives of size before those expressing color. Svenonius' work thus presents a principled and elegant criterion for when to use functional structure vs. other sorts of theoretical tools to explain word order facts.

Richard Larson and Hiroko Yamakido ("Ezafe and the deep position of nominal modifiers") examine so-called "Ezafe" marking on APs and other nominal modifiers in Modern Persian and Indo-Iranian languages, and argue that this marking supports an analysis of nominal modifiers as complements to D. Though in some respects this represents a radical departure from the standard syntactic analysis of these expressions, Larson and Yamakido observe that the proposal is semantically well grounded in Generalized Quantifier theory (Barwise and Cooper 1981) and allows for a very natural treatment of Ezafe as a kind of Case marking which licenses nominal modifiers in postnominal positions they would otherwise be unable to occupy. Larson and Yamakido suggest extending this Case marker analysis of Ezafe to similar phenomena in unrelated languages, including determiner spreading in Modern Greek, thus bringing a new perspective to a set of data which is otherwise quite puzzling given standard theoretical assumptions.

In "Meaning–form correlations and adjective position in Spanish," Violeta Demonte explores the relationship between the position of adjectives within DP in Spanish and their interpretation. Specifically, after providing a review of the distinctive properties of a comprehensive set of adjective classes in Spanish, she shows how these classes can be grouped into those whose members are non-predicative (and denote functions from properties to properties) vs. predicative (and denote properties of individuals); this latter class, in turn, can be further divided into those adjectives which are interpreted restrictively vs. nonrestrictively. Once the special case of focused adjectives is taken into account, this tripartite classification provides for an elegant account of facts which at first sight appear to defy any generalization about the syntax–semantics interface. Demonte then argues that these three classes combine in the syntax via (respectively) the operations Pair-Merge, external Merge, and internal Merge in the framework of Chomsky (2001a, b). The chapter by Demonte offers an example of how an independently motivated syntactic proposal can point the way towards a better semantic analysis.

Marcin Morzycki's contribution ("Nonrestrictive modifiers in non-parenthetical positions"), like Demonte's, is concerned with nonrestrictive modification, but in this case by adverbs rather than by adjectives. Morzycki begins by distinguishing restrictive vs. nonrestrictive readings of adverbs in English; he then shows that nonrestrictive readings are identified exclusively with preverbal position. Finally, he proposes a semantic analysis for the nonrestrictive readings based on Potts' 2005 "multidimensional" analysis of parentheticals: a semantic rule which is sensitive to linear order and composes nonrestrictive modifiers not as part of the main propositional content of the clause but rather as conventionally implicated content. Morzycki ends his contribution with the observation that order-sensitive semantic composition rules are not the norm. Note also the contrast between the English adverb facts and the Spanish adjective data discussed in Demonte's contribution: In Spanish, nonrestrictive readings are available for both pre- and postnominal adjectives; what is excluded is a restrictive reading for predicative adjectives in prenominal position. Altogether, the facts and the proposed analysis point to questions for future research: might recourse to an order-specific rule be avoided? And to what extent might a strict link be maintained between a semantic rule such as the one Morzycki proposes and the syntactic rule of internal Merge proposed by Demonte for nonrestrictive adjectival modifiers?

The subsequent four chapters in the volume are primarily concerned with lexical semantic issues. In "Adjectives and degree modification," Jenny Doetjes, like other contributors to the volume, integrates theory and detailed descriptive work. She uses the distribution of different classes of degree modifiers with different types of gradable expressions (adjectives, verbs, and nouns) as a probe on how best to understand and represent gradability semantically. She argues that gradable expressions form a continuum with adjectives at one extreme and plural (count) nouns at the other. This cross-categorial manifestation of gradability naturally raises the question of whether a degree argument should be postulated just for some gradable expressions (adjectives only, as has been commonly proposed since Seuren 1973, or adjectives plus the most adjective-like verbs), or for all gradable expressions. After considering the pros and cons of these various options for the purposes of explaining the distribution of degree modifiers, Doetjes suggests that the key to understanding the facts lies as much as or more in the nature of the scales associated with each type of expression: adjectives are special in being the only type of gradable expression consistently associated with scales whose standards are determined relative to a comparison class.

The relationship between gradability in the adjectival and verbal domain is also the subject of Christopher Kennedy and Beth Levin's contribution ("Measure of change: The adjectival core of degree achievements"). As mentioned above, in earlier work (Hay et al. 1999) they proposed that the telicity properties of so-called degree achievement verbs such as *to cool* (Dowty 1979), which are generally deadjectival, can be explained as a consequence of the different scale structures associated with the adjectives from which the verbs derive. However, their earlier proposal was subject to various criticisms (see e.g. Kearns 2007; Piñón, this volume) to which the present work responds. Kennedy and Levin propose that the derivation of verbs from adjectives is accompanied semantically by the introduction of what they term a "measure of change" function that turns the measure function on individuals denoted by the adjective into one that takes an individual and an event as arguments and returns the degree that represents the amount that the individual changes in the property measured by the adjective as a result of participating in the event. The chapter closes by suggesting that this analysis of degree achievements could form the basis for an analysis of other classes of verbs with variable telicity.

In his chapter ("Aspectual composition with degrees"), Christopher Piñón addresses precisely this question, and concludes that the degree-based analysis of variable telicity proposed in Kennedy and Levin's earlier work on degree achievements (Hay et al. 1999 and Kennedy and Levin 2002), as well as a related proposal by Caudal and Nicolas (2005), is insufficient as a fully general, compositional account of aspectual composition. Focusing on the case of "incremental theme verbs" like *eat*, *read*, and so forth, Piñón discusses a number of problems with the earlier degree-based analyses, central of which is the lack of an explicit account of the role of nominal reference in determining telicity: why a quantized object results in a telic event description (*eat an apple in ten minutes*) while a cumulative object derives an atelic one (*eat applesauce for ten minutes*). Piñón's proposal retains the underlying intuitions of the earlier accounts – that the semantics of verbs that show variable telicity involves a measure of the degree to which the affected object changes in some gradable property as a result of participation in the event – but differs crucially in its characterization of what exactly gets measured. Instead of measuring a "bare individual," verbs of gradual change – which denote what Piñón calls *incremental degree functions* – measure the degree to which an individual *as an individual of type O* changes, where *O* is the descriptive content of the incremental theme argument. Piñón provides an axiomatic treatment of aspectual composition based on this proposal and shows how it accounts for the relation between nominal and verbal reference.

Finally, Graham Katz ("Manner modification of state verbs") addresses a puzzle concerning the lexical semantics of manner adverbs, specifically, the ostensible inability of such adverbs to modify stative predicates. Katz argues that the modification facts constitute a strong argument against postulating a Parsonsian state variable in the logical representation of such predicates, contra Landman (2000) and Mittwoch (2005). In order for the argumentation to go through, Katz defends the position that the putative cases of manner modification brought to bear on the issue by Landman and Mittwoch (such as *to love passionately*) are only apparent, and can be instead reduced to one of three alternative kinds of modification: degree modification, idiomatic collocations (such as *to love deeply*), and what he terms "event-related" uses, on which the adverb describes not the state directly but rather an event which supports the existence of the state. Like the chapters by Doetjes, Kennedy and Levin, and Piñón, Katz's contribution offers yet another example of how a careful study of modification can provide insight into the basic lexical semantic properties of the modified expressions.

The remaining three chapters in the volume deal with aspects of the syntax and semantics of adjectives and adverbs that interact with facts about the discourse context. Each chapter takes as its starting point a case study in one or more classes of adjectives or adverbs, the analysis of which has implications for a general, integrated theory of the syntax, semantics, and pragmatics of the lexical categories in question.

Adam Wyner's contribution ("Towards flexible types with constraints for manner and factive adverbs") contrasts two approaches to the syntax and semantics of adverbs: what he terms the "fixed types" theory, on which the syntactic category and semantic type of an adverb are held to be unvarying, versus the so-called "flexible types" theory, on which any given adverb is allowed to range over a set of syntactic and semantic types. The former has problems accounting for the relative flexibility of adverb distribution without recourse to syntactic operations such as movement; the latter obviously runs the risk of making excessively weak predictions concerning that distribution. After reviewing some basic arguments for and against each type of approach, Wyner turns to establishing certain parallelisms between the conditions governing intersentential anaphora involving VPs and clauses and those governing the distribution and interpretation of factive and manner adverbs (such as *stupidly* and *quickly*, respectively). Wyner argues that a flexible types analysis for these adverbs can account for this parallelism, while a fixed types analysis cannot, thus showing how facts about the discourse context can be brought to bear on decisions about the syntax and semantics of adverbs.

In "Lexical semantics and pragmatics of evaluative adverbs," Olivier Bonami and Danièle Godard provide a new semantic and pragmatic analysis of what they term "evaluative" adverbs such as *unfortunately* and *strangely*. These adverbs have various distinguishing semantic and pragmatic properties; for example, they have been argued to make a contribution to the discourse which is independent of the main assertion of the clause in which they appear (see e.g. Bartsch 1976). Bonami and Godard discuss these properties, relate them to the semantics of the adjectives from which these adverbs derive, and argue against previous accounts of evaluatives on which they denote properties of facts, where facts are given a special ontological status distinct from propositions. As an alternative, Bonami and Godard propose a strictly pragmatic analysis of evaluatives on which they denote properties of propositions (like other sentential adverbs, they argue), but introduce a specific kind of dialogue move, which the authors term "ancillary commitment." Bonami and Godard's analysis thus seeks to maintain a simpler natural language ontology and greater uniformity in the lexical semantics of adverbs by placing some of the burden of explanation for the behavior of adverbs on an arguably independently necessary model of dialogue.

The volume closes with Gina Taranto's contribution, "Discourse adjectives," a study of the natural class of adjectives that includes *apparent, clear, evident,* and *obvious*. Taranto presents the distinctive syntactic and semantic characteristics of this class and proceeds to an analysis whose goal is to account for their apparent factivity and to explain the peculiar way in which these adjectives contribute informatively to discourse. Specifically, she argues that they fulfill an essentially metalinguistic function of helping to synchronize the common ground of the conversation. Taranto also discusses the consequences of the analysis for a theory of discourse and concludes on the basis of the facts that the discourse model must include a representation both of the conversation taking place (see Stalnaker 1998) and of the individual public and private commitments of the conversation participants (Gunlogson 2001).

2

The position of adjectives and other phrasal modifiers in the decomposition of DP

PETER SVENONIUS

2.1 Introduction

Patterns in adjective ordering have long been noted, and have been characterized in impressionistic semantic terms: "inherent" properties are expressed closer to the noun (Whorf 1945), or "objective" properties are (Hetzron 1978). Such characterizations have proven difficult to evaluate, but cross-linguistic examinations regularly show that similar patterns hold across languages to a striking degree (e.g. Sproat and Shih 1991). Cinque (1994) suggests that these orders can be captured in terms of a layered functional structure in the DP: different layers of nominal structure correspond to the attachment sites of different categories of adjective. Scott (2002) and Laenzlinger (2005) expand on Cinque's hierarchy of nominal functional projections with this aim in mind.

At the same time, expansions of DP-internal functional structure have been undertaken on independent grounds, for example by Vangsnes (1999); Zamparelli (2000); Rijkhoff (2002); Borer (2005a); Julien (2005) and others.

An important question is to what extent the decomposition of DP motivated by the order of adjectives matches the decomposition of DP motivated on independent grounds. In this article, I examine three different pieces of evidence concerning functional structure in the DP: the relative order of head-like elements such as articles, plural markers, and the noun; the relative order of phrasal modifiers such as adjectives, numerals, and (arguably) demonstratives; and the semantic arguments for layered structures put forth by Zamparelli (2000), Rijkhoff (2002), and others.

Overall, the independently motivated structures for DP decomposition do not provide the kind of fine-grained differentiation suggested by, for example, Scott (2002) for adjectival ordering (where, e.g., "length," "height," "depth," and "width" are all distinguished). However, they do provide a basic framework which, I suggest, goes a long way toward explaining the cross-linguistically valid generalizations that can be made regarding the order of attributive adjectives.

A side issue which is necessarily taken up in the course of this discussion is that of the order of DP-internal elements more broadly. In principle, there are three different factors which can affect word order: the basic hierarchical structure (which I assume is determined by something roughly like function–argument semantics), the order in which the function and the argument linearize when they combine, and movement. The first factor is generally taken to be invariant. Kayne (1994) has proposed essentially that the second factor is invariant as well, leaving movement as the only important factor in word order variation across languages.

To be plausible, this requires several additional assumptions. Consider, for example, the possibility that attributive adjectives attach inside DP in a way different from that of relative clauses. A language might exclusively rely on the relative clause strategy or the attributive strategy for modifying noun phrases, leading to a superficial difference between two languages which is not due to movement, but to facts about the inventories of functional items employed in the two languages, for example one has no relative head, or the other has no head that can be used to construct attributive adjectives.

In this chapter I outline such a model of cross-linguistic word order variation, concentrating on the noun phrase. Order in the noun phrase is in some ways easier to compare cross-linguistically than order in the clause, because fewer information-structural devices are employed (as noted by Cinque 2005).

The structure of the remainder of this chapter is as follows. To identify the functional structure in the noun phrase, I first examine articles and plural markers, which are attested in enough languages to give a good impression of the overall patterns possible. Then I examine some other categories that tend to be realized morphologically in the noun phrase, to give a fuller picture of the basic functional skeleton.

I then turn to the phrasal modifiers in DP, namely demonstratives, numerals, and adjectives, the ordering of which is famously characterized in Greenberg's (1963) *Universal 20*. Finally, the relative order of adjectives is discussed, completing the sketch of the functional structure of the noun phrase.

This sets the stage for the subsequent discussion of word order possibilities cross-linguistically and how to derive them. I argue that the order of adjectives can be understood as derivative of the order of the functional material and the fact that in some languages, the functional heads in the nominal projections form clusters (along lines developed in Svenonius 2007).

2.2 Mirror in nominal morphology

Many languages have articles which express definiteness, specificity, or indefiniteness (cf. Dryer 1989b). Another piece of nominal functional structure which is found in many languages is some overt marker of plurality (sometimes also duality or paucality; see Delfitto and Schroten 1991; Borer 2005a). If we compare the relative order of these markers across languages, the order Art > Pl > N emerges as the most plausible underlying hierarchy; some examples of Art–Pl–N order are provided in (1) (the glosses DEF, ART, and INDEF are retained from the original sources).

(1)   a.   hun-lii-štạan
           DEF-PL-armadillo
           "the armadillos"   (Misantla Totonac, from MacKay 1999: 312)

      b.   o   bi gotta
           ART PL tree
           "trees"   (Galela, from Rijkhoff 2002: 110)

      c.   ha   fanga pulu
           INDEF PL   COW
           "some cows"   (Tongan, Dryer 1989a: 875)

In many cases, prenominal articles and plural markers are not strictly adjacent to the noun (cf. Dryer 1989a), permitting adjectives and numerals, for instance, to intervene.

Another relatively common order is that in which the article precedes, but the plural marker follows, the noun (English is such a language). Some examples are given in (2).

(2)   a.   he pi'   miš̃ ʔaHkš̃
           the little boy PL
           "the little boys"   (Mixe, from Dryer 1989a: 875)

      b.   à-jɣab-c°a
           ART-girl-PL
           "the girls"   (Abkhaz, from Rijkhoff 2002: 79)

c. in coyō-meh
    the coyote-PL
    "the coyotes"   (Nahuatl, cf. Andrews 1975)

In these cases, the article is often separable from the noun by adjectives and other material, but the plural marker more rarely so; this suggests that N–Pl order may be the result of some kind of cluster formation (for discussion of cluster formation in the derivation of such orders see Svenonius 2007).

Finally, there are many examples of "mirror" order (the reverse of Art–Pl–N), in which N precedes Pl and both precede Art. These very often show cluster effects, with the three elements not allowing interruption by adjectives or other phrasal material.

(3) a. dàr-ì-dé
         gun-PL-DEF
         "the guns"   (Kotoko)

     b. säw-occ-u
         man-PL-DEF
         "the men"   (Amharic)

     c. hest-ar-nir
         horse-PL-DEF
         "the horses"   (Icelandic)

There are also cases in which articles are reported to appear inside plural markers. Under closer investigation, these seem to fall into two types: those in which the morpheme appearing closer to the noun than the plural is not actually an article, and those in which there is evidence for movement. I briefly describe one example of each type.

Basque is a language that is sometimes described as having an article inside the plural marker, as in *gizon-a-k* "man-DET-PL." However, the morpheme in question does not signal the semantic effects associated with articles; it is used, for example, on nouns in existential contexts (examples from Hualde and Ortiz de Urbina 2003: 120).

(4) a. Zigarro-a   nahi dut.
         cigarette-DET want AUX
         "I want a cigarette."

     b. Lekuederr-a-k   daude Bizkaian.
         beautiful.place-DET-PL are   Bizkaia.LOC
         "There are beautiful places in Bizkaia."

Thus the Basque suffix -*a* does not satisfy the usual criteria for an article. I will continue to assume that morphemes that consistently mark specificity or definiteness (including those which mark noun phrases as non-specific or indefinite) are articles, hierarchically located above plural markers.

Gungbe is a language which does exhibit the order N–Art–Pl (two different articles are illustrated here, from Aboh 2004: 77).

(5) a. távò ló
         table the
         "the specific table"

     b. távò ló lɛ́
         table the PL
         "the specific tables"

     c. távò ɖé lɛ́
         table DET PL
         "some specific tables"

Aboh argues that there is phrasal movement across Art. The projection of N which moves carries with it all modifiers and dependents of N (Aboh 2004: 78, 90).

(6) a. távò ɖàxó xóxó àtɔ̀n éhé ló lɛ́
         table big old three DEM the PL
         "these specific three big old tables"

     b. àgásá sín fɛ̀n   ɖàxó àtɔ̀n éhé ló lɛ́
         crab POSS pincer big three DEM the PL
         "these specific three big crabs' pincers"

Aboh develops a detailed roll-up analysis of the word order here, with the N moving first to the left of the adjective, the N–A sequence moving to the left of the Numeral, the N–A–Num sequence moving to the left of the Demonstrative, and the N–A–Num–Dem sequence crossing the plural marker and the article.

Thus, the order of morphemes cross-linguistically is compatible with the basic hierarchy Article > Plural > Noun, with a cluster formation rule (essentially like head movement) forming N–Pl and N–Pl–Art clusters in some languages, and more rarely, phrasal movement leading to other orders.

2.3 Classifiers

Many languages have head-like elements in the DP which are called "classifiers" (cf. Aikhenvald 2000 for an overview). These show a range of uses, from determiner-like (cf. Cheng and Sybesma 1999 on Chinese) to being involved in enumeration, quantification, or division of masses (Borer 2005a) and other functions.[1] Classifiers often serve two or more of these functions simultaneously and are often furthermore in complementary distribution with determiners or plural markers, making general statements about relative order difficult, but some generalizations emerge.

For example, the most typical classifier sorts nominal referents by characteristics such as shape (a "sortal" classifier), and makes them countable or quantifiable (a "numeral" classifier). Grinevald (2000) in particular argues that it is typical of numeral classifiers that they sort by shape. But a few languages differentiate the two functions, in which case the numeral classifier can be seen to be outside the sortal classifier, as in the Mayan language Akatek as described by Zavala (2000) (exx. here from his pp. 117 and 123).

(7) a. kaa-b'   sulan   aw-aan
         two-INAN SMOOTH A2-corncob
         "your two corncobs"

     b. 'ox-eb'   jilan   'aan
         three-INAN LONG.3D corncob
         "three corncobs"

     c. kaa-b'   b'ilan   poon yalixh-taj
         two-INAN SMALL.ROUND plum small-PL
         "two small plums"

Numeral classifiers in this language distinguish human, animal, and inanimate nouns (here only the inanimate one is shown). The sortal classifier distinguishes a dozen or more shapes ("smooth," "long three-dimensional," "erect," "half-circle," "round," "wide flat," "small spherical," "separate," etc.). Note in (7a–b) that the same noun can appear with different classifiers, depending on how the referent is perceived.

A third important type of classifier is the noun classifier, which typically sorts nouns by material qualities or essences (see Craig 1986, Grinevald 2000). These sometimes cooccur with sortal or numeral classifiers, and again, Akatek provides an example of cooccurrence. Akatek has a set of fourteen noun

---

[1] On the distinction between classifiers and markers of noun class or gender like the nominal prefixes of the Bantu languages, cf. e.g. Heine (1982), Dixon (1986).

classifiers ("man," "woman," "animal," "tree," "corn," "water," "salt," etc.) alongside the three numeral classifiers and the set of sortal classifiers. All three types are illustrated in (8) (adapted from Zavala 2000: 126–127).[2]

(8) a. 'ox-k'on   kupan   no'   wakax
        three-ANIM HALF.CIRCLE ANIMAL COW
        "three cows' (lying down)

    b. 'ox-eb'   kupan   'ixim paat
        three-INAN HALF.CIRCLE CORN tortilla
        "three (folded) tortillas"

    c. 'ox-eb'   xoyan 'ixim paat
        three-INAN ROUND CORN tortilla
        "three tortillas"

Noun classifier systems may resemble gender systems, in that a noun may be conventionally associated with a single noun classifier, and may develop into gender systems (Greenberg 1978, Corbett 1991). It is sometimes argued that nominal gender corresponds to a functional projection (cf. e.g. Spanish *abuelo* 'grandfather' ~ *abuela* 'grandmother' or *monje* 'monk' ~ *monja* 'nun'; cf. Ritter 1993 for references and a dissenting view). If so, it is clear that it is lower than number (cf. e.g. *abuelas* 'grandmothers' etc.).

In general, if a language has plural markers it does not have classifiers, and vice versa (see Borer 2005a: ch. 4 for references and discussion). In some languages, there are plural markers for animate nouns but classifiers for inanimates. In Akatek, the numeral classifier for inanimates, *eb'* (cf. 8b–c), is also used as a separate plural marker for human plurals, and may cooccur not only with numeral classifiers but also with noun classifiers, as in (9a–b) (Zavala 2000: 122–123; again, I have isolated noun phrases from sentences in context; see Zavala's paper for original sentences).

(9) a. kaa-wan   eb' naj winaj
        two-HUMAN PL MAN man
        "two men"

    b. 'ox-wan   eb' 'ix   'ix
        three-HUMAN PL WOMAN woman
        "three women"

---

[2] Zavala gives sentences from which I have isolated just the noun phrases; in each sentence, an existential predicate ("there is") precedes the noun phrase, and an adjectival predicate ("lying down" or "round") follows.

Nor is Akatek the only language in which a plural marker may cooccur with a numeral classifier. Allan (1977: 294) gives the following examples from Yucatec Mayan and Ojibway, respectively. In the Mayan example, the plural marker is optional, but in the Ojibway example, it has a semantic effect.

(10) a. oš   tul   maak   ~ oš   tul   maak-oob
         three ANIM person   three ANIM person-PL
         "three people' ~ "three people"

      b. nīšw-āttik kīšikk ~ nīšw-āttik kīšikk-ak
         two-STICK cedar   two-STICK cedar-PL
         "two pieces of cedar" ~ "two poles of cedar"

On the basis of these considerations, three levels of classifier can be identified; I will refer to the numeral classifier as UNIT, as this is the unit which is counted (it can be equated with Borer's 2005a #), and to the sortal classifier as SORT (like Borer's *Cl*); and I will refer to the noun classifier as *n*, following the discussion in Marantz (2001) of the nature of nominalizing affixes on roots.

In sum, the following hierarchy of classifier types can be discerned, though it should be stressed that most classifier languages have just one which spans two or more of these properties, as argued by Borer (2005a):[3]

(11)   UNIT > SORT > *n*

Putting these together with the Art > Pl > N hierarchy from section 2.2, it is relatively clear that Art is above these classifiers, while N is below. The exact position of Pl is partly a matter of guesswork due to the scarcity of clear cooccurrences, but the following seems to be a plausible hypothesis:

(12)   Art > UNIT > Pl/SORT > *n* > N

The category Pl/SORT suggests that those cases in which plurals are noted to cooccur with classifiers have involved either UNIT classifiers or noun classifiers, not SORT classifiers. It has repeatedly been argued that classifiers exist to individuate masses for quantification and counting (cf. in particular Borer 2005a).

At this juncture I leave these categories and turn to phrasal dependents in the DP, namely demonstratives, numerals, and adjectives.

---

[3] It should be noted that Grinevald (2000) argues for an additional type, the genitive classifier, which she argues is function-based (vehicle, edible, artifact, etc.) and is higher than the numeral classifier.

2.4 Greenberg's Universal 20

Greenberg's (1963) Universal 20 is stated as follows:

(13)   **Universal 20:** When any or all of the elements (demonstrative, numeral, and descriptive adjective) precede the noun, they are always found in that order. If they follow, the order is either the same or its exact opposite.

Subsequent work has confirmed the essentials of this observation (Hawkins 1983; Dryer 1992; Cinque 2005), though the order N–Dem–Num–A turns out not to be terribly common. The most common orders are apparently the following (judging from Hawkins 1983; Cinque 2005; and searches in the *World Atlas of Linguistic Structures*, Haspelmath et al. 2005):

(14)   a.   Dem Num Adj N

      b.   Dem Num N Adj

      c.   Dem N Adj Num

      d.   N Adj Num Dem

      e.   Num N Adj Dem

The most common orders are N-initial and N-final ones (273 languages in Haspelmath et al. 2005 have N preceding all of Dem, Num, and Adj, while another 191 have N following all three). The other three orders listed in (14) are about equally common (between fifty and seventy-five languages each in Haspelmath et al. 2005). No other orders are at all common.[4]

If we take as the null hypothesis that the most common order of phrasal elements directly reflects the underlying universal hierarchy, the hierarchy is Dem > Num > Adj > N. The order in (14b) is simply derived by moving N to the left of Adj. The order in (14c) is derived by combining that step with an additional step moving the [N–Adj] sequence across Num. And the order in (14d) involves yet another step, moving [[N–Adj]–Num] across Dem. Cinque (2005) notes that N-raising orders are all attested, for example Dem–N–Num–A, in which the N moves across the Num and A.

---

[4] Haspelmath et al. (2005) give the relative order of the noun and each dependent; thus, it can be determined, for example, that sixty-nine languages have Numeral before Noun, and Noun before both Adjective and Demonstrative; the database itself does not indicate how many of these sixty-nine are Num-N-Adj-Dem and how many are Num-N-Dem-Adj. Independent investigation shows that the former is much more common than the latter. See for example Hawkins (1983: 119), who lists seven Num-N-Adj-Dem languages and no Num-N-Dem-Adj ones. For a detailed analysis of this order in Semitic languages see Shlonsky (2004).

2.4.1 *Combining Dem–Num–Adj with Art–Pl–N*

How do these orders relate to the order of Art and Pl and N discussed in section 2.2, and to the order of classifiers discussed in section 2.3? I suggest that Dem, Num, and Adj are generally to be thought of as phrasal modifiers of functional projections in the DP. Demonstratives may lexicalize to D heads, and the numeral "one" in particular often seems to lexicalize as a head. Adjectival elements may also sometimes directly represent heads in the extended projection of N. But in the general case, a demonstrative can be thought of as modifying a DP, while a numeral can be thought of as modifying a PlP, and a typical adjective can be thought of as modifying an NP.

This would give an order something like Dem > Art > Num > Pl > Adj > N. The surface word order, however, is complicated by the facts of cluster formation; specifically, the tendency of heads like Pl to form a morphological cluster with N changes the linear order with respect to phrasal modifiers like adjectives. Despite such complications, a pattern like the expected one can be discerned. For example, in Rijkhoff's (2002) balanced survey of eighty-five languages, six allow Demonstrative to cooccur with an article; in three of those, the order is as given in (15a), and in three others it is as in (15b).

(15)   a.   Dem–Art–N: Abkhaz, Guaraní, Hungarian

       b.   Art–N–Dem: Berbice Dutch Creole, Galela, Samoan

A couple of illustrations are given in example (16).

(16)   a.   wɔy   á-jɣab
            that.one ART-girl
            "that girl"   (Abkhaz, Rijkhoff 2002: 183)

       b.   o   tahu manèna
            ART house this
            "this house"   (Galela, Rijkhoff 2002: 184)

Most typically, definite articles are in complementary distribution with demonstratives. According to Rijkhoff, four of the six languages which allow cooccurrence have a "stage II" article, in the sense of Greenberg (1978), that is not associated with definiteness, but with specificity.[5]

---

[5] Greenberg's four stages of the development of a demonstrative into a gender or noun marker are as follows:

(i)   a.   Stage 0: Demonstrative
      b.   Stage I: Definiteness
      c.   Stage II: Specificity
      d.   Stage III: Gender/Class or Noun Marker

However, Hungarian and Berbice Dutch Creole have definite articles which cooccur with the demonstrative.

(17) a. Az-t   a   filme-t   akarom megnézni.
          that-ACC the film-ACC I.want   watch
          "I want to watch that film."

      b. Azok-ról   az emberek-ről beszéltünk.
          those-DELAT the people-DELAT we.talked
          "We were talking about those people."   (Hungarian)

On the basis of these observations, I conclude that demonstratives are basically higher than articles (cf. also Julien 2005), but in languages like Galela (illustrated in (16b)) the [Art–N] sequence moves to the left of the demonstrative. It remains to be investigated what drives this movement, but it might be triggered by a requirement for N–Dem adjacency.[6]

Similarly, the order Num > Pl can be discerned in the typological data, in that a numeral is normally further from the noun stem than is plural marking, and in those cases where it is not, as in Gungbe (discussed above, §2.2), there are reasons to think that movement has occurred.

The relative position of Adjectives with respect to the Art–Pl–N hierarchy is the most difficult question. Clearly, most adjectives are lower than Art; rare cases of gradable descriptive adjectives higher than articles clearly involve movement (as in *how big a house*, with the *wh*-operator *how*). I will return to the question of the relative order of adjectives and plural markers, but for now will assume that adjectives are ordinarily below the plural. This gives a preliminary hierarchy as follows:

(18)   Dem > Art > Num > Pl > Adj > N

The categories which I have assumed are phrasal are interleaved with the categories which I have assumed are heads.[7]

---

[6] Brugè (2002) argues that demonstratives originate low and move to SpecDP. However, this is hard to reconcile with Greenberg's Universal 20. Most of Brugè's arguments are equally consistent with movement of a phrasal projection of N to the left of the demonstrative. Thanks to Klaus Abels and David Adger for discussion.

[7] There are interesting issues regarding head versus phrasal status of these elements; see, for example Bernstein (1993) for arguments that some attributive adjectives are heads, Svenonius (1994) for arguments that most attributive adjectives must be phrases, Sadler and Arnold (1994) for the suggestion that they must have a status in between phrase and head, and Starke (2004) for the claim that the distinction does not exist. I will continue to assume that there is a distinction and that attributive adjectives, in general, are phrasal, along with numerals (see Ionin and Matushansky 2005) and possibly demonstratives, though it seems likely that at least the latter are often recategorized as heads.

2.4.2 *Combining Dem–Num–Adj with* UNIT, SORT, *and* n

Turning to the classifiers, it is clear that the UNIT classifier is below numerals; it is presumably the same category identified by Szabolcsi (1994) as *Num*[ber], by Julien (2005) as *Card*[inality], or by Schwarzschild (2006) as *Mon*[otonicity]. Word order facts suggest that the UNIT classifier is above adjectives (see below). The *n*, on the other hand is lower, just above N; it comes close to being a gender or noun class marker (compare also Truswell's 2004 category *Same*). As suggested in section 2.3, SORT can probably be conflated with Pl; it can be compared with Delfitto and Schroten's (1991) treatment of the plural marker, or Borer's (2005a) *Cl*[assifier]. This gives an extended hierarchy as in (19):

(19)   Dem > Art > Num > UNIT > Pl/SORT > Adj > *n* > N

Muromatsu (2001) argues, in effect, that adjectives can be split into two classes, those which are sensitive to shape and merge above classifiers (here, SORT classifiers) and those which are not sensitive to shape and merge below. I will argue below for the same conclusion, and furthermore that adjectives can appear not only above and below Pl/SORT but also above and below *n*. For example, although in general adjectives follow classifiers in Chinese, certain adjectives can precede certain classifiers (examples from Cheng and Sybesma 1999: 516).

(20)   a.   yi   zhi da gou
            one CL big dog
            "a big dog"

       b.   yi   da zhang zhi
            one big SHEET paper
            "a big sheet of paper"

The adjective *da* 'big' in (20) follows the UNIT classifier *zhi* but precedes *zhang* 'sheet' which would be a SORT classifier. However, most adjectives, even in Chinese, are lower in the hierarchy than most classifiers, as suggested by (19).

   Before going into detail regarding the different attachment sites for different classes of adjectives, I turn to some issues regarding word order.

2.5 Word order

2.5.1 *Suffixal Pl and Art*

In many languages, although the individual subhierarchies such as Dem–Num–Adj and Art–Pl–N are respected, the complete hierarchical order is not evident on the surface; for example Norwegian could be characterized as having the order in (21), as illustrated in (22).

(21)   Dem–Num–Adj–N-*n*-Pl-Art

(22)   disse tre   funksjonelle projek-sjon-e-ne
       these three functional   project-ion-PL-DEF
       "these three functional projections"

I argue that this follows if *n*, Pl, and Art are heads, while Num and Adj are phrases, and cluster formation involves movements which ensure that certain heads wind up adjacent.

   If phrasal movement can derive N–Pl–Def order, then a Norwegian noun phrase like the one in (23) could have a structure something like that in (24) (see Vangsnes 1999, 2001; Julien 2002, 2005 on Norwegian DP structure).

(23)   disse tre   berømte bøk-e-ne
       these three famous book-PL-DEF
       "these three famous books"

(24)

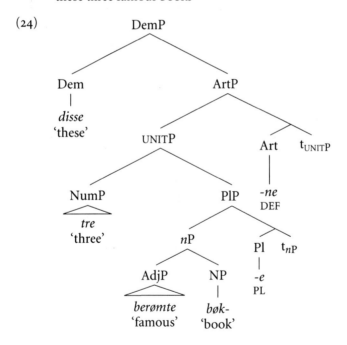

Note that the structure strictly observes the proposed universal hierarchy (leaving out some phonologically empty heads, to keep the tree small). I have represented the demonstrative as a head here, but nothing hinges on this. A pair of phrasal movements ensures that the suffixal Pl and Def (Art) heads are adjacent to N and Pl, respectively, which I take to be the essence of cluster formation (as argued in Svenonius 2007).

Icelandic provides an argument for movement of this type, as an overt demonstrative is in complementary distribution with a suffixal article, and the choice leads to word order differences. An overt demonstrative appears in the base Dem–Num–Adj–N order, as in Norwegian but with no definite suffix, while a definite noun phrase with no demonstrative shows the order Adj–N–Num (Sigurðsson 1992; Vangsnes 1999).

(25) a. Þessar Þrjár frægu bæk-ur
          these three famous book-PL
          "these three famous books"

     b. frægu bæk-ur-nar Þrjár
         famous book-PL-DEF three
         "the three famous books"

This is what would be expected if Pl attracts a large constituent, for checking of the N under adjacency, and Def attracts a relatively small constituent, perhaps even the PlP itself, as illustrated in (26). The fact that the movement (as identified by the reordering of the numeral) only occurs in the presence of the definite suffix suggests that the suffixal head is involved in triggering the movement.

(26)

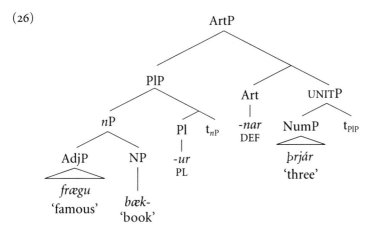

Prefixal plural morphology would involve movement of NP (or *n*P) to a position just below the plural morpheme. All else being equal, a noun with prefixal plural morphology should tend to precede adjectives, which would be crossed by the moving NP. Typological data supports this: of 104 languages listed in Haspelmath et al. (2005) as having prefixal plural marking, 80 have NA order, and only 18 have AN order (another 6 are listed as having no dominant order of N and A). This means that 80 percent of plural-prefixing languages are NA, whereas among plural-suffixing languages, the distribution is much more even (190 are AN and 204 are NA; there are 37 with no dominant order of N and A).

As Cinque (2005) argues, the attested word orders are generally those expected from a movement analysis.[8]

2.5.2 Classifiers and phrasal dependents in DP

Various surface orders can be observed with respect to classifiers. For example, Simpson (2005) notes the following orders among Southeast Asian languages.

(27) a. Chinese: Dem–Num–Cl–RC–Adj–N

     b. Thai, Khmer: N–Adj–RC–Num–Cl–Dem

     c. Burmese: Dem–RC–N–Adj–Num–Cl

     d. Hmong, Malay, Vietnamese: Num–Cl–N–Adj–RC–Dem

Simpson argues for an antisymmetric (Kayne 1994) movement analysis; he assumes that the various elements are heads, whereas I am assuming that adjectives and numerals, at least, are phrasal dependents. Modulo these differences, a movement account can be simply characterized in the following terms: Chinese reflects something like the base order.[9] In all of the other languages, N moves to the left of the adjective. If relative clauses are taken to be attached to the left just above adjectives, then the Thai/Khmer pattern (henceforth Thai) and the Hmong/Malay/Vietnamese (henceforth Malay) pattern

---

[8] Though see Abels and Neelam (2006) for a challenge. As noted above, many languages have the order in (14e), namely Num–N–Adj–Dem, which involves an unexpected (Num–Adj–Dem) order of modifiers, given the simplest assumptions about movement (see also Svenonius 2007). One possibility is that the Num in these cases is actually the head of the noun phrase, and moves to the left to combine with functional material. See for example Babby (1987); Franks (1994); Ionin and Matushansky (2005) on Russian, in which certain numerals determine the case on the accompanying noun and control subject agreement on a verb. Other examples of pattern (14e) may represent head-final structures in which the demonstrative is a head.

[9] I have added the relative clause position to the Chinese line-up; Simpson does not discuss relative clauses in Chinese. An example, from Zhang (2004), showing the order of modifiers:

(ii) *na   liang ge wo tidao   de nianqing ren*
    that two CL I   mention DE young   person
    "those two young people I mentioned"

also require an additional step of movement of [N Adj] to the left of RC. In Burmese and Thai, the [RC N Adj] constituent moves across the Num–Cl sequence. In Thai and Malay, a constituent containing the numeral moves to the left of the demonstrative. The Burmese pattern is outlined in tree form below, using the labels established above; in particular, the relative clause is taken to attach above SORT, and the classifier is assumed to be located in the head of UNIT.

(28)   Burmese:

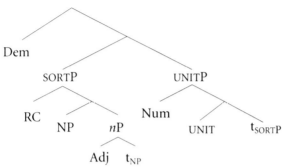

In the Malay pattern, I use a convention from Koopman and Szabolcsi (2000) of superscripting a "+" to the node which includes *n*P and a landing site for roll-up movement, simply in order to have labels for its trace.

(29)   Hmong, Malay, Vietnamese:

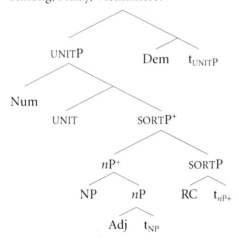

The Thai pattern combines both movements: the fronting of a projection of SORT, as in Burmese, and the fronting of a projection of UNIT, as in Malay. The order is the equivalent of right-adjoining the phrasal modifiers, except that the UNIT classifier follows the numeral.

(30)   Thai, Khmer:

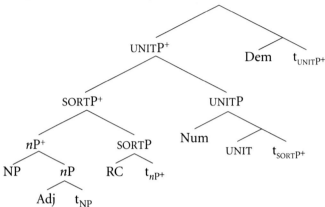

It is typical cross-linguistically of classifier languages that they normally do not separate the numeral and classifier (though it is not universally true; cf. Allan 1977, or example 20b above). If only maximal projections move, and the numeral is in the specifier of the classifier, then this is expected.

Note also that the position of the relative clause must be considered more carefully, and is identified here with sORTP only tentatively and for purposes of illustration.

2.6 Semantic arguments

The arguments regarding the decomposition of DP have so far been mainly based on observations regarding the order of morphemes and phrasal dependents. Various kinds of additional arguments have been developed as well, including lexical (Borer 2005a), cognitive (Rijkhoff 2002), and model-theoretic (Zamparelli 2000). I will not go into great detail here regarding those different models, but briefly outline the major motivations, the main categories postulated, and the relationship to the structures used here.

2.6.1 *Borer 2005a*

Borer (2005a) develops a model of the noun phrase in which the categories D, #, and Cl figure importantly. Each introduces an open value, represented by ⟨e⟩. Open values are assigned *range*, either by heads or by specifiers, which restrict their value. The lowest of the three important categories in the DP is $\langle e \rangle_{DIV}$, Div for "division" (Borer 2005a: 59) or "divided" (Borer 2005a: 95), of which one important manifestation is Cl. A noun in which $\langle e \rangle_{DIV}$ is assigned range is a count noun ($\langle e \rangle_{DIV}$ is absent from mass nouns).

Above $\langle e \rangle_{DIV}$ is the category Quantity, or $\langle e \rangle_{\#}$. This allows masses and count entities to be enumerated or quantified. $\langle e \rangle_{\#}$ may be assigned range by a quantifier, and is the level at which numerals and most determiners are introduced. Borer's system explicitly allows heads to assign range to more than one value, and determiners in general are introduced at the $\langle e \rangle_{\#}$ level but then move up to assign range to the next higher level, $\langle e \rangle_{d}$ (d for "determiner"), the highest important level in an ordinary noun phrase.

$\langle e \rangle_{d}$ can unproblematically be equated with the Article and Demonstrative here. Borer's category $\langle e \rangle_{\#}$ is the level at which numerals are introduced, and so could be equated with the category UNIT. Borer's category $\langle e \rangle_{DIV}$ and its manifestation Cl [assifier] are intended to capture properties both of the Asian classifier types and of English-style plurals. Thus, in the model here it is clearly Pl/SORT which is closest to Borer's $\langle e \rangle_{DIV}$.

Borer argues that Chinese classifiers can assign range to both $\langle e \rangle_{DIV}$ and $\langle e \rangle_{\#}$ (moving from the one to the other). Following this, I have suggested that many of the Asian classifiers are properly thought of as conflations of UNIT and SORT (if head-movement is an option, then a typical Asian classifier might move from SORT to UNIT, essentially as Borer suggests).

2.6.2 *Rijkhoff 2002*

Rijkhoff (2002) argues at length, on the basis of a typological study, for a layered DP in which the main categories are *Location*, *Quantity*, and *Quality*. He identifies demonstratives and articles with the category *Location*, and those also represent the outermost layer of the noun phrase here.[10] The intermediate layer, *Quantity*, is associated with numerals and quantifiers, and could be identified here with numerals and the UNIT category. The inner layer, *Quality*, is where adjectives typically reside, and so this would correspond to my SORT and *n*. Grinevald (2000) notes the correlation between noun classifiers and the categories relevant to Rijkhoff's *Quality*.

---

[10] Rijkhoff also locates relative clauses and possessors in this layer. I have not dealt with possessors at all and have only cursorily mentioned relative clauses. Possessors may move from a thematic position in NP to a licensing position higher up, so their exact position is complicated to determine (cf. Julien 2005 for extensive relevant discussion of Scandinavian possessors). Relative clauses, too, may be attached at different levels under different circumstances.

2.6.3 *Zamparelli 2000*

Zamparelli (2000) presents arguments for a compositional approach to nominal semantics in which a projection Ki[nd] plays a prominent role. This level is the level at which kinds in the Carlsonian sense (Carlson 1977) are determined. This category will play a role in the discussion in the next section. For present purposes it suffices to say that it cannot be higher than UNIT, nor lower than SORT, so if it is a distinct head it must be between the two.

2.7 Adjective ordering

Nearly all languages allow attributive adjectives to modify nouns; in fact, in many languages this is their only or primary function (Dixon 2004a). In some languages, attributive modification is limited to a single adjective phrase; additional adjectives must be coordinated, introduced by apposition, or introduced in relative clauses.[11] In other languages, such as English, multiple adjectives are possible, and in such languages there are very clear cross-linguistic tendencies in the ordering of attributive adjectives. By and large, the order of prenominal adjectives tends to be similar cross-linguistically, for example size before color. Languages with postnominal adjectives split, with some showing the same order as English (e.g. Irish: Sproat and Shih 1991) and other languages showing the mirror image (e.g. Hebrew: Shlonsky 2004, contra Sproat and Shih 1991). In many cases, there is a preferred ordering and a marked ordering, or two different interpretations for two different orders.[12]

2.7.1 *Fine-grained structure*

One approach that has been pursued is to identify individual adjective classes with specific functional heads, which are presumed to exist independently in the functional sequence. For example, Cinque (1994) observes various preferred orders, such as those in (31), and proposes the hierarchy in (32).

(31)   a.   numerous wonderful big American cars

       b.   various round black Egyptian masks

---

[11] For example: on Thai, Nung, and Indonesian: Simpson (2005: 834, n. 1), contra Sproat and Shih (1991); on Wolof, McLaughlin (2004: 254).

[12] See e.g. Demonte (this volume). Many languages have a kind of augment on each adjective, and it seems that this may yield relatively free ordering: cf. the discussion of Greek (Alexiadou and Wilder 1998), Hawrami (Holmberg and Odden 2005), Chinese (Sproat and Shih 1991; Paul 2005), and other languages. Compare Sproat and Shih's (1991) notion of "direct" versus "indirect" modification.

(32) Adj$_{quantification}$ > Adj$_{quality}$ > Adj$_{size}$ > Adj$_{shape}$ > Adj$_{color}$ > Adj$_{nationality}$

Scott (2002) expands on this, proposing the fine-grained hierarchy in (33).

(33) Ordinal > Cardinal > Subject Comment > Evidential > Size > Length
      > Height > Speed > Depth > Width > Temperature > Wetness > Age
      > Shape > Color > Nationality/Origin > Material

Laenzlinger (2005) suggests that Scott's inventory (with minor refinements)
can be organized into five subdivisions, as given in (34).

(34) [$_{QUANTIF}$ Ordinal > Cardinal] >
      [$_{SPEAK-ORIENT}$ Subject Comment > Evidential] >
      [$_{SCALAR PHYS. PROP.}$ Size > Length > Height > Speed > Depth > Width] >
      [$_{MEASURE}$ Weight > Temperature > Wetness > Age] >
      [$_{NON-SCALAR PHYS. PROP.}$ Shape > Color > Nationality/Origin > Material]

However, there are some concerns regarding these structures. For one thing,
the categories are not well-motivated outside of the adjectival ordering phenomenon that they are introduced to describe. That is, they do not carry much
explanatory force. Secondly, the actual observed orderings are not as rigid as
such an approach would seem to predict. What is desired is an independently
motivated hierarchy, with some way to fit adjectives into it in a way that
correctly predicts adjective ordering facts.

2.7.2 *Focused adjectives*

Steps have been taken in the right direction. Guttiérez-Rexach and Mallen
(2002), Giusti (2002), Truswell (2004), and Demonte (this volume), for example, adopt something like Zamparelli's (2000) Kind or Ki head, a level at which
"kind" concepts are formed, and suggest that Focused adjectives are above KiP.

(35) a. big square table; *square big table; SQUARE big table

      b. expensive wooden table; *wooden expensive table; WOODEN
          expensive table

      c. tasty French cheese; *French tasty cheese; FRENCH tasty cheese

This is illustrated in the tree below, making some assumptions (discussed
below) about attachment sites for different classes of adjectives.

(36)

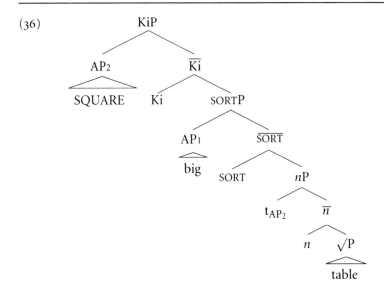

2.7.3 Idiomatic adjectives

Similarly, Marantz (2001) argues that the *n* level is the level of lexical idio-syncracy, so that idiomatically combined adjectives must attach below it. Expressions like those in (37) are illustrations; *wild rice* is a species of rice (*zizania palustris*), and need not have the properties conventionally associated with wildness. This contrasts, for example, with *wild tomato*, which has no idiomatic association and so would refer to an uncultivated (or ill-behaved, etc.) tomato. The idiom persists even when *wild rice* is modified by another adjective, such as *Minnesotan*, so that *Minnesotan wild rice* could be *zizania palustris*, when grown in Minnesota, for example.[13] However, if an adjective is inserted below *wild*, as in *wild Minnesotan rice*, the idiomatic reading is lost, and the rice must be conventionally "wild" (in the case of rice, this would most likely mean uncultivated).

(37)   a.   (Minnesotan) wild rice = *zizania palustris* (from Minnesota)

      b.   wild Minnesotan rice = compositional only: uncultivated rice from Minnesota

Along the same lines, *nervous system* is a kind of idiom, as is *French toast*; if regularly merged, compositional adjectives can only be merged outside *n*P, and these idiomatic adjectives are merged below, then the regular adjective cannot appear in between the idiomatic adjective and the noun.

---

[13]   A–N idioms can be distinguished from A–N compounds on the basis of stress; see e.g. Liberman and Sproat (1992). Compare the A–N idiom *wild ríce* to the A–N compound *wíld man*.

(38) a. (artificial) nervous system = system of nerves (which is artificial)

  b. nervous artificial system = compositional only

(39) a. (whole-wheat) French toast = fried battered bread breakfast dish
      (made with whole-wheat bread)

  b. French whole-wheat toast = compositional only

Note that under the right circumstances, idioms in general can be disrupted by adjoined material. For example, *ply X's trade* means "do X's usual work"; it can be applied to activities in which the word *trade* would not be used otherwise, for example as in (40).

(40) A team of young filmmakers plied their trade at the aquarium.

Even apart from the status of the possessive pronoun and the tense on the verb, an idiomatic noun like *trade* here can easily be modified by adjectives.

(41) A team of young filmmakers plied their glamorous trade at the aquar-
      ium.

Thus, it is not the case that idioms cannot be interrupted by non-idiomatic material (Nunberg et al. 1994; Svenonius 2005). Instead, if A can only have an idiomatic meaning in NP when it is merged below *n*, and if non-idiomatic A's must be merged above *n*, then the right results are achieved (in the diagram I depict the root as category-less, following Marantz; it could also be depicted as category N, as elsewhere in this chapter).

(42)

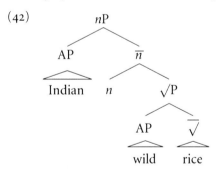

2.7.4 *Count adjectives*

The easy parts, as it were, have been picked off: focused adjectives off the top, and idiomatic adjectives off the bottom. The resulting situation is still a far cry from accounting for the observed tendencies in adjective ordering.

  Muromatsu (2001) and Truswell (2004) argue that dimension adjectives such as *big* and *tiny* must merge above the head which creates countable entities out of masses (Borer's Cl, Truswell's Div, my SORT). This prevents them from appearing at all with mass nouns, which lack the appropriate kind of SORT.

(43)   a.   red liquid, expensive salt, French mustard

     b.   *big liquid, *tiny salt, *long mustard

Dimension adjectives consistently precede color, origin, and material adjectives.

(44)   a.   a big expensive vase; *?an expensive big vase

     b.   tiny red hats; *?red tiny hats

     c.   long French shoes; *?French long shoes

This is explained if color, origin, and material adjectives merge below SORT, for example to *n*P.

(45)

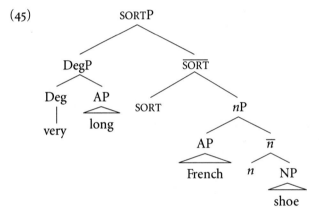

As for why such adjectives merge low, I suggest the following. Modification of *n*P is essentially intersective. Therefore only predicates of the same semantic type as *n*P can modify it. I suggest that this is the type of non-gradable predicates, including the origin reading of *French*, the material reading of *wooden*, the geometric reading of *square*, and so on.

All of these adjectives can also be gradable, through combination with a Degree head (Abney 1987; Corver 1990; Grimshaw 1991; Kennedy 1999b; Svenonius and Kennedy 2006). In that case they must be interpreted in terms of a scale, which affects the way they are understood (e.g. *French* meaning "typical of France" rather than literally "from France," etc.).

SORTP modification occurs in a different way from *n*P modification: it is crucially subsective, cf. Higginbotham (1985) for example. A DegP, I suggest, can be used for subsective modification of sortP, but not a simple (non-gradable) AP.

Thus I concur with Scott (2002) when he argues that APs in general are permitted to merge in whatever position makes sense for their interpretation. For example, when *French* is an evaluative adjective, as in *a very French attitude*, rather than an origin adjective, the same lexeme *French* might be merged in a higher position.

Where I break with Scott, however, is in the fine-grainedness of the structure supporting the adjectival modification. I have suggested here that the independently motivated layers of the DP provide several different parameters of adjectival meaning (focused, count, subsective, idiomatic), and that gradability provides another parameter of meaning. These factors, combined, should account for the adjectival orderings which are actually observed, and extralinguistic factors should account for the rest. On the account proposed here, it is difficult to see how, for example, length and width could be distinct functional heads. Scott proposes these in order to account for the pattern in (46).

(46)   a.   a long thin knife

     b.   * a thin long knife

However, the solution seems too tailored to the example. Consider the examples in (47)–(48), where *thick* is presumably an adjective of width and *lengthy* presumably an adjective of length.

(47)   a.   a long thick rope

     b.   a thick long rope

(48)   a.   a lengthy thin cord

     b.   a thin lengthy cord

Scott's proposed hierarchy does not seem to admit the necessary flexibility. Even *thin long* is not completely impossible.

(49)   a.   thin long strands of pasta

     b.   a thin long charm necklace

     c.   thin long legs

Suppose, with Kayne (1994), that each head supports at most one specifier. If that is the case, then there cannot be more than one modifier per functional head in the DP (as suggested by Cinque 1994). This would mean that the possibilities for attachment reduce as more adjectives are added. For example, perhaps *big* can in principle attach to SORTP, but if some other adjective is attached there, then *big*, if introduced, must attach either above or below.

(50)

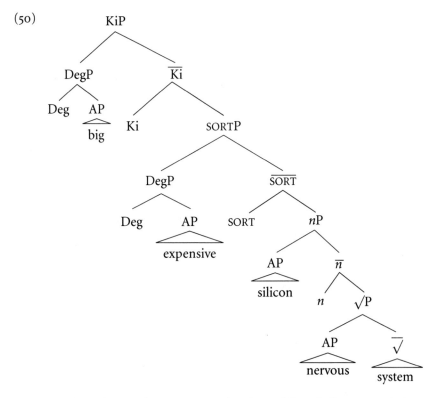

This would produce rather constrained orders while, I believe, permitting a great deal of the actually observed variation. A language like English does seem to allow multiple instantiations of the same category, as in *brave clever man* ∼ *clever brave man*, discussed by Dixon (1977) (cf. also discussion of this example in Scott 2002). On the view taken here, this would require a language-specific innovation, perhaps the innovation of a particular functional head. Principles of economy might favor fitting adjectives into the independently motivated structure when possible, leading to favored orders but admitting reverse orders when motivated.

2.8 Conclusion

In conclusion, Cinque's general idea that the fine syntactic structure of the DP can be put to use to constrain adjectival ordering is superior to any alternative thus far available. However, it does not seem necessary to go so far as to introduce dedicated functional heads for each adjective encountered.

The idea advanced here is that Universal Grammar (UG) dictates a structure for argumental noun phrases that necessarily involves a fair amount of functional structure, following Zamparelli (2000), Baker (2003), Borer (2005a), and others. The layers of functional structure represent stages of building referential argumental DPs from the abstract concepts associated with roots. Languages may then (and generally do) invent ways to modify the different layers of structure. A typical modifier for the DP level is a demonstrative, though other kinds of modifiers are possible; Zhang (2004) argues, in effect, that Chinese has a way of modifying the D layer with a relative clause. A demonstrative may be grammaticized as a D head when a reanalysis takes place from the demonstrative being a phrasal adjunct to DP in one generation to being a head of D in another.

Similarly, a language may over time invent a way to modify the UNITP level, with various quantifiers or numeral phrases. Again, some of these may become grammaticized as heads of UNITP.

And so on down the line. UG provides the basic ingredients for the category Adjective, and all languages appear to avail themselves of it in one form or another. The adjective turns out to make a particularly suitable modifier for some of the lower levels of the DP, but exactly how this is done varies substantially from language to language. What is most common, judging from Dixon's (2004a) typological survey, is that adjectives expressing dimension, age, value, and color are developed and combined with some functional structure to create nP modifiers or SORTP modifiers.

There seem to be at least two ways in which this might occur.[14] If the functional structure takes the adjective as complement, changing its type into that of a modifier of, say, SORTP, then the adjective may be able to apply iteratively within a projection. This is the case, for example, in Jarawara, according to Dixon (2004b), which has only fourteen adjectives but may use more than one in a single DP, with apparently free ordering. Another possibility is that a language might use the nominal structure itself to introduce the adjectival modifier, e.g. by allowing n or SORT to take an adjectival specifier. In such cases, a single adjective (of any given type) would be the norm. This seems to be the situation in Wolof, as described by McLaughlin (2004), where an

---

[14] See discussion in Truswell (2004), including discussion there of work by Albert Ortmann, which I have not read.

adjective may cooccur with a relative clause, but two adjectives cooccur only if coordinated.[15]

Eventually, a language might innovate ways of modifying each layer of the DP, either with specialty inventories of modificational elements for each layer, or, as in English, with a large class of adjectives being compatible with more than one functional option. The impression of a large class of adjectives comes then from the fact that there are many roots that can be used as adjectives, and from the fact that the functional heads introducing NP, *n*P, and sortP modifiers are not morphologically distinct. The impression of strict ordering comes mainly from the fact that sortP modifiers are strictly ordered before *n*P modifiers (and both are strictly ordered before NP modifiers), and that iteration within a layer is avoided when possible. Thus, pairs of adjectives will normally be arranged, in English, so that one is an *n*P modifier and the other is a sortP modifier. The one which is the most sensitive to shape, or the one which is the most robustly gradable, will then appear as the sortP modifier.

Acknowledgments

Thanks to the audience at the Workshop on the Semantics of Adjectives and Adverbs in Barcelona in 2005, where I was able to present some of this work, in the form of comments on Larson and Yamakido (this volume) and Demonte (this volume), under the title "What can decomposition do for you?" Thanks also to the organizers of that event, in particular Louise McNally, and to Chris Kennedy for comments on an earlier draft.

---

[15] Interesting in this regard is the characterization of Chinese presented in Sproat and Shih (1991), where it is claimed that direct (i.e. without *de*) modification of a noun is possible for exactly one adjective expressing size or quality, and one expressing color or shape, and if the two cooccur it is in strict order: quality/size > shape/color. This would suggest that Chinese provides a position for a single quality or size adjective above sort, and a position for a single shape or color adjective below sort. The element *de* makes iteration possible.

3

Ezafe and the deep position of nominal modifiers

RICHARD LARSON AND HIROKO YAMAKIDO

3.1 Introduction

In languages exhibiting the Ezafe construction, such as Modern Persian, nominal modifiers generally follow the noun, and a large class of nominal modifiers, including APs, NPs, some PPs, but not relative clauses, require a "linking" element, referred to as *Ezafe*. Thus in (1a), the noun *otâq* 'room' is modified by the adjective phrase *besyar kuchik* 'very small.' The Ezafe vowel *é* appears in between, suffixed to the noun. In (1b), the noun *xune* 'house' is followed by a restrictive PP, *kenar-é dærya* 'on the beach.' The two are connected by Ezafe, which also appears internally, between the preposition and its object. Finally (1c) shows the noun *otâq* modified by the relative clause *î- ké bozorg ast* 'that is big.' No Ezafe appears in this case; the relative clause initial *-î* is a distinct morpheme.[1]

(1) a. otâq-é   besyar kuchik
         room-EZ very   small
         "very small room"   (AP)

     b. xune-yé [kenar-é dærya]
         house-EZ next-EZ sea
         "house on the beach"   (PP)

     c. otâq-î   ké bozorg ast
         room-REL that big   is
         "room that is big"   (CP)

The Ezafe construction raises a number of interesting questions, not the least of which is: What is the Ezafe morpheme? What is its status under current grammatical theory?

---

[1] All data in this paper are drawn from either Samiian (1994) or Ghozati (2000).

In this chapter we develop a proposal advanced by Samiian (1994) that Ezafe is a case-marker, inserted to case-license [+N] elements. After introducing Ezafe, and reviewing Samiian's arguments for its case-marker status, we go on to consider two simple questions that arise from her results:

- Why do modifiers require Case?
- What is their Case-assigner?

Case-marking (as opposed to agreement) is typically associated with argument status; however, the Ezafe-marked items in (1a) and (1b) are modifiers. Why would modifiers need case? We suggest an answer to these questions based on an articulated "shell structure" for DP proposed by Larson (2000c). Under this account, (most) nominal modifiers originate as arguments of D, a view defended in classical transformational grammar by Smith (1964), and in generalized quantifier theory by Keenan and Stavi (1994). We also relate our account to other cases of postnominal APs, including English indefinite pronoun constructions and the Greek "poly-definiteness" construction, and to adjectival inflection in Japanese, following Yamakido (2005, 2007). If correct, our conclusions suggest a return to the early transformationalist view of nominal modifiers as complements of the determiner that originate in the position of relative clauses.

3.2 The Ezafe construction

The Ezafe construction is found in Modern Persian (Farsi), in Kurdish (Kurmanji and Sorani) and in Zazaki. Ezafe occurs with various kinds of modifiers, but not typically with RCs.

3.2.1 *Farsi (Samiian 1994; Ghomeshi 1997; Ghozati 2000; Kahnemuyipour 2000)*

Farsi shows the basic Ezafe pattern in a simple form. The language contains prenominal demonstratives (2a) and numerals (2b); superlatives seem to be the only case of prenominal adjectives (2c).

(2) a. on mard
       that man

    b. sé tá dokhtar
       three CL daughter

    c. kûechektarin mive
       smallest   fruit

Otherwise all modifying elements occur postnominally and typically require Ezafe, including APs (3a), descriptive NPs (3b, c), genitive NPs (3d), and some PPs (3e). The construction is recursive, insofar as multiple modifiers of these kinds trigger multiple occurrences of Ezafe (3f).

(3) a. otâq-é   besyar kuchik
         room-EZ very   small
         "very small room"   (AP)

     b. del-é   sang
         heart-EZ stone
         "stone heart"   (NP)

     c. shahr-é Tehran
         city-EZ Tehran
         "city of Tehran"   (NP)

     d. manzel-é John
         house-EZ John
         "John's house"   (NP)

     e. xune-yé [kenar-é dærya]
         house-EZ next-EZ sea
         "house on the beach"   (PP)

     f. ketâb-é sabz-é   jâleb
         book-EZ green-EZ interesting
         "interesting green book"   (AP-AP)

As noted earlier, relative clause modifiers, which are also postnominal, do not trigger Ezafe (4). They are introduced by a relative morpheme (î) that may be historically related to Ezafe, but is considered synchronically distinct by Persian grammarians.

(4) otâq-î   ké bozorg ast
     room-REL that big   is
     "room that is big"   (*CP)

3.2.2 What is Ezafe? (Samiian 1994)

The presence of the Ezafe "linking" morpheme raises a simple and very natural question. What is Ezafe? What function does Ezafe serve in the grammar of Persian and languages like it? In an interesting article, Vida Samiian (1994) argues that Farsi Ezafe is a *case marker*, inserted before complements of [+N] categories, including Ns, As, and some Ps. Samiian supports this claim by observing that the use of Ezafe extends considerably beyond modification. Many contexts where English would use the (genitive) case-marking preposition *of* are ones in which Ezafe occurs, including complements of N (5a–c), complements of A (6a–c), and certain partitive constructions (7a, b).

(5)   Complements of N

    a.   tæxrib-é   shæhr
        destruction-ez city
        "destruction of the city"

    b.   hordan-é   âb
        drinking-ez water
        "drinking of water"

    c.   forushandé-yé ketâb
        seller-ez   books
        "seller of books"

(6)   Complements of A

    a.   asheq-é   Hæsæn
        in love-ez Hasan
        "in love with Hasan"

    b.   negæran-é bæche
        worried-ez child.PL
        "worried about the children"

    c.   montæzer-é Godot
        waiting-ez   Godot
        "waiting for Godot"

(7)   Partitives

    a.   tamâm-é-în manzelhâ
        all-ez-DEF   houses
        "all (of) the houses"

    b.   hardo-yé-în manzelhâ
        both-ez-DEF houses
        "both (of) the houses"

The role played by *of* in the counterpart English cases is to case-mark the complement following adjectives, nouns, and partitives. Samiian suggests that Ezafe plays the same role here.

Perhaps the most persuasive piece of evidence Samiian gives is the behavior of the category P, which initially looks like a problem for Samiian's proposal. Since prepositions are typically analyzed as $[-N,-V]$ elements, PP would not be expected to require Ezafe marking; furthermore, P would not be expected to require Ezafe to case-license its object, contrary to what we observed in (1b)/(3e). However, Samiian shows that the class of prepositions in Farsi is not uniform with respect to Ezafe. As shown in (8), some prepositions reject Ezafe (call these *Class 1*). By contrast, as shown in (9) and (10), other prepositions either permit Ezafe, or require it (call these *Class 2*):

(8)   Class 1 Ps (reject Ezafe)

   a.   be (*-yé) Hæsæn
        to (-EZ) Hasan
        "to Hasan"

   b.   æz   (*-é) Hæsæn
        from (-EZ) Hasan
        "from Hasan"

   c.   ba   (*-yé) Hæsæn
        with (-EZ) Hasan
        "with Hasan"

   d.   dær   (*-é) Hæsæn
        in/at/on (-EZ) Hasan
        "in/at/on Hasan"

(9)   Class 2 Ps (permit Ezafe)

   a.   zir(-é) miz
        under (-EZ) table
        "under the table"

   b.   ru (-yé) miz
        on (-EZ) table
        "on the table"

   c.   bala (-yé) divar
        up   (-EZ) wall
        "up the wall"

   d.   jelo   (-yé) Hæsæn
        in front of (-EZ) Hasan
        "in front of Hasan"

(10)   Class 2 Ps (require Ezafe)

    a.   beyn-é   mæn-o to
         between-EZ me-and you
         "between you and me"

    b.   væsæt-é   otâq
         in.the.middle-EZ room
         "in the middle of the room"

    c.   dor-é   estæxr
         around-EZ pool
         "around the pool"

    d.   bæqæl-é dær
         by-EZ   door
         "by the door"

Samiian shows that whereas Class 1 prepositions are true function words
equivalent to English Ps, Class 2 prepositions are really noun-like elements.
For example, Class 1 prepositions require an object, whereas Class 2 Ps do not
(11a, b). Class 2 Ps can occur after determiners and can even bear plural morphology (whose function is apparently intensification) (11c, d), whereas Class
1 prepositions cannot. Finally, only PPs headed by Class 2 prepositions appear
in case positions and are joined to nominals by Ezafe; Class 1 prepositions do
not (11e, f).

(11)   a.   ræft ba   *(Hæsæn)
           went with Hasan
           "went with Hasan"

       b.   ræft bala (-yé deræxt)
           went up -EZ tree
           "went up (the tree)"

       c.   in   ru
           this top
           "up here"

       d.   un   zir-a
           that under-PL
           "way down there"

       e.   æks-é   ru-yé miz
           picture-EZ on-EZ table
           "picture on the table"

f. *æks-é   dær-é ganje
   picture-EZ in-EZ closet
   "picture in the closet"

The upshot is that, instead of being a counterexample to the case marker hypothesis, Farsi PPs appear to provide further support for it. It is exactly the noun-like (and presumably [+N]) prepositions that trigger the Ezafe phenomenon – exactly the prepositions that would not be expected to assign case, and whose projections would require it. As a point of comparison with English, we might note that Class 2 prepositions in Farsi appear to resemble complex English Ps like (12a, b), which contain an internal nominal element (*cause*, *spite*) and require an internal genitive case-assigner (*of*).

(12) a. [be [cause]] *(of) that fact
         (historically: by-cause-of)

    b. [in [spite]] *(of) his reluctance

We find Samiian's analysis of Ezafe convincing; however, if the analysis is correct, important additional questions arise. Accepting that Ezafe occurs to case-mark complements of non-verbal elements, how do modifiers fit in? For example, even if adjectives, as [+N] categories, are case-bearing elements, why would modifiers need case?

3.3 Projecting DP-structure

The answer we suggest is based on the theory of DP structure originally proposed in Larson (2000c), which takes DP to be projected from the thematic structure of determiners, much like VP is projected from the thematic structure of verbs. A core element in this account is the semantic analysis of determiners introduced by Barwise and Cooper (1981) and Keenan and Stavi (1994), according to which determiners express relations between sets.

(13) **Relational view of D:** Determiners express relations between sets.

Familiar determiner relations are given in (14a–e). Thus, the ALL-relation holds between two sets iff the second contains the first; the SOME-relation holds iff the two have a non-empty intersection, etc.[2]

(14) a. ALL(X,Y) iff $Y \subseteq X$

    b. SOME(X,Y) iff $Y \cap X \neq \emptyset$

---

[2] Standard relational notation R(X,Y) takes Y to be the first/internal argument of R, and X to be the second/external argument; hence with relational Ds, Y corresponds to the first/internal argument – the nominal restriction – and X corresponds to the second/external argument – the scope.

c.   NO(X,Y) iff Y ∩ X = ∅

d.   MOST(X,Y) iff |Y ∩ X| > |Y − X|

e.   THE(X,Y) iff Y ⊆ X & |Y| = 1

3.3.1 *A thematic analysis of DP*

In DP quantification, the set Y is normally given by the internal argument of D: the nominal that D combines with, usually referred to as "the restriction on quantification." The set X is given by the external argument of D: the expression that DP is adjoined to, usually called "the scope of quantification." Larson (2000c) suggests that notions like scope and restriction be understood as thematic roles assigned by determiners to their set arguments, and ordered into a hierachy as shown in (15a). On this proposal, there is a hierarchy of θ-roles for D, parallel to, but distinct from, the hierarchy of θ-roles for V (15b).

(15)   a.   D: $^{\theta}$SCOPE > $^{\theta}$RESTRICT > $^{\theta}$NOBLIQUE ("Nominal Oblique")

b.   V: $^{\theta}$AGENT > $^{\theta}$THEME > $^{\theta}$GOAL > $^{\theta}$OBLIQUE

The parallel thematic analysis of D and V allows for a parallel account of structure. In the shell theory of Larson (1988, forthcoming), transitive VPs receive a simple binary branching structure (16a), whereas ditransitive Vs receive a structure containing a phonetically null "light verb" that triggers V-raising (16b).

(16)   a.

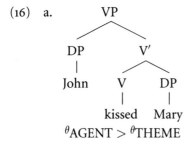

$^{\theta}$AGENT > $^{\theta}$THEME

b.

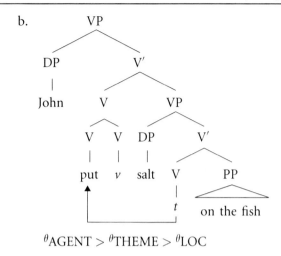

$^\theta$AGENT > $^\theta$THEME > $^\theta$LOC

In both cases, arguments appearing higher in structure (as expressed by c-command) receive θ-roles that are correspondingly higher on the thematic hierarchy.

In a similar way, DPs can be assigned a structure that reflects the thematic hierarchy for D. Simple quantificational DPs correspond to transitive structures and receive the binary branching structure in (17a). "Ditransitive" (that is, triadic) determiners like *every...except* or *more...than* receive a structure containing a phonetically null "light determiner" that triggers D-raising (17b).

(17) a.

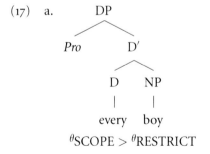

$^\theta$SCOPE > $^\theta$RESTRICT

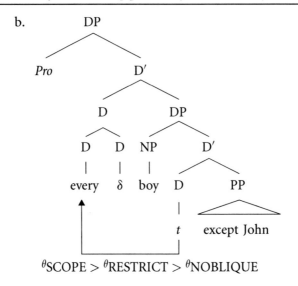

$$\theta\text{SCOPE} > \theta\text{RESTRICT} > \theta\text{NOBLIQUE}$$

Here *Pro* is a pro-predicate argument corresponding to the scope, whose content is given by the phrase that DP is sister to at LF (18a–d).

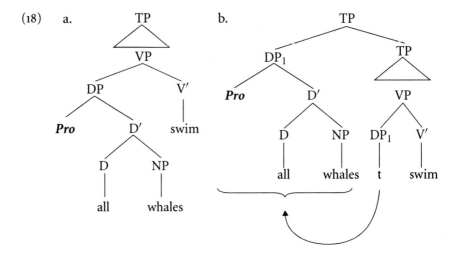

c.

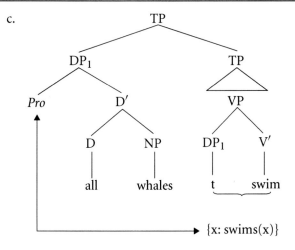

d. $[_{DP_i} Pro[_{D'} D\ NP]]\ [_{XP}\ldots t_i\ldots]$

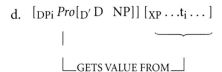

The same analysis applies straightforwardly to examples with a quantified DP object. Again note that in (17a, b) (set) arguments appearing higher in structure (as expressed by c-command) receive θ-roles correspondingly higher on the thematic hierarchy.

3.3.2 *The position of modifiers*

Within this general framework, verbal and nominal modifiers like those in (19) are not analyzed as adjuncts, attached high on the right, but rather as oblique complements, which actually combine with the head before other arguments.

(19)   a.

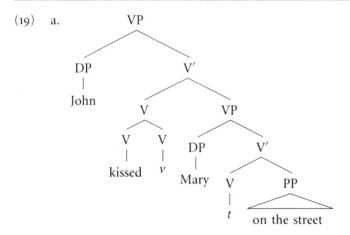

$^\theta$AGENT > $^\theta$THEME > $^\theta$LOC

b.

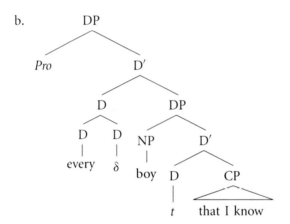

$^\theta$SCOPE > $^\theta$RESTRICT > $^\theta$NOBLIQUE

This approach has a variety of advantages. For example, it allows us to capture certain discontinuous dependencies that appear to hold between the head (V or D) and a modifier. Thus (20a–d) give various cases in which a verb and an oblique PP form a notional unit that is discontinuous in surface syntax. (21a–d) and (22a–c) give familiar parallel cases for DP. The first is Kuroda's observation that indefinite nouns like *way* are licit with a demonstrative determiner, but not with a simple definite; however, the combination of a definite determiner and a restrictive modifier are acceptable with such a noun.

(22a–c), noted by Jackendoff, make a similar point in connection with proper nouns.

(20) a. $_{VP}$ **treat** John **with kid gloves** ("treat carefully")   MANNER

b. $_{VP}$ **rub** John **the wrong way** ("bother")   MANNER

c. $_{VP}$ **put** John **on the spot** ("confront")   LOCATION

d. $_{VP}$ **kill** John **with kindness** ("be very solicitous toward")

INSTRUMENT

(21) I earned it ...

a. ... **that** way.

b. ... *the way.

c. ... **the old-fashioned** way.

d. ... **the** way **that one should.**
    (from Kuroda 1969)

(22) a. *the Paris

b. **the old** Paris

c. **the** Paris **that I love**
    (from Jackendoff 1977)

Under the shell theory both receive a similar treatment: the elements forming a notional unit comprise an underlying syntactic unit as shown in (23a, b); the latter is subsequently broken up when the overt head raises to the light head.[3]

---

[3] The idea of relative clauses as semantic D arguments is first proposed (to our knowledge) by Bach and Cooper (1978), who suggest, within the framework of Montague Grammar, that alongside standard IL translations like (ia–c), Ds be assigned interpretations like (iia–c). Here R is a variable over properties that is "filled in" by the denotation of an RC or other restrictive modifier.

(i) a. *every* $\lambda Q \lambda P \forall x [Q(x) \rightarrow P(x)]$
     b. *some* $\lambda Q \lambda P \exists x [Q(x) \rightarrow P(x)]$
     c. *the* $\lambda Q \lambda P \exists y \forall x [[Q(y) \leftrightarrow y = x] \wedge P(x)]$

(ii) a. *every* $\lambda Q \lambda P \forall x [[Q(x) \& R(x)] \rightarrow P(x)]$
      b. *some* $\lambda Q \lambda P \exists x [[Q(x) \& R(x)] \rightarrow P(x)]$
      c. *the* $\lambda Q \lambda P \exists y \forall x [[[Q(y) \& R(x)] \leftrightarrow y = x] \wedge P(x)]$

In Larson (2000c) restrictive D arguments are accommodated semantically by means of a valence-changing operation defined over binary determiner meanings. Specifically, if δ is a binary determiner, then we can define δ' a ternary determiner, such that for all α, β, γ of type $< e, t >$, $\delta'(\gamma)(\beta)(\alpha)$ iff $\delta(\zeta)(\alpha)$, where $\zeta' = \lambda x[\beta'(x) \& \gamma'(x)]$. This relation is defined over two-place determiners, whether basic or derived, hence if δ is a three-place D that has already combined with a restrictive argument,

(23) a. [$_{VP}$ ... [$_{V'}$ *v* [$_{VP}$ John [$_{V'}$ **put** [$_{PP}$ **on the spot**]]]]]

   b. [$_{DP}$ ... [$_{D'}$ δ [$_{DP}$ **way** [$_{D'}$ **the** [$_{CP}$ **that one should**]]]]]

3.3.3 *The problem of prenominal modifiers*

The view sketched above can be extended to other postnominal modifiers including PPs, as in (24a), reduced relative clauses, as in (24b), and combinations of them as in (24c). The latter involve recursive DP shells and multiple raising to light heads, as shown in (25).

(24) a. the man [$_{PP}$ at the podium]

   b. three women [$_{RC}$ capable of lifting a sofa]

   c. every book [$_{PP}$ on the shelf] [$_{RC}$ published since WWII]

(25) [$_{DP}$ *Pro* [$_{D'}$ every$_i$ [$_{DP}$ book [$_{D'}$*t$_i$* [$_{DP}$ [$_{PP}$ on the shelf]
   [$_{D'}$*t$_i$* [$_{RC}$ published since WWII]]]]]]]]

But what about prenominal modifiers, APs like those in (26), which are semantically equivalent to copular relative clauses?[4]

(26) a. the tall woman   (cf. *the woman who is tall*)

   b. every beautiful house   (cf. *every house that is beautiful*)

   c. three blind mice   (cf. *three mice that are blind*)

One possibility is base generation along the lines in (27).

---

there will be a δ' that adds another set-argument to it. This accommodates the recursive character of restrictive D-arguments.

 [4] We are not suggesting, of course, that all prenominal modifiers are equivalent to relative clauses. In fact there are well-known differences between them. For more on this topic see Larson (1998) and Larson and Takahashi (2007).

(27)   **Base Generation ??** ⇒

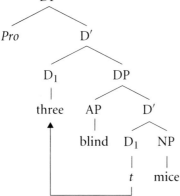

On reflection, however, this idea is problematic. Given a θ-role-based approach, in order to project AP in the site shown in (27), we would apparently have to allow for an optional oblique θ-role between two obligatory roles in our hierarchy, as in (28).

(28) $^{\theta}\text{SCOPE} > (^{\theta}X) > {}^{\theta}\text{RESTRICT}$

Worse yet, given the wide range of modifiers available in the prenominal site, we would seem to have to allow for a very large number of optional oblique θ-roles between our two obligatory ones (29). This looks unpromising.

(29)   a.   three **German** mice

b.   three **blind German** mice

c.   three **grey blind German** mice

d.   three **furry grey blind German** mice

e.   three **small furry grey blind German** mice

f.   three **excellent small furry grey blind German** mice

The only plausible alternative we see is that prenominal position is not a base position for adjectives in English, but rather a derived one. That is, we are led to resurrect the view of early transformationalists: that intersective attributive APs originate in the position of RCs, and obtain their surface position by movement, along the lines shown in either (30a) or (30b).

(30)   a.

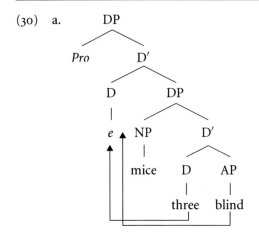

   b.

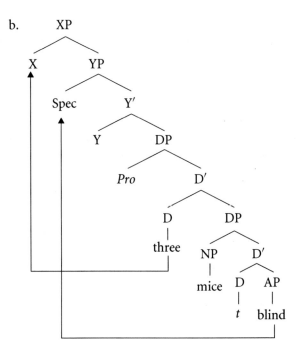

However, this raises the natural question as to why restrictive adjectives must move from their base position. Why can't they remain in postnominal position like PPs, finite and reduced relative clauses?

3.4 Case in DP

We believe the Ezafe construction suggests an answer to this question. On the picture sketched above, DP is like VP in that:

- D selects thematic arguments.
- DP syntax is right-descending.
- DP modifiers are lowest complements of the head – all begin in post-head position.

Suppose now that DP is also like VP in deploying its own system of Case-marking; specifically suppose that:

- [+N] complements of D need Case – they bear a Case feature that must be checked.
- D/δ can (in general) check Case on its internal argument, just as V/v checks one Accusative on an internal argument of V.

Then we will have the following consequences:

- D will in general check Case on its NP restriction.
- DP-modifiers that do not have Case features to be checked (PPs, CPs, and disguised CPs) will remain *in situ*.
- DP-modifiers that bear Case features (APs) will be required to move to a site where they can check Case (e.g., by Concord).

So the general picture we have is as in (31). The determiner *every* checks its one structural Case on its nominal restriction (*woman*), exhausting its Case-checking potential. English postnominal PPs and CPs do not bear Case features, and therefore can stay in their base position. Likewise for reduced relative clauses, which we analyze as covert CPs, following Kayne (1994).[5] However APs that do not occur inside reduced relatives cannot remain in place, and must move to a site where their Case can be checked.[6]

---

[5] "Reduced relative clause" is not a uniform notion. English reduced RCs appear to be full finite clauses, as evidenced by the fact that they can contain a clausal negation licensing negative polarity items (e.g., *the men [not present in any of the pictures]*). Under a number of proposals, the presence of clausal negation always implies a c-commanding tense (Laka 1990; Zanuttini 1996, 1997). By contrast, in many languages, including nearly all with prenominal relatives (e.g., Turkish), reduced RCs are clearly less than full finite CPs (see Krause 2001).

[6] The mechanism of case-checking for languages with prenominal APs is discussed in Larson (2006), for the eastern Indo-Iranian language Pashto, which behaves like English in relevant respects. The derivation of a Pashto nominal *agha tɔge peghla* 'that thirsty girl':

(31)

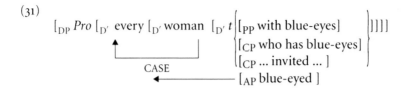

$[_{DP}$ *Pro* $[_{D'}$ every $[_{D'}$ woman $[_{D'}$ *t* $\left\{\begin{array}{l}[_{PP}\text{ with blue-eyes}]\\ [_{CP}\text{ who has blue-eyes}]\\ [_{CP}\text{ ... invited ... }]\end{array}\right\}$ $]]]]$

CASE

$[_{AP}$ blue-eyed $]$

3.4.1 *Ezafe construction again*

Suppose now that a language had in its D-system the equivalent of a "generalized genitive preposition" – an item that could be inserted to check Case on [+N] determiner complements. A single, additional Case would then become available for each such Case-marker, allowing APs/NPs/nominalPPs to remain *in situ*. Relative clauses and non-nominal PPs would not require such an element, and so none would appear.

We propose that this is what's happening in the Ezafe construction. Modifying NPs, APs, and (nominal) PPs are selected by D and generated postnominally as usual. As [+N] elements they bear Case features, and are Case-licensed by Ezafe in their base-position. We will tentatively consider Ezafe to form an XP phrase with its complement, but to cliticize onto the preceding [+N] element for phonological reasons. So the picture, for a simple Farsi NP like (32a), is as in (32b). The definite determiner *in* checks its one Case feature on its restriction. Ezafe is inserted and licenses the remaining modifiers in their base positions.

(32)   a.   in   ketâb-é sabz-é   jâleb
         DEF book-EZ green-EZ interesting
         "the interesting green book"

   b. $[_{DP}$ *Pro* $[_{D'}$ in$[_{DP}$ ketâb $[_{D'}$ *t* $[_{DP}[_{XP}$ é sabz] $[_{D'}t[_{XP}$ é jâleb$]]]]]]]$

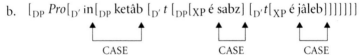

CASE   CASE   CASE

(i)   a. $[_{DP}\ [_{NP}$ peghla] $[_{D'}$ agha $[_{AP}$ tɔge]]]   *Merge Initial arguments of D; D agrees with AP on T*

   b. $[_{dP}$ d $[_{DP}\ [_{NP}$ peghla] $[_{D'}$ agha $[_{AP}$ tɔge]]]]   *Merge little d*

   c. $[_{dP}$ agha-d $[_{DP}\ [_{NP}$ peghla] $[_{D'}$ agha $[_{AP}$ tɔge]]]]   *Raise D*

   d. $[_{dP}\ [_{AP}$ tɔge] $[_{d'}$ agha-d $[_{DP}\ [_{NP}$ peghla] $[_{D'}$ agha $[_{AP}$ tɔge]]]]]   *d attracts AP*

   e. $[_{dP}$ d $[_{dP}\ [_{AP}$ tɔge] $[_{D'}$ agha-d $[_{DP}\ [_{NP}$ peghla] $[_{D'}$ agha $[_{AP}$ tɔge]]]]]]   *Merge d*

   f. $[_{dP}$ agha-d-d $[_{dP}\ [_{AP}$ tɔge] $[_{D'}$ agha-d $[_{DP}\ [_{NP}$ peghla] $[_{D'}$ agha $[_{AP}$ tɔge]]]]]]   *Raise head*

   g. $[_{dP}$ *Pro* $[_{D'}$ agha-d-d $[_{dP}\ [_{AP}$ tɔge] $[_{D'}$ agha-d $[_{DP}\ [_{NP}$ peghla] $[_{D'}$ agha $[_{AP}$ tɔge]]]]]]]
                                                           Project DP Subj

The crucial parametric property of Pashto (and, by extension, English) is hypothesized to be an EPP/Edge feature on little *d*. For details see Larson (2006).

Again, relative clauses (CPs) and non-nominal PPs do not require Case. Hence they can appear in their base site (like English RCs and PPs) without the need for a licensing Ezafe.

Under this proposal, Ezafe languages are special insofar as they reveal the deep position of all nominal modifiers. They can do so because they have a special Case-marking device.

Interesting evidence for the tie between D and Ezafe comes from Kurmanji, which also has the Ezafe construction, but which differs from Farsi in important subtleties. In brief, Kurmanji exhibits an alternation in the form of Ezafe according to definiteness. Kurmanji definite DPs with iterated modifiers show so-called *primary Ezafe* between the noun and its first modifier, but a distinct *secondary Ezafe* thereafter (33a). By contrast, Kurmanji indefinite DPs with iterated modifiers show *secondary Ezafe* throughout (33b).

(33) a. kitêb-ên   bas-î   nû
          book-1EZ(PL) good-2EZ(PL) new
          "the good new books"

      b. xani-n-e   bas-î   nû
          house-INDEF(PL)-2EZ(PL) good-2EZ(PL) new
          "some good, new houses"

Definiteness is very widely held to be an interpretable/meaningful property of determiners insofar as it is the semantics of D that establishes whether a nominal is definite or indefinite (Barwise and Cooper 1981; Diesing 1992; Keenan and Stavi 1994). Thus Kurmanji, which exhibits a distinct Ezafe for definiteness, would seem to indicate a relationship between Ezafe and D. In the theory developed here, the relation between Ezafe and (null definite/indefinite) D is in fact selectional: D selects EzP, hence this link is captured directly.

3.4.2 *Extending the analysis*

Our analysis has consequences beyond languages with the Ezafe construction. We will consider here three further extensions: to English, to Modern Greek, and to Japanese.

3.4.2.1 *Postnominal adjectives in English*   English shows one environment where adjectives that normally occur only prenominally can occur after N. This is the so-called indefinite pronoun construction (IPC).[7]

---

[7] The terminology "indefinite pronoun" is adopted here from the literature (see, for example, Haspelmath 1997), despite our reservations about expressions like *everything* and *nothing* being referred to as "pronouns."

Thus adjectives like *interesting* and *tall* normally must occur prenominally (34); however, when they occur with indefinite pronouns like *everything/something/anything/nothing, everyone/someone/anyone/no one*, etc., they must occur in postnominal position, as seen in (35).

(34) a. i. every **interesting** book
           ii. *every book **interesting***

      b. i. a **tall** person
          ii. *a person **tall***

(35) a. i. ***interesting** everything*
           ii. everything **interesting**

      b. i. ***tall** someone*
          ii. someone **tall**

Many have tried to analyze the postnominal adjectives with indefinite pronouns as prenominal adjectives that have been stranded by N-raising (36):

(36) [$_{DP}$ every -thing [$_{NP}$ interesting [$_{NP}$__]]]

(Abney 1987, Kishimoto 2000)

However, as Larson and Marušič (2004) show, this analysis cannot be correct: adjectives in indefinite pronoun constructions do not behave like underlying prenominal adjectives, but as underlying postnominal adjectives.

To give an illustration of the arguments, English measure adjectives show a difference in inflection when they occur pre- vs. postnominally, as noted by Sadler and Arnold (1994). In postnominal position, the unit phrase shows plural inflection (37a, 38a), whereas in prenominal position, it is uninflected (37b, 38b). If adjectives with indefinite pronouns were stranded prenominal modifiers, we would expect the inflectionless form (39). But this is not what we see. The form we get is the inflected one, characteristic of postnominal adjectives (40). This argues against the N-Raising analysis.

(37) a. a rope [23 **inches** long]

      b. a [23 **inch** long] rope

(38) a. a river [two **miles** wide]

      b. a [two **mile** wide] river

(39) [$_{DP}$ any **thing** [$_{NP}$ **23 inch long** [$_{NP}$ __]]]

(40) a. anything 23 **inches** long /*23 **inch** long

      b. everything two **miles** wide/*two **mile** wide

Another problem for the raising analysis concerns modifier recursion. Although indefinite pronoun constructions allow adjectives to occur post-nominally that ordinarily could not occur there, only a single such form is permitted. As (41a, b) show, more than one such adjective yields ungrammaticality. Two postnominal adjectives are permitted when one of them would independently be allowed in the postnominal slot, as in (42a) and (43a), but here again there is a restriction. The adjective that is ordinarily disallowed in postnominal position must occur adjacent to the indefinite pronoun (42b, 43b).

(41) a. everyone **tall** (*heavy*)

      b. everyone **heavy** (*tall*)

(42) a. everyone [**tall**] [**present**] (cf. every woman present/*tall)

      b. *everyone [**present**] [**tall**]

(43) a. something [**large**] [**spotted**] (cf. some object spotted/*large)

      b. *something [**spotted**] [**large**]

None of this is predicted by the stranding analysis. Since adjectives stack in the prenominal position it is a mystery why two prenominal adjectives would be forbidden postnominally: the noun should just be able to raise around them (44).

(44) *[DP every **one** [NP **tall** [NP **heavy** [NP __]]]]

(cf. *every tall heavy person*)

Likewise, it's unclear why there should be any ordering restriction.

   Our Case-analysis permits a surprisingly simple account, however. Suppose that a determiner's NP restriction – its internal argument – could incorporate into it, just as verbs are known to be able to incorporate their objects. Following Baker's (1988) analysis of object incorporation in Southern Tiwa, we might expect the determiner's single Case feature to be "freed up" for checking on a single additional argument.

   We propose that this is what is happening with APs in English IPCs. The indefinite N (*-one, -thing, -place, -where*) incorporates into D, freeing its single Case feature for alternative checking. Exactly one AP is then licensed in the postnominal position by the free Case feature, as displayed in (45):

(45)   [DP *Pro* [D′ every-one [AP tall]]]

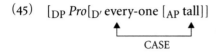

CASE

The ordering restriction we observe on the postnominal adjectives can then be understood as a version of the usual adjacency/minimality requirement on Case-checked items vis-a-vis their Case-checkers (46):[8]

(46)   [DP *Pro* [D′ every-one [CP ... present ...]][AP tall]]

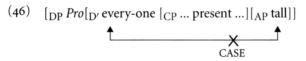

CASE

3.4.2.2 *Polydefiniteness/D-spreading in Modern Greek*   Like English, Modern Greek shows prenominal restrictive adjectives that cannot typically appear postnominally. This is illustrated in the contrast between (47a) and (47b).[9]

(47)   a.   to meghalo petrino spiti
            the big   of.stone house
            "the big stone house"

       b.   *to spiti   meghalo petrino
            the house big   of.stone

But postnominal APs can be licensed in Modern Greek definite DPs via the phenomenon of "determiner spreading," in which the definite determiner is essentially duplicated between each of the modifiers. Thus either (48a) or (48b) is possible (Androutsopoulou 1994, 1995; Alexiadou and Wilder 1998; Kolliakou 1998; Marinis and Panagiotidis 2004).

(48)   a.   **to** spiti **to** meghalo **to** petrino
            the house the big   the of.stone
            "the big stone house"

       b.   **to** spiti **to** petrino **to** meghalo
            the house the of.stone the big
            "the big stone house"

Interestingly, the possibility of D-spreading imposes at least two constraints. First, the adjective must be interpreted restrictively. Second, only intersective/predicating As are permitted. These facts are illustrated in (49–51). In

---

[8]   By contrast, postnominal modifiers that do not require case are predicted to stack freely and show no ordering restrictions.

[9]   Chris Kennedy (p.c.) raises the interesting question of whether verb-copying is available for case-marking in the verbal domain as well. The phenomenon of verb serialization in West African languages suggests a possible general analogy.

(49a) (from Marinis and Panagiotidis 2004) the prenominal A *ikani* 'competent' appearing in the boldfaced DP is interpreted either restrictively or unrestrictively. Thus DP can be understood as referring only to the competent researchers, or to all the researchers (who are understood to be competent). By contrast in (49b), with D-spreading, only the former, restrictive interpretation is available for the postnominal A.

(49)   a.   O dhiefthindis dhilose oti **I**   **ikani**
             the manager   declared that the competent

             erevnites   tha eprepe na   apolithun.
             researchers FUT had.to SUBJ fired.3PL

             "The manager declared that the competent researchers should be fired." (restrictive or non-restrictive interpretation)

      b.   O dhiefthindis dhilose oti **I**   **erevnites** **I**
             the director   declared that the researchers the

             ikani   tha eprepe na   apolithun.
             competent FUT had.to SUBJ fired.3PL

             "The manager declared that just the competent researchers should be fired." (only restrictive interpretation)

The second constraint – that only intersective/predicating As can appear - is demonstrated in (50) and (51) (from Alexiadou and Wilder 1998). (50a, b) show that the non-intersective adjective *ipotithemenos* 'alleged' can appear in prenominal position, but not in the D-spreading construction. Similarly for (51a, b), which involve the non-predicating nationality adjective *italiki* 'Italian'.

(50)   a.   o   **ipotithemenos** dolophonos
             the alleged   murderer
             "the alleged murderer"

      b.   *o dolophonos o **ipotithemenos**
             (cf. *O dolophonos itan ipotithemenos. "The murderer was alleged.")

(51)   a.   i   **italiki** isvoli
             the Italian invasion
             "the Italian invasion"

      b.   *i isvoli   i   **italiki**
             the invasion the Italian
             (cf. * I isvoli stin Alvania itan italiki. "The invasion of Albania was Italian.")

The facts of Modern Greek raise simple and immediate questions: How does D-spreading license a postnominal A that would have otherwise been disallowed? And why must A be read restrictively/predicatively? Again the D-shell analysis offers an attractive answer.

On our proposal, multiple modifiers involve multiple DP-shells through which D raises recursively. Suppose that as D raised through the DP-shells, it were permitted to leave behind a copy whose formal but not semantic features were active. Assuming, as we have, that D checks the Case features on its complements, we would expect a single additional D Case to become available for each copy of D, allowing an AP to remain *in situ* for each copy.

We suggest that this is exactly what is happening in the Greek polydefiniteness construction. When definite D raises, it has the option of leaving copies behind (52a); this licenses exactly one AP/NP in each shell by each copied head (52b).

(52)

a.   [DP *Pro*[D′ to [DP spiti [D′ to [DP [AP meghalo] [D′ to [AP petrino]]]]]]]

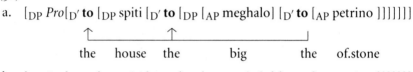

    the   house   the   big   the   of.stone

b.   [DP *Pro*[D′ to [DP spiti [D′ to [DP [AP meghalo] [D′ to [AP petrino]]]]]]]

    CASE   CASE   CASE

In the case where no copies are left, no Case is assigned to the APs/NPs, and they must raise (53a, b).

(53)   a.   **to**   meghalo petrino spiti
         the big   of.stone house
         "the big stone house"

      b.   *****to** spiti   meghalo petrino
         the house big   of.stone

3.4.2.3 *Japanese adjectival morphology*   The Ezafe construction and the general approach to DP structure pursued here suggest many intriguing connections, of which we will sketch just one. The Indo-Iranian language Zazaki exhibits the Ezafe construction in a significantly more complex form than Modern Persian. Whereas Ezafe is invariant (up to phonological alternation) in Persian, in Zazaki the Ezafe element inflects according to the number (SG/PL) and the gender (MASC/FEM) of the modified noun. Furthermore, and

TABLE 3.1. Zazaki Ezafe morphemes

	Descriptive	Genitive
Masculine Cons. Stem	*-o*	*-e*
Masculine Vowel Stem	*-yo(2)*	*-y*
Feminine Cons. Stem	*-a*	*-a*
Feminine Vowel Stem	*-ya*	*-y(a)*
Plural Cons. Stem	*-e*	*-e*
Plural Vowel Stem	*-y*	*-y*

more importantly for our purposes, Zazaki distinguishes between a *descriptive Ezafe*, which links a modified noun with an adjective, and a *genitive Ezafe*, which links a noun to another noun in the possessive relation. Table 3.1 gives the set of Zazaki Ezafe forms, drawn from Todd (1985).[10] Examples are provided in (54–55) also from Todd (1985).

(54) a. ban-**e**   min
          house(MASC)-EZ me(OBL)
          "my house"

     b. ling-**a**   min
          foot(FEM)-EZ me(OBL)
          "my foot"

     c. ling-**e**   min
          feet(PL)-EZ me(OBL)
          "my feet"

(55) a. pirʿtok-**o**   find
          book(MASC)-EZ good
          "good book"

     b. top-**a**   wer'd-i
          ball(FEM)-EZ small-FEM
          "small ball"

     c. pirʿtok-**e**   gird-is
          book(PL)-EZ big-PL
          "big books"

---

[10] Table 3.1 leaves out what Todd labels the *subordinated* Ezafe series, which occur in the context of certain oblique case environments. That Ezafe alternates in this circumstance again suggests that it is a form of case-marking. See Larson and Yamakido (2005) for more on subordinated Ezafe.

Under the view of Ezafe as a Case-marker, this suggests that Zazaki distinguishes at least two cases within the nominal: one with which it marks NP/DP modifiers in a genitive relation N (54), and a second that it uses for adjectival modifiers in a descriptive relation (55).

Given this result, it is interesting to observe that Japanese appears to make a very similar distinction in its system of marking for prenominal modifiers. Japanese contains a morpheme *-no* that is used to link a noun with an NP/DP in a genitive or modifying relation (56a–c).

(56)   a.   Taroo-**no** kyoodai
Taroo-GEN sibling
"Taroo's siblings"

   b.   Taroo-**no**   hon
Taroo-GEN book
"Taroo's book"

   c.   Nihonzin-**no** gakusee
Japanese-GEN student
"Japanese student (student who is Japanese)"

In addition, Japanese contains morphemes that are used to link a noun with an attributive AP, an AP in a descriptive/modifying relation. There are in fact two such morphemes, *-i* and *-na*, corresponding to the two classes of Japanese adjectives, so-called "true adjectives" (57a, b) and "nominal adjectives" (57c, d).

(57)   a.   utukusi-**i**   tori
beautiful-? bird
"beautiful bird"

   b.   taka-**i**   hon
expensive-? book
"expensive book"

   c.   kiree-**na** uti
clean-?   house
"clean, tidy house"

   d.   sizuka-**na** umi
quiet-?   sea
"quiet sea"

While the morpheme *-no* in (56) is standardly classified in Japanese grammar books as a genitive case-marker, the status of *-i* and *-na* has been much more controversial. A large number of linguists have assumed that these morphemes represent tenses, copulas, or tensed forms of the copula, implying that (57a–d) all represent covert relative clause constructions (58a–d).

(58) a. utukusi-i   tori
          beautiful-cop bird
          "bird that is beautiful"

      b. taka-i   hon
          expensive-cop book
          "book that is expensive"

      c. kiree-na   uti
          clean-cop house
          "house that is clean, tidy"

      d. sizuka-na umi
          quiet-cop sea
          "sea that is quiet"

However, Yamakido (2000, 2005, 2007) argues convincingly that the relative clause analysis cannot be correct. One simple piece of evidence is the existence of non-predicating Japanese AP constructions like (59a, b).

(59) a. huru-i tomodati
          old   friend
          "longtime friend" (cf. # "friend who is longtime")

      b. kanzen-na baka
          complete   fool
          "complete fool" (cf. # "fool who is complete")

If the adjectival linking morphemes are not tenses, copulas, or tensed copulas, then what are they? Yamakido (2005) argues that these elements are in fact case morphology. Hence if she is correct, then not only do -*no*, -*i*, and -*na* form a set, their pattern (abstracting from number and gender) is essentially identical to that of Zazaki: -*no* represents the Japanese genitive Ezafe morpheme used to link a noun with a modifying NP/DP in a possessive relation, and -*i*/-*na* represents the Ezafe morpheme used to link a noun with a modifying AP in a descriptive relation.

3.5 Summary

In this chapter we introduced the Ezafe construction, in which NPs, APs, and some PPs are "unexpectedly" postnominal. We explored a theory of DP structure in which all DP modifiers begin postnominally as complements of D, and we suggested that Case is behind pre-/postnominal distribution: APs, NPs, and nominal PPs need Case, but can't normally get it *in situ*.

We analyzed Ezafe as a special device for making Case available in the base site, thus allowing the underlying postnominal position of nominal modifiers to emerge. We argued that our Case-theoretic approach has potential relevance not only to "exotic" Indo-Iranian languages with the Ezafe construction, but also to the peculiar distribution of postnominal adjectives in the English indefinite pronoun construction, and to the polydefiniteness construction of Modern Greek. These represent alternative case-mechanisms allowing the [+N] modifiers to remain in place. The first was suggested to represent a case of NP incorporation, parallel to object incorporation in the verbal domain. The second was proposed to represent a case of copy raising. Finally, we suggested that reflection on more complex forms of the Ezafe construction offers interesting analytical possibilities for other languages. In particular the distribution of Ezafe in Zazaki nominals containing a modifying NP or AP appears remarkably similar in pattern to Japanese inflection in nominals containing a possessive nominal or a descriptive AP. These elements, whose analysis is otherwise problematic, can be viewed as Case-marking, following Yamakido (2005, 2007).

4

Meaning–form correlations and adjective position in Spanish

VIOLETA DEMONTE

4.1 Introduction

This chapter addresses the empirical generalization in (1), which raises puzzling questions about the putative correlation between meaning and syntax.

(1) In Spanish, a language in which adjectives appear pre- and postnominally, there are systematic (although sometimes not easily describable) interpretive differences associated with the position of adjectives in the nominal domain.

These differences in meaning can be provisionally described, as is usual in descriptive grammars, as an opposition between the restrictive (R) and nonrestrictive (NR) readings of adjectives.[1]

(2) a. Encontré *las llaves viejas.*
         Lit. I found the keys old. (i.e., the subset of keys which are old)

     b. Encontré *las viejas llaves.*
         Lit. I found the old keys. (i.e., I found certain keys and they are old.)

There are other oppositions cross-cutting the opposition R vs. NR, which I will consider – for the sake of argument and with the provisions below – as falling under the same general principle. Namely, I will assume, first, that modal adjectives have an "implicit relative" reading in postnominal position yet a "direct modification" reading when prenominal. In the implicit relative reading, as opposed to the direct modification reading – the distinction is Larson's (2000a, 2000b) –, the adjective does not modify the noun directly but rather does so indirectly through an implicit relative clause. See (3):

---

[1] I consider mainly object-denoting nouns.

(3)   a.   Tuvo en cuenta *la salida posible* en la parte de atrás.
           Lit. He kept in mind the way out possible in the back.
                             (i.e. as feasible/possible for him)

      b.   Atendió a todos *los visitantes posibles*.
           "He received all the visitors it was possible for him to receive."
                             (Implicit relative reading; Larson 2000b)

      c.   Tuvo en cuenta *la posible salida* en la parte de atrás.
           Lit. He considered the possible way out in the back.
                             (i.e. the possible/potential way out in the back)

      d.   Atendió a todos *los posibles visitantes*.
           "He attended to all the people that were possible visitors."
                             (Direct modification meaning; Larson 2000b)

I will also assume that non-intersective and intersective adjectives have preferred positions within DP, namely prenominal and postnominal position,
respectively:

(4)   a.   El buen abogado
           Lit. The good lawyer (good as a lawyer)   (Non-intersective reading)

      b.   El abogado bueno
           Lit. The lawyer good (good as a human being[2])
                             (Intersective reading)

Nonetheless, this view might be controversial. While it is generally accepted
that intersective adjectives occur postnominally in Romance, since they are
a subclass of predicative adjectives (Knittel 2005), it is less obvious what the
situation is regarding non-intersective adjectives. At first sight it appears that
adjectives like *bueno* 'good,' *malo* 'bad,' or *grande* 'big,' clearly non-intersective
when preceding an N (5a), can also have this reading in postnominal position:
(5b) is ambiguous between the intersective and the non-intersective reading.
However, if we look at a larger set of data we find that the non-intersective
reading is standard in prenominal position (see 5c vs. 5d) and it survives in
postnominal position mainly when the alternative reading is not possible for
independent reasons (see 5e vs. 5f).

(5)   a.   Búscate un buen abogado.
           "Get a good lawyer." (Good as a lawyer)

      b.   Búscate un abogado bueno.
           "Get a good lawyer." (Good as a lawyer/good person)

---

[2] But see the qualification immediately below.

c. Irina es una atractiva bailarina.
    "Irina is an attractive dancer." (attractive person or attractive as a dancer, the latter preferred)

d. Irina es una bailarina atractiva.
    (Only "attractive person")

e. Fernando es un eficaz colaborador.
    "Fernando is an efficient co-worker." (Only "efficient as a co-worker")

f. Fernando es un colaborador eficaz.
    (Only "efficient as a co-worker")

A way to dispense with these apparent problems is, first, to claim that the ambiguity in (5c) derives from the nominal and propose, following Larson 1998, that the source of the "as a" reading is a result of the modification of an event argument in NP/DP. Second, the presence of a non-intersective reading in (5b) can be considered as a singular fact, perhaps a result of displacement of the adjective for prosodic reasons (see below).

It appears, then, that to correctly depict the whole paradigm some qualifications are in order. To do this let us return to the R–NR distinction. Observe that there are examples like those in (6) in which, similarly to (5), it seems to be the case that both interpretations are allowed in postnominal position.

(6) a. Los amigos pretenciosos de Laura llegaron tarde.
         Lit. The friends pretentious of Laura were late (Ambiguous: a subset of Laura's friends are pretentious, or all of Laura's friends are pretentious).

     b. Los pretenciosos amigos de Laura llegaron tarde.
         Lit. The pretentious friends of Laura were late (All of Laura's friends are pretentious).

Note, however, that such an ambiguity is present in very restricted contexts and that there appear to be semantic and pragmatic factors triggering the shift from the R to an NR interpretation. For example, (7a) appears to be a potential counterexample to the generalization in (1) since only the NR interpretation appears postnominally.

(7) a. Me gusta tocar las manos suaves de María. [NR]
         Lit. I like to touch the hands soft of Maria

     b. Me gusta tocar las suaves manos de María. [NR]
         Lit. I like to touch the soft hands of Maria

Contrast now (7) with (8):

(8) a. Me gusta tocar las manos suaves / los tejidos suaves. [R]
        I like to touch the hands soft / the fabrics soft
        "I like to touch soft hands/fabrics."

     b. Me gustan mucho las suaves manos *(de María). [NR]
        Lit. I like a lot the soft hands *(of Maria)

     c. Me gustan mucho los suaves tejidos *(de la India).
        Lit. I like a lot the soft fabrics *(of India)

What (8a) shows is that the NR interpretation of the postnominal adjective in (7a) disappears when the possessive complement restricting the reference of the noun is absent. It is fair to think, then, that in *las manos suaves de María* the postnominal adjective has an NR interpretation due to the fact that Maria's hands cannot have a subset. (8b–c) suggest that an NR interpretation is difficult to obtain, even in prenominal position, when the referent cannot be identified as unique.

(9) also appears to be an exception to the generalization in (1) since an R interpretation can also be found in prenominal (and sometimes in marked postnominal) position, with certain adjectives:

(9) a. Las FÉRTILES [R] verdes praderas de Irlanda lo deslumbraron.
        "He was astonished by Ireland's FERTILE meadows."

     b. Odio los MALOS [R] vinos.
        "I hate the bad wines (not the good ones)."

     c. Adora los coches rojos largos MARAVILLOSOS.
        adores the cars red long wonderful
        "He/she adores MAGNIFICENT long red cars."

However, given their interpretation and phonological properties, one can claim that the prenominal/postnominal R adjectives in (9) are (contrastively) focused, both semantically and phonologically, and thus their distribution is determined by specific prosodic and syntactic conditions.

The conclusion that can be drawn from this set of data is that syntactic position does in fact determine semantic interpretation (Bolinger 1967; Bouchard 1998, 2002; Larson 1998, among others). Strictly speaking, in the case of the relation between nouns and modifying adjectives, there appear to be three canonical interpretations associated with three syntactic environments: R in postnominal position, NR in prenominal position and (restrictive) F in prenominal focus positions.[3]

---

[3] There is also a second, right-focus position which I will consider later on.

In this chapter I give theoretical support to this preliminary conclusion. In the following sections, I provide evidence for the hypothesis that there is a systematic correlation (with the caveats just made) between syntactic position and logical types of adjectives. Pretheoretically speaking, the supposition I will take as a point of departure is that adjectives have a lexical meaning which contributes to their logical type, but the latter is ultimately determined configurationally.

Finally, another crucial working hypothesis is that when R or NR interpretations appear in non-canonical positions this is due to interferences from other factors, either semantic or pragmatic, external to the syntax of the noun–adjective relation.

4.2 Logical types of adjectives and meaning relations in pre- and postnominal positions

4.2.1 *Logical types of adjectives*

In languages in which adjectives appear both pre- and postnominally, adjectives establish different meaning relations with N. Descriptively, we can say that prenominal adjectives "modify components internal to N" (Bouchard 1998). Though I will not provide a fine-grained analysis of these internal components of the lexical structure of nouns, I will assume, with the minimal qualifications to be made below, that nouns contain referential and event variables that can be saturated by different types of predicates, and that they also contain a qualia structure (Pustejovsky 1995); both can be modified by adjectives.

The crucial point underlying the observation just made is that a given adjective can have different readings (R or NR) depending on the position it occupies. One way of approaching this double behavior is to think that its source is the semantic structure of the adjective. Alternatively, we might attribute the double reading to the semantic structure of N, to the extent that this structure is available to the adjective. The second view is the one that I take in this chapter. This approach is in line with the assumption that syntax plays a role in the composition of the meaning of phrases.

More specifically, in our idealization of the meaning relation between adjectives and nouns in prenominal syntactic position, the semantics of noun modification by adjectives can be described in the following four ways: (a) modifying the denotation assignment function; (b) modifying central properties; (c) modifying a temporal interval; (d) expressing an extreme property.

4.2.1.1 *Modifying the denotation assignment function (a)*   As is the case in (10), adjectives can modify the denotation assignment function of nouns, and "indicate that some postulated assignment may not be in the present world or may even be false" (Bouchard 1998: 143–144). This is the case of modal and "epistemic" adjectives:

(10)   el {posible, necesario, presunto, supuesto, falso, presumible} asesino
       the {possible, necessary, alleged, supposed, false, presumed} murderer

4.2.1.2 *Modifying central properties (b)*   Adjectives can also, as in (11), modify one or more central properties of N,[4] asserting either that they are completely or exclusively satisfied by N, or that the noun – which must have a perfectly identified referent – can efficiently fulfill such property/ies. The first function corresponds to Quirk's "restrictive" adjectives[5] like *perfecto* 'perfect,' and to "degree and quantifying" adjectives[6] like *verdadero* 'real,' *simple* 'utter,' or *completo* 'complete';[7] the second one corresponds to qualitative-evaluative adjectives like *bueno* 'good,' *pequeño* 'little,' *sagrado* 'sacred,' *suave* 'gentle,' *amable* 'kind,' and color, form, and taste adjectives like *verde* 'green,' *acido* 'acidic'.

(11)   a.   **Restrictive and degree/quantifying adjectives:**
           {completo / rotundo / perfecto / verdadero / simple / puro / mero / exclusivo / único} fracaso
           '{complete / total / perfect / true / simple / pure / mere / exclusive / only} failure'

       b.   **Qualitative–evaluative adjectives:**
           el {*buen/pobre*} *abogado* 'a good (with respect to his qualities as a lawyer) / poor (who evokes pity) lawyer'; *el despiadado crítico* 'the merciless critic'; *las pequeñas ovejas* 'the little sheep'; *la ácida ensalada* 'the acidic salad'; *la última suave curva* 'the last gentle/easy bend'; *los blancos palacios* 'the white palaces'

Following standard assumptions it might be difficult to accept that these two sets of adjectives belong to the same logical type since restrictive adjectives,

---

   [4] "Modifier of central properties" is an informal way to describe what is usually called "reference modification."

   [5] The term "restrictive adjective" is taken from Quirk et al. (1978: §7.35), where it refers to those adjectives orienting the interpretation towards the uniqueness of the referent.

   [6] Degree and quantifying adjectives indicate "the degree to which the property expressed in the head nominal applies in a given case" (Pullum and Huddleston 2002: 555).

   [7] Larson (1998: 10) also says that *utter, mere,* and *complete* "cannot be analyzed as simple, univocal predicate of events [like *former*]. Rather they appear to be forms whose relation to N parallels the relation of a degree modifier to an associated A."

and those of degree, are usually considered predicate modifiers (functions from properties to properties) while qualitative adjectives generally denote properties. What I want to emphasize with this regrouping is the fact that most adjectives in (11) license the entailment "NP is N" ("a good lawyer is a lawyer") but they do not license the entailment that "NP is Adj" ("a good lawyer is not necessarily good in general terms"). In a similar way, *a complete failure* is a failure which is complete as a failure, and *un verdadero coche* is a car which satisfies the properties which distinguish cars within a larger domain. Neither of them implies, respectively, *el fracaso es completo* "the failure is a subset of the 'complete things' " or *el coche es verdadero* "the car is real."

Different with regard to this entailment are qualitative evaluative adjectives, specifically sensorial quality adjectives such as *white, acidic, round*, etc.: a white palace is obviously a white object. In traditional grammars of Spanish it is usual to call these color, shape, and taste adjectives *epithets*, as they emphasize the prototypical elements in the meaning of the noun, and this is the main characteristic of the attributive NR interpretation when resulting from the use of these forms:

(12)   *la blanca paloma* 'the white dove,' *la redonda esfera* 'the round sphere,' *la olorosa rosa* 'the fragrant rose,' *las verdes praderas* 'the green meadows'

In fact, these adjectives cannot be prenominal in certain Romance languages like French (Laenzlinger 2005, Knittel 2005, among others). Even in Spanish these adjectives are not frequent in prenominal position. These lexical sub-types of adjectives (color, form, taste, and other sensorial properties) tend to be used postnominally, and are typically predicative, since they are intersective. Nevertheless, their function when used prenominally is not that of intersecting the class of objects denoted by the noun and the property expressed by the A, but rather that of "affecting" the denotation of the unique object(s) expressed by N. Observe the contrast between the sensorial adjectives in (13):

(13)   Me gustaban las *amargas* hojas del arce y los sabores *ácidos* de las primeras fresas de junio.
        "I loved the bitter leaves of the maple and the acidic flavors of the first strawberries in June."
        = Me gustaban las hojas del arce, que son (por naturaleza) amargas, y los sabores que son ácidos de las primeras fresas de junio.
        "I loved maple leaves, which are (naturally) bitter, and the early June strawberry flavours that are acid."

In (13) both taste adjectives occur in very similar contexts, [N+PP_{restrictive}], but the first is prenominal and the second postnominal. They are both predicates that denote properties of N; however, the first one has to be glossed through an appositive relative clause while the postnominal one is equivalent to a restrictive relative.

In this sense prenominal sensorial adjectives (the epithets) have an interpretive role very similar to that of 'restrictive' and degree adjectives (cf. 11). At least as a speculation it can be said that in both cases (non-intersective restrictive–degree adjectives and prenominal qualitative–evaluative adjectives) the adjectives modify a hidden parameter of N. We might claim, as in Pustejovsky (1995), that "every category expresses a qualia structure" and that certain nouns (and the NPs containing them) encode information about particular activities or properties associated with them. In this framework, restrictive degree modifiers and qualitative epithetic adjectives can be considered modifiers of the *formal* quale of N, namely, "the aspects of a word's meaning that distinguish (the object) within a larger domain" (Pustejovsky 1995: 76). I will come back to this aspect of the semantic relation between N and A in section 4.4.1.1, where I will present some speculations about why these structural meanings appear mainly when the adjective occurs in prenominal position.

Finally, the class of prenominal adjectives that I describe as modifiers of a central property can have this function only when the DP identifies unique referents (recall 8b). This is the reason why these prenominal adjectives are more common in definite DPs and require modifiers restricting the reference of NP (14a). Without the modifier, the sentences are acceptable if the DP refers to a previously introduced referent. In the same vein, they are normal in singular and plural indefinite expressions (14b), since these DPs introduce referents in the discourse:

(14)   a.   Mostraron los hermosos libros #(de medicina).[8]
            "They showed the beautiful books (of medicine)."

       b.   Mostraron un hermoso libro / unos hermosos libros.
            "They showed a beautiful book / some beautiful books."

4.2.1.3 *Modifying a temporal interval (c)*   In (15) the adjective modifies a temporal interval of N. This is the case of deictic and event-temporal modifier adjectives.

---

[8] An anonymous reviewer asks whether *libros de medicina* can be considered a fixed expression. As a matter of fact, a similar oddness is found with a very wide variety of different PP modifiers:

(i)   Nos mostró los bonitos libros #con tapas azules.
      "He/she showed us the beautiful books with blue covers."

(15)   *la futura reina* 'the future queen,' *el antiguo acuerdo* 'the old agreement,' *el actual presidente* 'the current president,' *los nuevos coches* 'the new cars,' *mi anterior marido* 'my previous husband,' *un largo viaje* 'a long trip'

4.2.1.4 *Expressing an extreme property (d)*   In (16) we have the logical type of what I call "extreme degree adjectives": certain of Dixon's human disposition adjectives (*horrible* 'horrible,' *necio* 'stupid,' *espantoso* 'awful') and qualitative superlative adjectives (*maravilloso* 'wonderful,' *hermosísimo* 'very beautiful,' *magnífico* 'magnificent') correspond to this type.[9] Considering their function we may call them "appositive" because they serve to express a distinctive or central property of N, as if it were added as a supplement to its denotation.

(16)   *el/un horrible concierto* 'the horrible concert,' *los maravillosos sombreros* 'the wonderful hats,' *los aburridísimos hombres* 'the very boring men,' *la débil voz* 'the soft voice'

My assertion is that these adjectives are predicative nonrestrictive modifiers, different in this sense from the three preceding types. This is so because in all syntactic contexts in which they occur they do not refer to a subset of the class of objects denoted by N. Moreover, they can be paraphrased as parenthetical or as nonrestrictive relatives. The examples in (16) (recall also 7a) can be paraphrased as in (17):

(17)   a.   Asistí a un (horrible) concierto (horrible). = Asistí a un concierto, {y fue horrible / que fue horrible}.
            "I went to a horrible concert."

       b.   La (débil) voz (débil) apenas se oía. = La voz, que era débil, apenas se oía.
            "The soft voice could hardly be heard."

       c.   Los (aburridísimos) hombres (aburridísimos) nos dejaron exhaustos. = Los hombres, que eran aburridísimos, nos dejaron exhaustos.
            "The very boring men left us exhausted."

Superlative nonrestrictive adjectives like *maravillosos* in *sus/los maravillosos sombreros* are usually prenominal in definite expressions; #*Sus sombreros maravillosos* is less frequent. The reason is that, by default, superlative evaluative adjectives do not serve to delimit a subset of objects; they cannot classify objects in the world since they express not objective properties but rather

---

[9] Knittel (2005: 193) names these "subjective comment" adjectives. She rightly asserts that these adjectives can be both prenominal and postnominal, and they can be modified by subjective adverbs like *verdaderamente* 'truly' or *realmente* 'really.'

subjective evaluations. Note that the DP *los sombreros maravillosos* (where the superlative adjective is postnominal) is acceptable especially when it refers to a set of hats that has not previously been mentioned (see section 4.2.2.4 below). In my view, these adjectives fall under the subsidiary generalization I established in the first section: there are semantic and pragmatic reasons which sometimes cause the shifting from the expected R to an NR interpretation when these adjectives are found in postnominal position. I will come back to these, explaining this in terms of focalization as external predicates to the right of NP.

Summarizing, the adjectives in the first three subgroups, from (a) to (c), can be argued to form a single group from a semantic and syntactic point of view. This unification is supported by the assumption that they scope over subparts of the meaning of N, a question to which I will return briefly in section 4.4.1.1.

In contrast to the three subgroups just mentioned, postnominal adjectives (as in 18) normally modify "the individuals determined by all the properties of N" (Bouchard 1998: 143).

(18)   *la manzana roja* 'the red apple,' *dos mariposas negras* 'two black butter-flies,' *el abogado bueno* 'the good lawyer,' *el hombre pobre* 'the poor (not rich) man,' *la sobrina antipática* 'the nasty niece,' *las señoras amables* 'the kind ladies'

Briefly summarizing what we have seen up to this point: the distinction R–NR in interpretation correlates with syntactic position in two senses. First, a reduced set of adjectives are assigned either a restrictive or a nonrestrictive interpretation depending on their position (*pobre, completo, simple, antiguo*, etc.): I refer to the contrast between *el pobre hombre*, where the prenominal adjective means "pitiable" vs. *el hombre pobre*, where *pobre* is "not rich." Second, most adjectives are interpreted one way or another depending on their position, as we will see in section 4.2.2.

4.2.2 *Some diagnostics for the logical types of adjectives*

There are at least four diagnostics which typically distinguish the adjectives in classes (a), (b), and (c), i.e. prenominal adjectives, from postnominal adjectives like those in (18). First, the members of each set differ as to their ability to be used in copular predicative structures. Second, they behave differently with respect to tests that make explicit the "subset property" (Pullum and Huddleston 2002). Third, gradable adjectives with different scalar properties ("absolute" and "relative" ones in the sense of Kennedy and McNally 2005) do not always accept degree modification in prenominal position. And fourth, the two positions also mark the difference between the non-specific and specific readings. I will now provide some evidence for these differences.

4.2.2.1 *Occurrence as predicative complements in copular structures*   Regular qualitative adjectives that can be used both pre- and postnominally can occur as predicates of copular sentences; see (19). As has frequently been noted, in this construction they only retain the restrictive meaning typical of postnominal adjectives, as the comments in the glosses are meant to show:

(19)   Dame los libros interesantes. = Dame los libros que son interesantes.
       "Give me the books that are interesting."

In other words, in *los libros que son interesantes* the predicative adjective has the same restrictive meaning that we find in *los libros interesantes*. The sense of "modification of a central property or modification of the reference" which we find in *los interesantes libros* does not appear in the copular construction.

   In the case of human disposition adjectives, the adjective appearing in copular constructions generally refers to a temporary or stage level-like property; this is the meaning we find in postnominal position (20a) in contrast with the individual level reading in (20b), where the adjective is prenominal.

(20)   a.   El crítico despiadado no la saludó. = El crítico que fue/estuvo despiadado no la saludó.
            "The critic who was merciless did not greet her."

       b.   El despiadado crítico no la saludó.
            "The critic is merciless and he did not greet her."

The remaining adjectives appearing in prenominal position – modal (*posible*), restrictive (*mero*), degree/quantifying (*total*), and event modifier/deictic (*futuro*), are either banned from occurring in predicative structures or when they do occur in such structures they have a different meaning which corresponds to the one they receive as postnominal modifiers of N, when they appear in such a context. Let us consider some cases that illustrate these contrasts.

   Observe, first, in (21), that in the cases in which modal adjectives appear as predicates of copular sentences, they are either unacceptable (the examples in 21a–b) or have an implicit relative reading (21c).

(21)   **Modal:**
       a.   *El culpable es presunto.
            "The guilty person is alleged."

       b.   *El defensor es supuesto.
            "The defender is supposed."

   c. Los acuerdos son falsos.
      "The agreements are untrustworthy."

The meaning in (21c) is the same we find in *los acuerdos falsos*, which is different from the one in *los falsos acuerdos*, the latter being fake agreements or agreements that do not have the properties required to be considered as agreements.

In fact, Larson (2000b: 3) noted that *the possible candidate* is ambiguous between meaning 'the potential candidate' (= a direct modification reading) and 'the X which Y considers as a possible candidate' (= implicit relative reading). In Spanish, as expected, this analysis does not hold for *el posible candidato*, which only means 'the potential candidate'. There is also no ambiguity in copular constructions: *El ataque es posible* does not refer to 'the potential attack' but rather entails that 'X considers that the attack is feasible', the same meaning we find in *el ataque posible* and different from that in *el posible ataque*. Observe that we can say *El ataque es posible/viable pero arriesgado* 'the attack is possible (=feasible) but risky' (i.e., there are constraints on its feasibility) but not #*El ataque es posible pero no hay modo de hacerlo* 'the attack is possible (=feasible) but there is no way to launch it' – here there is a contradiction.[10] The contrast in (22) illustrates the same contrast with *falso* and completes the series in (21):

(22)   a. *Los acuerdos falsos son verdaderos/de toda confianza.
         "The untrustworthy agreements are true / deserve to be trusted / are worthy of trust."

     b. Los falsos acuerdos son verdaderos/de toda confianza.
         "The fake agreements are true / deserve to be trusted / are worthy of trust."

Restrictive, degree/quantifying, and deictic/event modifier adjectives are usually not possible either in postnominal position or in copular structures. In case they appear postnominally, a different reading usually obtains; we find the same in copular structures. Let us consider both cases separately.

In the case of restrictive and degree/quantifying adjectives, the meaning contrast evokes the opposition non-intersective/intersective. While the non-intersective reading appears in prenominal position, the intersective reading appears in postnominal position and copular sentences (see the second series of examples in 23a). In the case of deictic adjectives, the deictic function

---

[10] In this regard there appear to be differences with English and Italian where both interpretations are possible in copular sentences.

sometimes cannot be expressed through postnominal modification[11] and even less so through copular predicative structures (see the first series in 24). When deictic adjectives appear postnominally it would perhaps be better to think of them as polysemic: adjectives like *nuevo* "new," *antiguo* "old," *viejo* "old" are interpreted postnominally not as deictic but as qualitative adjectives.

(23)　**Restrictive and degree-quantifying adjectives**

　　a.　*El hecho es mero.
　　　　*"The fact is mere."

　　b.　El desacuerdo es total.
　　　　"The disagreement is complete." (i.e., they disagree in all respects, not "the act of disagreeing is such that represents a clear case of disagreement", namely the reading found in *el total desacuerdo*)

　　c.　La solución es perfecta.
　　　　"The solution is perfect." (i.e., it belongs to the set of perfect acts; cf. *la solución perfecta*, different from the meaning the adjective has in *una perfecta solución*, i.e., perfect as a solution/a solution in all respects).

(24)　**Deictic adjectives:**

　　a.　*La reina es futura.
　　　　*"The queen is future."

　　b.　*El alumno es último.
　　　　"The student is last."

　　c.　El acuerdo es antiguo.
　　　　"The agreement is old." (not "previous" as in *el antiguo acuerdo*)

(25)　**Event modifier adjectives:**
　　　　El viaje fue largo y entretenido.
　　　　"The trip was long and entertaining" (as in *el viaje largo y entretenido*)

4.2.2.2 *The subset property*　Only DPs with postnominal adjectives can be used in response to the question "What kind of an N is X?" For example, if somebody were to ask *What kind of lawyers are Rodrigo and Pedro?*, a possible answer would be *Rodrigo y Pedro son abogados competentes* 'Rodrigo and Pedro are competent lawyers' but not *??Rodrigo y Pedro son competentes abogados.*

---

[11] The reason for this remains obscure to me. Perhaps these forms are not non-predicative adjectives but rather close to deictic determiners.

Another context in which we can test the subset property is provided by what we may call *set-making verbs* like *distinguir* 'distinguish,' *diferenciar* 'differentiate,' *dividir* 'divide,' or *agrupar* 'group.' When we say *Distingo entre sueños posibles e imposibles* 'I can distinguish between possible and impossible dreams' we mean that dreams can be classified as possible and impossible, and we suppose that a distinction can be made between dreams that are candidates to become materialized and those that are simply out of reach. **Distingo entre posibles e imposibles sueños* sounds awkward if not ungrammatical because the subset reading is not possible. The following is another example in the same line (note that the strangeness in (26b) goes away if *luminosas mañanas* and *tormentosas mañanas* is interpreted as "echoed discourse").

(26) a. Mis mañanas infantiles se dividen en mañanas luminosas y mañanas tormentosas.
"My childhood mornings divide between bright mornings and stormy mornings."

b. ?Mis mañanas infantiles se dividen entre luminosas mañanas y tormentosas mañanas.

In sum, the subset property shows in those cases when adjectives are used restrictively because they serve to denote a class: a subset of the set mentioned by the N head. Prenominal adjectives usually are not qualified to trigger this interpretation.

4.2.2.3 *Degree modification on pre- and postnominal adjectives*   Of course, gradability is not a property which distinguishes between different logical types of adjectives. There are modal adjectives that are gradable: *el muy posible acuerdo* 'the very possible agreement' (but: **el muy supuesto asesino* 'the very alleged murderer') or even event/deictic modifiers which accept degree modification: *el muy anterior suceso* 'the very much earlier event.' However, for the sake of my argument in this work, I will consider gradability as a property of basically two classes of adjectives: pure qualitative ones (*los ojos tan limpios* 'such clear eyes,' *el niño menos feliz* 'the least happy boy,' *los más altos cipreses* 'the tallest cypresses,' *la muy seca piel de la niña* 'the girl's very dry skin') and deverbal ones (*el muy discutido asunto* 'the much debated topic,' *el área completamente protegida* 'the fully protected area').

Kennedy and McNally (2005) have convincingly argued that gradable adjectives can be partitioned into two semantic classes: relative vs. absolute adjectives. These two classes capture the fact that adjectives, by virtue of their lexical features, have different scalar properties. Absolute adjectives like *awake*, *open*, *full*, or *straight* have a non context-dependent standard of comparison:

"they simply require their arguments to possess some minimal [or maximal] degree of the gradable property they introduce" (ibid.: 14). Relative adjectives like *tall* or *expensive* have a context-dependent standard: there is a contextual standard of comparison. In other words, absolute adjectives have a "closed" scale structure while relative adjectives have an "open" scale structure.

There are many interesting properties which differentiate these two types of adjectives.[12] Here, I will concentrate only on the fact that contextual standard of comparison and scale structure affect the grammatical behavior of the degree modifiers which can be applied to gradable adjectives. According to the aforementioned authors, degree modifiers like *very*, *much*, and *well/completely* are sensitive to standard type and scale structure. More strictly, the degree modifier *very* is restricted to relative adjectives, while absolute adjectives, in normal usage, reject modification by this adverb:

(27)   a.   The international space station is very expensive.

       b.   ??They were very able to solve their own problems.
            (Kennedy and McNally 2005: 65)

In contrast, degree modifiers like *well* or proportional modifiers like *completely* combine with adjectives that have closed scales (28a) and (28b), but not with adjectives that have open scales (28c).

(28)   a.   We are well aware of the difficulties.

       b.   We are completely aware of the difficulties.

       c.   *This book is well/completely expensive.

Let us consider now the two series of Spanish adjectives in (29). Those in (29a) are relative adjectives with an open scale and they accept modification by *muy* 'very' but not by the proportional modifier *completamente* 'completely.' Those in (29b) are absolute adjectives with a closed scale such that they can be modified by *completamente* 'completely.'[13]

(29)   a.   muy/*completamente {inteligente, ágil, triste, tranquilo,[14] orgul-
            loso}
            'very/*completely {intelligent, agile, sad, calm, proud}'

---

[12]   See Kennedy and McNally (2005) for a detailed analysis of relative and absolute adjectives.

[13]   When modified by *very* in special contexts, a fact that I do not consider here, they probably change their scalar properties and denote the average degree of the property of an object, thus behaving like relative adjectives.

[14]   Observe that the adjective *tranquilo* can be modified by *completamente* when it is used as a stage-level predicate (*Juan está completamente tranquilo* vs. **Juan es completamente tranquilo*). I thank Olga Fernández for this observation.

   b.   completamente {seca, descuidada, incapaz, abierta, insensible}[15]
        "completely {dry, careless, incapable, open, insensitive}"

When relative adjectives with an open scale (29a) are modified by *muy*, this modifier boosts the (contextual) standard of the property with respect to the objects to which the adjective applies (Kennedy and McNally 2005). When absolute adjectives are modified by *completamente* this modifier fixes the degree of the property at an endpoint in the structure of the scale that a gradable adjective uses as a basis for ordering objects in its domain.[16]

   Both types of adjectives can precede or follow N in Spanish DPs. However, the occurrence of both types of adjectives in pre- and postnominal position shows restrictions that depend precisely on the presence of the aforementioned degree modifiers. (In the following judgments, I disregard generic contexts where these distinctions do not hold.)

   Observe the facts in (30)–(35). They show that there is a kind of complementary distribution between the two classes: relative adjectives modified by *muy* are felicitous in prenominal position; however, such a modification sounds awkward – or has to be qualified – when they are postnominal (examples 30, 31, and 32). In contrast, absolute adjectives modified by *completamente* are almost impossible prenominally, their standard position being the postnominal one (examples 33, 34, and 35) (of course NPs containing prenominal adjectives preceded by *completamente* are perfectly grammatical if the adverb is removed).

   Relative adjectives:

(30) a.   El muy inteligente profesor esquivó la respuesta.
           "The very intelligent teacher avoided the answer."

      b.   ??El profesor muy inteligente esquivó la respuesta.

(31) a.   Los muy ágiles atletas llegaron a la meta.
           "The very agile athletes reached the finish line."

      b.   ?Los atletas muy ágiles llegaron a la meta.[17]

(32) a.   El muy torpe electricista provocó un cortocircuito.
           "The very clumsy electrician caused a short circuit."

      b.   ok/?El electricista muy torpe provocó un cortocircuito.

---

[15] I am very grateful to Isabel Pérez Jiménez for the examples in the two series.

[16] Of course, *completamente* has other uses which are equivalent to *very*. Such cases will not be considered here.

[17] *Los atletas muy ágiles* and *el profesor muy inteligente* sound appropriate under two conditions: a) when the DP has been previously mentioned, and b) when *muy* 'very' is equivalent to *más* 'most.'

Absolute adjectives:

(33)   a.   *El completamente seco paisaje da mucha tristeza.

       b.   El paisaje completamente seco da mucha tristeza.
            "The completely dry landscape causes much sadness."

(34)   a.   *El totalmente ineficaz médico se llama José.

       b.   El médico totalmente ineficaz se llama José.
            "The totally inefficient doctor is called José."

(35)   a.   *La completamente insensible cantante es mi prima.

       b.   La cantante completamente insensible es mi prima.
            "The completely insensitive singer is my cousin."

I consider it reasonable to assert that such contrastive behavior constitutes further evidence that pre- and postnominal adjectives have different semantic relations to the N they modify. I am unable to go as far as to establish exactly why fixing of a value on the scale (the function of *completamente*) helps to fulfill the restrictive function of postnominal adjectives and, at the same time, makes the adjective invalid to be an NR modifier. Perhaps the reason is that absolute adjectives modified by degree adverbs become stage-level predicates and stage-level predicates are not possible prenominally but only postnominally.

In contrast, it is more evident, at least intuitively, in what sense relative adjectives modified by *muy* help to delineate the central property expressed by the adjective (cf. 11): if the standard of the property is above the normal standard for the N, this property is more likely to be considered central or distinguished.

4.2.2.4 *The specific/non-specific distinction and the position of evaluative adjectives*   In section 4.2.1.4 above, examples (16) and (17), I described "extreme degree" or superlative adjectives as an exception to the correlation between position and N/NR interpretation. Since they express subjective judgments they are NR in both positions and they do not serve to establish partitions among classes or subsets. However, there are interpretive differences that depend on the position in which they surface.

Knittel (2005: §2.2) (following Waugh 1977) noted that adjectives such as *magnificent*, when postnominal, are used to introduce new information, while their prenominal position indicates that they are part of an anaphoric NP. The following French sentence illustrates this observation:

(36)   J'ai vu *un éléphant énorme*. Cet *énorme éléphant* buvait de l'eau.
       Lit. I have seen an elephant huge. This huge elephant was drinking
       water.
       (Waugh 1977: 132, apud Knittel 2005: 190)

This apparent generalization does not hold in Spanish. The examples in (37) show contexts where new information is introduced when the adjective of subjective evaluation occurs prenominally:

(37)   a.   –¿Qué os dio de comer?
            "What did he give you for lunch?"
            -Puso de primer plato *una riquísima paella*.
            "He served a delicious paella as a first course."

       b.   –¿Qué le vas a regalar?
            "What will you give her as a present?"
            -Pienso regalarle un *enorme ramo* de flores.
            "I will give her a huge bunch of flowers."

I understand that the contrast in (36) is a subcase of another much noted and important distinction involving prenominal adjectives, namely the fact that, in indefinite contexts, DPs with prenominal adjectives have a specific reading as can be see in (37). On the other hand, DPs with postnominal adjectives are ambiguous between a specific and a non-specific interpretation (Picallo 1994; Bosque 1996; Demonte 1999). Presupposition of existence of the journalist is clear in (38a), which can be continued as indicated; the same continuation is not acceptable in (38b) because the DP with an adjective following N gets a non-specific reading:

(38)   a.   Ana cree que una *muy importante periodista* le solicitará una entre-
            vista. Esa periodista es Marisa Fernández.
            "Ana believes a very important journalist will ask her for an inter-
            view. This journalist is MF."

       b.   Ana cree que una *periodista muy importante* le solicitará una entre-
            vista. #Esa periodista es Marisa Fernández.

Consider now the sentences in (39):

(39)   a.   Ana sabe que todos los conferenciantes se entrevistaron con una
            muy importante periodista.
            "Ana knows that all the speakers had an interview with a very
            important journalist."

  b. Ana sabe que todos los conferenciantes se entrevistaron con *una periodista muy importante.*

As is known, a DP is specific if it always takes wide scope, even when embedded under a quantifier under which the DP would not normally be able to scope. In (39a), where the nominal with indefinite article and prenominal adjective is embedded under a universal quantifier, we find the referential/quantificational ambiguity characteristic of indefinites (Fodor and Sag 1982). The DP is specific on the referential reading and it takes wide scope. In (39b), which corresponds to the same sentence with the embedded nominal constructed with a postnominal adjective, the indefinite DP has only the expected narrow scope quantificational reading. Fodor and Sag (1982: 359) noted that "richness" of the NP correlates with referential understanding and loss of narrow scope quantifier interpretation for indefinites. Unexpectedly, a prenominal adjective appears to contribute to the referential reading of the indefinite. It is far from the objectives of this chapter to provide an explanation for these interesting facts. I only want to remark that (36), (37), (38), and (39) show again that there are reasons to assert that adjectives have a meaning contribution to DP which is due to configurational factors.

4.2.3 *A generalization: two positions, two classes of adjectives*

Following a long tradition (Bolinger 1967; Chierchia and McConnell-Ginet 2000), I will label the two subclasses of pre- and postnominal adjectives as non-predicative and predicative, respectively.[18] These two types of adjectives differ as to their denotation. A non-predicative adjective denotes a function from adjective denotations to adjective denotations; it maps properties to properties. A predicative adjective denotes a function from individuals to truth values or a property of individuals.

  Adjectives that can be analyzed as properties of individuals can also be analyzed as functions from properties to properties, and as also noted by Chierchia and McConnell-Ginet, "the differences in logical type may actually explain certain distributional properties of classes of expression and thus constitute a substantive component of their behavior" (2000: 466). In other words, a large number of adjectives belong to both categories of predicative and non-predicative adjectives: adjectives like *alegre* 'funny,' *rojo* 'red,' *prudente* 'wise,' *sabio* 'learned,' *estúpido* 'stupid,' *redondo* 'round,' *saludable* 'healthy,' etc., can appear both pre- and postnominally without any

---

[18] Many authors use the term *attributive* to refer to adjectives that Chierchia and McConnell-Ginet call *non-predicative.*

significant change in their lexical meaning but with the previously analyzed differences in reading.

Given this background, the following questions arise: Are such configurations and interpretations due to the intrinsic meaning of the adjectives? Or are they rather due to the syntax of the expression, or perhaps to the combination of both factors? As I have anticipated, I think the latter is the right answer.

In section 4.4 I discuss the syntax which underlies the lexical semantic facts elaborated so far.

4.3 Theoretical background

To explain the syntax of pre- and postnominal adjectives I adopt the basic assumptions of the Minimalist framework as outlined in Chomsky (2001a, b). In this approach the fundamental syntactic operations are "Merge" and "Move." (External) Merge, the operation of basic-structure building, is an operation imposed by the recursive nature of language: it takes two syntactic objects, A and B, and creates a new object consisting of the two {A, B}. Move (also called "internal Merge") takes an element B already constructed by external Merge and places it under the c-command of a probe A. As to the motivation for Move, it is considered to be necessary in derivational approaches to express the fact that certain elements appear in non-theta positions for reasons of scope, or to manifest informational or discourse-oriented properties.

Internal and external Merge are both facets of so called "Set-Merge." In addition to Set-Merge, another way of yielding syntactic objects out of already constructed units can be conceived. In fact, "Pair-Merge" or adjunction is such an operation. Pair-Merge is asymmetric: it takes two elements (one of which is already built) and adjoins one of them to the basic projection, taking its label. Pair-Merge "has no selector and is optional" (Chomsky 1998: 51).[19]

In a strict minimalist system, every device employed has to be sustained on "conditions of computation efficiency and the interface conditions that the [linguistic] organ must satisfy for it to function at all" (Chomsky 2001b: 3). If this quite strong position holds, any syntactic derivation D should provide a pair of forms legible by the Phonetic and Semantic levels or interfaces which are respectively accessed by the sensory motor and the

---

[19] According to Chomsky (2001b: 16) the interface condition which imposes Pair-Merge appears to be the necessity to produce "composition of predicates."

conceptual–intentional (C-I) systems. These systems impose conditions on the operations which are active in narrow syntax. As for Merge and its relation to the semantic module SEM, if it "comes free" (Chomsky 2001a: 3), and if it has to provide units easily mapped onto the interface level SEM, it is conceivable that there could be a correlation between the semantic properties required by the C-I interface and the structures provided by the operations in narrow syntax.

The fundamental interface semantic properties discovered and elaborated along the history of formal grammar are (i) properties related to theta-theoretic relations, namely, to predicate–argument and predicative relations; (ii) properties deriving from the "composition of predicates;" and (iii) discourse-related properties. Theta-theoretic relations express s-selection and obey c-command; composition of predicates expresses the necessity of a predicate to act as an A' operator binding a variable when no subject is available; discourse-related properties are A or A' relations resulting from the way information is organized.

It appears that the category labeled Adjective manifests these three semantic properties and therefore gives rise to the three operations. The proposal I will elaborate on in the following section shows three possibilities.[20] The first one is based on the idea that certain adjectives (externally merged in DP) will be interpreted as expressing, roughly speaking, theta-theoretic requirements: they will be predicates selecting Ns as their "subjects." This is the case of predicative adjectives – usually postnominal in Romance languages – cf. (40) below. As a second possibility, other adjectives, those which interact with a functional category above NP (nP) as their adjuncts, will have the semantic properties associated with the "composition of predicates"; I understand as such the operation of one-place predicates that modify elements in N. This is the case of non-predicative adjectives – usually prenominal ones – cf. (41) below. In the third possibility, adjectives with a predicative interpretation may be moved from NP to the edge of nP to receive a focus interpretation (cf. (45) below).

The semantic relations between adjectives and nouns result then from the configuration obtained when certain lexical categories are merged with the appropriate heads. In other words, the interaction between lexical-semantic interpretable (valued) properties of adjectives and the configurations in which they appear provides the interpretation of DPs containing adjectives. I claim, moreover, that adjectives come from the lexicon encoding uninterpretable formal features (gender and number) and (valued) semantic

---

[20] Demonte (2005) contains a more comprehensive elaboration of this hypothesis.

features. Adjectives will end up with a specific semantic interpretation, predicative or non-predicative: [+p] or [−p], according to their position after external Merge. Of course, [+p] or [−p] are only convenient ways to represent the many nuances of the two distinct but not always univocal semantic interpretations that adjectives may receive in pre- and postnominal position.

Regarding the structure of DP, I assume a quite strict – although not total – parallelism with VP (see sections 4.4.1. and 4.4.2.2. below) and I propose that, besides NP and DP, there must be an nP category whose head is a light n (Carstens 2000; Adger 2003). This head contains uninterpretable phi-features and may project a possessive "agent" in its Spec. This head becomes a probe to delete the (un)interpretable gender and number features of a goal N. I assume that, aside from nP and from conceptually and empirically necessary functional projections like, perhaps, DemP, there are no other functional categories in DP.

4.4 Merge of adjectives in DP

4.4.1 *Types of syntactic N–A relations*

Given the assumptions adopted earlier, we expect to find basically two types of syntactic relations between nouns and adjectives (for the time being, I leave aside internal Merge for reasons of focalization):

(a) There is a structure in which adjectives are recursively adjoined to nP – a functional phrase that perhaps may simply be called FP – as in (40); this is the case of non-predicative adjectives.

(b) There is a configuration obtained by the merging of adjectives as predicates of N within the c-command domain of the N head, as in (41) – this is the case of predicative adjectives.

I would also like to claim that the difference between languages in which adjectives may be both pre- and postnominal and languages like English, where adjectives occur only prenominally, is due to the lack of overt N-movement in languages of the latter type (a question I will not consider in this chapter). Similarly to what occurs with V to I movement, this type of movement might ultimately be related to the morphophonological content of the functional head. Still, this assumption is controversial since I am claiming that N to n – as opposed to V to v – is not universal.

(40)   Non-predicative (prenominal) adjectives

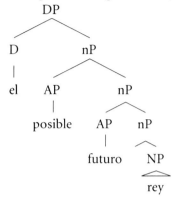

(41)   Predicative (postnominal) adjectives

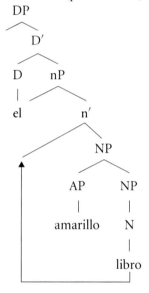

Now let us consider the reasons for the two representations just proposed.

4.4.1.1 *Non-predicative (prenominal) adjectives*   First, consider (40). Recall that it has been shown in section 4.2 that [−p] and [+p] adjectives differ interpretively. Given (40), it can be claimed that [−p] adjectives receive the aforementioned intensional interpretation at SEM (the semantic module) once they Pair-Merge with nP. As a consequence of this merge, the members of the pair are then sent to Spell-Out, the last step in the derivation, and, at the same time, are interpreted according to both their intrinsic meaning and the position they occupy in the syntactic hierarchy.

Secondly, note that in section 4.2 we distinguished two subtypes of [−p] or prenominal adjectives, which give rise to the following readings: (i) modal and event modifier adjectives, with an intensional reading, as in (42) (recall also (10) and (15); and (ii) qualitative adjectives with a non-restrictive reading, as in (43) (recall also 11).

(42) El *posible futuro rey* llegó tarde.
      "The possible future king arrived late."

(43) a. Se abrirán las *anchas alamedas*.
          "The wide tree-lined avenues will be opened." (The tree-lined avenues will be opened, and they are wide).

      b. Las *deliciosas galletas* están en el coche.
          "The delicious cookies are in the car." (The cookies are in the car, and they are delicious.)

These two types of readings have been described by Higginbotham (1985) as a case of (modal, intensionally oriented) modification of the attribute indicated by N, as in (43a), and as a case of "autonymous theta-marking," where the adjective saturates a denotational variable in N, as in (43b).

The relevant question now is how syntax (Pair-Merge) lays the basis for semantic interpretation. My claim is that in DPs with pair-merged adjectives these predicates combine semantically with elements in the semantic structure of n due to the effect of independent compositional rules that apply straight-forwardly in adjunction configurations.[21] More precisely, adjunction is the suitable syntactic correlate for certain compositional rules to the extent that adjuncts syntactically have a binding capacity, and semantically can be taken as one-place predicates whose arguments are present in the nominal. Descrip-tively speaking, these interactions between adjunct adjectives and nouns entail the following possibilities: First, the adjectives will have scope over spatio-temporal event arguments (e.g., circumstantial adjectives like *antiguo* 'old'). Second, the adjectives will have scope over denotational variables (e.g., non-restrictive qualitative adjectives like *bonita* 'nice/pretty') or over the "attribute" expressed by N (e.g., modal adjectives like *presunto* 'presumed' or restric-tive adjectives like *completo* 'complete'). Among the just mentioned putative

[21] A piece of evidence that these prenominal adjectives are adjuncts with a binding capacity – as opposed to postnominal adjectives – is that they have scope requirements that are violated if they do not occur in a given order.

elements in the semantic structure of N, event arguments do not need specific motivation. Nevertheless, it is obvious that the notion of "denotational variable" is left (deliberately) vague. Since it refers to the various aspects covered by the intension of the noun (tentatively: (i) properties "mentioned" by N, in the case of modal modification; and (ii) "distinguished" or particular properties of N, in the case of evaluative adjectives) we might think that this "denotational" variable is the R argument claimed to be bound by determiners when dealing with referential expressions (Longobardi 1994) or perhaps a world argument.[22]

The configuration in (40) correlates with this semantics since it involves, as in the case of Ernst (2002) for the treatment of adverbs, a scope-based approach to the position of non-predicative adjectives. This approach states that, in general, these adjectives must be the sister of (i.e., be adjoined to) a constituent with which they can establish the appropriate semantic relation (e.g., an eventive reading if n has an event argument). In this sense, the relation shown in (40) could be well adjusted to satisfy requirements of SEM at C-I.

4.4.1.2 *Predicative (postnominal) adjectives*   As for the set of [+p] adjectives, I claim that the appropriate representation for this type of relation is similar to the one found in (secondary) predication within VP, namely, when a predicate merges above the maximal lexical projection of N, as in (41).

In standard approaches to (secondary) predication this relation has been termed an adjunction relation. However, I will assume that there exists a distinction between true adjunction or Pair-Merge and Merge for predication purposes between AP and NP. In predication – as has been classically argued (Williams 1980) – predicative adjectives select for the category they modify. A (mutual) c/m-command relation should hold for the predication relation to be established. The question is then how to express c/m-command and what basic relation is expressed by c/m-command in (41).

Under the hypothesis of minimal search and restriction on bare phrase structure (Chomsky 2001b), we may contend that a head noun – and its maximal projection – can be extended through (a series of) second or subsequent merges. The unit so merged would be, strictly speaking, a special kind of Spec or, in my descriptive terms, an Adjunct/Spec. By definition, Specifiers must satisfy the Extended Projection Principle (EPP) feature of the head (internal Merge) or be semantically selected by the head (external Merge). In certain cases, they have to undergo Agree (where a head contains a probe seeking

---

[22] One referee, wondering about the justification of this denotational variable, suggested that this notion could be implemented within a semantics where nouns do not have world arguments and where intensionality is handled in some indirect way. Unfortunately, for lack of space I cannot develop this suggestion any further.

a goal with matching features). In the case of predicative adjectives they are not selected by N (instead the adjective would select for N, in a certain sense), and the relation between nouns and predicative adjectives in DP is not one of Agree. I stipulate that the relation between N and the predicative adjective in (41) is Concord (Carstens 2000). Concord is assumed to take place when pairing among features is required, as a part of Merge, but there is no matching of features with the resulting pied-piping and deletion. I will not take a position as to whether Concord delimits a second type of specifier, but there are independent reasons to assert that the relation between AP and NP in (41) is closer to the Spec–head relation than to the adjunct–XP relation. As we will see immediately below, the weak constraints on the ordering among restrictive adjectives also appear to provide some support for this hypothesis.

If these assumptions are tenable, predicative adjectives are then merged in DP as (multiple) specifier-like elements. In other words, I assume that the syntactic relation between N and the predicative adjectives modifying it is similar to the one that is established in secondary predication, namely, the AP merges higher than NP within the same maximal projection and the configuration does not preclude m-command as would be the case if we were dealing with an adjunction relation. At the SEM module this way of combining the adjective with the noun will be read, then, as the intersection between the denotations of N and A. Merge of predicative adjectives in DP will not be subject, on this view, to any other restrictions, and lexical incompatibilities between N and A will produce deviance and not ungrammaticality.

4.4.1.3 *Focused adjectives in DP*   Let us turn to the cases of (epithetic) appositive adjectives like *la blanca paloma* 'the white dove' (recall (11b) and (12) above), or the case of contrastively stressed restrictive adjectives (recall (9)).

(44)   las ESPANTOSAS tristes jornadas
        "the HORRIBLE sad journeys" (i.e. the journeys had the distinguishing characteristic of being sad; moreover, they were horrible – not melancholic or simply different from regular ones)

I propose that what we have here is raising of a predicative adjective from Spec of NP up to a Focus position above nP (see 45).

(45)

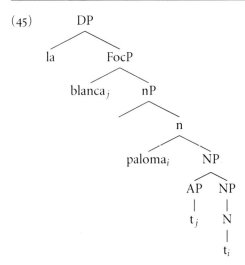

Bolinger wrote of examples like *Los españoles que vinieron en opuesta dirección* 'the Spaniards who came in the opposite direction,' where it is not expected for a restrictive adjective like *opuesta* to appear in such a position, that "when [somebody] says it, [he/she] de-accent[s] *dirección*" (1967: 91). I share this assessment and claim that focalization (coupled with previous de-stressing of other focused constituents) is deeply bound up with the marked meaning of certain prenominal adjectives that appear postnominally (when they are restrictive instead of nonrestrictive).[23]

At this point, we may ask whether the configuration in (45) is also used to derive nominal predications with exclamative meaning, as in (46a), similar to English (46b):

(46) a. ¡(Muy) Guapo tu novio!
          Lit. (Very) Handsome your boyfriend

      b. How tall a man

The construction in (46b) has been analyzed as movement of a DP modifier to a Focus position at the edge of DP (Dikken 1998). At first sight it might be claimed that the Spec-FocP at the edge of nP in (45) could be the same position where adjectives are found in (46). Now, the ban against degree modifiers in constructions like the ones in (44) (*la muy ESPANTOSA triste jornada*), but not in cases like (46a) indicates that we are dealing with two different configurations. The focused A(P) in (46a) and (46b) could be the

---

[23] Scott (2002) also claims that certain adjectives may be preposed into some sort of Focus phrase within DP.

predicate of a small clause predicative DP structure (Trombetta 2002) and be, in fact, moved to a FocP at the edge of a PredP. In a similar vein, these cases of "extraposed" degree adjectives are analyzed by many authors as constituent fronting to the left periphery of the noun phrase:

(47)   [$_{DP}$ [How tall] [$_{DP}$ a man]] is your friend?

Consequently, the facts in (46) show that there could be two Focus positions within DP, a lower one related to the nP domain, where qualitative adjectives move past nP, and a higher one related to degree evaluation. In (48) both possibilities are attested:

(48)   [$_{DP}$[$_{FocP}$Muy guapo][$_{DP/PredP}$[tu[$_{FocP}$[ENCANTADOR]][$_{nP}$riquísimo novio]]]
Lit. Very handsome, your CHARMING wealthy boyfriend.

But there is still another set of facts that falls within the hypothesis that Merge of A at a FocP plays a significant role in accounting for the position and interpretation of adjectives within DP. Cinque (1994) identified a class of "predicative" adjective structures which appear after a series of adjectives, or after a PP complement of N, with a contrastive interpretation. Italian, Spanish, and French are similar in this regard. English has the same construction, with the specific condition that this position is restricted to "heavy" adjectives. Observe the series in (49). (49a–c) are taken from Laenzlinger (2005: 671) and the postposed adjective in (49d) is not supposed to be a contrastive focus).

(49)   a.   una macchina rossa italiana, (veramente) BELLISIMA

b.   une voiture rouge italienne, (vraiment) MAGNIFIQUE

c.   un coche rojo italiano, (verdaderamente) FANTASTICO
"a really beautiful/magnificent/fantastic red Italian car"

d.   a red Italian car, suitable for large families

The usual analysis for this construction (see Bernstein 1991 or Campos and Stavrou 2003) is the Cinquean one, that is, it is assumed that a predicative projection (a PredP to the right of a postnominal adjective) hosts the contrastively marked adjectives in (49). We can extend this analysis to Spanish (49c), which will simply add another structural position to the one already proposed. However, I would like to highlight two distinctive properties of the phrases in (49a–c). One is the fact that, like (44), they receive a contrastive interpretation. The other is that this position is usually restricted to evaluative gradable adjectives generally carrying subjective meaning.

I agree, then, with Laenzlinger (along the lines of Bernstein 2001) in that there is a specific predicative/focus projection in a very high position within the noun phrase. However, I differ from Laenzlinger in not assuming the pied-piping/snowballing FPAgr(NP) movement within NP. Given my analysis, a FocP in the higher part of the DP (recall 48) could host the contrastive predicates in (49). The process yielding this result is an external Merge that strands an XP constituent on the right of DP. As a result, we have, as usual, two types of focus: one resulting from internal Merge, and another coming from external Merge.

To summarize, the three derivations for adjectives modifying N in DP appear to be just those which are possible according to general principles of constituent structure formation, and they adapt straightforwardly to interface conditions. They also adapt correctly to the types of adjective meanings identified in section 4.2.

4.5 Summary and Conclusions

In the first part of this chapter I presented a new classification of non-predicative and predicative adjectives and introduced a series of generalizations showing that the semantic interpretation and logical types of adjectives strongly correlate with syntactic position. In the second part, I justified the proposal that the modifying relation that adjectives establish with Ns is created by the three operations for forming phrase structure that are provided by the hypothesis of narrow syntax developed in Chomsky (2001a,b): external Merge, internal Merge (both cases of Set-Merge) and Pair-Merge. My claim is that non-predicative adjectives, [−p], receive such an interpretation at SEM when they Pair-Merge, or adjoin, to the maximal projection of N; predicative adjectives, [+p], receive their interpretation when they form a predication structure through external Merge. Adjectives which "preserve" their predicative interpretation in prenominal position or are non-restrictive in postnominal position have been displaced to a Focus position above NP, which constitutes a case of internal Merge. These three operations are the only options. By adhering to a narrow set of assumptions and minimal analyses, we thus illuminate aspects of the syntax–semantics interface.

Acknowledgments

The research underlying this work has been partly supported by the research project BFF2003-06053, funded by the Spanish DGI (Ministry of Science and Education) – FEDER. I would like to thank Olga Fernández, Cristóbal Lozano, Louise McNally, and Isabel Pérez for their kind advice and help on various versions of this article. I owe a special debt of gratitude to Chris Kennedy and an anonymous reviewer for their thoughtful and insightful comments and suggestions which undoubtedly contributed to the improvement of this chapter. Of course, all errors and shortcomings are only mine.

5

Nonrestrictive modifiers in non-parenthetical positions

MARCIN MORZYCKI

5.1 Introduction

The systematic but often subtle semantic differences between prenominal and postnominal adjectives first noted by Bolinger (1967) in many respects remain poorly understood. There remains a similar murkiness surrounding some of the systematic but often subtle semantic differences between preverbal and postverbal adverbs, of the sort noted by Jackendoff (1972), Bellert (1977), Ernst (1984, 2002), and Cinque (1994), among many others. This chapter focuses on one difference of this sort that occurs in both these murky domains: for both adjectives and adverbs, nonrestrictive interpretations are possible without resort to parenthetical intonation only in pre-head positions.[1]

The proposal is to derive this striking parallel from a broader principle governing how nonrestrictive interpretations are built up. More precisely, I will suggest that the semantic mechanism that gives rise to these interpretations – understood here more or less in the framework of Potts (2005) – is characterized by a fundamental structural asymmetry that prevents it from assigning such interpretations to constituents on right branches. This is in one respect a surprising proposal: linear precedence normally has no effect on semantic interpretation, and it's not altogether clear that information about linear precedence should be present at LF at all. What this may reveal is that such nonrestrictive, non-truth-conditional meaning is fundamentally quite different from ordinary meaning. One of the broader questions that underlie the proposal here, then, is how and where truth-conditional and nonrestrictive

---

[1] The term 'nonrestrictive' does not have a precise self-evident definition. I use it here essentially as a convenient label for the problem, in part because it is widespread in the literature. References cited in section 5.4.1 provide a fuller picture of how one might understand it.

meaning interact. The other broader question that will frame the discussion is the general empirical one of how modifier position and interpretation relate.

Section 5.2 relates the contrast in the availability of nonrestrictive interpretations between prenominal and postnominal adjectives to the corresponding contrast among adverbs. Section 5.3 shows that these facts are not easily explained away by independent assumptions about modifier syntax, focus/information structure, or prosody. Section 5.4 proposes a nonrestrictive counterpart of the rule of intersective modifier interpretation and argues that it is inherently structurally asymmetric. Section 5.5 concludes.

5.2 The phenomenon

5.2.1 *The contrast in adjectives*

It is now fairly well established that the position of an adjective correlates with its interpretation in a variety of diverse ways (Bolinger 1967; Sproat and Shih 1988; Valois 1991; Bernstein 1993; Cinque 1994; Laenzlinger 2000; Mcnally and Boleda 2004, among many others, and work in the typological tradition including Hetzron 1978 and Dixon 1982). One such contrast is reflected in the Bolinger examples in (1) and (2), in which the prenominal adjectives most naturally receive (something like) an individual-level interpretation and the postnominal ones (something like) a stage-level one (Larson 1998; Larson and Marušič 2004; Larson 1999).

(1)   a.   the visible stars   (Bolinger 1967)

     b.   the stars visible

(2)   a.   the navigable river   (Bolinger 1967)

     b.   the river navigable

There are other clear distinctions in this domain, though. In (3a), for example, the most natural interpretation involves a person who is both religious and socially masochistic; in (3b), the most natural interpretation involves a person who is both social and religiously masochistic.

(3)   a.   a religious social masochist

     b.   a social religious masochist

And of course there are a variety of semantically based ordering restrictions on adjectives – many of them discussed in other papers in this volume – including in English a requirement that color adjectives precede size adjectives (*the big red balloon* vs. *the red big balloon).

The corner of this larger picture that is of immediate interest here is reflected in (4a), which has both a restrictive and nonrestrictive interpretation, and in (4b), which has only the restrictive one.

(4)   Every *unsuitable word* was deleted.   (Larson and Marušič 2004)

   a.   **Restrictive:** Every word that was unsuitable was deleted.

   b.   **Nonrestrictive:** Every word was deleted; they were unsuitable.

(5)   Every *word unsuitable* was deleted.   (Larson and Marušič 2004)

   a.   **Restrictive:** Every word that was unsuitable was deleted.

   b.   *__Nonrestrictive:__ Every word was deleted; they were unsuitable.

A similar ambiguity is observed in this variation on the familiar incantation that appears at the end of acknowledgment footnotes, where the nonrestrictive reading is the most natural: *All the inevitable errors are solely the author's responsibility.*

This effect is not always easy to demonstrate – in part because English adjectives don't generally like to be postnominal – but with a sufficiently heavy AP it can also be perceived in judgments of pragmatic oddness:

(6)   a.   Every *needless and thoroughly reprehensible war crime* should be prosecuted.

   b.   #Every *war crime needless and thoroughly reprehensible* should be prosecuted.

The postnominal position in (6b) gives rise to the feeling that the speaker does not regard all war crimes as needless and reprehensible.

This effect is not limited to English, and is in fact perhaps more easily seen in Romance, where adjective position is not restricted quite so severely. The generalization, though, takes a slightly different form. While in English postnominal adjectives are unambiguously restrictive, in Spanish *pre*nominal adjectives are unambiguously *non*restrictive:[2]

(7)   *los* sofisticados   amigos *de María*   (Mackenzie 2004)
       the sophisticated friends of María

   a.   *__Restrictive:__ those of María's friends who are sophisticated

   b.   **Nonrestrictive:** María's friends, all of whom happen to sophisticated

---

[2] The facts are actually interestingly more complicated – nonrestrictive postnominal readings are subject to further restrictions. The absence of *de María* in (7b) can force the restrictive reading, for example (Violeta Demonte, p.c.).

(8)   los *amigos sofisticados* de María   (Mackenzie 2004)

    a.   **Restrictive:** just those friends of María who are sophisticated

    b.   **Nonrestrictive:** María's friends in general (who all happen to be sophisticated)

Italian works the same way:[3]

(9)   Le *noiose lezioni di Ferri se   le   ricordano tutti.*   (Cinque 2003)
    the boring lectures of Ferri REFL PRON remember all

    a.   *****Restrictive:** Everybody remembers just Ferri's classes which were boring.

    b.   **Nonrestrictive:** Everybody remembers Ferri's classes, all of which were boring.

(10)   Le *lezioni noiose* di Ferri se le ricordano tutti.   (Cinque 2003)

    a.   **Restrictive:** Everybody remembers just Ferri's classes which were boring.

    b.   **Nonrestrictive:** Everybody remembers Ferri's classes, all of which were boring.

The difference between Romance and English in this respect is expected, given that Romance nouns move higher in their projection than they do in English.

5.2.2 *The contrast in adverbs*

Just as with adjectives – perhaps more so, or at least more famously – the position of an adverb also correlates with its interpretation (Jackendoff 1972; Bellert 1977; McConnell-Ginet 1982; Wyner 1994, 1998a; Geuder 2000; Ernst 1984, 2002; Cinque 1999; Alexiadou 1997; Rawlins 2003, and many others). To take just two examples, the interpretation of each instance of *happily* in (11) is different, and in (12), only (12c) has the manner reading presumably intended:

(11)   Happily, Clyde would happily play the tuba happily.[4]

(12)   a.   #Lavishly, Josie has furnished the house.   (McConnell-Ginet 1982)

    b.   #Josie lavishly has furnished the house.

    c.   Josie has furnished the house lavishly.

Again, then, the effect of interest here is part of a larger and more complicated picture.

---

[3]   These paraphrases are Cinque's.
[4]   This is built around an example due to Jackendoff (1972).

There is an adverbial version of the restrictive–nonrestrictive contrast. Peterson (1997) observes the ambiguity in examples along the lines of (13):

(13)   The Titanic('s) rapidly sinking caused great loss of life.

    a.   **Restrictive:** The Titanic's sinking being rapid caused great loss of life.

    b.   **Nonrestrictive:** The Titanic's sinking, which was rapid, caused great loss of life.

Peterson doesn't relate this contrast to the structural position of the modifier, though – in fact, he suggests postverbal manner adverbs like the one in (14b) have nonrestrictive readings too. But as Shaer (2000, 2003) points out, the availability of such nonrestrictive readings is doubtful.[5]

(14)   The Titanic('s) sinking rapidly caused great loss of life.

    a.   **Restrictive:** The Titanic's sinking being rapid caused great loss of life.

    b.   ***Nonrestrictive:** The Titanic's sinking, which was rapid, caused great loss of life.

This may be clearer in embedded contexts, as in (15), or – paralleling the adjectival cases more closely – in antecedents of conditionals that restrict a quantificational adverb, as in (15).

(15)   a.   It is regrettable that the Titanic *slowly sank*.

    b.   It is regrettable that the Titanic *sank slowly*.

(16)   a.   If a ship *slowly sinks*, it is always regrettable.

    b.   If a ship *sinks slowly*, it is always regrettable.

Unlike the (a) sentences, the (b) sentences unambiguously express regret that the relevant ship-sinking wasn't faster.

To sharpen these intuitions a bit, suppose that I make the wager in (17):

(17)   I'll bet you $80 that Floyd, who has read a lot of medical books, could *easily perform* a successful nose job in a moving taxi.

If it turns out that Floyd has in fact read *no* medical books, I don't lose the bet – indeed, if he has read no medical books but nonetheless manages to perform a successful nose job in a moving taxi, I win it. If, though, Floyd manages to perform a successful nose job in a moving taxi, but it was not easy, a quandary

---

[5] The * here is mine.

results – it is not clear whether I win or lose the bet. This is expected, because the *easily* in (17) has both the restrictive and nonrestrictive readings, and it is not clear which was intended in the original bet. On the restrictive reading, I lose. On the nonrestrictive one, I win.

If nonrestrictive interpretations were in general possible postverbally, we would expect the same uncertainty to arise if the terms of the bet had instead been (18):

(18)   I'll bet you $80 that Floyd, who has read a lot of medical books, could perform a successful nose job in a moving taxi easily.

But this is not so. If this is the bet we had made, and it had in fact required some effort for Floyd to perform the nose job, I clearly lose. So a nonrestrictive reading is not possible here.

5.3 Some analytical possibilities

5.3.1 *Blaming focus*

One natural analytical intuition that quickly arises with respect to these facts – particularly in their adverbial form – is that this phenomenon is ultimately an effect of focus: focused modifiers are restrictive; non-focused ones are nonrestrictive (Göbbel 2004).

Certainly, there seems to be a connection here, and prosodic considerations more generally seem to be relevant. But this kind of explanation, at least in its most obvious form, doesn't seem to be sufficient on its own to explain the contrasts.

Wrong predictions   One difficulty is that no matter how one manipulates focus in the betting example with a postverbal adverb in (18), I lose:[6]

(19)   a.   I'll bet you $80 that Floyd, who has read a lot of medical books, could perform a SUCCESSFUL nose job in a moving taxi easily.

   b.   I'll bet you $80 that Floyd, who has read a lot of medical books, could perform a successful NOSE JOB in a moving taxi easily.

   c.   I'll bet you $80 that Floyd, who has read a lot of medical books, could perform a successful nose job in a MOVING taxi easily.

If the restrictive reading were only possible when the adverb is focused, it would be necessary to suppose that *easily* is in fact focused in all of these

---

[6]   Barbara Abbott (p.c.) points out that this argument is built around contrastive focus, which may not be the variety of focus that would be involved here – and indeed perhaps distinguishing more finely among different varieties of focus might diminish the force of the other arguments presented below as well. I leave this to future research.

examples, and indeed that it is not possible *not* to focus it in this position. This seems undesirable.

Some adjectives require focus?   Perhaps what's happening here, as Göbbel's (2004) approach might imply, is that phrasal prosody is somehow directly driving the placement of focus. But there does not appear to be any phonological difference between English and Spanish that would suffice to achieve this. At best, perhaps it might conceivably be able to rule out nonrestrictive readings in medial positions in (7b) and (8b), wrongly (Anne-Michelle Tessier, p.c.).

Some adjectives forbid focus?   An account that relies entirely on focus would require that prenominal adjectives in Spanish and Italian generally *cannot* be focused, since these are generally nonrestrictive. Such a uniform ban would be quite odd, and would in itself require some kind of explanation.[7]

Feels like more than focus   A final argument against a purely focus-based account is simply that these effects involve intuitions that don't seem to be the ones ordinarily evoked by focus. These effects are typically described using terms like "nonrestrictive," "double assertion" (Peterson 1997), or "parenthetical," and they are naturally paraphrased using *incidentally* or *by the way*. This is not how expressions that simply lack focus are normally described. So on these grounds too, much more would have to be said. Whatever role focus ought to play in the analysis, then, it seems likely that it could not be a substitute for some independent assumptions about how nonrestrictive meaning is computed.

5.3.2 *Assimilating these to other effects of modifier position*

Another natural approach to these observations is to suppose that the solution should follow straightforwardly from a general theory of modifier position – from whatever determines the relative order of evaluation, color, and size adjectives, for example, or pragmatic, subject-oriented, and manner adverbs. This is in some respects appealing, but it is not clear what its content would be without committing to a particular theory of this sort.

General theories in this domain are hard to come by (ones that aspire to high degrees of empirical breadth include Ernst 2002; Cinque 1999; Alexiadou 1997; Morzycki 2005). The most familiar of these, and perhaps the only one in which an account of these facts would be available straightforwardly, is the

---

[7] Certainly, it is not clear that this result would follow purely from facts about the distribution of phrasal stress, for example.

framework of Cinque (1999), in which particular positions in a tree are idio-syncratically associated with particular modifier classes. Might there be, then, a single spot associated with nonrestrictive modification, understandable per-haps in a vaguely Cinquean (Cinque 1994, 1999, and many others) treatment as in (20)?

(20)   A More-or-Less Cinquean Possibility

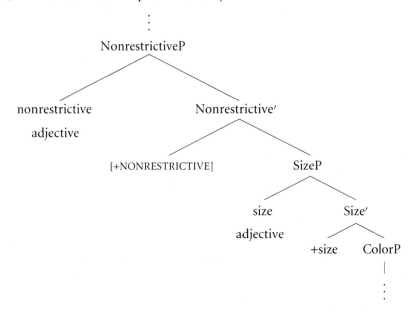

Perhaps. But there are reasons to think that these facts about nonrestrictive readings are of a different sort.

One is that, as Shaer points out, the restrictive/nonrestrictive distinction in adverbs cuts across adverb classes. Both the subject-oriented adverb *acciden-tally* and the (pure) manner adverb *softly* manifest the contrast, for example:

(21)   a.   Clyde softly / accidentally muttered something offensive.

  b.   Clyde muttered something offensive softly / accidentally.

This distinction similarly cross-cuts adjective classes as well.

Another difficulty with such an approach is that the restric-tive/nonrestrictive contrast targets multiple modifiers at a time, grouping together members of different classes:

(22)   I'm positively tickled pink to meet your charming lovely Norwegian wife.

Here, all the prenominal adjectives are most naturally interpreted nonrestrictively – this does not suggest that the addressee has any other wives, or that any of them are anything other than charming, lovely, and Norwegian.[8]

5.4 Modifier position in computing expressive meaning

5.4.1 *Expressive meaning*

Crucial to what needs to be captured in building an account of these facts is the sense of "double assertion." A natural way to do this is to take the nonrestrictive modifiers at issue here to involve a species of expressive meaning (Kratzer 1999; Potts 2005, and references there), as nonrestrictive relative clauses and numerous other constructions do.

Among the identifying characteristics of expressive meaning are:

- It is speaker oriented, in the sense that it conveys the speaker's commentary on what is being said.
- It always takes maximally wide scope. That is, an expression that contributes expressive meaning cannot occur under the scope of any scope-bearing expression. Thus the expressive meaning contributed by *hopefully* cannot be incorporated into a sentence such as *Every monkey that hopefully is housebroken can sleep in the living room*, in which *hopefully* would have to occur inside the scope of *every* – this sentence cannot be used to convey a desire that all relevant monkeys be housebroken.
- Unlike conversational implicatures, expressive meaning does not arise from the context of use and principles such as the Gricean maxims. Indeed, it is often associated with a particular lexical item. At least for current purposes, one can identify expressive meaning with *conventional* implicature.

5.4.2 *Potts 2005: Some theoretical machinery and* damn *expressive adjectives*

To serve as a foundation for an account, I will adopt the general framework of Potts (2005) for representing expressive meaning. In this framework, expressive meaning (conventional implicatures) and ordinary truth-conditional ("descriptive") meaning are computed compositionally, in parallel, and along distinct dimensions of semantic representation.

---

[8] Curiously, it seems to be the case that when one prenominal adjective is interpreted nonrestrictively, all of them tend to be. I have no explanation of this, apart from the speculation that it may be a psycholinguistic effect of some sort.

Potts proposes an analysis of nonrestrictive adjectives that focuses on adjectives that lexicalize a nonrestrictive meaning, e.g., *damn* and *fucking*.[9] In these representations, a syntactic tree such as the one in (23a) is understood to correspond to a semantic one, as in (23b), that represents its interpretation.

(23)   a.

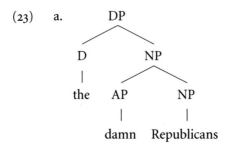

   b.

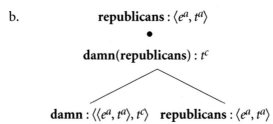

Importantly, the node in (23b) corresponding to *damn Republicans* has two tiers, divided by a bullet. The higher of these represents ordinary descriptive meaning. The lower represents expressive meaning. For each formula in (23b), its type is explicitly indicated to the right of the colon.

It is this type system that is the essence of how expressive meaning is represented. The core innovation is that (non-functional) types come in two flavors: one associated with an ordinary descriptive meaning (indicated with superscript a) and another with an expressive meaning (indicated with superscript c).[10] A rule of semantic composition – CI Application[11] – puts descriptive and expressive denotations together in the way (23b) reflects. This rule is roughly the expressive counterpart of the standard functional application rule. In (23b), then, the fact that *damn* contributes expressive meaning is reflected in its type. It is a function from ordinary properties (e^a, t^a) to expressive

---

[9] He calls these "expressive" adjectives, using the term in a more narrow sense than I will here. He suggests, though, that analogous nonrestrictive uses of e.g. *lovely* work roughly similarly.

[10] One might worry a bit about this. It does suggest, in a way that seems troubling, that there is a fundamental sortal distinction in the ontology between, for example, truth values of type t^a and t^c.

[11] "CI" is for "conventional implicature."

truth values (t^c), and thus applies to the denotation of *Republicans* to yield an expressive truth value. Because of how the CI Application rule works, the ordinary meaning of *Republicans* is simply passed on to *damn Republicans*, reflecting the fact that, apart from expressive meaning, these expressions are synonymous.

This of course reflects only how semantic composition proceeds. Substantively, Potts suggests that *damn* denotes a function that predicates of the *kind correlate* of its argument, specifically, that it denotes some kind of generalized disapproval predicate whose exact nature is irrelevant to the combinatorics, as in (24) (where $^\cap$ is the nominalization function of Chierchia 1984, which maps a predicate to a corresponding kind, and τ is an arbitrary type):

(24)   *damn* $\rightsquigarrow \lambda X . \mathbf{bad}(^\cap X) : \langle\langle \tau^a, t^a \rangle, t^c \rangle$

Very roughly, this says that *damn* is true of a property iff things that have that property are bad. Thus (24) could be spelled out more fully as (25):

(25)

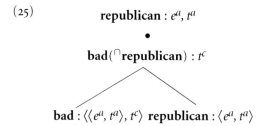

$$\mathbf{republican} : e^a, t^a$$
$$\bullet$$
$$\mathbf{bad}(^\cap\mathbf{republican}) : t^c$$

$$\mathbf{bad} : \langle\langle e^a, t^a \rangle, t^c \rangle \quad \mathbf{republican} : \langle e^a, t^a \rangle$$

5.4.3 *Some bumps in the road and a positive prediction*

At least two significant challenges present themselves in directly extending this approach to the phenomena of interest here.

Problems with what is modified   As Potts himself observes, there are many uses of expressive adjectives of this sort – in fact, of *damn* in particular – for which something more must be said. What he proposes to deal with these cases, though, proves to be of limited help with respect to the current goals.

A clear problematic case is (26):

(26)   The damn machine didn't come with an electric plug.   (Potts 2005)

Given (24), the predicted interpretation here would be one in which *damn machine* expresses generalized disapproval of machines as a kind:

(27)

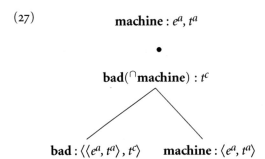

This isn't the desired result, though. One can very naturally talk about a *damn machine* without having the sentiment that machines are bad.

What Potts proposes to deal with this is that *damn* in these instances receives a clause-modifying adverbial interpretation, and actually gives rise to a semantic representation like (28):

(28)

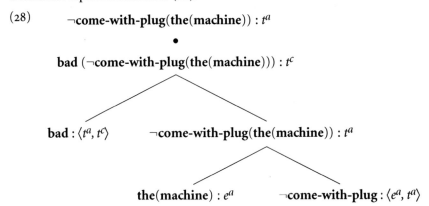

Importantly, this proposal has some firm empirical grounding – various adjectives can, under particular and somewhat mysterious circumstances, receive "adverbial" readings. The most familiar such case may be *The occasional sailor walked by* (Stump 1981; Larson 1999; Zimmerman 2000), in which the contribution of *occasional* is paraphrasable with an adverb as *Occasionally, a sailor walked by*.

However, the predicted interpretation for this sentence still raises some difficulties. The expressive meaning now assigned to the sentence is one that might otherwise be conveyed by uttering *Damn. The machine didn't come with an electric plug*. Certainly, this is an improvement. But with respect to a sentence like (29), it predicts an unattested adverbial reading:

(29)   The fucking people next door finally stopped playing their accordion.

The adverbial reading here can be represented as in (30):

(30)   **bad (finally-stop-playing-accordion(the(people-next-door)))** : t^c

This would be a reading in which the sentence communicates disapproval of the cessation of accordion playing. This is nearly the opposite of the actual reading. The kind-modifying approach is of no help here either, because *people next door* – being an inherently indexical expression – has no kind counterpart, as the oddness of, for example, #*People next door are widespread* reflects (Carlson 1977). Nor would it help to attach *fucking* below *next door*, since that would predict a reading in which the sentence communicates disapproval of people in general. This is a possible reading, perhaps, but certainly not the natural one. So this approach predicts one interpretation for (29) that is not in fact possible, and does not predict its actual interpretation.

Problems with other modifiers   If either version of this approach were simply applied as-is to most of the adjectives and adverbs of interest here, the wrong interpretation would result. Neither of the predicted interpretations expressed in (31a) and (31b) properly characterize the contribution of the adjective:

(31)   Every unsuitable word was deleted.

    a.   "Words (as a kind) are unsuitable."

    b.   "Unsuitably, every word was deleted."

The situation is similar with respect to adverbs, though it is not entirely clear what an "adverbial reading" of an adverb would be:

(32)   It's regrettable that the Titanic slowly sank.

    a.   "Sinkings (as a kind) are slow."

    b.   #? "Slowly, it's regrettable that the Titanic sank."

Positive prediction   In light of these problems, why go down this road? It is of course possible that the behavior of inherently expressive modifiers such as *damn* and *fucking* is in some essential way unrelated to how garden-variety modifiers can be interpreted nonrestrictively. But despite the obstacles to connecting these phenomena directly, drawing such a connection does make a surprising and desirable prediction.

It is part of the lexical semantics of *damn* and *fucking* that they can receive expressive interpretations only – they have no meaning apart from this, and there is no way to interpret them as contributing ordinary descriptive meaning. If what is banned from post-head positions is exactly this kind of meaning, then it should be the case that *damn* and *fucking*, having no non-expressive meaning to contribute, should be unable to occur in such positions at all. This is in fact the case:[12]

(33) a. He fucking ate the whole goddamn thing.

   b. *He ate the whole goddamn thing fucking.

(34) a. He'll damn well invade Iran.

   b. *He'll invade Iran damn well.

As (33) demonstrates, adverbial *fucking* is restricted to leftward positions in exactly this way. And this is the case for *damn well*, the adverbial analogue of *damn*, as well, as (34) shows.

5.4.4 *Building an alternative: An analogy to definite descriptions*

An essential problem here is this: It seems to be a fundamental property of expressive meaning (or conventional implicatures) that a constituent with such an interpretation can't contain a variable inside it that is bound from outside it. (Karttunen and Peters 1975 termed this the "binding problem.") The way around this is to suppose that nonrestrictive modification always involves reference, or at least some form of quantificational independence. The problem faced here is that in, for example, *unsuitable word* or *damn Republican*, the modified expression is property-denoting. So how then to reconcile this with the need to keep expressive and at-issue meaning apart from each other in the right way? What *do* expressive modifiers modify?

To address this question, it may help to momentarily revisit an old analytical intuition: that expressive meaning (or in any case nonrestrictive modification) involves, in some sense, interleaving two utterances, one commenting on or elaborating the other. Seen in this light, perhaps the Larson and Marušič (2004) paraphrase of (35a) in (35b) is not only apt, but also revealing:

(35) a. Every unsuitable word was deleted.

   b. Every word was deleted. They were unsuitable.

What's special about (35a) (on the relevant reading) is that it is a way of saying both sentences of (35b) at once. And the linguistic trick that makes (35b) possible is using *they* to refer back to a plural individual consisting of the set quantified over by *every*.

Thus an answer to the question just raised presents itself: Maybe what these nonrestrictive modifiers modify is a potentially plural discourse referent such as the one the pronoun in (35b) refers to.

---

[12] Setting aside an irrelevant verbal reading in (33) and an irrelevant manner reading in (34).

Importantly, the anaphora (35b) would not be possible with a singular pronoun:

(36)   *Every word$_i$ was deleted. It$_i$ was unsuitable.

That is, (36) can't mean "Every word was deleted and unsuitable." A natural assumption about why this anaphora is nonetheless possible in (35b) is that this *they* is an E-type pronoun, and consequently is interpreted like a definite description (Heim 1990):

(37)   Every word was deleted. *The words* were unsuitable.

This approach helps avoid an interpretation that includes an element such as "words were unsuitable," because, unlike kinds, definite descriptions involve a contextual domain restriction.

What's being quantified over in the unsuitable-words example is not, of course, all words, but only the contextually relevant ones – a fact I'll reflect here using a contextually supplied resource domain variable C (Westerstahl 1985; von Fintel 1994), as in (38) and (39).[13]

(38)   a.   Every unsuitable word$_C$ was deleted.

　　　b.   "Every word$_C$ was deleted. The words$_C$ were unsuitable."

　　　c.   "For every word x in C, x was deleted, and the sum of the words in C was unsuitable."

(39) $\forall x[[\textbf{word}(x) \wedge x \in C] \rightarrow \textbf{deleted}(x)] : t^a$

$$\bullet$$

$\textbf{unsuitable}(sup(\lambda y.\textbf{words}(y) \wedge y \in C)) : t^c$

Roughly analogous assumptions are possible for adverbs:[14]

(40)   a.   If a ship slowly sinks$_C$, it's always regrettable.

　　　b.   "Every ship-sinking$_C$ is regrettable. The sinkings$_C$ (i.e., the relevant sinkings) are slow."

　　　c.   "For every ship-sinking event e in C, e is regrettable, and the sum of all the ship-sinking events in C is slow."

(41) $\forall e[[\textbf{ship-sinking}(x) \wedge e \in C] \rightarrow \textbf{regrettable}(e)] : t^a$

$$\bullet$$

$\textbf{slow}(sup(\lambda e'.\textbf{ship-sinking}(e') \wedge e' \in C)) : t^c$

---

[13] In addition to contextual domain restrictions, these rough interpretations introduce a supremum operator that loosely corresponds to the definite determiner in the paraphrases. This is not as significant a move, however. Indeed, the Chierchia (1984) nominalizing type-shift $\cap$ itself has this general kind of semantics (at least extensionally). Note also that I am placing the resource variable C directly in the syntax, as a subscript on the head.

[14] There is a certain amount of sleight of hand taking place in (40) to avoid intensionality.

Striving to assemble these interpretations may be a step toward a more adequate general understanding.

It also provides an alternative way of understanding the *damn/fucking* facts in the previous sections. On this view, *the damn machine* will convey disapproval of only the machine relevant in the context, and *the fucking people next door*, disapproval of contextually relevant people next door.

5.4.5 *Expressive predicate modification*

The problem remains, however, of building up the interpretations in the previous section compositionally, and of doing so in a way that captures the syntactic constraints on where such nonrestrictive readings are available.

The rule   Since this is a two-dimensional semantics, with distinct dimensions of meaning being computed and distinct composition rules assembling them, perhaps rules that introduce expressive meaning may look quite different in principle from ones that do not. Specifically, maybe rules that introduce expressive meaning can be directly sensitive to precedence in a way ordinary non-expressive meaning is not. This would accord naturally with the intuition that nonrestrictive modifiers are in some sense secondary or additional, extra comments on the current utterance that happen to be interleaved with it.

In view of this, we can adopt the rule in (42). Potts' framework already has a rough counterpart to standard function application that operates in the expressive-meaning dimension – namely, the rule of Conventional Implicature Function Application mentioned earlier. Adopting (42) would maintain the parallelism by adding an expressive counterpart to a rule of intersective modifier interpretation.[15]

(42)   Expressive Predicate Modification

$$\beta : \langle e^a, t^a \rangle$$
$$\bullet$$
$$\alpha(\sup (\beta)) : t^c$$

$$\alpha : \langle e^a, t^a \rangle \quad \beta : \langle e^a, t^a \rangle$$

... where the relative order of α and β is as indicated

---

[15] This is slightly simplified, in that strictly speaking, it should reflect that the daughters can themselves have expressive meaning. This makes no substantive difference in this framework.

This rule can be understood to do three things:

- The *sup* operator picks out the largest plural individual in the extension of the modified expression (β).
- The denotation of the modifier (α) is predicated of this plural individual. Crucially, this happens in the expressive dimension of interpretation.
- The ordinary descriptive meaning of the modified expression is simply passed up as the ordinary descriptive meaning of the whole.

How this works   This rule will give rise to interpretations such as (43) and (44).[16]

(43)   a.   [Every [unsuitable word$_C$]] was deleted.

   b.

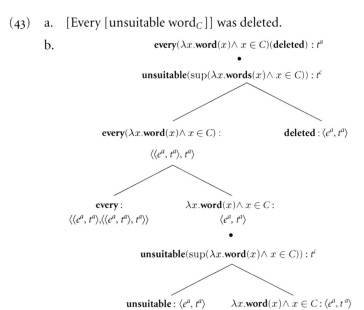

This mirrors the Larson and Marušič (2004) paraphrase. We obtain similar results for the adverbial cases:

---

[16] I am adopting the conventions that events (or, as would ultimately be necessary, situations) are of type s and that (i) holds:

(i)   for any a
      $a_C \rightsquigarrow \lambda x.a(x) \wedge x \in C$

(44)   a.   [If [a ship slowly sinks$_C$]] [it is always regrettable].

b. $\mathbf{always}(\lambda e.\mathbf{ship\text{-}sinking}(e) \wedge e \in C)(\mathbf{regrettable}) : t^a$

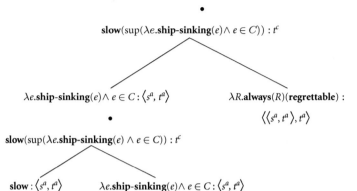

It bears pointing out here that I am assuming that C is interpreted on the head noun rather than on the determiner. This is crucial. It is this that ensures that the extension of the NP is whittled down appropriately *before* the nonrestrictive modifier applies to it.

How is this intersective?   In what sense is this a rule of intersective modifier interpretation? True, nothing is conjoined. But this does capture the same intuitive content of such a rule, and shares some of its essential properties. The expressions it combines must both be of the same semantic type, for example. As with predicate modification, they must in fact both denote properties. Moreover, because sup(β) must satisfy both α and β (the latter by definition), the conjunctive character of such a rule is implicitly captured.

In fact, the way (44) is formulated *requires* that it target only intersective modifiers. This makes a substantive prediction: that nonrestrictive readings of the relevant kind should be possible only for intersective modifiers. This seems to be the case. Certainly, it is difficult to see how the modifiers in (45) could get nonrestrictive interpretations:

(45)   a.   Every alleged mistake was deleted.

b.   Most possible students visited for a few days.

c.   The ship was probably sinking.

This may actually serve as a useful diagnostic for intersective modification in cases which remain unclear, such as subsective adjectives generally (Siegel 1976b; Landman 2001; Larson 1998).

5.4.6 Is "left branch" good enough? Will head movement break this?

Now that the proposal has been laid out, it is possible to more directly address a thorny question that has been lingering in the background. The generalization as it was presented early on was about the relative surface order of heads and modifiers. But of course there are a number of structures that can derive any particular order – a modifier might wind up to the right of a head, for example, even though it occupies a left branch. So perhaps it is simplistic to state the generalization as a simple matter of left branches versus right branches, as the proposed rule in (42) does. A related question, essentially a more specific form of it, is how this all interacts with head movement, which can change the relative surface order of modifier and head.

In fact, though, this kind of characterization may be an advantage. Among its important properties is that it may make it possible to derive the variation in the form it takes from one language to another via head movement. Returning to Romance for a moment, the generalization there is not that postnominal adjectives must be restrictive, but that prenominal ones must be nonrestrictive. Taking into account the independent fact that Romance nouns move higher in their NP (Bernstein 1993; Cinque 1994; others), at least half this generalization follows. The reason both readings are available in surface postnominal positions is that there are both left and right branches that are spelled out right of the noun.

Moreover, there is actually more flexibility with respect to head movement in (42) than there may seem. It can actually restrict the availability of nonrestrictive interpretations on the basis of the position of the head in a more fine-grained way. More often than not, the position in which heads are interpreted doesn't matter for the semantics, and usually it's convenient to assume they are interpreted in their base position. But nothing requires this, and one could equally well suppose that (some) heads are interpreted in their surface position and semantically reconstruct, binding so-called "big" – that is, high-type – traces. In light of (42) and the binding properties of expressive modifiers, this has consequences. The trace of a head inside the scope of an expressive modifier, if bound from outside its scope, would bring about the (independently) ruled-out binding-across-dimensions configuration. Thus a head can't bind its trace in the expressive meaning from inside the ordinary-meaning dimension. In turn, this and the left-branch requirement together create a system in which these nonrestrictive modifiers can only occur left of *wherever a head is interpreted.*

Given all this, some subtle predictions arise with respect to English as well. Assuming that verb movement in English is present but short (Johnson 1991) and that verbs are interpreted in their base positions, adverbs in English *should* admit nonrestrictive readings, even though right of the verb at the surface, if the verb has moved past them. This may be right:

(46)   If a government transfers prisoners secretly *t* to Syria, it's always

inexcusable.

In (46), the verb moves from the position indicated by the trace. Consequently, *secretly* should be able to get a nonrestrictive interpretation.

5.4.7 *An alternative approach*

Quite clearly, the proposal laid out here rests on a highly unorthodox and in some respects odd idea: that once fundamental distinctions are made among different tiers or layers of meaning, it makes sense to ask whether even the very basic notion that semantics is insensitive to linear order should necessarily carry over from standard descriptive meaning. But this must at this point be regarded as a kind of conjecture – alternative explanations of these facts are possible.

Chris Kennedy (p.c.) suggests one alternative route. Potts' proposal, and consequently the proposal here that builds on it, would place the burden of relating expressive and at-issue meaning squarely on the shoulders of the semantics. Instead, one might place more of the explanatory burden on the syntax, thereby simplifying the semantics. Rather than a separate rule of Expressive Predicate Modification or CI Application, one might instead suppose there is a functional head E, that takes APs as specifiers and NPs as complements, or AdvPs as specifiers and VPs as complements. Semantically, it would do what Expressive Predicate Modification does:

(47) $\text{E} \rightsquigarrow \begin{bmatrix} \lambda f \lambda g . f : \langle e^a, t^a \rangle \\ \bullet \\ \lambda f \lambda g . g(\text{sup}(f)) : t^c \end{bmatrix}$

(48)

$$\rightsquigarrow \begin{bmatrix} \lambda x . \textbf{word}(x) \wedge x \in C : \langle e^a, t^a \rangle \\ \bullet \\ \textbf{unsuitable}(\text{sup}(\lambda x . word(x) \wedge x \in C)) : t^c \end{bmatrix}$$

This has several advantages. First, and most relevant here, it is more semantically conservative – it doesn't commit to any notion that the semantics must be sensitive to linear order. Second, the place where linear order is expressed on this view is in the *syntax* of E, which seems natural. Third, this accounts for cross-linguistic variation in a fairly direct way. Languages that differ in the positions in which nonrestrictive modification is possible can be understood to differ either in the position in the sentence E occupies or in its headedness. And perhaps the greatest advantage of this approach is that it is consistent with a stronger notion of compositionality. Expressive Predicate Modification introduces elements of semantics – such as the supremum operator – that correspond to no linguistic expression and nothing in the syntax.

These are significant, of course. But of course they don't come for free. Most obviously, while this alternative approach is clearly more conservative in terms of the architecture of the grammar, it is certainly less syntactically conservative. Of course, if an overt expression of E could be discovered – or some other independent syntactic evidence could be brought to bear on the issue – this would be an appealing approach. And taking a syntactic leap in this way has the methodological advantage of compelling one to look for such evidence. Precisely because of that, though, it removes any pressure to look harder for evidence of semantic sensitivity to linear order, so this method-ological argument could cut either way.

Another difficulty with this approach is that it embodies essentially the Cinquean conception that proved problematic in section 5.3.2. As pointed out there, the nonrestrictive/restrictive contrast seems to cross-cut other semanti-cally based adjective and adverb classes. Thus, even though this is essentially a Cinquean approach, in a curious way it would be difficult to reconcile with a broader Cinquean model – one would have to find principled answers to questions like: Should a nonrestrictive evaluative adjective occupy the speci-fier position associated with evaluative adjectives or expressive adjectives, or somehow both? This would be an odd state of affairs in another respect, too. The principal motivation for the hypothesis that modifiers occupy specifier positions to functional heads is that this may provide a means of understand-ing otherwise mysterious restrictions on modifier order. But nonrestrictive modifiers don't seem to be associated with a fixed position relative to other adjectives in quite the same way other adjectives are.

That said, at present there does not appear to be any data in this domain that could serve as a case against the alternative approach in (47) and (48).

5.5 Final remarks

The core empirical argument here has been that both adjectives and adverbs can receive nonrestrictive interpretations only in leftward positions, and that they contribute expressive meaning (just as nonrestrictive relatives do).

I suggest an understanding of this in which a nonrestrictive modifier is predicated of something like a contextually restricted definite description. In this way, such modifiers receive an interpretation that loosely mirrors E-type anaphora. I also introduce a rule of semantic composition, Expressive Predicate Modification, as the expressive counterpart of the ordinary predicate modification rule. The proposed rule makes direct reference to linear order, requiring an expressive modifier to be on a left branch.

It's worth noting that throughout this system, syntactic and semantic constituency coincide. Among the other advantages of this approach is that it seems to get the right interpretation for nonrestrictive leftward modifiers in a way that is appropriately sensitive to what the modifier is modifying, and that creates parallel interpretation rules in both semantic dimensions. And, in providing an account that parallels a discourse anaphora effect, it has the virtue of corresponding to a natural paraphrase of what such nonrestrictive modifiers mean and of relating these structures to another (somewhat surprising) linguistic phenomenon. There is a somewhat unnerving big-picture question lurking here, though. Semantic rules are now standardly thought to be unable in principle to refer to linear order. But in light of multidimensional semantic theories such as that of Potts and others (notably Chierchia 2001), who treats scalar implicatures in a compositional multidimensional way, and of course theories of focus such as Rooth 1985), perhaps it is worth asking afresh whether in fact this standard view should extend to all levels of meaning – or, to put things another way, if these entirely distinct dimensions are genuinely necessary, maybe we should *expect* them to be fundamentally different in various respects.

Acknowledgments

For comments on various incarnations of this work, thanks to Adam Wyner, Alan Munn, Angelika Kratzer, Anna Maria di Sciullo, Anne-Michelle Tessier, Barbara Abbott, Ben Shaer, Brigid Copley, Chris Kennedy, Chris Piñón, Cristina Schmitt, Gina Taranto, Grover Hudson, Iannis Thomadakis, Louise McNally, Peter Svenonius, Tom Ernst, Violeta Demonte, and audiences at the Workshop on the Semantics of Adjectives and Adverbs at Universitat Pompeu Fabra, at Michigan State University, and at the 2005 LSA Annual Meeting, and to the various people I'm no doubt forgetting.

6

Adjectives and degree modification

JENNY DOETJES

6.1 Introduction

Adjectives are often considered to be the prototypical example of a "gradable" category.[1] Degree expressions such as *too* are restricted to adjectives and morphological comparatives, and superlatives are found for adjectives and not for other categories. This has led several linguists to assume that gradability is a distinctive property of adjectives (see, among others, Jackendoff 1977), while others rather insist on the fact that gradability is found across categories (see Bolinger 1972; Bresnan 1973; Doetjes 1997; Neeleman et al. 2004). This chapter investigates the relation between gradability and the category "adjective," as opposed to other categories, on the basis of the distribution of degree expressions.

Even though it is clear that certain degree expressions are adjectival modifiers only, it is also clear that other degree expressions have a much broader use. Consider the paradigm in (1), which compares French *trop* and English *too*.

(1)	a.	**trop** grand	**too** big	[ADJECTIVE]
	b.	**trop** apprécier	to appreciate **too much**	[GRADABLE VERB]
	c.	**trop** danser	to dance **too much**	[EVENTIVE VERB]
	d.	**trop** de soupe	**too much** soup	[MASS NOUN]
	e.	**trop** de livres	**too many** books	[COUNT NOUN]

Whereas the distribution of *too* suggests that adjectives (1a) differ from other categories and are the only gradable ones, *trop* combines also with nouns and verbs, and rather suggests that adjectives are not special at all.

[1] In this chapter I will not make a distinction between adjectives and those adverbs that have adjective-like behavior in the sense that they can be modified by, for instance, *very* (that is, for English, most of the adverbs ending in *-ly*, and a few other ones such as *well*).

The tension between the distributions of *trop*-like expressions, on the one hand, and of those that behave like *too*, on the other, will be the point of departure for this chapter. I will argue in section 6.2 that degree expressions form a continuum based on their distributions, roughly corresponding to compatibility with the categories in (1a–e). If a degree expression is compatible with category (a) it may be compatible with category (b), which is adjacent to (a) on this continuum. It cannot be compatible with an expression of the category (e), which is not adjacent to (a), unless it is compatible with all of the categories in between. For instance, there exist degree expressions that are limited to adjectives and abstract verbs (e.g. *terribly*), but no degree expressions that have the distribution of both *too* and *many*, as nouns and adjectives are not adjacent categories on the degree expression continuum. The continuum allows us to formulate the special relation between adjectives and gradability in a more precise way: adjectives are at one end of the continuum, and not somewhere in the middle.

Section 6.3 explores two ways in which the special position of adjectives at one end of the continuum could be accounted for. The first involves the lexical representation of adjectives. It has been claimed in the literature that expressions such as English *too* make use of a degree variable that is part of the lexical meaning of adjectives, while other categories lack such a degree variable. The second way to look at the relation between adjectives and gradability is based on scale structure (see Kennedy and McNally 2005). Instead of claiming that adjectives are associated with scales while other categories are not, it is hypothesized that certain types of scales are typically adjectival in the sense that they are incompatible with other categories. On this view, degree expressions that typically combine with adjectives are sensitive to adjectival scales, rather than to the category adjective itself.

6.2 The distribution of degree expressions

6.2.1 *The degree expression continuum*

The data discussed so far give a rather simple view of the distributions of degree expressions. According to the examples in (1), they are either compatible with different categories or they are compatible with adjectives only. It turns out that the distributional patterns are far more complex when we start looking outside of the adjectival system. This section will give further insight into these patterns, on the basis of which I will claim that the distributions of degree expressions form a continuum. A rough first version of this continuum, based on the examples in (1), is given in Table 6.1.

TABLE 6.1. The degree expression continuum (first version)

I	adjectives	**type A** very[E]	**type B** erg[D]			**type 0** −
II	gradable verbs	**type D** beaucoup[F]	**type E** veel[D]	**type C** trop[F] less[E] minder[D]	**type F** a mountain[E]	**type 0** −
III	eventive verbs					
IV	mass nouns					**type 0** −
V	plural nouns					**type G** many[E]

It seems to be the case – and this view will be motivated on the basis of a large number of examples below – that degree expressions do not cover several non-adjacent fields of the continuum in Table 6.1. That means, for instance, that an expression of type 0, found with gradable verbs and with mass nouns but nothing else (see the gray coloured cells in Table 6.1) is predicted to not exist.

Table 6.1 only contains the types of expressions given in (1). It will turn out later in this section that the classification in the table is incomplete. For instance, adjectives may be used as eventive predicates. In that case they fall in class III. Also, the table does not include comparatives, while these can be modified by a degree expression (e.g. *much bigger*). Comparatives combine with type D and type E expressions rather than type A or B (*beaucoup/*très plus*[F] */ veel/*erg meer*[D] 'much/*very more'), which suggests that they are situated somewhere near the gradable verbs.[2] In the remainder of this section I will give examples of the different types that are given in Table 6.1, mainly in English (E), Dutch (D), and French (F). Section 6.2.2 discusses the particular properties of French *très* 'very.' A revised version of Table 6.1 will be given in section 6.2.3, which concludes the discussion of the distribution of degree expressions.

Type A modifiers are typically adjectival modifiers. There are some clear cases of these modifiers in English and Dutch. The properties of French type A look-alikes, and more specifically those of *très*, the French counterpart of *very*,

---

[2] Degree expressions such as *completely*, *fully*, and *half*, which are associated with the presence of an endpoint on a scale or path, will not be taken into consideration. They differ in several respects from the modifiers looked at here, for instance in the fact that they can be used as path modifiers with PPs (Zwarts 2004). For discussion of the distribution of these expressions in various domains, see also Hoekstra (2004) and Vanden Wyngaerd (2001) (for verbs and event structure) and Kennedy and McNally (2005) (for adjectives).

will be treated in section 6.2.2 below. In addition to modifiers such as *very* and *as*, type A also includes comparative and superlative morphemes, as these usually combine with adjectives only.[3] Quite generally it seems to be the case that morphological comparatives and superlatives combine with adjectives, while analytic comparatives tend to have a larger distribution (cf. *-er* versus *more* in English).

(2)   a.   very dirty, too tired, as easy, smaller/est   (E)

      b.   te   moe, even gezellig, klein-er/st   (D)
            too tired, as   cosy,   small-er/est

The interpretations that we find for type A modifiers are equal degree (*as*, *even*), excessive degree (*too*, *te*), comparative (*-er*), superlative (*-(e)st*), high degree (*very*).

Obviously, it is not the case that all adjectives allow for the use of modification by one of these modifiers. As noted by Bolinger (1972), among many others, it is by no means true that all adjectives are intensifiable. As expected, the unintensifiable ones are incompatible with type A expressions. Moreover, Kennedy and McNally (2005) argue that the possibility of using *very* depends on the presence of a relative standard. I will get back to the role of the relative standard and of scalar properties of adjectives at various points below.

At first sight type A expressions are compatible with PPs as well, as in *very in love*. However, the possibility of using these PPs in typically adjectival positions (3a) suggests that they should be considered to be adjectives "in disguise," on a par with collocations such as *forget-me-not*, which behaves syntactically as a noun rather than a verb phrase (see Neeleman et al. 2004).

(3)   a.   a very in love couple

      b.   a [forget-me-not]$_N$

      c.   very [in love]$_A$

Type B expressions are usually interpreted as intensifiers and, according to the data discussed so far, they are compatible with adjectives and gradable verbs. Some examples are given in (4):

(4)   a.   terribly happy, to miss someone terribly   (E)

      b.   erg gelukkig, iemand   erg   missen   (D)
           very happy,   someone very/a lot miss
           "very happy," "to miss someone a lot"

---

[3] In this chapter I will remain neutral about the syntax of these expressions. See Neeleman et al. (2004) and Doetjes (1997) for arguments in favor of the idea that expressions that only combine with adjectives and those that may modify other categories as well occupy different syntactic positions. I will briefly discuss some of our arguments in section 6.3.2 below.

c. terriblement heureux, quelqu'un lui   manque terriblement
    terribly   happy,   someone to-him lacks   terribly
    "terribly happy," "he misses someone terribly"   (F)

The typical meaning of these expressions is either extreme degree or high degree. In this respect, this class is more restricted than type A. The source of these expressions is usually an adverb that has inherently a (very) high degree meaning, such as *horribly*. The lexical interpretation of these adverbs seems to fade away, resulting in an extreme degree or high degree modifier. The Dutch word *erg* originally meant *serious*, as in *een erge ziekte* 'a serious illness.' In some contexts only the high degree interpretation is left, as illustrated by *erg gelukkig* 'very happy.' In many cases a slight connotation remains that usually reflects the original meaning of the word. French *atrocement* 'cruelly, brutally' can be used nowadays in expressions such as *des murs atrocement blancs* 'extremely white walls,' but the use of *atrocement* still introduces a negative connotation. On the other hand, there are cases such as Dutch *geweldig*, which is derived from the word *geweld* 'violence,' but nonetheless has a positive connotation in modern Dutch.

The expressions of this type may also be used to modify predicative nouns, such as *honger/faim* 'hunger' and *dorst/soif* 'thirst' in the Dutch and French examples in (5).[4]

(5) a. Jan heeft verschrikkelijk honger/dorst.   (D)
        Jan has   terribly   hunger/thirst

     b. Jean a   terriblement faim/soif.   (F)
        Jean has terribly   hunger/thirst

In section 6.2.2, which concerns French *très*, it will be argued that these gradable predicative nouns form a subclass between adjectives and gradable verbs.

Type C expressions are the first type discussed here that can be used both as intensifiers and as expressions indicating a degree of quantity. The degree of quantity interpretation occurs with nouns and eventive verbs. For instance, when these expressions are combined with a plural noun such as *books*, they

---

[4] Next to these examples, the corresponding attributive adjectives may be used inside of a noun phrase:

(i) a. Hij heeft verschrikkelijke honger.
        he has terrible+AGR hunger

    b. Il a   une faim   terrible.
        he has a   hunger terrible

In the Dutch example the presence of the adjectival agreement morpheme *-e* shows that *verschrikke-lijke* is an attributive adjective and not an adverb (cf. 5a). Degree modification of this type, inside an argumental noun phrase containing a gradable noun, is limited to attributive adjectives corresponding to the type B expressions, and will be left out of consideration here.

indicate the degree of quantity of books. In combination with an eventive verb, the degree expression indicates the degree of quantity corresponding to the event (see Bach 1986 and Krifka 1986 for arguments in favor of representing nominal and verbal quantity in a similar way). Degree expressions typically combine with plural and mass terms, which both have cumulative reference.

Type C includes French *trop* as well as English *more* and *less*, all of which combine with adjectives, verbs and nouns alike (cf. 1):

(6) a. more difficult, to walk more, more books   (E)

    b. minder interessant, minder dansen, minder boeken   (D)
        less   interesting, less   dance, less   books

    c. trop/plus difficile, parler trop/plus   que...,   (F)
        too/more difficult, talk   too much/more than...,
        trop/plus de   livres
        too many/more books

The different interpretations obtained in these three contexts can be illustrated on the basis of the examples in (6a). *More* in *more difficult* indicates that the intensity of the difficulty exceeds a certain point, while *more* in *to walk more* and *more books* indicates that the degree of quantity corresponding to *walking* and *books* respectively exceeds a certain amount or quantity.

Even though type C is not widespread in English and Dutch, where it is mostly restricted to *more, less,* and *enough,* Romance languages manifest a large variety of type C expressions, including the counterpart of several type A expressions in English. Examples include Portuguese *muito* 'very, much/many' and Spanish *demasiado* 'too (much/many).' Consider for instance the examples in (7):

(7) a. muito grande, muito trabalhar, muitos libros   (P)
        "very big, to work a lot, many books"

    b. demasiado grande, demasiado trabajar, demasiados libros   (S)
        "too big, to work too much, too many books"

The typical meanings of type C expressions are the same as the typical meanings of type A: comparative (non-morphological), superlative (non-morphological), excessive degree (French *trop* 'too (much)'), high degree (Portuguese *muito* 'very, much').[5]

Note that the comparative *more* in English is exceptional in the sense that it cannot combine with all scalar adjectives. Its use with adjectives is

---

[5] Type A and type C roughly correspond to the class-1 and class-2 expressions in Neeleman et al. (2004).

phonologically restricted. The use of the comparative suffix -*er* is restricted to adjectives of at most two syllables, while *more* combines with other adjectives and also with nouns and verbs (see Di Sciullo and Williams 1987 for an account of this in terms of blocking).

In general, type C expressions combine with plurals and with mass nouns alike. There are some cases of type C expressions that do not combine with plural nouns, however. The class of small amount expressions such as *a bit* in English, *een beetje* in Dutch, and *un peu* in French systematically resist the use with a plural noun. Interestingly, there do not seem to be expressions that combine with plurals, with verbs and/or adjectives, and that are incompatible with mass nouns.

Type D expressions are similar to type C expressions. However, even though they can be interpreted as "intensifiers" this use is not freely available in combination with adjectives, and is usually restricted to abstract verbs. Examples are English *a lot* and French *beaucoup*, as well as *autant* 'as much' and *tant* 'so much.' In Dutch there are no clear cases of this type.

(8) a. to appreciate a lot, to walk a lot, a lot of books   (E)

 b. beaucoup apprécier, beaucoup se promener, beaucoup de livres (F)

Again we may observe that the meanings we find are fairly similar to the ones we have found for types A and C.

An interesting member of this class is English *much*.[6] Kennedy and McNally (2005) discuss the distribution of English *much* in the adjectival domain. They argue that *much* is compatible with those adjectives that introduce a lower closed scale, but not with others. This is illustrated by the contrast in (9). The adjective *tall* in *a tall man* indicates that the man is taller than an expected value (the relative standard), rather than a zero value on a scale of tallness. As a result, *not tall* does not imply a zero level on the scale of length. However, in the case of *appreciated*, we are dealing with a lower closed scale, which means that *not appreciated* corresponds to a lack of appreciation.

(9) a. *a much tall man

 b. a much appreciated man

The semantic differences between adjectives that take *very* and the ones that take *much* will be further discussed and clarified in section 6.3.3.

Type E is not very common. Unlike type D, this type is incompatible with gradable non-eventive verbs. If combined with a verb, it can only indicate a

---

[6] Note that *much* and *little* are not used with plurals, which seems to be due to competition with *many* and *few*.

degree of quantity, and therefore the verb has to denote an activity or a plural event (see the discussion on type C above). The difference between what I call here type D and type E was first observed by Obenauer (1984) for French *beaucoup* (type D) and German *viel* (type E). Dutch *veel* is similar to German *viel* in this respect. Contrary to their French and English counterparts in (8), *veel* and *viel* cannot be used to modify gradable non-eventive verbs.

(10)   veel wandelen, veel boeken, *veel waarderen, *veel aardig   (D)
       "walk a lot, a lot of books, to appreciate a lot, very nice"

The typical meaning of expressions of this type is one of high degree. Their existence in Dutch and German seems to be related to the existence of a neutral high degree expression of type B. Dutch *erg* and German *sehr* are used with adjectives and gradable verbs, and have a neutral high degree meaning as illustrated in (11).

(11)   erg aardig, erg waarderen   (D)
       "very nice, to appreciate a lot"

It seems that the type B neutral high degree expression *erg* blocks the use of *veel* in this context (see Doetjes 1997 for an account in terms of the Elsewhere Condition). As a result, the only meaning type that exists for this type is one of neutral high degree.

   Interestingly, comparative adjectives are modified by *veel* rather than by *erg* in Dutch:

(12)   veel/ *erg groter   (D)

This suggests that comparatives pattern with eventive verbs rather than with adjectives and/or gradable verbs.

   It is interesting to compare the use of comparatives in combination with degree modifiers to their use with measure phrases such as *two meters*. It turns out that degree modification is not completely parallel to modification by a measure phrase. Consider for instance the case of *tall*, which may be modified by measure phrases indicating length (e.g., *two meters tall*). The same type of measure can be used with the comparative form of the adjective, as in *two centimeters taller*. In the case of degree words, the positive and the comparative do not behave alike, as shown by the pairs *very tall* (type A)/*much taller* (type C/D) and *erg groot* (type B)/*veel groter* (type E). Kennedy and McNally (2005) analyze the difference between *much* and *very* in these examples in terms of presence versus absence of a lower closed scale. The comparative adjective *taller* introduces a lower closed scale, while the adjective *tall* does not (cf. the contrast between 9a and 9b). This cannot explain the Dutch facts, however. *Erg* is compatible with adjectives such as *gewaardeerd*, which are argued to introduce a lower bound and as such require the use of *much* in English (cf. 9b). Thus the use of *veel* rather than *erg* in *veel groter* has to be explained in a different way.

The difference between degree modifiers and measure phrases can be further illustrated by the French facts in (13). In French, degree modifiers of the relevant type (not A or B) may modify the comparative directly, while measure phrases introduce a different syntax:

(13) a. Il est *deux mètres grand/grand de deux mètres.   (F)
          he is two   meters tall/tall   of two meters

      b. Il est deux centimètres plus grand/plus grand de deux
          he is two centimetres more tall/more   tall   of two
          centimètres.
          centimetres

I will not further discuss the issue of measure phrases here. As for degree modification, the facts discussed above indicate that the comparative patterns with eventive verbs.

A final context where we find type E expressions rather than type A or B expressions is that of predicative eventive adjectives. Consider the contrast between *veel ziek* and *erg ziek* in (14).

(14) a. Jan is veel ziek.   (D)
          Jan is a lot ill

      b. Jan is erg ziek.
          Jan is very ill

In (14a) the global amount of the event of being ill is modified, while (14b) indicates that Jan is seriously ill. Similarly, in French *beaucoup malade* corresponds to *veel ziek/ill a lot*, while *très malade* corresponds to *erg ziek/very ill*. In the final version of the degree expression continuum presented at the end of this section, comparatives and eventive adjectives will be classified along with eventive verbs.

Type F expressions are found with nouns only. They are compatible with plurals and mass nouns, that is, nominal expressions that have cumulative reference, and as such introduce a scale of quantity. Some examples are given in (15).

(15) a. a mountain of books   (E)

      b. een berg boeken   (D)

      c. une montagne de livres   (F)

This type includes many expressions that are based on a measure word, such as *mountain*, which both indicates high degree and provides information on, for instance, the shape of the quantity involved, or indicates a type of container. As one reviewer has noticed, it may not be fully appropriate to list these expressions as a separate category in the degree expression continuum, given that they may have different syntactic properties. However, Doetjes and Rooryck (2003) argue on the basis of agreement facts that *une montagne de livres* is structurally ambiguous between a structure in which *une montagne* is the head of the noun phrase (singular agreement with *montagne*) and another in which *une montagne* acts as a modifier and *livres* behaves like the head of the noun phrase (plural agreement with *livres*). In this second case *une montagne* may get a pure high degree interpretation and lose its lexical meaning of "a mountain" or "a stack." It is this second use of *une montagne* that I am interested in here.

A further reason to treat this class here is that many degree expressions that are used outside of the nominal system start out historically as measure phrases indicating high degree of quantity in the nominal system. The lexical part of the interpretation of the measure word may bleach. Once the lexical meaning has entirely disappeared, these expressions often widen their distribution and may be used outside of the nominal system. An example is English *a lot*. In most cases where *a lot* is used, only the high degree meaning is left, and *a lot* has shifted towards a type D expression. A similar process seems to be going on with Dutch *een hoop*. It is marginally possible to say things such as *een hoop wandelen* 'to walk a lot.' Other modifiers, such as *een berg* 'a mountain' are less easily used in a high degree reading in the nominal system, and cannot be used with verbs at all. Thus, *een berg wandelen* 'walk a mountain' is completely excluded. French *beaucoup* and *trop* (type C) also illustrate this phenomenon, as they are etymologically derived from measure expressions. *Beaucoup* comes from *beau* 'good' and *coup* 'blow' while *trop* is etymologically related to *troupeau* 'herd' (for the historical development of *beaucoup* in French, see Marchello-Nizia 2006).

Type G expressions include, for instance, English *many* and *few*. They only combine with plural nouns, but they do have a clear degree interpretation. The existence of *many* and *few* seems to block the use of *much* and *little* with plural nouns. It is not completely clear how this type of blocking process works, as *a lot* combines with both plurals and mass nouns. French *une foule* in its pure high degree reading is also a case in point. The use of *une foule* with this interpretation is illustrated in (16), taken from Doetjes and Rooryck (2003). Its use with a mass term, as in *une foule de soupe*, is excluded.

(16)   Une foule   de problèmes se   sont produits.
a   crowd of problems   REFL are   occurred
"A host of problems have occurred."

A further interesting member of class G is Dutch *tig*, which has recently been discussed in great detail by Norde (forthcoming). For most speakers of Dutch, *tig*, which has derived from the suffix *-tig* '-ty,' as in *twintig* 'twenty,' may be used as a very high degree modifier of plural nouns, and is restricted to plural contexts. Examples are *tig boeken* 'very many books,' *tig keer* 'again and again.' Norde shows that some speakers also use *tig* as a degree modifier with other categories, including gradable adjectives and comparatives. Interestingly, the meaning of *tig* is one that is usually found for type B expressions. This may have been the reason for the confusion of *tig* 'terribly many' with *ontzettend veel* 'terribly much/many,' resulting in *tig veel* 'a whole lot.' In this form, *tig* is used as a modifier of *veel*, which in terms of degree modification behaves like a gradable adjective. This in turn might have been the source of further changes in the distribution of *tig*, which is attested not only with other gradable adjectives, as in *tig leuk* 'extremely nice,' but also with comparatives (*tig sneller* 'a whole lot faster'), participles (*tig bedankt* 'thanks a whole lot'), and with mass nouns (*tig rotzooi* 'a whole lot of rubbish'). Even though the numbers of occurrences are so small that it is hard to judge on the basis of corpus information whether all predicted combinations are found, it seems that the use of *tig* as an intensifier has been at the source of an extension of its use in combination with other categories as well, and that the reason for the change is the unstable situation in which one and the same item acts like a type A and like a type G expression at the same time.

Norde assumes that the first step of the change was the analogy between *veel* and *tig*, both of which can modify plurals. As *veel* is also used with comparatives, the use of *tig* would have been extended to that context via syntactic reanalysis of [*tig* [*betere oplossingen*]] 'a very large number of better solutions' to [[*tig betere*] *oplossingen*] 'far better solutions.' This, in turn, might have been the source of the use of *tig* as an intensifier. As shown above, degree modification of adjectives and of comparatives is not similar in Dutch, so a change from a modifier of comparatives into a modifier of adjectives is not based on an analogy similar to the one causing the first step in the change. Moreover, it may be observed that *tig veel* is by far the most frequent context in which non-standard *tig* is used.[7] This is not surprising if we assume that the (erroneous) use of *tig veel* replacing the original *tig* is at the origin of the other

---

[7] On the internet, *tig veel* is about fifty times more frequent than *tig leuk*, while *veel* is only four to five times as frequent as *leuk*. This is a very rough indication, based on Google searches.

extensions, as I suggested above. In any case, *tig* seems to be an example of a type G expression that for some speakers has turned into a type C expression.

In the next subsection some particular characteristics of French *très* will be discussed, after which we will turn to a revised version of Table 6.1.

6.2.2 *French* très: *a case study*

As I already mentioned in the previous section, the distribution of French *très* is not completely parallel to that of Dutch and English type A expressions. Besides cases such as *très à la mode* 'very fashionable,' which are analogous to the example *very in love* discussed in (3) above, there are a number of other contexts in which *très* is found, and where type A expressions are excluded (cf. Abeillé et al. 2004; Gaatone 1981). Some of these contexts might be adjectival after all, while for some others this is clearly not the case. In this section, I will compare the distributions of type A expressions in Dutch and English to the distribution of *très*, and I will argue that *très* is starting to have the properties of a type B expression.

In the examples in (17) *très* modifies a noun in a predicative position (the examples have been found on the internet):

(17)   a.   C'est une ville très sport.
             it-is a   city very sport

       b.   Moi qui étais très voiture française j'ai   largement changé
            I   who was very car   French   I-have greatly   changed
            d'avis   depuis cet achat.
            my mind since   this purchase
            "I used to be very much into French cars, but I have changed a lot
            since I made this purchase."

Even though similar structures are excluded in English and Dutch (**too French car*), it has to be noted that this type of predicative use of nouns is also excluded in these languages. A possible way to look at this is to assume that French has a conversion rule creating adjectives from nouns, as in (18):

(18)   a.   une ville très [sport]$_A$

       b.   [sport]$_N$ "sports" $\Rightarrow$ [sport]$_A$ "sportif"

       c.   [voiture française]$_{NP}$ "French car" $\Rightarrow$ [voiture française]$_A$ "who
            likes French cars"

The derivation in (18c) might seem at first sight implausible, but a morphological rule that operates on the basis of a phrase is not excluded, as the Dutch examples in (19) show.

(19) a. [Franse auto]$_{NP}$ + gek$_N$ ⇒
    [Franse autogek]$_N$ (≠ [Franse [autogek]]$_{NP}$
    "someone crazy about   "French person crazy
      French cars"   about cars")

b. erg huis -tuin   -en -keukenachtig
    very home-garden -and -kitchenlike
    "very ordinary"

A further difference between *très* and the English and Dutch type A expressions is that *très* may modify passive participles, as opposed to past participles of active verbs (Creissels 2000; Carlier 2002):[8]

(20) a. La maison a été beaucoup/très photographiée.
    the house has been a lot/very   photographed

b. On a   beaucoup/*très photographié cette maison.
    they have a lot/very   photographed this house

c. Son histoire a été très racontée.
    his story   has been very told

d. On a   beaucoup/*très raconté son histoire.
    they have a lot/very   told   his story

According to Creissels (2000), the passive sentences are homonymous with resultative sentences, in which the passive participle is reanalyzed as an adjective, which explains the use of *très*, which he considers to be a diagnostic for adjectivehood. In order to further motivate this claim, he shows that passive participles are compatible with modifiers such as *depuis trois jours* 'since three days,' modifiers that cannot be used in the corresponding active sentence:

(21) a. Les coupables sont arrêtés depuis trois jours.
    the guilty.ones are arrested since   three days

b. *On a   arrêté les coupables depuis trois jours.
    they have arrested the guilty.ones since   three days

---

[8] There is a slight meaning difference between *beaucoup* and *très* in the (a) cases, which can be illustrated on the basis of the pair in (i). *Ce journal* 'this journal' in (ia) is not easily interpreted as a token, and refers to, for instance, *Le Monde* rather than to a crumpled newspaper laying on the table. Somehow, the use of *très* suggests that we are dealing with an intrinsic characteristic of the newspaper. I leave this issue for further research.

(i) a. Ce journal a été très lu ?(par les jeunes).
    "This newspaper (type) has been read a lot by young people."

b. Ce journal a été beaucoup lu.
    "This newspaper (type/token) has been read a lot."

Note that the use of a temporal modifier introduced by *depuis* is not limited to stative sentences. Clear passives can also accept this type of modifier, as illustrated in (22).

(22) Les coupables avaient été arrêtés par la police depuis trois jours
the guilty-PL had been arrested by the police since three days
avant qu' on ne les ait laissés parler à leur avocat.
before that one NE them has-SUBJ let speak to their lawyer
"The guilty ones were arrested by the police for three days before they were allowed to speak to their lawyer."

According to Carlier (2002) the past participle is still completely verbal and a true passive participle. She argues that the impersonal *il*-construction is incompatible with adjectives, but can be formed on the basis of passives with a "resultative" interpretation (Creissel's adjectival resultatives). The sentence in (23a) has clearly such an interpretation, and indeed this sentence can give rise to an impersonal construction as in (23b). This is excluded for real adjectives, as shown in the pair in (23c, d).

(23) a. Trois chansons sont enregistrés sur chaque face.
three songs are recorded on each side

b. Il est enregistré trois chansons sur chaque face.
it is recorded three songs on each side

c. Trois enfants sont trop timides pour rentrer.
three children are too shy for enter-INF

d. * Il est trop timide pour rentrer trois enfants.
it is too shy for enter-INF three children

Note however that the use of *très* is never possible in the impersonal cases. Consider, for instance, the pair in (24):

(24) Il a été beaucoup/ *très parlé de cet endroit.
it has been a lot/ very spoken of this place
"A lot has been said about this place."

If it is true that the impersonal construction can distinguish verbs from adjectives, the impossibility of *très* in (24) is a reason to believe that whenever the past participle combines with *très* it has to be analyzed as an adjective. I will leave this issue for further research. At this point the use of *très* in combination with a passive participle is not a reason to distinguish it from type A expressions in English and Dutch, given that passive participles might be analyzed as adjectival expressions.

However, there are two contexts where *très* is used and where type A expressions are prohibited. Contrary to the cases discussed above, we are clearly not dealing with independent differences between French on the one hand and Dutch and English on the other. As shown in (20) above, only passive participles have been claimed to have adjectival properties in French. Active past participles of eventive verbs do not allow modification by *très*. However, when we consider gradable verbs, we may observe that both the passive participle and the past participle of the active form may be modified by *très*, as well as the infinitive. Note that the use of *très* in the examples in (25b, c) is colloquial and will not be accepted by all speakers. What is important here is that there is a strong contrast between the use of *très* in (25b, c), and (20b, d) above.

(25) a. Le film   a   été   beaucoup/très apprécié   par le public.
          the movie has been a lot/very   appreciated by the audience

      b. Le public a   beaucoup/² très apprécié   le film.
          the public has a lot/very   appreciated the movie

      c. Il a l'air de beaucoup/²très apprécier le débat.
          he seems to a lot/very   appreciate the debate

Even though the modification of gradable verbs is limited, the data seem to suggest that *très* might well be in the process of changing into a type B expression. Sentences such as the one in (25b) are clearly less common than the one in (25a), but they can be found easily on the internet: *a très apprécié* yields about 400 Google hits (Sept. 2006). Infinitives are slightly harder to find – *très apprécier* turns out to contain most often a misspelled participle – but they do occur as well, and according to a native speaker I consulted the example in (25c) sounds even slightly better than the one in (25b).[9]

An additional type B context that allows for the use of *très* is illustrated in (26). *Très* may be used in a restricted number of light verb constructions with a bare nominal predicate.[10] Note that there are lexical restrictions on this use, as (26c) is excluded. This use of *très* is quite common, even though the dictionary *Le Trésor de la Langue Française* labels it as "improper."

(26) a. Elle a   très soif/faim.
          she has very thirst/hunger

---

[9] I have not found any cases where *très* follows the verb, and liaison (pronunciation of the final /z/ of *très* in front of a vowel) seems to be obligatory. These latter properties may reflect the properties of *très* in its more usual contexts.

[10] Those who reject the adjectival analysis of *sport* and *voiture française* in (18) may want to assume that these cases are similar to the ones in (26), and involve modification of a gradable nominal predicate.

   b. Cela me fait   très plaisir.
       that me does very pleasure

   c. *Cela porte très bonheur.
       that brings very luck

To conclude, the data in (25) and (26) are evidence in favor of the claim that French *très* is developing in the direction of a type B expression, which accounts for the clear non-adjectival contexts in which the modifier is used. As the context in (26) is much more common than the use of *très* with active past participles and infinitives of gradable verbs, the data suggest that these two contexts are ordered with respect to each other, the predicative nouns in (26) being closer to adjectives than the gradable verbs.

6.2.3 *Summary*

Given the discussion so far, we can introduce a completed version of the degree expression continuum in Table 6.2. It is important to realize that the different types are not meant to be an exhaustive inventory of static types. In many cases individual members may have slightly different properties at the "borders" of their distribution. An example is English *much*, which usually does not combine with plurals, unlike the other members of type D, and which also combines with certain adjectives (see section 6.3.3 below). Also, an expression

TABLE 6.2. The degree expression continuum (final version)

I	gradable adjectives	**type A** very[E]			très[F]	
IIa	gradable nominal predicates		**type B** erg[D]		↓	
IIb	gradable verbs			**type C**	↓	**type 0** –
III	eventive verbs, eventive adjectives, comparatives	**type D** beaucoup[F]		trop[F] less[E] minder[D]		
IV	mass nouns		**type E** veel[D]			**type 0** –
V	plural nouns				**type F** a mountain[E]	**type G** many[E]

might have the distribution of a type C expression except for the fact that it is incompatible with plurals; this is actually the case for *mycket* 'a lot' in Swedish (Muriel Norde, p.c.).

The semantic properties of the different types can be summarized as follows. There are no obvious meaning differences between types A, C, and D. Type B (*erg, horribly*) is clearly distinct from a semantic point of view (see also the discussion on Dutch *tig* above). This seems to be due to the origin of these expressions, which are bleached adverbial modifiers with a high or very high degree interpretation. Similarly, most type F expressions contain a measure word (e.g. *a mountain of*) and have a high degree (of quantity) meaning. Type E (e.g. Dutch *veel*) seems to be in complementary distribution with type B and therefore inherits the meaning restrictions on type B.

6.3 The status of adjectives

6.3.1 *Stating the problem*

It has been shown in the previous section that there are quite a number of different types of degree expressions, one of which is typically used with adjectives or, to be more precise, with a subclass of adjectives (cf. Kennedy and McNally 2005). The question is now what the degree expression continuum tells us about the status of adjectives with respect to gradability. Are adjectives special or not?

Given the fact that adjectives are found at one end of the continuum in Table 6.2, one could argue that they are non-special and special at the same time: non-special because they behave similarly to other categories in being part of the continuum, and special in being at one end of it. This allows us to reformulate our initial question as follows: Why are adjectives at one end of the continuum and what restricts the distribution of type A expressions to adjectives?

A first, rather naive, hypothesis about the status of adjectives is based on the difference between quantities and qualities. Adjectives denote qualities, and as such adjectival modifiers correspond to intensifiers. One could assume that type A expressions are restricted to adjectives because they fail to indicate a quantity. Verbs and nouns introduce a quantity and combine with expressions that indicate a degree of quantity, while adjectives correspond to qualities and as such are modified by intensifiers:

(27) a. a mountain/a lot of books ((degree of) quantity)

     b. He walked miles and miles/a lot.

     c. very interesting (degree of quality/ intensity)

However, if one type of degree expressions is sensitive to the distinction between quantity and quality, it is rather type B than type A (cf. *to appreciate to a certain degree/extent*), and type B is not restricted to adjectives (I will come back to this below).

Note that the difference between a quality and a quantity is not always obvious. Gradable abstract nouns such as *success* and *patience* behave like mass nouns (*much success, a lot of patience*) with respect to the degree expressions they combine with. However, intuitively, these nouns correspond to a scale that is qualitative rather than quantitative. Similarly, it is not even obvious that adjectives are always associated with "qualitative scales," as illustrated by the examples in (28):

(28)   a.   A different slant on a very photographed subject![11]   (E)

      b.   C'est un lieu très photographié.   (F)
            "It is a very photographed place."

In this type of example *very* and *très* have an interpretation that is similar to *often*.

The next two sections will consider the special status of adjectives as opposed to other categories from two different angles. Section 6.3.2 discusses the possible presence versus absence of a degree variable, and section 6.3.3 explores the idea that certain types of scales are typically found with adjectives rather than with other categories.

6.3.2 *The presence/absence of a degree variable*

One way to account for the special status of adjectives is to assume that scalar adjectives differ from other categories because they contain a degree variable. Under this assumption, modifiers that typically combine with adjectives are modifiers that depend on the presence of a degree variable. In this view the idea that adjectives are more "gradable" than other categories is directly implemented in the lexical representation of adjectives.

In their study of the scale structure of deverbal adjectives, Kennedy and McNally (2005: 365) assume that the structure of the scale of the derived adjective is created "by mapping from a set of potentially complex events that can be ordered in an algebraic structure as proposed in, for example, Link (1983), Landman (1989), or Lasersohn (1995)." Even though the event

---

[11] This example has been cited from the internet, and similar examples can be easily found by searching for the string "a very photographed." However, not all speakers like modification of an adjectival *photographed* by *very*. Similar examples are not found in Dutch (*een *erg/*even /(even) veel gefotografeerde kerk* 'a very/ as/(as) much photographed church'), which might be understood if we assume that English allows passive participles to shift to adjectives more easily than Dutch does.

structure of a verb is at the basis of the scale structure of the corresponding deverbal adjective, the presence of the scale is assumed to be a property of the adjective, not of the verb it is derived from. One could assume that degree expressions modifying verbs and nouns are interpreted with respect to the algebraic structures these correspond to, while modifiers of adjectives perform an operation on a scale that is part of the linguistic representation of the adjective.

The hypothesis that adjectives should be treated as relations between individuals and degrees is often made in the literature (see Seuren 1973; Cresswell 1977; Hellan 1981; von Stechow 1984; Bierwisch 1989; Klein 1991; Kennedy and McNally 2005). An adjective such as *difficult* is to be seen as a relation between individuals and degrees, as in (29).[12]

(29) $[\![difficult]\!] = \lambda d \lambda x.\mathbf{difficult}(x) = d$

If the presence of a degree variable is typically adjectival, one has to assume that expressions such as *much* and *many* when used to modify mass nouns and plurals and *very*, which is used to modify an adjective, have a different semantics. Whereas *very* operates on the value of a degree variable, *much* and *many* should rather be seen as quantity predicates that contain a degree variable themselves (cf. Hackl 2000):[13]

(30) a. $[\![much]\!] = \lambda d \lambda x.\mathbf{much}(x) = d$

 b. $[\![many]\!] = \lambda d \lambda x.\mathbf{many}(x) = d$

The difference between a degree expression that directly operates on a degree variable and one that makes use of a quantity predicate is illustrated in (31). The meaning of the type A expression *as* in (31a) has been taken from Kennedy and McNally (2005: 269) and the one of *as much* in (31b) is composed of *as* applied to the quantity predicate *much*.

(31) a. $[\![as \; as \; d_c]\!] = \lambda G \lambda x. \exists d [d \succeq d_c \wedge G(d)(x)]$

 b. $[\![as \; as \; d_c]\!]([\![much]\!]) = \lambda x. \exists d [d \succeq d_c \wedge [\![much]\!](d)(x)]$

Given (31a), application of *as* to a gradable adjective yields a property to a degree d which equals at least d_c, the degree introduced by the *as*-clause. The

---

[12] I will not consider an alternative analysis in which the scalar adjective is seen as a partially ordered set of individuals. In such an approach scalar and non-scalar adjectives have the same representation; the difference between the two is the presence versus absence of a partial ordering of the domain. This type of approach has been advocated by Klein (1980). For arguments against such a view, see Kennedy (1999a, b).

[13] I define *much* and *many* in the same way as the scalar adjective *difficult* in (29), that is, as a predicate. For ease of exposition, I will disregard the differences between predicative adjectives on the one hand and attributive adjectives and adverbs derived from adjectives on the other.

way a degree reading is obtained by *as much* is very different. The quantity predicate *as much* would combine through intersection with another predicate. A similar analysis would hold for *as many*. As such, *as many books* denotes a set of plural objects that have the property of being books and the property of having a quantity that at least equals a contextually given degree of quantity d_c.

In what follows I will discuss two consequences of this approach. In the first place, if *as* has a semantics as in (31a) and *as much* a semantics as in (31b), one might wonder what type of semantics has to be assumed for type C expressions such as *more* and *trop*, which may be used with nouns and verbs, but also with adjectives. In the second place I will consider the question of how to analyze gradable predicates that are not adjectival (e.g., gradable verbs such as *to appreciate* and gradable nouns such as French *faim* 'hunger'). Are there reasons to assume that these expressions contain a degree variable as well? Obviously, the next question is whether one would like to claim that all categories in Table 6.2 contain degree variables (see Cresswell 1977).

Under the assumption that adjectives contain a degree variable and other categories do not, we need two meanings for *more* in order to account for its ability to modify both adjectives and other categories. One of these meanings is similar to the one of *as* and the other to that of *as much* in (31). The idea that expressions that modify adjectives, but that also occur with for instance nouns, are ambiguous has been proposed in the literature by Jackendoff (1977). In order to explain that degree expressions such as *as* are only used with adjectives, while *more* can be used with other categories as well, Jackendoff assumes that *more* is ambiguous between a degree expression Deg (*more₁*) and quantifier Q (*more₂*). In what follows, I will call the two readings of *more* "Deg" and "Q" for ease of exposition.

Ambiguity is unproblematic if it is accidental. Once it is not, one would like to know why it exists. Some general process creating ambiguity should be at the source of any systematic ambiguity. It is clear that we are not dealing with accidental ambiguity in the case of *more*. As shown above, type C expressions constitute a large class, including French *trop* 'too (much/many),' *moins* 'less,' *plus* 'more,' *un peu* 'a bit,' English *more, less, a bit*, Dutch *minder* 'less,' *een beetje* 'a bit,' Portuguese *muito* 'a lot, very,' and Italian *molto* 'a lot, very,' etc. Given the generality of the phenomenon, one would like these expressions to be unambiguous, and if not, there should be a general mechanism that can account for the existence of the ambiguity.

One question is in what sense the two interpretations of *more* are connected. Is there a derivation of Deg towards Q or the other way around? There is historical evidence in favor of the idea that Q may be at the source of Deg. A first indication is the case of Portuguese *muito*. In older stages of Portuguese, *muito* would function as a type D expression (similar to *a lot* and *beaucoup*) and it would alternate with *mui*, which occurred with adjectives. The type A expression *mui* became obsolete and *muito* extended its distribution (João Costa, p.c.). A second indication are cases such as *trop* and *a bit*, which derive from measure constructions (meaning 'a heap' and 'a bite' respectively). Measure constructions are at first used in the nominal system (see section 6.2.1 above). Once they have a pure degree interpretation they may extend their distribution and become type D or type C expressions. This suggests that there is a diachronic mechanism that allows a Q to turn into a Deg by abstracting over the quantity predicate. The definition of Deg in (32) is taken from Kennedy and McNally (2005: 367), where R is a restriction on the degree argument of the adjective.

(32) $[\![Deg]\!]([\![much]\!]) = \lambda x.\exists d[R(d) \wedge [\![much]\!](d)(x)]$
    $\rightarrow \lambda G \lambda x.\exists d[R(d) \wedge G(d)(x)]$

The examples in (33) give the Deg and the Q interpretations for *more* and for *less*:

(33) a. *more₁* "-er"
         $[\![more_1 \ than \ d_c]\!] = \lambda G \lambda x.\exists d[d \succ d_c \wedge G(d)(x)]$

     b. *more₂ = much + -er*
         $[\![more_2 \ than \ d_c]\!] = \lambda x.\exists d[d \succ d_c \wedge [\![much]\!](d)(x)]$

     c. *less₁* "reversed -er"
         $[\![less_1 \ than \ d_c]\!] = \lambda G \lambda x.\exists d[d \prec d_c \wedge G(d)(x)]$

     d. *less₂ = little + -er* or *much + reversed -er*?
         i. $[\![less_2 \ than \ d_c]\!] = \lambda x.\exists d[d \succ d_c \wedge [\![little]\!](d)(x)]$
         ii. $[\![less_2 \ than \ d_c]\!] = \lambda x.\exists d[d \prec d_c \wedge [\![much]\!](d)(x)]$

The case of *more* is rather simple. The basic *more* (*more₂*, the Q) is built out of *much* + the comparative morpheme *-er*. In order to form *more₁*, *much* is replaced by an abstraction over a gradable predicate by application of the rule in (32), and we are left with a synonym of *-er*. The case of *less* is more complicated. The Q *less*, *less₂*, could have two meanings, one of which involves *much*, the other *little*. If one assumes *less* is a comparative of *little*, which is at first sight straightforward, one cannot simply abstract over *little* in order to get to *less₁* because then *less₁* would have the same meaning as *more₁* and the comparative suffix *-er*. This might be seen as evidence for the assumption that *less* is based on *much*, and includes a degree item with the meaning of a "reversed" *-er*, which is lexicalized in English by *less₁*. This would also hold for German *weniger*, from *wenig + -er* 'little' + "-er". As *weniger* may be combined with adjectives (e.g. *weniger klug* 'less smart'), one has to assume that alongside the compositional meaning in (33d.i) *weniger* can also have the equivalent meaning in (33d.ii). This in turn may undergo the rule in (32), resulting in the meaning of "reversed *-er*."

In any case, the formation of *less$_{1'}$*, which would be derived from the representation of *less$_2$* in (33d.i) by an abstraction rule along the lines of (32), and which would have the same meaning as *more$_1$*, has to be blocked. As Chris Kennedy has pointed out to me, the abstraction rule in (32) might be blocked by the presence of *little*. Given that *little*, being the antonym of *much*, can be seen as a negative quantity predicate, that is, a predicate that gives information about the quantity an object does not have, it seems reasonable to assume that only the positive quantity predicate may be abstracted over by a rule such as (32).

The derivation of *less$_1$* shows that in order to derive it we need an abstract operator with the meaning of *less$_1$*, that is, *less$_2$* cannot be seen as a suppletive form of two morphemes that independently exist in the language: this would be true for *more* and for the first definition of *less$_2$*, but not for the second one, which is the one we need in order to derive *less$_1$*. Note that the quantity predicate in for instance French *trop* 'too much' does not correspond to a lexical item either, given that *beaucoup*, the French counterpart of *much/many*, may not be modified by degree expressions, as illustrated by the ungrammaticality of **très beaucoup* 'very much.' The same is true for Spanish *mucho* 'much,' as illustrated by the impossibility of **muy mucho* 'very much.' The absence of a lexical quantity predicate seems to correlate with the wealth of type C expressions in these languages.

The case of *less* in English (and its counterparts *weniger* and *minder* in German and Dutch) is quite interesting, because in Germanic languages there is a strong tendency to lexicalize type A expressions separately, and to construe type C expressions by combining a type A expression and *much*. As such, if *less* is considered to be a combination of reversed *-er* and a quantity predicate (abstract *much*) as in (33d.ii), the non-existence of a separately lexicalized type A expression with the meaning of a reversed *-er* is intriguing.

The ambiguity of type C expressions might also have consequences for their syntax, given the claim that type A are syntactic heads while type C expressions are adjuncts (Doetjes 1997; Neeleman et al. 2004). If these syntactic differences are related to the semantic differences between the two types of expressions, one expects type C expressions to have a different syntax depending on whether they combine with an adjective or not.

The idea that type A expressions are syntactic heads of a Degree phrase was first put forward by Corver (1990) and Zwarts (1992). Zwarts explicitly argues that the projection of a degree phrase hosting a type A expression in its head is related to the semantic representation of the adjective, which contains a degree variable. The structure proposed by Zwarts (1992: 32) is given in (34), where $\underline{Th}$ corresponds to the variable x and G_i to the variable d in (31a).

(34)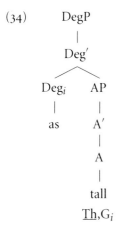

Type C expressions, on the other hand, have been claimed to be adjuncts rather than heads. Doetjes (1997) and Neeleman et al. (2004) argue that expressions such as *as much* are adjuncts, rather than heads, and that this is why they are not sensitive to the categorial properties of the expression they modify. Type A expressions are heads and as such categorially select an AP, while type C expressions are adjoined to an XP of any category, provided that this category is semantically compatible with the scalar interpretation of the degree expression.

   Given the hypothesis that degree variables are typically adjectival, the syntactic difference between degree expressions involving a quantity predicate (type C) and the ones that directly operate on the meaning of an adjective (type A) might be related to the different type of semantic operation that is needed in order to interpret them (Chris Kennedy, p.c.). From a semantic point of view, *as* combines with an adjective through function application, while *as much* is a quantity predicate, and combines with another predicate through intersection (see 31). It is not implausible that this semantic difference corresponds to head versus adjunct syntax. Moreover, it would allow us to do away with the idea of categorial selection, and view the facts as an instance of semantic selection after all. If this idea is adopted, it implies that the ambiguity issue discussed above also concerns the syntactic position the degree expression occupies. That is, *less₁* and *more₁* would occupy a head position when used with a gradable adjective, and an adjunct position elsewhere. This in turn predicts that a type C expression used with a gradable adjective syntactically should behave like a type A expression. However, a closer look at the data motivating the difference in syntactic status of type A and type C expressions shows that this prediction is not borne out.

Neeleman et al. show that there are a number of differences between type A and type C expressions (their class-1 and class-2) all of which obtain in the context of adjectives.[14] For instance, adjectives may be stranded in the context of a type C expression, but not in the context of a type A expression:

(35) a. *Intelligent is hij te   om enigszins   normaal te functioneren.
           intelligent is he too for more-or-less normally to function
           "He is too intelligent to function more or less normally."

     b. Intelligent is hij minder dan de gemiddelde Nederlander.
           intelligent is he less   than the average   Dutch person
           "He is less intelligent than the average Dutch person."

A second case of different syntactic behavior of type A and type C expressions concerns the various positions the complement of an adjective may occupy in Dutch. As the example in (36) shows, the complement of an adjective in Dutch may scramble to a position to the left of this adjective (see also Corver, 1997):

(36) a. Hij is afhankelijk van zijn vader's goedkeuring.
           he is dependent of   his father's approval

     b. Hij is van zijn vader's goedkeuring afhankelijk.
           he is of   his father's approval   dependent

As shown in (37), the presence of a type A expression blocks scrambling to a position in between the degree modifier and the adjective, while scrambling to a position to the left of the degree expression is possible:

(37) a. *Hij is te van zijn vader's goedkeuring afhankelijk om een eigen
           he is too of his father's approval   dependent for a   own
           zaak   te beginnen.
           business to start

     b. Hij is van zijn vader's goedkeuring te afhankelijk om een eigen zaak
           te beginnen.
           "He is too much dependent on his father's approval to start his own
           business."

[14] Neeleman et al. also discuss the possibility of topicalization of a type C expression in the context of an adjective. As predicted, type A expressions, being heads, may not undergo topicalization. Even though topicalization of a type C expression is certainly not as bad as topicalization of a type A expression, it is not straightforwardly possible in any given sentence (see Neeleman et al. 2004 for examples). As similar problems occur with topicalization of a degree expression modifying a noun, there is no contrast between an adjectival and a non-adjectival context.

Neeleman et al. argue that the ungrammaticality of (37) is due to an adjacency requirement of the head Deg and the head of its complement. Interestingly, type C expressions such as *more* do not impose this requirement:

(38)   a.   Hij is van zijn vader's goedkeuring meer afhankelijk dan je
            he is of his father's approval   more dependent than you
            dacht.
            thought

       b.   Hij is meer van zijn vader's goedkeuring afhankelijk dan je dacht.
            "He is more dependent on his father's approval than you might
            think."

For Neeleman et al., the contrast between (37) and (38) corroborates their claim that *meer* 'more' (type C, their class-2) is an adjunct, while *te* 'too' (type A, their class-1) is a head. Unlike the relation between an adjunct and a following adjective, the head–complement relation between a Deg and an adjective is blocked by an intervening scrambled complement of the adjective. This is in accordance with their claim that the only difference between *too* and *too much* is syntactic: *too* is claimed to categorially select an adjective and the insertion of *much* is seen as insertion of a dummy that is necessarily present in order to make *too* syntactically compatible with categories other than adjectives.[15] Under the ambiguity approach sketched above, and assuming the appealing hypothesis that the semantic difference between modifiers of adjectives and modifiers of other categories is reflected in syntactic structure, the contrasts in (35) and (36)–(38) are not expected to exist. The syntactic differences between type A and type C expressions seem to be independent of whether the type C expression combines with an adjective or with another category. If they are due to a head/adjunct contrast, as argued by Neeleman et al., this contrast does not seem to be a reflection of the two different semantic structures illustrated in (31).

Up to this point it has been assumed that the semantics of type A expressions makes them sensitive to the presence of a degree variable, and that this is why they combine with adjectives rather than with other categories. The

---

[15] Note that in certain approaches to categorial selection, semantic properties of the category trigger this selection. Zwarts (1992) tries to connect the syntactic structure in (32), in which the Deg selects an adjectival projection, to semantic properties of adjectives (the presence of a degree variable). In Doetjes (1997) and Neeleman et al. (2004) we rather assume that categorial selection of adjectives is a purely formal issue. Under this assumption, the main question addressed in this chapter might be formulated as follows: Why do degree expressions categorially select adjectives rather than some other gradable category, e.g. gradable verbs or gradable nominal predicates? In this chapter I explore semantic properties of adjectives that may be related to the distribution of type A expressions, rather than develop an argument either for or against the existence of categorial selection.

second most restricted type of degree expression at the top of the continuum in Table 6.2 is type B, which is not restricted to adjectives, as it is also compatible with gradable expressions of other categories.

As shown in (39), verbs such as *to appreciate* do not seem to have a quantity interpretation (see also section 6.3.1):

(39)   a.   John appreciated the comments less than he should.

        b.   John appreciated the comments to the degree d where $d \prec$ the degree to which he should appreciate the comments.

The possibility of having a degree interpretation and not a quantity interpretation in the case of modification of the verb *to appreciate* indicates that postulation of a quantity predicate as in (31b) is not enough to explain all the uses of degree modifiers outside of the adjectival domain. The facts can have two explanations: either there has to be a mechanism that modifies the degree of appreciation in (39a) and that does not make use of a degree variable, or all expressions modified by a type B expression contain a degree variable. If the latter explanation is correct, the idea that the availability of a degree variable alone is what determines the distribution of Type A expressions must be wrong. If, on the other hand, another mechanism is involved in determining the degree of appreciation in (39a), one may wonder why type A expressions do not make use of this mechanism. It is clear that in order to maintain the hypothesis that only adjectives contain degree variables, independent evidence in favor of a linguistic difference between gradable adjectives on the one hand and the other gradable predicates in Table 6.2 on the other is necessary.[16]

So far we have considered limiting degree variables to the contexts where either type A or type B expressions are found. A third obvious possibility is to assume that degree variables are found in the context of type C expressions, that is, for all categories in Table 6.2. On such an approach, all degree expressions have similar meanings.[17] This view is not new either. Cresswell (1977) and von Stechow (1984) argue in favor of such an analysis, in particular with respect to mass nouns. On this view, lexical items such as *more* and *trop* are not ambiguous, and have a meaning similar to that of type A expressions. All

---

[16] Such evidence might come from restrictions on the use of antonyms in comparatives. See Kennedy (1999a, b), who argues on the basis of the distribution of antonymous adjectives in comparatives that the semantics of gradable adjectives needs to make reference to degrees. I will leave this issue for further research.

[17] Cf. Doetjes (1997) and Neeleman et al. (2004). Bresnan (1973) argues that degree modifiers always have the form Deg + *much*, and may apply to adjectives, nouns, and verbs alike. In the context of an adjective, however, *much* is deleted. Given the discussion at the beginning of this section, it is quite appealing to see this deletion of *much* as an instance of rule (32), which would imply that her proposal is actually very close to the one in Jackendoff (1977) and very different from the type of analysis advocated by Cresswell.

degree expressions act on a degree variable, but this variable corresponds to a qualitative scale in the case of adjectives such as *difficult*, and to a quantitative scale in the case of nouns. The adjective *difficult* and the nouns *books* and *soup* would then all have a degree variable, as in (40):

(40) d-difficult
      d-books
      d-soup

Cresswell illustrates this approach with the example in (41) for the noun *water*, which is analyzed as a two-place predicate, such that x is an amount of water with volume y. The sentence in (41a) gets the interpretation in (41b):

(41) a. More water ebbs than mud flows.

      b. The degree of the totality of ebbing water is greater than the degree of the totality of flowing mud.

The interpretation in (41b) could also be paraphrased as: the quantity of ebbing water exceeds the quantity of flowing mud, where quantity is expressed as a degree on a scale. I will not attempt to provide a full analysis along these lines here. Note that both Cresswell and von Stechow only talk about mass nouns. *More* in combination with a mass noun has the same semantics as *more* modifying an adjective. Given the much larger distribution of *more*, it seems plausible that this idea should be extended to other contexts where *more* is found. An advantage of such an approach is the uniform semantics that can be adopted for degree expressions. However, within this type of approach the presence or absence of a degree variable is totally independent of the distribution of degree expressions, and we are left without an answer to the question of why adjectives are at one end of the degree expression continuum.

6.3.3 *Adjectival scales*

The last idea that will be explored with respect to the special properties of adjectives is that adjectives are associated with certain types of scales while degree modifiers may be sensitive to properties of scales. Kennedy and McNally (2005) argue that this type of analysis explains the distribution of degree expressions in the adjectival domain, specifically, the distribution of *much* and *very*. Whereas the meaning of *much* makes reference to a lower closed scale, *very* is defined with respect to a relative standard.

Kennedy and McNally's proposal can be made more general. It might be hypothesized that certain scale types are typically adjectival, and that degree expressions that are sensitive to them are for that reason restricted to the adjectival system. On this view, adjectives differ from other categories in terms of the type of scales they are associated with. One might argue then that adjectives are more "gradable" than other categories in the sense that they are compatible with a wider array of scales. Expressions that select "typical" adjectival scales are the ones that are only found for (a subset of) adjectives and not for other categories. A further consequence of such an approach is that we predict that there are two types of adjectives: the ones that have typically adjectival scales and therefore combine only with expressions that cannot be used outside of the adjectival system (e.g. *very*) and those that have more common scales, which makes them compatible with expressions that are also used outside of the adjectival system (this would be the case of the adjectives introducing a lower bound and combining with *much*).

Let us first have a closer look at the work of Kennedy and McNally (2005) in order to gain a better understanding of the differences between types of scales. As already said above, the types that are relevant with respect to the distribution of *much* as opposed to *very* are the lower closed scale pattern and the scales that are characterized by a relative standard.

The test for a lower (but not fully) closed scale pattern is illustrated in (42). Expressions that have a lower closed scale are themselves incompatible with expressions such as *completely* and *fully* that need an upper closed scale. However, given their lower bound, their antonyms will have upper closed scales, and as such the antonyms will be compatible with *completely* and *fully*.

(42) a. ??The pipe is fully bent.

  b. The pipe is fully flat.

  c. ??That author is completely famous.

  d. That author is completely unknown.

Given the data in (42) one may conclude that the adjectives *bent* and *famous* have lower closed scales, while their antonyms *flat* and *unknown* have upper closed scales. Antonyms of adjectives introducing fully open or fully closed scales are parallel to one another. Either both antonyms are incompatible with *completely* (open scale) or both are compatible with *completely* (fully closed scale). This is illustrated in (43) for the open scale adjectives *tall* and *short* and the closed scale adjectives *open* and *closed*:

(43) a. ??Her brother is completely tall/short.

  b. The door is completely open/closed.

The second aspect of scale structure that enters into play is the presence of a standard of comparison. This notion can be illustrated on the basis of an adjective with a relative standard, such as *tall*. Being tall means being tall to a degree *d* that exceeds a contextually defined degree, corresponding to what is expected in the given context (this usually involves formation of a comparison class, Klein 1980). The contextually defined degree of tallness that has to be taken into account in order to judge a sentence with *tall* is the standard of comparison. The presence of a relative standard can be tested by means of negation. Some examples are given in (44).

(44)   a.   The door is not large $\not\models$ The door is small

     b.   The door is not small $\not\models$ The door is large

     c.   The table is not expensive $\not\models$ The table is cheap

     d.   The table is not cheap $\not\models$ The table is expensive

If a table is not cheap, it means that its cost is not lower than expected in a given context. This does not imply that its cost is higher than expected or expensive.

The standard of comparison is not always relative (context-dependent) as in the examples in (44). It may also be absolute (cf. Yoon 1996 and Rotstein and Winter 2004, who call adjectives with an absolute standard "total adjectives" as opposed to "partial adjectives," which have a relative standard). Absolute standards may be maximal or minimal. A maximal standard corresponds to the upper bound of an upper or fully closed scale. A minimal standard corresponds to the lower bound of a lower or fully closed scale. The presence of an absolute standard may be tested by making use of negation as well: the negation of an adjective with an absolute standard entails its antonym. This is illustrated in (45) for the antonyms *open* and *closed*. Recall that both are fully closed scale adjectives (cf. 43b above). The absolute standard is minimal in the case of *open*, and maximal in the case of *closed*. This is illustrated by (45c). Even if a door is minimally open, it is open. On the other hand, a door needs to be maximally closed in order to be closed.

(45)   a.   The door is not open $\models$ The door is closed

     b.   The door is not closed $\models$ The door is open

     c.   The door isn't closed/#open but it's ajar

Kennedy and McNally argue that *very* boosts the value of a relative standard. The relative standard for *tall*, for instance, is computed on the basis of the expected length. A tall person is taller than the average in a given context. By using *very tall* rather than *tall* the comparison class changes. Not all contextually relevant persons are taken into account but only those that are tall. As a result, a very tall person is someone who is tall as compared to other tall persons, while a tall person is tall with respect to other persons that may be tall or short or something in between (see also Klein 1980). The degree modifier *much* indicates a high degree on the basis of a lower bound, and is therefore incompatible with open scale adjectives.[18]

Given the analysis of *very*, it is important to know under what conditions a relative standard may be present. Kennedy and McNally argue that gradable adjectives associated with totally open scales always have relative standards. Totally or partially closed scales usually have absolute standards, but they may have relative standards as well in certain contexts, as illustrated in (46b) for the closed scale adjective *full*.

(46)   a.   The beaker is completely full.

   b.   Whoops! This beaker is very full. I'd better pour out some of that liquid.

The presence of a relative standard for comparison seems to be disfavored when there is already an absolute standard that corresponds to the minimal or maximal value on a partially or fully closed scale. As open scales lack a minimum or a maximum value that may be mapped onto an absolute standard, these scales are condemned to having relative standards. This accounts for the fact that relative standards are relatively rare and strongly context-dependent in the case of (partially) closed scale adjectives.[19]

Let us now turn to the idea that certain types of scales are restricted to adjectives, and as such restrict the distribution of certain degree expressions to the adjectival domain. More in particular, I would like to postulate that open scales, as well as relative standards, are typically adjectival, while lower closed scales are found both in the adjectival domain and outside of it. Consider for instance the data in (47). When negation is applied to a noun or an eventive verb, there is a "zero" reading, typical for a lower closed scale.[20]

(47)   a.   John read no books. (no books = zero books)

   b.   John did not read. ('zero' reading by John)

---

[18] A reviewer wonders why it is not possible to use *much open*, as *open* introduces a lower bound. It should be noted that *open* also introduces an upper bound, given that a door can be completely open, and this seems to be the reason why *much open* is excluded. The only way to get a high degree interpretation for an upper closed adjective seems to be insertion of a relative standard, as illustrated for *full* in (46).

[19] Neeleman et al. (2004) argue that the application of the rules introducing the equivalent of a relative standard is forced by the fact that without applying them the sentence is usually a truism. A sentence such as *John is tall* would mean that John has height, which is already presupposed by the use of the adjective *tall*.

[20] See also the discussion on the mapping of event structure to scale structure in Kennedy and McNally (2005: 361–365). They argue that in all cases this mapping yields lower closed scales.

According to (47a), John read zero books, and similarly, there is "zero" reading by John in (47b). In the case of abstract verbs such as *to appreciate* a zero point seems to be available as well. As it is hard to determine what antonym to use, I will use a slightly modified form of the test, making use of the absence of the relative standard in comparatives. This form of the test can be illustrated for *tall* in (48a) and for *to appreciate* in (48b):

(48)   a.   John is not tall, but he is taller than Peter

      b.   #John did not appreciate the movie, but he appreciated it more than Peter did

The example in (48a) is clearly not contradictory at all, while the example in (48b) is strange.

    In the remainder of this section, I would like to briefly discuss two questions that are relevant for the hypothesis that certain types of scales are typically adjectival. The first is what happens after conversion from one category to another. The second question is whether it is possible to account for the distribution of all type A expressions in this way.

    There is some evidence that a noun, when turned into an adjective, switches from a lower closed scale to an open scale with a relative standard. This is illustrated by the examples in (49) for the Dutch pair *geduld* 'patience' and *geduldig* 'patient.' The adjective *geduldig* is derived from the noun *geduld* by suffixation of *-ig*.

(49)   a.   #Jan heeft geen geduld, maar hij heeft wel iets meer geduld dan Piet.
        "Jan has no patience but he does have a bit more patience than Piet."

      b.   Jan is niet geduldig, maar hij is wel iets geduldiger dan Piet.
        "Jan is not patient, but he is slightly more patient than Piet."

The sentence in (49a) is a contradiction. If Jan has no patience, he cannot possibly have more of it than Piet. If he is not patient, however, it does not mean that he has no patience at all, it just means that he is less patient than most people. This is corroborated by the intuition that the degree of Jan's impatience is greater for *Jan heeft geen geduld* than for *Jan is niet geduldig*. These data suggest that in fact the type of scale changes with the change of category. I will leave this issue for further research, but the data in (49) indicate that category and scalar properties do in fact interact.

    As for the second question, if the distribution of *very* is determined by its interpretation (it boosts a relative standard), one would like to know what happens to the type A expression *as*, which is not sensitive to the presence of a relative standard. It seems that *as* is in fact more easily compatible with adjectives such as *needed* and *praised*, even though *as needed/praised* and *as much needed/praised* are both available. This suggests that *as* is in fact sensitive to the class of adjectives as a whole, while *much* and *as much* are sensitive to the presence of a lower bound.

The discussion in this section shows that the idea of using scale structure in order to better understand the distribution of degree expressions on the one hand and the status of adjectives as opposed to other categories on the other, is promising, even though more research is needed in order to make it possible to use this for explaining the distribution of all type A expressions. However, it seems to be true that only a subclass of the types of scales found for adjectives is found for other categories as well. This is in particular clear for mass nouns, plurals, and eventive verbs, which are at the bottom of Table 6.2. The scalar properties of nominal and verbal gradable predicates (*faim* 'hunger' and *to appreciate*) constitute an issue for further research, and this issue is connected to the question of whether one would like to assume a degree variable in their representation or not.

6.4 Conclusions

This chapter started out with the question of how adjectives and gradability are related to one another, and I have looked at this question from the perspective of the distribution of degree expressions. It has been argued that the categories degree expressions may combine with form a continuum in the sense that degree expressions cannot combine with two categories that are not adjacent on this continuum, unless they may be combined with all categories in between as well. Some degree modifiers can be used in all contexts (e.g., *trop*) while others are only compatible with adjectives (e.g., *too*) or with plural nouns (e.g., *many*). In between these extreme cases all sorts of "intermediate" distributions are found.

In the second part of the chapter I explored several aspects of the continuum in relation to the status of adjectives. First I explored different hypotheses concerning the presence vs. absence of degree variables. A first possibility is to assume that gradable adjectives contain a degree variable, while other gradable categories do not. This allows us to assume that type A expressions have a semantics that makes them incompatible with expressions that do not offer a degree variable. This approach would force us to postulate systematic ambiguity for type C expressions (the expressions that can be used with all categories). It has been shown that this type of approach does not account for syntactic differences between type A and type C expressions in the context of adjectives. A second possibility is to assume that all contexts that are compatible with type B expressions (gradable adjectival, nominal, and verbal predicates) are sensitive to the presence of a degree variable. This would have the (possibly) desirable result that abstract gradable verbs such as *to appreciate* and gradable adjectives obtain their degree reading in a similar way. Finally, one could assume that all degree expressions are sensitive to the presence of a degree variable that would then be available cross-categorially (see Cresswell 1977). This would allow us to do away with the ambiguity of expressions such as *more* and *less*. In the latter two scenarios (degree variable in all gradable predicates and degree variable everywhere), the special behavior of adjectives remains unexplained.

A second way to look at the distribution of type A expressions involves scale structure. Building on Kennedy and McNally (2005), it has been hypothesized that certain types of scales are typically adjectival. This type of approach is actually compatible with different views on the presence versus absence of a degree variable. On the one hand scale structure might explain certain distributional patterns within a Cresswellian approach to the degree variable. On the other hand, under the assumption that only adjectives contain degree variables, the special scalar properties of adjectives might be related to the presence of this degree variable.

Acknowledgments

I would like to thank the audiences at the Workshop on the Semantics of Adjectives and Adverbs in Barcelona and the *Journée d'Études sur l'analyse formelle des adjectifs*. More particularly, I would like to thank Chris Kennedy and an anonymous reviewer, both of whom gave very constructive remarks on a previous version of the chapter, as well as Camelia Constantinescu, Mélanie Jouitteau, Louise McNally, Ora Matushansky, Muriel Norde, Johan Rooryck, Maaike Schoorlemmer and Kateřina Součková. The support of NWO, the Dutch Organisation for Scientific Research (grant 276-70-007) is gratefully acknowledged. All usual disclaimers apply.

7

Measure of change: The adjectival core of degree achievements

CHRISTOPHER KENNEDY AND BETH LEVIN

7.1 Introduction

Current theories of aspect acknowledge the pervasiveness of verbs of variable telicity, and are designed to account both for why these verbs show such variability and for the complex conditions that give rise to telic and atelic interpretations. Previous work has identified several sets of such verbs, including incremental theme verbs, such as *eat* and *destroy*; degree achievements, such as *cool* and *widen*; and (a)telic directed motion verbs, such as *ascend* and *descend* (see e.g., Declerck 1979; Dowty 1979, 1991; Krifka 1989, 1992; Tenny 1994; Bertinetto and Squartini 1995; Levin and Rappaport Hovav 1995; Jackendoff 1996a; Ramchand 1997; Filip 1999; Hay et al. 1999; Rothstein 2004; Borer 2005b). As the diversity in descriptive labels suggests, most previous work has taken these classes to embody distinct phenomena and to have distinct lexical semantic analyses. We believe that it is possible to provide a unified analysis in which the behavior of all of these verbs stems from a single shared element of their meanings: a function that measures the degree to which an object changes relative to some scalar dimension over the course of an event. We claim that such "measures of change" are based on the more general kinds of measure functions that are lexicalized in many languages by gradable adjectives, and that map an object to a scalar value that represents the degree to which it manifests some gradable property at a time (see Bartsch and Vennemann 1972, 1973; Bierwisch 1989; Kennedy 1999b; Piñón 2005). In this chapter we focus on the analysis of degree achievements, which provide the first step towards this goal. As verbs for the most part derived from gradable adjectives, they most transparently illustrate the semantic components that we claim are involved in determining variable telicity.

We begin this chapter with a detailed examination of variable telicity in degree achievements. We explore both the general role of adjective meaning in the composition of predicates that express changes along a scalar dimension and the specific effects of idiosyncratic features of adjective meaning, in particular the structure of the scale that represents the gradable property measured by the adjective. The set of facts we delineate allows us to evaluate the two major kinds of semantic analyses that have been proposed for degree achievements – what we call the "positive" and "comparative" analyses – and to highlight the strong and weak points of each. We then present our own analysis in terms of measure of change, which represents a synthesis of the best features of the positive and comparative analyses, and show how it explains the semantic behavior of degree achievements. We conclude with a sketch of how the analysis can be extended to an account of variable telicity in the other verb classes mentioned above.

7.2 Variable telicity in degree achievements

7.2.1 *Telicity and vagueness*

Vendler (1957) distinguishes atelic predicates (activities) like *run* from telic predicates (accomplishments) like *run a mile* on the basis of whether they entail of an event that a "set terminal point" has been reached. Most studies of variable telicity focus on contrasts like *run for/??in four minutes* vs. *run a mile in/??for four minutes*, because they show that compositional interactions between a verb and its argument(s) can affect the telicity of the predicate (Verkuyl 1972; Mourelatos 1978; Bach 1986; Krifka 1989). Degree achievements (DAs) present a special challenge, however, because they may have variable telicity independently of the properties of their arguments, as first observed by Dowty (1979). Consider for example the uses of *cool* in (1a–b).[1]

(1)   a.   The soup cooled in 10 minutes.   (TELIC)

       b.   The soup cooled for 10 minutes.   (ATELIC)

The acceptability of the *in*-PP in (1a) shows that *cool* can be telic, and indeed this sentence is true of an event only if it leads to an endstate in which the affected participant has come to be cool. However, the acceptable *for*-PP in

---

[1] We will focus primarily on inchoative forms of DAs in this chapter, even though most have causative variants as well, as it is the semantics of the "inchoative core" that is crucial to capturing variable telicity. That is, telicity does not correlate with causativity: if a DA shows variable telicity at all, then it shows it in both its causative and inchoative forms (Hay et al. 1999). Since for deadjectival verbs the semantics of the latter are part of the former (on standard assumptions about causative/inchoative alternations; though see Koontz-Garboden 2007), it must be the case that it is the latter on which telicity is based.

(1b) shows that *cool* can also be atelic, and this example implies neither that the endstate associated with (1a) ("coolness") has been reached, nor that a sequence of distinct change of state eventualities has taken place (as in iterated achievements like *Kim discovered crabgrass in the yard for six weeks*; see Dowty 1979). Similarly, whether or not the progressive form in (2a) entails the perfect in (2b) depends on whether we understand *cool* in (2a) only as implying that the temperature of the soup is getting lower (atelic; (2b) entailed), or as implying that the temperature of the soup is moving towards an understood endstate of being cool (telic; (2b) not entailed).

(2)   a.   The soup is cooling.

      b.   The soup has cooled.

The challenge then is to identify the factors which lead to variable telicity in DAs. Building on ideas in Dowty (1979), Abusch (1986) proposes that the variable telicity of DAs (her "vague inchoatives") is parasitic on a different kind of variability in the meanings of the expressions that describe the endstates such verbs imply (in their telic uses). Following Dowty, Abusch takes the lexical meaning of an inchoative verb to be as in (3a), where P is a property of individuals, with truth conditions as in (3b).[2]

(3)   a. $\lambda x \lambda e.\text{BECOME}(P)(x)(e)$

      b. $\text{BECOME}(P)(x)(e) = 1$ iff $P(x)(init(e)) = 0$ and $P(x)(fin(e)) = 1$, where $init(e)$ and $fin(e)$ are the initial and final parts of e.

Abusch observes that what is special about DAs like *cool* is that P corresponds to a vague predicate: what counts as cool is a matter of context, and there will typically be some things for which it is impossible to say whether they are cool or not (so-called "borderline cases"). Building on the analyses of vague predicates in Kamp (1975) and Klein (1980) (see also McConnell-Ginet 1973 and Fine 1975), Abusch analyzes adjectival *cool* as a function **cool** from contexts to properties of individuals, and proposes that the variability of verbal *cool* depends on whether the contextual argument of **cool** is fixed to the context of utterance, as in (4a), or is bound by an existential quantifier, as in (4b).

(4)   a. $\lambda x \lambda e.\text{BECOME}(\textbf{cool}(c_u))(x)(e)$

      b. $\lambda x \lambda e.\exists c [\text{BECOME}(\textbf{cool}(c))(x)(e)]$

In (4a), $\textbf{cool}(c_u)$ is the property of being cool in the context of utterance. This is the meaning of the positive (unmarked) form of the adjective, which

---

[2] Abusch does not assume an event semantics; (3b) simply restates the interval-based semantics for BECOME that she assumes (based on Dowty 1979) in terms of an event argument; cf. Krifka (1998b); Parsons (1990).

is true of objects that are at least as cool as some contextual "standard" of temperature. (The standard can vary both on properties of the object and on properties of the context: cool lemonade is normally cooler than cool coffee, and coffee that counts as cool relative to one's desire to drink it in the morning with a bagel is typically warmer than coffee that counts as cool relative to one's desire to pour it over ice without turning the whole thing into a watery mess.) Saturation of the individual argument x derives a property that is true of an event just in case x is not as cool as the contextual standard at the beginning of the event, and is at least as cool as the standard at the end of the event; the requirement that this transition be made renders the predicate telic.

In (4b), the context variable is existentially bound, which means that the predicate is true of an event just in case there is some context such that x is not cool relative to that context at the beginning of the event and is cool relative to the context at the end of the event, that is, that x has a coolness that is below the standard of comparison for that context at the beginning of the event, and above it at the end. But this merely requires an increase in coolness (which amounts to a decrease in temperature, since *cool* is a "polar negative" adjective; see Seuren 1978; Bierwisch 1989; Kennedy 2001), and there is no entailment that a particular endstate is reached. Assuming an arbitrary number of contextual interpretations of vague predicates, differing only in where along a gradable continuum they draw the line between the things they are true and false of, (4b) is true of any subevent of an event that it is true of. In other words, it has the "subinterval property," and so is atelic (Bennett and Partee 1982).

Abusch's analysis predicts that DAs in general should behave like *cool*, having either telic or atelic interpretations depending on whether the adjectival root is analyzed in a "positive" sense as in (4a) or a "comparative" sense as in (4b).[3] One potential problem for this analysis comes from the fact that many DAs have default telic interpretations. Such verbs have atelic uses, but in the absence of explicit morphosyntactic or contextual information forcing such interpretations, they are treated as telic. This is illustrated by the examples in (5).

(5)   a.   The sky darkened (?but it didn't become dark).

   b.   The shirt dried (??but it didn't become dry).

   c.   The sink emptied (??but it didn't become empty).

---

[3] Abusch's analysis of the atelic interpretation is often characterized as involving a "comparative" semantics, and we will continue to use this label here, but with caution: this characterization is not quite accurate. Abusch's semantics is similar to e.g. Klein's (1980) analysis of comparatives in that it involves existential quantification over contextual interpretations of vague predicates, but it is crucially different in not introducing an explicit standard of comparison (the expression contributed by the *than* constituent in an English comparative construction).

As observed by Kearns (2007), the most natural interpretations of examples like these are ones in which the affected objects reach the endstate named by the positive form of the adjective, as illustrated by the oddity of the completions in parentheses. These completions do not result in true contradictions, showing that the telic interpretation is not obligatory, but they do result in degraded acceptability.[4] In particular, they have the feel of "garden path effects," suggesting that the verbs in (5) have default telic positive interpretations, and the completions require reanalysis to the atelic, comparative ones.

A potential explanation for this default is a pragmatic one: since the telic interpretation entails the atelic one, it is more informative and therefore stronger. In the absence of information to the contrary – which could in principle be implicit (contextual), compositional (such as modification that is consistent only with atelicity), or even lexical (word-based defaults) – the strongest meaning should be preferred, resulting in a preference for telic interpretations (cf. Dalrymple et al.'s (1998) analysis of interpretive variability in reciprocals).

Although we will end up adopting a version of this proposal to explain the fact that verbs like those in (5) have default telic interpretations, it is not enough to save Abusch's analysis from a more serious second problem: there are DAs which appear to have only atelic interpretations. For example, (6a–b) show that DAs derived from the dimensional adjectives *wide* and *deep* accept only durative temporal modifiers:

(6) a. The gap between the boats widened for/??in a few minutes.

   b. The recession deepened for/??in several years.

In addition, entailment from the progressive to the perfect is automatic, as shown by the fact that (7a–b), unlike e.g. (8a–b), are contradictory.

(7) a. #The gap is widening, but it hasn't widened.

   b. #The recession is deepening, but it hasn't deepened.

(8) a. The soup is cooling, but it hasn't cooled.

   b. The shirt is drying, but it hasn't dried.

These facts are unexpected if a DA such as *widen* is ambiguous between the two meanings in (9), comparable to those for *cool* in (4).

---

[4] Kearns points out that this effect is gradient, with some verbs (like *darken*) showing it mildly and others (like *empty*) showing it quite strongly. However, even verbs like *empty* can take on atelic interpretations when the context is rich enough or other components of the sentence force such readings, as in the case of post-verbal modification by *quickly* (Kearns 2007):

(i) The sink emptied quickly (but we closed the drain before it became empty).

(9)   a. $\lambda x \lambda e[\text{BECOME}(\textbf{wide}(c_u))(x)(e)]$

      b. $\lambda x \lambda e.\exists c[\text{BECOME}(\textbf{wide}(c))(x)(e)]$

In particular, if (9a) were an option, then *widen* should have a telic interpretation equivalent to *become wide*, namely "come to have a width that is at least as great as the minimum width that counts as wide in the context of utterance."[5] It would then be possible to simultaneously assert that something widens in the sense of (9b) while denying that it widens in the sense of (9a) (this is Zwicky and Sadock's (1975) "test of contradiction"), since an object can increase in width without becoming wide. But this is not the case: if it were, then the examples in (7) would fail to generate a contradiction. That is, there would be an interpretation of, for example, (7a) in which the occurrence of *widen* in the perfective form is understood to mean the same as *become wide*, not *become wider*, in which case there would be no incompatibility with the progressive assertion: a gap could be increasing in width without having become wide (see note 5). We can therefore conclude that DAs like *widen* and *deepen* resist interpretations parallel to (9a), a fact that deserves explanation.[6]

A final problem with Abusch's analysis involves the interpretation of measure phrases in DAs. Consider the following examples:

(10)   a.   The soup cooled 17 degrees.

       b.   The gap widened 6 inches.

The measure phrases in these examples specify the amount that the respective subjects change in temperature and width as a result of participating in the event described by the verbs, and in doing so, render the predicates telic (a point to which we will return below). However, it is difficult to see how this result can be achieved given the options in (4) and (9). It might seem reasonable to modify the account so that the measure phrase and adjectival base together provide the value of the inchoative predicate, but this would predict that (10a–b) should have the meanings in (11a–b).

[5] Even if the exact value of such a width is vague or unknown (or unknowable; see Williamson 1992, 1994), it remains the case that (9a) should be semantically telic, since it imposes exactly the same kind of requirement on an event that a DA like *cool* does in its telic sense in (4a). This is confirmed by the absence of an entailment from the progressive to the perfect for *become wide*, as shown by (i).

(i)   The gap is becoming wide(r), but it hasn't become wide.

Modification of *become wide* with an *in*-PP is not particularly felicitous, but this is presumably due to the vagueness of *wide*, and therefore not indicative of atelicity.

[6] While this conclusion is justified based on the clear contrast between the examples in (7) and those in (8), we suspect that it may be possible under special circumstances and with strong contextual support to understand DAs like *widen* in a telic, "positive" sense comparable to (9a). The analysis that we present in section 7.3.2 will allow for this possibility as a (highly) marked option, while at the same time explaining why the atelic "comparative" sense is the default.

(11) a. ??The soup became 17 degrees cool.

   b. The gap became 6 inches wide.

This prediction is obviously incorrect: *cool* is a gradable adjective that does not combine with measure phrases (see Schwarzschild 2005 and Svenonius and Kennedy 2006 for recent discussion of this issue), and (11b) does not accurately convey the meaning of (10b). Instead, (10a–b) are more accurately paraphrased by (12a–b).

(12) a. The soup became 17 degrees cooler (than it was at the beginning of the event).

   b. The gap became 6 inches wider (than it was at the beginning of the event).

These paraphrases show that measure phrases in DAs express "differential" amounts, just like measure phrases in comparatives: instead of specifying the total amount to which an object possesses some measurable gradable property (as in (11b), where *six inches* is used to describe the total/maximal width of the gap), such measure phrases convey the extent to which two objects (or the same object at different times) differ along some gradable continuum. An analysis of variable telicity in DAs that is based strictly on the vagueness of the positive form, such as Abusch's, is not equipped to convey this kind of meaning. (See von Stechow 1984 for a discussion of the problem differential measure phrases present for a semantics of comparatives based on the analysis of vagueness in Kamp 1975 and Klein 1980, on which Abusch builds her analysis of DAs.)

7.2.2 *Telicity and scale structure*

Our discussion of Abusch's work shows that any account of DAs must explain three factors: 1) the (strong) default telic/positive interpretation of verbs like *darken*, 2) the lack of a telic/positive meaning for verbs like *widen*, and 3) the differential interpretation assigned to measure phrase arguments. Recent analyses of DAs have attempted to account for these factors by adopting a semantics for DAs that is more directly "scalar," importing features from degree-based semantic analyses of gradable adjectives. We hold off on providing a full overview of scalar semantics until section 7.3 when we introduce our own account (which is also a scalar one); here we highlight the crucial advantages – and shortcomings – of existing scalar analyses.

   The first explicitly scalar analysis of DAs, and the one on which the analysis we will present in section 7.3.2 is based, is provided by Hay et al. (1999). Hay et al. provide in effect a purely "comparative" semantics for DAs, treating them as predicates of events that are true of an object if the degree to which it possesses the gradable property encoded by the source adjective at the end of the event exceeds the degree to which it possessed that property at the beginning of the event by some positive degree d. The degree argument, which Hay et al. refer to as the *difference value*, is a measure of the amount that an object changes as a result of participating in the event described by a DA, and is precisely that which is overtly expressed by the measure phrases in (10) that were problematic for Abusch's analysis. The meanings assigned to these examples in the Hay et al. analysis are exactly those specified above in (12), thus solving one of the three problems.

The difference value is furthermore the crucial factor determining the telicity of the predicate. If it is such that a particular degree on the adjectival scale must be obtained in order for the predicate to be true of an event, then a terminal point for the entire event can be identified, namely that point at which the affected object attains that degree (which is equivalent to the initial degree to which it possessed the property plus the degree specified by the difference value); the result is a telic interpretation. If, however, the difference value is satisfied by any positive degree, this computation isn't possible and no terminal point can be identified; in this case, the predicate is atelic.

In some cases, such as the examples with measure phrases above, the difference value is explicit and the predicate is telic. When the difference value is implicit, contextual and lexical semantic factors determine its value and in turn the telicity of the predicate. Hay et al. take advantage of the latter to explain the different aspectual properties of DAs like *widen* and *deepen* on the one hand, and those like *darken, dry*, and *empty* on the other. In particular, they observe that these two classes of DAs differ with respect to the structures of the scales associated with their adjectival bases: *wide, deep*, etc. use open scales (scales that lack maximal elements); *dark, dry*, etc. use closed ones (scales with maximal elements).

According to Hay et al., verbs derived from closed scale adjectives are by default telic due to a preference for fixing the difference value in such a way as to entail that the maximal value on the scale must be reached. In effect, since the structure of the scale allows for the possibility of increase along the adjectival scale to a maximal degree ("maximal change"), and such a meaning is stronger than (entails) all other potential meanings, it should be selected, resulting in a telic interpretation. This explanation has obvious similarities to the account of default telicity presented above in the context of Abusch's analysis; where the Hay et al. proposal stands apart is in the explanation of obligatory atelicity for DAs derived from open scale adjectives like *widen*. Because the adjectival root *wide* uses a scale that does not have a maximal degree, there is no possibility for an interpretation involving maximal change, so the difference value is existentially closed. The result is that *widen* is true of an event and an object as long as it undergoes some increase in width, which derives an atelic interpretation.

Similar analyses have been developed by Kearns (2007) and Winter (2006), which differ slightly in detail but ultimately face a similar challenge. To set the stage for this challenge, we must first address a specific criticism of Hay et al.'s account of default telicity for verbs based on closed scale adjectives, discussed in Kearns (2007). Kearns argues that the telos for such verbs need not be a maximum value on the relevant scale, but is rather the standard used by the corresponding adjective, whatever that is. As support for this claim, she presents examples like (13a–b) to show that the telic interpretations of DAs based on (unmodified) closed scale adjectives do not actually entail maximality, as indicated by the acceptability of the *not completely* continuations (numbers in square brackets refer to the example numbers in Kearns 2007).

(13)   a.   The sky darkened in an hour, but it wasn't completely dark. [37a]

       b.   The fruit ripened in five days but it wasn't completely ripe. [38a]

While we agree with Kearns' claim that the telos for verbs like *darken* and *ripen* should be identified with the standard of the corresponding adjectives (and that the Hay et al. analysis fails to adequately explain this connection), we do not agree that the data in (13) show that this value is not a maximal degree on the relevant scales. Instead, we claim that the apparent non-maximality of the adjectival standards in the second conjuncts of (13a–b) is an artifact of the fact that the definite descriptions that introduce the affected arguments in the first conjuncts can be interpreted imprecisely, allowing for the possibility that the verbs do not apply to subparts of the objects that the descriptions are used to refer to. In other words, what is being denied in the second conjunct of (13a) is that all parts of the sky are dark, not that the parts of the sky that the verb does in fact apply to fail to become maximally dark.

Evidence in favor of this interpretation of the data in (13) comes from a couple of sources. First, if we eliminate the possibility of an imprecise interpretation of the definite in the first conjunct by making it explicit that the entire object is affected, we get a contradiction with a *not completely* interpretation:

(14)   a.   #All of the sky darkened in an hour, but it wasn't completely dark.

       b.   #The entire fruit ripened in five days, but it wasn't completely ripe.

These examples show that the second conjunct can have an interpretation in which the adverb is in effect modifying the subject (*not all of it*) rather than picking out a maximal value on the scale, which in turn shows that Kearns' examples do not counterexemplify Hay et al.'s claims that telic DAs entail maximum degrees.

Second, if we modify the second conjunct to make it explicit that the intended interpretation is one in which a maximal degree is not achieved, we get a contradiction:

(15)   a.   #The sky darkened in an hour, but no part of it was completely dark.

   b.   #The fruit ripened in five days, but no part of it was completely ripe.

These examples provide positive evidence that telic DAs like *darken* and *ripen* do in fact entail that their affected arguments achieve maximal degrees of the properties measured by the adjectives. If this were not the case, then there would be no incompatibility between the two conjuncts: the assertion that no part of the sky is completely dark in the second conjunct of (15a), for example, should be perfectly consistent with the first conjunct if the verb merely required something close to complete darkness for whatever parts of the sky (possibly all of them) are assumed to be affected.

These considerations show that telic interpretations of DAs based on closed scale adjectives do in fact entail movement to a maximal degree, contrary to Kearns' claims; however, they do not argue against her position that the telos is the "standard endstate" associated with the adjectival form, if in fact the adjectival standard is itself a maximal degree.[7] This position is in fact argued for in detail by Rotstein and Winter (2004), Kennedy and McNally (2005) and Kennedy (2007), a point that we will discuss in detail in the next section. Although this result is not inconsistent with Hay et al.'s analysis, it is important to acknowledge that the analysis does not actually derive it in a principled way.

The problem is that Hay et al. do not provide an explicit mechanism for fixing the difference value for verbs like *darken*, *ripen*, etc. in such a way as to ensure that the predicate actually entails of its argument that it becomes maximally dark, ripe, etc., saying only that the existence of a maximal value on the scale "provides a basis" for fixing the difference value in the appropriate way (see Piñón's contribution to this volume for detailed discussion of this point). This problem threatens to undermine the whole analysis: without a principled account of the conditions under which the difference value can

---

[7] Kearns is correct that the DA *cool* – and presumably some others like it – has a conventionalized non-maximal endpoint. When this verb is used telically without context, as in (i), the endpoint is assumed to be room temperature, presumably because food normally can't cool further without being put in a refrigerator or in some other cold place.

(i)   The soup cooled in ten minutes.

We discuss the case of *cool* in more detail below.

and cannot correspond to particular degrees, we lose the explanation of the difference in (default) telicity between DAs derived from adjectives with open scales and those derived from adjectives with closed scales. In short, we have no explanation of why it is possible to fix the difference value to a degree that entails movement to the end of the scale in the case of the latter class of DAs, but not possible to fix the difference value to a degree that entails movement to a contextual standard in the case of the former class (see Kearns 2007 for the same criticism). Such a move would result in a telic interpretation of, for example, *widen* with a meaning comparable to *become wide*, which as we have shown is not an option (or is at best a highly marked one).

Kearns' solution to this problem is to claim that the contextual standard associated with adjectives like *wide* is "insufficiently determined" to serve as a telos. Although this explanation has intuitive appeal, it seems unlikely given the fact that *become wide* is telic (see note 5), and more generally, given the fact that speakers must have access to the contextual standard in order to assign truth conditions to sentences containing the positive form of the adjective. Winter (2006) takes a different approach: he defines the mapping from scalar adjectives to (corresponding) DAs in such a way that the verbal form has a telos based on a lexically specified adjectival standard *if one is specified*, and (building on proposals in Rotstein and Winter 2004) posits that such standards are specified only for closed scale adjectives. While this analysis achieves the desired result, it has a couple of undesirable features. First, it simply eliminates the possibility of a contextual standard by stipulation; an analysis in which this restriction follows from more general principles is preferable. Second, it predicts that DAs based on closed scale adjectives like *straighten* should have only telic interpretations, since in the Rotstein and Winter semantics for scalar adjectives, *straight* is specified as having a standard associated with the endpoint of the scale. The fact that DAs based on closed scale adjectives can also have atelic interpretations (see note 4 and Kearns 2007) then remains unexplained.

At a more general level, Winter's analysis raises the question of why it is just the closed scale adjectives that are conventionally associated with fixed standards. If we can answer this question, and also provide an answer to the question of why fixed standards can give rise to telic interpretations of DAs while context-dependent ones (of the sort involved in the interpretation of an open scale adjective like *wide*) cannot, then we will have the basis for a truly explanatory account of the relation between scale structure and telicity in DAs. In the next section we present an analysis of the semantics of degree achievements in which the answers to these two questions are in fact the same.

7.3 Measure of change

7.3.1 *Scale structure and standard of comparison*

Our analysis builds on the same core hypothesis that underlies the Dowty/Abusch analysis: the variable aspectual properties of DAs derive from the semantic properties of the adjectival part of their (decomposed) lexical meanings. However, we begin from different assumptions about how to capture the semantics of gradability and vagueness. Whereas Abusch's analysis is built on a semantics of gradable predicates in which they denote (context-dependent) properties of individuals, we start from the assumption that such expressions do not themselves express properties, but rather encode measure functions: functions that associate objects with ordered values on a scale, or degrees.[8]

In particular, we follow Bartsch and Vennemann (1972, 1973) and Kennedy (1999b) and assume that gradable adjectives in English directly lexicalize measure functions.[9] We further assume following Hay et al. (1999) (cf. Piñón 2005) that such measure functions can be relativized to times (an object can have different degrees of height, weight, temperature, etc. at different times), so that the adjective *cool*, for example, denotes a function **cool** from objects x and times t that returns the temperature of x at t. A consequence of this analysis is that a gradable adjective by itself does not denote a property of individuals, but must instead be converted into one so that composition with its individual argument results in a proposition; this is the role of degree morphology: comparative morphemes, sufficiency/excess morphemes, intensifiers, and so forth.

Among the set of degree morphemes is a null degree head (or possibly a semantically equivalent type-shifting rule) that is involved in the

---

[8] Following Kennedy and McNally (2005), we take scales to be triples $\langle S, R, \delta \rangle$ where S is a set of degrees, R an ordering on S, and δ a value that represents the dimension of measurement. Scales may vary along any of these parameters: the structure of S (e.g., whether it is open or closed), the ordering relation ($\prec$ for increasing, "positive" adjectives like *warm*; $\succ$ for decreasing, "negative" adjectives like *cool*), and the dimension (temperature, width, depth, linear extent, temporal extent, etc.). Semantic differences between gradable adjectives are primarily based on differences in the kinds of scales they use.

[9] An alternative (and more common) analysis of gradable adjectives is one in which they do not directly denote measure functions, but incorporate them as part of their meanings (see e.g. Cresswell 1977; von Stechow 1984; Heim 1985, 2000; Klein 1991). On this view, a gradable adjective like *cool* expresses the relation between degrees and individuals in (i), where **cool** is a measure function.

(i) $[[[_A \ \text{cool}]]] = \lambda d \lambda x.\mathbf{cool}(x) \succeq d$

Our proposals in this chapter can be made consistent with this analysis of gradable adjectives by simply assuming that measure functions correspond not directly to adjective denotations, but rather to more basic units of meaning, which are part of the lexical semantic representations of both gradable adjectives and verbs of gradual change.

interpretation of the so-called positive (morphologically unmarked) form, which denotes the function **pos** in (16).[10]

(16) $\mathbf{pos} = \lambda g \in D_{\langle e,d \rangle}\lambda t \lambda x.g(x)(t) \succeq \mathbf{stnd}(g)$

Here **stnd** is a function from gradable adjective meanings to degrees that returns a standard of comparison for the adjective in the context of utterance: the minimum degree required to "stand out" in the context relative to the kind of measurement expressed by the adjective (Kennedy 2007; Bogusławski 1975; Fara 2000; cf. Bartsch and Vennemann 1972, 1973; Cresswell 1977; von Stechow 1984). The positive form of *wide*, for example, denotes the property in (17), which is true of an object (at a time) just in case its width exceeds the standard, that is, just in case it stands out in the context of utterance relative to the kind of measurement represented by the measure function **wide** ("linear extent in a horizontal direction perpendicular to the perspective of reference," or something like that).

(17) $\mathbf{pos}(\mathbf{wide}) = \lambda t \lambda x.\mathbf{wide}(x)(t) \succeq \mathbf{stnd}(\mathbf{wide})$

The truth of a predication involving the positive form of a gradable adjective thus depends on two factors: the degree to which it manifests the gradable property measured by the adjective (in this case, its width), and the actual value of the standard of comparison in the context (here the degree returned by **stnd**(**wide**)). The latter value is a function both of (possibly variable) features of the conventional meaning of the adjective (such as its domain, which may be contextually or explicitly restricted to a particular comparison class; see Klein 1980; Kennedy 2007), and of features of the context (such as the domain of discourse, the interests/expectations of the participants in the discourse, and so forth).

However, there is an asymmetry in the relative contributions of conventional (lexical) and contextual information to the determination of the standard of comparison. Rotstein and Winter (2004), Kennedy and McNally (2005), and Kennedy (2007) provide extensive empirical arguments that when an adjective uses a closed scale (a feature of its conventional meaning), the standard of comparison invariably corresponds to an endpoint of the scale: the minimum in some cases (*bent, open, impure*, etc.) and the maximum in others (*straight, closed, pure*, etc.). In other words, the standards of comparison of closed scale adjectives are not context-dependent.

---

[10] At the risk of confusion, we follow descriptive tradition and use "positive form" to refer to the morphologically unmarked use of a predicative or attributive adjective. This sense of "positive" is distinct from the one used to refer to adjectival polarity, e.g. the characterization of *warm* as a (polar) positive adjective and *cool* as a (polar) negative one.

Kennedy (2007) argues that this distinction follows from the semantics of the positive form: specifically from the fact that the standard represents the minimum degree required to stand out relative to the kind of measure encoded by the adjective. The difference between adjectives that use closed measurement scales and those that use open ones is that the former come with "natural transitions": the transition from a zero to a non-zero degree on the scale (from not having any degree of the measured property to having some of it) in the case of an adjective with a lower closed scale, or the transition from a non-maximal to a maximal degree (from having an arbitrary degree of the measured property to having a maximal degree of it) in the case of an adjective with an upper closed scale. Kennedy proposes that what it means to "stand out" relative to a property measured by a closed scale adjective is to be on the upper end of one of these transitions. In the case of adjectives with lower closed scales like *wet*, *impure*, and so forth, this means having a non-zero degree of the measured property; in the case of adjectives with upper closed scales like *dry* and *pure*, this means having a maximal degree of the measured property.[11]

Scale structure explains why the endpoints of closed scale adjectives are potential standards (only closed scale adjectives have scales with endpoints), but it does not explain why they are the actual standards. There is nothing inherently incompatible between a closed scale and a context-dependent, non-endpoint-oriented standard, so the fact that closed scale adjectives default to endpoint-oriented standards must follow from some other constraint. According to Kennedy, this constraint is the principle of Interpretive Economy stated in (18).

(18)   **Interpretive Economy:** Maximize the contribution of the conventional meanings of the elements of a sentence to the computation of its truth conditions.

The effect of Interpretive Economy is to make a contextual standard a "last resort": since the natural transitions provided by the endpoints of a closed scale provide a basis for fixing the standard of comparison strictly on the basis of the conventional (lexical) meaning of a closed scale adjective, they should always be favored over a context-dependent standard. In contrast, nothing inherent to the meaning of an open scale adjective beyond its dimension of measurement (e.g. width vs. depth) provides a basis for fixing the standard. This means that contextual factors such as the domain of discourse,

---

[11] Adjectives with totally closed scales are somewhat more complicated: some can have either maximum or minimum standards (e.g. *opaque*), which is expected given the considerations articulated above, but others have only maximum standards (e.g. *full*). See Kennedy (2007) for discussion.

the interests and expectations of the discourse participants, and so forth must be taken into consideration when determining how much of the measured property is enough to stand out, resulting in the familar context-dependent, vague positive form interpretations of adjectives like *wide* and *deep*.

7.3.2 *The semantics of scalar change*

The assumptions outlined in the previous section (or something very much like them) are necessary to account for the semantics of the positive form, given a degree-based analysis of gradable adjectives.[12] They are not sufficient on their own, however, to explain the semantic properties of DAs in terms of the semantic properties of the adjectival parts of their meanings. To implement this hypothesis directly – essentially providing a scalar version of the Dowty/Abusch analysis – we would posit (19) as the meaning of a DA based on a gradable adjective g.

(19) $\lambda x \lambda e.\text{BECOME}(\textbf{pos}(\textbf{g}))(x)(e)$

Here **pos(g)** is equivalent to the meaning of the positive form of a gradable adjective **g**. In the case of DAs based on adjectives whose positive forms make use of maximal standards (adjectives with upper closed scales), such as *straight, dry,* and *dark,* we almost get the right results. The DA *straighten,* for example, would have the denotation in (20).

(20) $\lambda x \lambda e.\text{BECOME}(\textbf{pos}(\textbf{straight}))(x)(e)$

(20) is true of an individual x and an event e just in case **pos(straight)** is false of x at the beginning of e and true of x at the end of e. Since the measure function **straight** uses a scale with a maximum value, **pos(straight)** is true of x just in case it has maximal straightness, which in turn means that (20) holds of an event just in case x undergoes a change from non-maximal to maximal straightness. (20) fails to hold of subevents in which x ends up less than completely straight, and so is correctly predicted to be telic. However, this analysis will run into the same problems as Winter's account: it predicts that *straighten* is never atelic, contrary to fact.

This simple implementation fares even worse for DAs based on adjectives that do not have upper closed scales and maximum standards, however. Consider the case of *widen,* based on the open scale adjective *wide,* which should have the denotation in (21) according to (19).

---

[12] This is true regardless of whether we assume that such adjectives are of type $\langle e, d \rangle$ or type $\langle d, \langle e, t \rangle \rangle$, as described in note 9. The latter approach also requires a null positive morpheme, type-shifting rule, or saturation principle to map a function of type $\langle d, \langle e, t \rangle \rangle$ to a property of individuals.

(21) $\lambda x \lambda e.\text{BECOME}(\textbf{pos}(\textbf{wide}))(x)(e)$

The problem is essentially the same as the problem discussed in section 7.2.1: **pos(wide)** denotes the property of having a width that exceeds the standard of comparison for the context of utterance (whatever amount is enough to stand out relative to the measure function **wide**), so *widen* should have a meaning equivalent to *become wide* (which it doesn't) and it should be telic (which it isn't). For the same reason, a DA like *cool* is predicted to have only a telic interpretation equivalent to *become cool*; (19) does not provide a means of deriving the atelic interpretation parallel to *become cooler*.

One response to these problems would be to assume instead a version of Abusch's "comparative" semantics as in (22).

(22) $\lambda x \lambda e.\text{BECOME}(\textbf{more}(\textbf{g}))(x)(e)$

Strictly speaking, **more** in (22) cannot encode exactly the same meaning as the morpheme involved in comparative constructions, since the latter needs to combine with both an adjective and a standard of comparison (provided by the *than*-constituent in English) in order to derive a property of individuals. Instead, the **more** in (22) should really be thought of as shorthand for something that leaves us with a property that is true of an object x and an event e just in case x ends up being "more **g** at the end of e than it was at the beginning;" this is essentially the analysis of DAs proposed in Hay et al. (1999) and Winter (2006) (minus the culmination stipulation in the latter). (22) correctly captures the atelic interpretations of *widen* and *cool*, but fails to adequately account for the telic interpretation of the latter or to adequately explain why DAs like *straighten* and *darken* have default telic interpretations.

It appears, then, that basing the semantics of DAs on a degree semantics of gradable adjectives fares no better than the Dowty/Abusch analysis. If we assume that DAs have only "positive" meanings like (19), we fail to account for atelic interpretations of *widen, cool, straighten*, and so forth. If we assume that DAs have only "comparative" meanings like (22) (essentially the position taken in e.g. Hay et al. 1999), we fail to derive the telic interpretations of *straighten, darken*, etc. Finally, if we assume that DAs are ambiguous between (19) and (22), the fact that *widen*, etc. do not have both atelic and telic interpretations (absent a measure phrase) becomes mysterious.

As a solution to this apparent paradox, we present a kind of synthesis of the "positive" and "comparative" analyses, which differs from both the Dowty/Abusch approach and the analyses of Hay et al. (1999), Kearns (2007), and Winter (2006) in the following crucial respect: instead of treating the adjectival part of the meaning of a DA as identical to the meaning of the adjectival base (a vague property for Abusch and Dowty; a measure function or the equivalent for Hay et al., Kearns, and Winter), we propose that the adjectival core of a DA is a special kind of derived measure function that measures the degree to which an object changes along a scalar dimension as the result of participating in an event.

Our analysis builds on a non-standard semantics of comparatives discussed in Kennedy and McNally (2005) (see also Faller 2000; Neeleman et al. 2004; Rotstein and Winter 2004 and Svenonius and Kennedy 2006; see Schwarzschild 2005 for a similar idea).[13] Noting that comparatives and deverbal adjectives with lower closed scales accept the same kinds of degree morphemes (e.g., both can be modified by *much*, as in *much taller* and *much appreciated*, which is indicative of a lower closed scale), Kennedy and McNally propose that comparatives should be analyzed as derived measure functions, which are just like the functions expressed by the base adjective except that they use scales whose minimum values are determined by the denotation of the *than*-constituent – the "comparative standard." Generalizing this idea, we can define for any measure function $\mathbf{m}$ a corresponding DIFFERENCE FUNCTION $\mathbf{m}_d{}^{\uparrow}$ that is just like $\mathbf{m}$ except that the degrees it returns for objects in its domain represent the difference between the object's projection on the scale and an arbitrary degree d (the comparative standard): a positive value when there is a positive difference, and zero otherwise. This idea is made explicit in (23).

(23)   **Difference functions:** For any measure function $\mathbf{m}$ from objects and times to degrees on a scale S, and for any $d \in S$, $\mathbf{m}_d{}^{\uparrow}$ is a function just like $\mathbf{m}$ except that:

   i.   its range is $\{d' \in S \mid d \preceq d'\}$, and

   ii. for any x, t in the domain of $\mathbf{m}$, if $\mathbf{m}(x)(t) \preceq d$ then $\mathbf{m}_d{}^{\uparrow}(x)(t) = d$.

In the case of comparatives, the hypothesis is that the comparative morphology turns a basic measure function into a difference function with a scale whose minimal element – the "derived zero" – corresponds to the degree introduced by the comparative standard. So if *wide* denotes the measure function **wide**, *wider than the carpet* denotes the difference function $\mathbf{wide}_{\mathbf{wide(c)}}{}^{\uparrow}$, which returns values that represent the degree to which an object's width exceeds that of the carpet (represented here as **wide(c)**, which suppresses the temporal argument for perspicuity): positive values if the argument's width is greater than that of the carpet, and zero (relative to the derived scale)

---

[13] The "standard" semantics for comparatives is one in which *more than X* is a quantifier over degrees that targets the degree argument of a gradable adjective; see Heim (2000) for a representative implementation.

otherwise.[14] A consequence of this analysis is that like morphologically bare adjectives, comparative adjectives are of type $\langle e, d \rangle$ and so need to combine with **pos** to derive a property of individuals. The denotation of the bracketed comparative predicate in (24a) is (24b), which is an abbreviation for the property in (24c) (which spells out the result of composition with **pos**).

(24) a. The table is [wider than the carpet].

   b. $\mathbf{pos}(\mathbf{wide}_{\mathbf{wide}(c)}{}^{\uparrow})$

   c. $\lambda x \lambda t.\mathbf{wide}_{\mathbf{wide}(c)}{}^{\uparrow}(x)(t) \succeq \mathbf{stnd}(\mathbf{wide}_{\mathbf{wide}(c)}{}^{\uparrow})$

Given the semantics of the positive form discussed in the previous section, in particular the meaning contributed by **stnd**, (24c) is a property that is true of an individual if it stands out relative to the kind of measurement expressed by the difference function $\mathbf{wide}_{\mathbf{wide}(c)}{}^{\uparrow}$. Crucially, for any measure function **m**, a difference function $\mathbf{m}_d{}^{\uparrow}$ based on **m** always uses a lower closed scale: one whose minimal element is d. Since measure functions with lower closed scales are systematically associated with minimum standards when they combine with **pos**, as discussed in section 7.3.1, the result is that (24b) denotes a property that is true of an object x if the degree we get by applying the difference function to x is non-zero relative to the scale of the difference function, that is, is greater than **wide**(c). In other words, *wider than the carpet* is true of an object just in case its width exceeds the width of the carpet, which is exactly what we want.

   Returning now to the semantics of DAs, we propose that the adjectival core of a degree achievement is a special kind of difference function: one that measures the amount that an object changes along a scalar dimension as a result of participating in an event. We make this idea explicit in (25), which defines for any measure function **m** from objects and times to degrees on a scale S a new MEASURE OF CHANGE function $\mathbf{m}_\Delta$. (Here *init* and *fin* return the initial and final temporal intervals of an event.)

(25) **Measure of change:** For any measure function **m**, $\mathbf{m}_\Delta = \lambda x \lambda e.$
   $\mathbf{m}_{\mathbf{m}(x)(init(e))}{}^{\uparrow}(x)(fin(e))$

In prose, a measure of change function $\mathbf{m}_\Delta$ takes an object x and an event e and returns the degree that represents the amount that x changes in the property measured by **m** as a result of participating in e. It does this by mapping

---

[14] We do not address here the question of how this degree is derived compositionally, though we see no obstacles to adapting any of a number of current proposals for the syntax and semantics of the comparative clause. Most analyses agree that the comparative clause denotes some sort of maximal degree (see e.g. von Stechow 1984; Rullmann 1995; Heim 2000; Bhatt and Pancheva 2004), which is all that we need to build the derived scale.

its individual argument x onto a derived scale whose minimal element is the degree to which x measures **m** at the initiation of e. The output is a degree that represents the positive difference between the degree to which x measures **m** at the beginning of e and the degree to which it measures **m** at the end of e; if there is no positive difference, it returns zero.[15]

Like other measure functions, a measure of change must combine with some degree morphology (or undergo a type shift) in order to ensure that we ultimately end up with a property of events. We will consider overt instances of such morphology below; in order to complete the semantic analysis of DAs we follow Piñón (2005) and posit a verbal positive form morpheme **pos**$_v$ with the semantic properties stated in (26). (Here D_{m_Δ} represents the domain of measure of change functions – functions from individuals to functions from events to degrees.)

(26)   **pos**$_v = \lambda g \in D_{m_\Delta} \lambda x \lambda e.g(x)(e) \succeq \textbf{stnd}(g)$

Combining **pos**$_v$ with a measure of change function returns (27), which we claim represents the core (inchoative) meaning of a DA: a DA based on a measure of change function $\textbf{m}_\Delta$ is true of an object x and an event e just in the degree to which x changes as a result of participating in e exceeds the standard of comparison for $\textbf{m}_\Delta$.

(27)   **pos**$_v(\textbf{m}_\Delta) = \lambda x \lambda e.\textbf{m}_\Delta(x)(e) \succeq \textbf{stnd}(\textbf{m}_\Delta)$

Before showing how this analysis derives the facts discussed in section 7.2, we want to elaborate on two intuitions that underlie our proposal that DAs are based on measure of change functions, rather than basic measure functions encoded by (non-comparative) gradable adjectives. The first is that any change necessarily entails a shift along some dimension, and that when that dimension is a scalar one, the change corresponds to a difference in degree. In this sense, a measure of change function generalizes (and directly encodes) the "transition" feature of Dowty's BECOME operator (where the shift from 0 to 1 represented by BECOME is just the limiting case where the scale has no intermediate values). The second is that a fundamental part of what it means to make an adjective "verbal" is to introduce an event argument.

---

[15] Strictly speaking, (25) is not quite correct, because it does not ensure that what is measured is the degree to which x changes *as a result of participating in e*. That is because *init* and *fin* just return times, and not necessarily parts of e. This means that $\textbf{m}_\Delta$ can measure differences in an object relative to **m** over the time span of arbitrary events, rather than just events of x changing relative to **m**. We can fix this problem by assuming that *init* and *fin* return the minimal situations that correspond to the initial and final parts of e, and revising our semantics of measure functions accordingly, so they map individuals and situations to degrees, rather than individuals and times. We are grateful to Mark Gawron for pointing this out to us.

Thus the difference between a pure measure function or a comparative difference function (both adjectival roots) and a measure of change function (a verbal root) involves a difference in domain: the former are functions from objects and times to degrees; the latter is a function from objects and events to degrees. In the next section, we will show that this analysis both captures the truth conditions of DAs and accounts for their observed patterns of telicity in terms of the scalar properties of the measure of change function.

7.3.3 *Capturing (a)telicity*

Recall from the discussion in section 7.3.1 that the standard of comparison involved in the truth conditions of the positive form of a gradable predicate – the value returned by applying the standard-identifying function **stnd** to a measure function **m** in a context of utterance – represents the minimum degree required to stand out relative to the kind of measurement encoded by **m**. This value is further regulated by the principle of Interpretive Economy which requires truth conditions to be based on the conventional meanings of the constituents of a sentence whenever possible, allowing for context-dependent truth conditions only as a last resort. A consequence of this principle is that when **m** is a function to a closed scale, the standard of comparison must be endpoint-oriented. In particular, the positive form of an adjective with a lower closed scale is true of an object just in case it has a non-zero degree of the measured property, and the positive form of an adjective with an upper closed scale is true of an object just in case it has a maximal degree of the measured property. Context-dependent standards are available only for the positive form of adjectives that denote measure functions to open scales (or perhaps also when contextual information is strong enough to force such a result as a marked reading for a closed scale adjective).

These considerations form the basis of our account of variable telicity in degree achievements. According to the semantic analysis outlined in the previous section, an (unmodified) DA is a kind of positive form gradable verb whose meaning is based on a measure of change function. Crucially, since a measure of change function is a special kind of difference function, and since all difference functions use scales with minimum elements (see the discussion of adjectival comparatives above), our analysis predicts that a DA should always permit a minimum standard interpretation whereby it is true of an object and an event as long as the measure of change function the DA encodes returns a non-zero degree when applied to the object and event; that is, as long as the object undergoes some positive change in the measured property as a result of participating in the event. In other words, all DAs are predicted to allow "comparative" truth conditions, in which all that is required is that the affected argument undergo some increase in the measured property as a result of participating in the event. As we have already shown, such truth conditions correspond to atelic predications, so all DAs are predicted to allow atelic interpretations, which is in fact the case.

At the same time, some DAs encode measure of change functions that make use of scales with maximal as well as minimal elements. In particular, given the definition of measure of change functions in (25), this will be the case for any DA whose corresponding adjectival form uses a scale with a maximum element, such as *straighten, darken, fill, empty,* and so forth. Since the scale for the measure of change function is derived from the scale for the adjectival measure function, it will always "inherit" a maximal element if there is one; the crucial difference between the adjectival measure function and the verbal measure of change function involves the obligatory presence of a (derived) minimum value in the latter. For example, the scale for the measure of change function **straight**$_\Delta$, on which the DA *straighten* is based, is that subpart of the **straight** scale whose minimum value is the degree to which the (internal) individual argument of the verb is straight at the beginning of the event. But since the **straight** scale has a maximum element (the degree that represents complete straightness), the **straight**$_\Delta$ scale does too.

Importantly, on the analysis proposed here, the availability of the maximum standard/telic interpretation is a consequence of more general principles governing the interpretation of the positive form, which apply equally to a gradable adjective like *straight* and a DA like *straighten*. In the case of the DA, there are two potential standards of comparison that are consistent with Interpretive Economy: one based on the minimal element of the derived scale, resulting in the "comparative" truth conditions described above and an atelic predicate, and one based on the maximal element of the scale, resulting in truth conditions that are similar to the "positive" interpretation discussed in section 7.2. On this latter interpretation, a DA like *straighten* is true of an object and an event just in case the value returned by applying the measure of change function **straight**$_\Delta$ to the object and the event equals the maximal degree of the **straight**$_\Delta$ scale, in other words, just in case the object ends up completely straight. As we have already seen, this results in a telic predicate. As in the Dowty/Abusch analysis, the preference for a telic interpretation can be explained in terms of pragmatic principles: since the maximum standard, telic interpretation of *straighten* entails the minimum standard, atelic one, it is more informative, and is therefore preferred unless there are contextual, compositional, or lexical reasons to avoid it.[16]

This account of default telicity of DAs based on closed scale adjectives is an improvement over the analysis in Hay et al. (1999), where the telic interpretation of the DA has no direct connection to the maximum standard interpretation of the adjective. It is also an improvement over the analysis in Winter (2006), where the culmination requirement of DAs based on closed scale adjectives is stipulated. Finally, our analysis directly captures Kearns' (2007) intuition that the telos of the verb equals the standard of the adjective. While we disagree with Kearns about where on the scale the standard falls (she denies that it is a maximal degree, though we feel that the evidence in section 7.2.2, together with an account of imprecision, supports the position that it is one), we agree completely that the adjective/verb pairs like *straight* and *straighten* should pattern together. Our analysis derives this result because the two forms have the same core meaning: one that involves a relation to a standard based on the maximal element of the **straight/straight**$_\Delta$ scale, which is the same value. The DA differs from the adjective in using a scale with a derived minimum value, which allows for the possibility of a minimum standard, "comparative," atelic interpretation alongside the – preferred – maximum standard "positive," telic interpretation.

Turning now to the case of *widen*, our analysis explains both why this verb and others like it have only atelic interpretations, and why true context-dependent positive interpretations (equivalent to *become wide*) are impossible (or at least highly marked). The crucial fact is that such DAs are related to adjectives that denote measure functions to open scales; this is why the positive form of *wide* has a context-dependent standard of comparison. However, according to our analysis the DA *widen* is not based on the open scale measure function **wide**, but on the measure of change function **wide**$_\Delta$. There is no maximal degree on the **wide** scale, so there is no maximal degree on the **wide**$_\Delta$ scale, eliminating the possibility of a maximum standard/telic interpretation. However, there is a minimum value on the **wide**$_\Delta$ scale: the degree to which the affected argument is wide at the beginning of the event. This value supports

---

[16] A question that arises from this analysis is why comparative forms of closed scale adjectives, such as *straighter*, do not have maximum standard interpretations as well as their minimum standard ones. (Recall for a comparative like *straighter than this rod*, a minimum standard meaning requires positive (non-minimal) straightness relative to the subpart of the **straight** scale whose (derived) minimal value is *this rod's* straightness.) A plausible explanation for this is that if the comparative form were assigned a maximum standard interpretation, it would have identical truth conditions to the positive form (maximal straightness); since the comparative is more complex than the positive, this interpretation is blocked. In the case of DAs, however, there is no competing form, so both the maximum and minimum standard interpretations are accessible.

a minimum standard, atelic interpretation on the basis of the lexical semantic (scalar) properties of the verb; Interpretive Economy then rules out the possibility of a contextual standard (which is the only option for the adjective) and an interpretation equivalent to *become wide*.

In short, Interpretive Economy rules out a telic, "positive" interpretation of DAs like *widen*, because given the option of a conventionalized, scale-based standard and a contextual, norm-based one, it forces the former to be chosen. What is crucial, though, is the conventional/contextual distinction, rather than the scale/norm distinction per se. The structure of the scale used by a measure function is one aspect of conventional meaning that can be used to fix a standard, but our analysis allows for the possibility that some adjectives/verbs and the measure functions they encode could, as a matter of conventional meaning, identify particular values on their scales as standards of comparison. This, we assume, is what happens in the case of *cool*: in addition to a norm-based meaning that requires its argument to have a temperature below some contextual standard, it has a purely conventionalized meaning along the lines of "has a stabilized temperature" or "at room temperature." It is the availability of this conventionalized but non-scale-based standard that licenses a telic interpretation of *cool*, albeit one that does not entail movement to a scalar maximum, unlike what we see with DAs based on true closed scale adjectives (Kearns 2007).[17]

We conclude the presentation of our analysis by showing how it accounts for examples involving measure phrases like (28a–b), as well as examples with various kinds of degree modifiers such as (29a–b).

(28)   a.   The soup cooled 17 degrees (in 30 minutes).

       b.   The gap widened 6 inches (in 1 hour).

(29)   a.   The basin filled completely/halfway/by one third (in 10 minutes).

       b.   The basin filled partially/a bit/slightly (??in 10 minutes).

As noted in section 7.2.1, the fact that examples like (28a–b) are telic is unsurprising given their truth conditions: (28a), for example, entails that the soup undergoes a decrease in temperature of 17 degrees; the event description will fail to hold of subevents in which the soup cools less than this, resulting in a telic interpretation. The question that we need to answer is whether

---

[17] The existence of adjectives and verbs like *cool*, which have conventionalized but non-scale-based standards, is not unexpected in the general approach to the semantics of the positive form articulated in Kennedy (2007), which we have adopted here. That said, such cases appear to be rare: we know of no other adjectives/verbs that are like *cool* in this respect, though presumably there are some.

our analysis of DAs fares any better than Abusch's analysis in deriving this meaning.

In particular, recall from the discussion in section 7.2.1 that examples like (28a–b) posed a problem for Abusch's account because it was not clear how to ensure that the measure phrases are interpreted as differential terms, measuring the change in temperature/width that the affected objects undergo, rather than their "absolute" temperature/width. Since our semantics of DAs is based on a measure of change function, it avoids this problem (the degrees returned by the measure of change function are differential measures); but it faces another one: how do we compositionally integrate the measure terms into the semantics of the verb?

Our solution to this problem builds on the analysis of measure phrases in Svenonius and Kennedy (2006). According to Svenonius and Kennedy, measure phrases saturate degree arguments that are introduced by a special degree morpheme μ, which combines with a measure function to produce a relation between degrees and individuals, as shown in (30).

(30) $[\![\mu]\!] = \lambda g \in D_{\langle e,d\rangle}\lambda d\lambda x\lambda t.g(x)(t) \succeq d$

On this view, the interpretation of the phrase in (31a) (which by hypothesis contains the degree head μ) is (31b), which is true of an object if its height is at least as great as 2 meters. (Here we assume for simplicity that measure phrases denote degrees, though the analysis is consistent with alternative assumptions in which they are quantifiers over degrees or predicates of degrees.)

(31) a. $[_{\text{DegP}}$ 2 meters $\mu\,[_{\text{A}}$ tall $]\,]$

   b. $[\![\mu]\!]([\![\text{tall}]\!])([\![2\text{ meters}]\!]) = \lambda x.\text{tall}(x) \succeq \mathbf{2\ meters}$

Svenonius and Kennedy motivate this analysis by showing that it provides a means of accounting for cross-linguistic and language-internal restrictions on adjective/measure phrase combinations, via the selectional restrictions on μ. One of the general properties of this morpheme, however, is that it can always combine with difference functions.[18] Since the measure of change functions that underlie DAs on our analysis represent a special type of difference function, the only move we need to make to extend our account to cover examples like those in (28) is to assume that there is a verbal version of μ to go along with the verbal version of **pos** that we posited above, with the denotation in (32).

---

[18] Svenonius and Kennedy suggest that this is precisely because such functions use scales with (derived) minimal elements. This feature of μ accounts for the fact that cross-linguistically, even languages that do not permit measure phrases with unmarked adjectives (such as we find in the English example in (31a)) do permit them with comparatives, which denote difference functions. See Schwarzschild (2005) for detailed discussion of this point and an alternative analysis.

(32) $\llbracket \mu_v \rrbracket = \lambda g \in D_{m_\Delta} \lambda d \lambda x \lambda e. g(x)(e) \succeq d$

Given these assumptions, an example like (28a) will express the event description in (33), which has exactly the properties we want: it is true of an event *e* if the degree returned by applying the measure of change function **cool**$_\Delta$ to *the soup* and *e*, which represents the amount that the soup decreases in temperature as a result of participating in the event, is at least as great as 17 degrees.

(33) $\lambda e.$**cool**$_\Delta$(the soup)$(e) \succeq$ 17 degrees

Finally, the contribution of adverbs such as those in (29) can be incorporated into our analysis if we follow Piñón (2005) and treat these on a par with **pos** and μ, that is, as degree modifiers that have both "adjectival" and "verbal" denotations (so that we can handle *completely/slightly/... full* along with *fill completely/slightly/...*). The denotation assigned to an arbitrary verbal degree modifier *mod*$_v$ will in general be one that relates the degree returned by applying the measure function encoded by a verb to its individual and event arguments to some arbitrary standard determined by the modifier (cf. Kennedy and McNally's 2005 analysis of adjectival degree modifiers). For example, *completely*$_v$ should have a denotation along the lines of (34a), where **max** is a function that returns the maximal element of the scale used by its measure function argument, and *slightly*$_v$ should have a denotation like (34b), where **min** returns the minimum value on the measure function's scale and **small** is a context-dependent function that returns a low degree on the scale.

(34)   a. $\llbracket$completely$_v\rrbracket = \lambda g \in D_{m_\Delta} \lambda d \lambda x \lambda e. g(x)(e) =$ **max**(g)

     b. $\llbracket$slightly$_v\rrbracket = \lambda g \in D_{m_\Delta} \lambda d \lambda x \lambda e.$**min**$(g) \succ g(x)(e) \succeq$ **small**(g)

Whether a particular adverb results in a telic interpretation or not is dependent on the kind of relation it encodes: given the denotations in (34), *completely*$_v$ V will be a telic predicate, while *slightly*$_v$ V will be an atelic one, which is exactly what we want.

7.4 Looking ahead

This chapter has presented an analysis of variable telicity in degree achievements that is similar to the analysis originally proposed by Dowty and Abusch (and advocated more recently in a different form by Kearns and Winter) in that it links telicity to the semantic properties of the gradable adjective meanings on which the verbs are based, in particular to the calculation of a standard of comparison. It differs from the Dowty/Abusch analysis in adopting a scalar semantics for gradable adjectives, and it differs from previous scalar analyses in assuming that the adjectival meanings that underlie DAs are measure of change functions, rather than the more general kinds of measure functions involved in (non-comparative) adjectival forms. The latter move allows us to provide an explanation of the relation between the scalar properties of a measure of change function and the telicity of the corresponding DA that is based on exactly the same semantic and pragmatic principles that determine the standard of comparison for an adjectival predicate as a function of the scalar properties of the measure function it encodes, as described in Kennedy (2007).

The account presented here leaves a number of important questions unanswered, however. First, we have said nothing about the morphosyntax of DAs and the larger verbal projections in which they appear, something which should be part of a fully comprehensive analysis. However, it is worth pointing out one interesting morphological property of DAs that our analysis may provide an explanation for. Based on a survey of roughly twenty languages, Bobaljik (2006) has identified the following generalization about the form of DAs (his "change-of-state verbs"):

(35)   If the comparative degree of an adjective is built on a suppletive root, then the basic corresponding change-of-state verb (inchoative or causative) will also be suppletive.

In our analysis, there is a direct link between comparatives and DAs: both are based on difference functions, rather than on the more general measure functions that are involved in (non-comparative) adjectival predications. While it remains to be shown how our semantic analysis connects to a theory of the morphosyntax of adjectives, comparatives, and DAs, the fact that our analysis relates comparatives and DAs in terms of such a basic notion – the kind of measure function they encode – suggests that it can provide the basis for an explanation of Bobaljik's generalization.

Second, although we started out this chapter with the broad aim of providing an account of variable telicity in several different classes of verbs – "classic" incremental theme verbs, verbs of directed motion, and degree achievements – we have thus far only provided a detailed analysis of the latter. It therefore remains to be shown that our proposals will extend to the other classes of verbs as well. In the case of directed motion verbs like *ascend, raise,* and so forth, we believe that the account we have presented here carries over entirely: such verbs encode measure of change functions over scales that measure directed movement along a path. While they do not always have corresponding adjectival forms, the kinds of meanings they express are identical to the kind of meanings we have described here for verbs directly related to gradable adjectives.

Incremental theme verbs are not so simple. The analysis of the meanings of these verbs proposed by Rappaport Hovav (to appear) suggests that many – if not all – of these verbs do not themselves lexicalize a measure of change, but rather the measure of change is introduced compositionally by the objects of these verbs. (This proposal is consistent with Rappaport Hovav and Levin's (2005) study, which shows that these verbs behave differently from change of state verbs, including degree achievements.) Nevertheless, once introduced, the measure of change function will give rise to meanings comparable to those postulated here for degree achievements. Assuming that the referential properties of the arguments that introduce the measure of change function determine the scalar properties of the measure of change function (in the spirit of Krifka 1989, 1992), our account of variable telicity in DAs should carry over directly. Demonstrating that this is the case, and exploring further extensions of our proposals, will be the focus of future work.

In closing, we draw attention to one feature of our analysis of degree achievements that bears on the analysis of verb meaning and verb behavior more generally. Although we have provided a general account of degree achievements, it is one that accommodates differences among the degree achievements that reflect differences in the scale structure of the adjectives themselves. The observation that the meaning of individual lexical items has a part to play in the explanation of their properties is consistent with what Rappaport Hovav and Levin have noticed in other verbal domains: a lexical item's so-called "root" or "core" meaning contributes to its behavior, though within the behavioral confines defined by the verb's semantic class-specific meaning.

Acknowledgments

We are grateful to Hagit Borer, Hana Filip, Mark Gawron, Jen Hay, Louise McNally, Chris Piñón, Malka Rappaport Hovav, Susan Rothstein, Steve Wechsler, and Yoad Winter for discussion of the issues discussed in this chapter over the long course of its gestation, as well as to audiences at Georgetown, Michigan State, MIT, Stanford, UCSC, and the 75th Annual Meeting of the Linguistic Society of America in Washington, DC. This chapter is based upon work supported by the National Science Foundation under Grants No. 0094263 and 0618917 to Chris Kennedy.

8

Aspectual composition with degrees

CHRISTOPHER PIÑÓN

8.1 Introduction

Approaches to aspectual composition (most notably Krifka 1989, 1992; Verkuyl 1993) have generally focused on how to account for contrasts such as those in (1) and (2), where compatibility with a temporal *in*-adverbial is taken to indicate a *telic* interpretation, and compatibility with a temporal *for*-adverbial to signal an *atelic* interpretation, of the phrase that the adverbial attaches to. Nothing hinges on the use of the terms *telic* and *atelic* here, and for present purposes, *bounded* and *unbounded* would do equally well.

(1)   a.   Rebecca ate an apple in five minutes.

    b.   #Rebecca ate an apple for five minutes.

(2)   a.   *Rebecca ate apples in thirty minutes.

    b.   Rebecca ate apples for thirty minutes.

(3)   a.   Rebecca ate a bowl of applesauce in five minutes.

    b.   #Rebecca ate a bowl of applesauce for five minutes.

(4)   a.   *Rebecca ate applesauce in five minutes.

    b.   Rebecca ate applesauce for five minutes.

Although the prevailing view has been that sentences such as those in (1b) and (3b) are unacceptable, it is also clear that the corresponding sentences in (2a) and (4a) are less acceptable by comparison. The present view, in agreement with Smollett (2005), is that the sentences in (1b) and (3b) are acceptable but require more contextual support than the corresponding ones in (1a) and (3a). Thus, out of the blue (1a) requires no special effort, whereas acceptance of (1b) might lead one to imagine that Rebecca is a small child who hardly ever finishes the apples she is given to eat.[1] In contrast, the sentences in (2a) and (4a) are considered to be unacceptable.

One task of an aspectual theory is to determine the content of terms such as *telic* and *atelic*. In Krifka's (1989, 1992) approach, a VP is telic if the corresponding event predicate is *quantized*, whereas it is atelic if the corresponding event predicate is *cumulative*:

(5) $\mathbf{qua}(P) \overset{\text{def}}{=} \forall a \forall b (P(a) \wedge P(b) \rightarrow \neg(a \sqsubset b))$ ▷ *P* is quantized

(6) $\mathbf{nuniq}(P) \overset{\text{def}}{=} \exists a \exists b (P(a) \wedge P(b) \wedge \neg(a = b))$ ▷ *P* is non-unique

(7)   ▷ *P* is cumulative

$$\mathbf{cum}(P) \overset{\text{def}}{=} \mathbf{nuniq}(P) \wedge \forall a \forall b ((P(a) \wedge P(b)) \rightarrow P(a \oplus b))$$

In these definitions, *P* is a one-place predicate of *events* or *ordinary individuals* (thus *a*, *b* stand for events or ordinary individuals), $\sqsubset$ denotes the *proper part* relation, and $\oplus$ designates the *sum* operation. In prose, *P* is quantized just in case it never applies both to an event or an individual and to a proper part of that event or individual, *P* is non-unique only if it applies to at least two events or individuals, and *P* is cumulative just in case it is non-unique and applies to the sum of two events or individuals whenever it applies to each of the two events or individuals independently. Observe that quantization and cumulativity form contraries, hence if *P* is quantized, it is not cumulative, but *P* may be neither quantized nor cumulative. Moreover, if *P* is not quantized, then it is non-unique.[2]

To illustrate how quantization and cumulativity are applied, consider the examples in (1) and (2). In general, tense will be ignored, because it is not crucially relevant to the issues discussed in this chapter. The telic VP *eat an apple* in (1a) is taken to denote the set of (minimal) events in which an apple is (completely) eaten. Since no such event in which an apple is eaten properly contains an event in which an apple is eaten, the denotation of this VP is quantized (therefore not cumulative). In contrast, the atelic VP *eat apples*

---

[1] Observe that judgments improve if the object NP is definite:

(i)   Rebecca ate the apple for five minutes (before dropping it on the floor).

(ii)   Rebecca ate her apple for five minutes (before dropping it on the floor).

(ii), in particular, seems unobjectionable. Arguably, the difficulty in (1b) and (3b) is that we need a *specific* apple or bowl of applesauce that is repeatedly partially affected, and yet an existential reading of the object NP does not (automatically) yield this. Once a specific reading is forced (cf. *a certain apple*), the judgments pattern more readily like those of (i) and (ii).

[2] The definition of cumulativity in (7) is not quite equivalent to either the notion of *cumulativity* or that of *strict cumulativity* in Krifka (1989, 1992). The present definition of cumulativity, which appeals to non-uniqueness, ensures that quantization and cumulativity form contraries, even if the denotation of *P* is empty.

in (2b) is assumed to denote the set of events in which one or more apples are eaten. Since the sum of any two events in which one or more apples are eaten is also an event in which one or more apples are eaten, the denotation of this VP is cumulative (hence not quantized), assuming that it is non-unique. The reasoning is analogous for the telic VP *eat a bowl of applesauce* in (3a) (quantized) versus the atelic VP *eat applesauce* in (4b) (cumulative). According to this line of thinking, the atelic interpretation of *eat an apple* in (1b) should be cumulative, which would be the case if the VP on this reading denoted the set of events in which a specific apple is partly eaten.[3] This would hold because the sum of two events in which a specific apple is partly eaten is again an event in which that apple is partly eaten: since a specific apple is at issue, it is kept constant.[4]

Beyond characterizing sentences such as those in (1)–(4) in terms of telicity and atelicity and clarifying that these two notions correspond to quantization and cumulativity, respectively, another task of an aspectual theory is to show how these results are achieved compositionally. For example, how does the telicity of *eat an apple* follow from the meaning of *eat* and that of *an apple*? The same may be asked about the atelicity of *eat apples*. Moreover, why does *eat apples* not allow for a telic reading, whereas *eat an apple* does allow for an atelic reading? In Krifka's approach, these results – again, with the exception of examples such as (1b) and (3b), which are considered to be unacceptable – depend on essentially two factors:

(i) whether the NP representing the internal argument of the verb is quantized (e.g., *an apple*) or cumulative (e.g. *apples*);
(ii) whether or not the internal argument of the verb is an *incremental theme* (e.g., *eat* versus *like*; see also Dowty 1991).

The factor mentioned in (i) is reasonably straightforward, once given the definitions of quantization and cumulativity and an appropriate analysis of the NPs in question. In contrast, the criterion described in (ii), namely, the characterization of an incremental theme, is somewhat involved and is formulated in terms of certain properties of *thematic relations*, where a thematic relation is treated as a two-place relation between ordinary individuals and events. The three central properties of incremental themes for Krifka are *uniqueness of*

---

[3] Since Krifka's approach takes sentences such as those in (1b) and (3b) to be unacceptable, this extension is mine.

[4] See note 1 in this connection. For the paraphrase to work, *partly* should be understood in the sense of *improper part*, thus a partial eating of an apple is compatible with a complete eating of it. Observe also that if *an apple* were interpreted existentially, the VP would not be cumulative, even if it meant "partly eat an apple," because in this case the choice of apple might well vary between the two events initially selected.

objects, mapping to objects, and *mapping to events.* Without diving into the formal details, uniqueness of objects states that if x is an incremental theme of e, then x is the unique incremental theme of e. Mapping to objects says that if x is an incremental theme of e, then every subevent e' of e has a part x' of x as its own incremental theme. Conversely, mapping to events states that if x is an incremental theme of e, then every part x' of x is an incremental theme of a subevent e' of e. These three properties specify the core of what it means for a thematic relation to be an incremental theme.[5] Assuming this setup and excluding an iterative interpretation, it can be shown that a VP is telic (or its corresponding event predicate is quantized) if the verb takes an incremental theme and the NP corresponding to the incremental theme is quantized, as in (1a) and (3a). Furthermore, a VP is atelic (or its corresponding event predicate is cumulative) if the verb takes an incremental theme and the NP corresponding to the incremental theme is cumulative, as in (2b) and (4b).[6]

Another aspectual problem, first succinctly described by Dowty (1979, sect. 2.3.5) and then freshly addressed by Hay, Kennedy and Levin (1999) and Kennedy and Levin (2002), is posed by *degree achievements:*[7]

(8) a. Rebecca lengthened the rope for twenty minutes.

    b. The soup cooled for ten minutes.

    c. The boat sank for forty minutes.

    d. The submarine ascended for thirty minutes.

For Dowty, the problem posed by these examples was how to treat vagueness and gradual change with his sharp and instantaneous **become** predicate, a puzzle that he never really managed to solve. Hay et al. and Kennedy and Levin, equipped with an analysis of gradable adjectives (that Dowty lacked), propose a treatment of degree achievements that aims to do justice to their deadjectival character and to account for their telic uses as well.[8]

---

[5] The incremental theme of verbs of consumption (*eat*) and creation (*write*) additionally satisfy *uniqueness of events*, which states that if x is an incremental theme of e, then x is an incremental theme of no other event but e.

[6] This is a fairly high-level summary of Krifka's account – see Krifka (1989, 1992) for the details.

[7] The term "degree achievement" is due to Dowty. It is retained for the sake of tradition, but note that degree achievements are actually a kind of accomplishments and not achievements.

[8] Kennedy and Levin distinguish verbs of directed motion (*sink, ascend*) from degree achievements (*lengthen, cool*), whereas Dowty, as far as I can tell, would regard them all as degree achievements. For present purposes, I take verbs of directed motion to be a species of degree achievements and do not discuss them as a separate class, though they could certainly receive separate attention in a more elaborate treatment.

(9) a. Rebecca lengthened the rope in twenty minutes.

    b. The soup cooled in ten minutes.

    c. The boat sank in forty minutes.

    d. The submarine ascended in thirty minutes.

Although the account that Hay et al. and Kennedy and Levin propose will be discussed in detail in section 8.2.1, their idea is that degree achievements have a "degree of change" argument d that measures a change in the extent to which an individual has a certain gradable property. Depending how d is specified, the resulting VP is either atelic or telic. For instance, in (8b) there is an unspecified degree of change in the extent to which the soup becomes cool (this corresponds to the existential binding of d), which yields an atelic (cumulative) interpretation, whereas in (9b) the degree of change in the extent to which the soup becomes cool is contextually determined (e.g., the value of d is large enough so that the soup becomes cool enough to eat without the risk of burning one's mouth), which results in a telic (quantized) interpretation.

At first glance, there does not appear to be so much in common between the data in (1)–(4) and those in (8)–(9). More strikingly, perhaps, there seems to be even less in common between Krifka's account and the one proposed by Hay et al. and Kennedy and Levin. Nevertheless, Hay et al. and Kennedy and Levin claim that their degree-based account can be naturally extended to deal with data such as those in (1)–(4) and that it can even do so without the mapping properties that Krifka appeals to in order to characterize incremental themes. As Kennedy and Levin (2002: 2, 12) put it, "In our analysis, quantization/telicity follows completely from the structure of the degree of change argument" and "Telicity is determined solely by the semantic properties of the degree of change." In section 8.2.1, I set out to evaluate Kennedy and Levin's claim and conclude that their account is incomplete as an analysis of aspectual composition. The question then arises about how to remedy this, and in section 8.3 I offer a degree-based alternative that fills in some of the missing details. Along the way, in section 8.2.2, I take a brief look at Caudal and Nicolas' (2005) degree-based account and conclude that it is both conceptually and formally problematic and therefore not yet ready as a viable alternative.

Viewing the matter more broadly, the advantage of a unified degree-based account of aspectual composition would not merely reside in providing a common framework for the treatment of data such as those in (1)–(4) and (8)–(9), but it would also serve to capture more explicitly the intuition that verbs with an incremental theme are *gradable*. This intuition is present in Krifka's analysis, but it is expressed in a way that tends to *conceal* rather than to reveal how this sort of gradability is related to gradability in the adjectival domain. Furthermore, an advantage of having an explicit representation of degrees is that it would make it easier to talk about the degree to which an event type is realized, something that is tricky to formulate in Krifka's approach without introducing degrees in the first place.[9]

In addition to degree achievements and verbs with an incremental theme, degrees have other potential applications in the verbal domain. To mention several, Kiparsky (2005) argues that the choice of structural case in Finnish (Accusative versus Partitive) depends on the gradability of the verbal predicate. Tamm (2004) proposes that the choice between Total and Partitive case in Estonian is also sensitive to the gradability of the verbal predicate (though Estonian and Finnish differ in certain details). Martin (2006: chap. 8.2) considers the possibility of treating the intriguing difference between French *convaincre* 'convince' and *persuader* 'persuade' in terms of gradability. In previous work (Piñón 2000, 2005), I appealed to degrees to account for *gradually* and adverbs of completion (see also Kennedy and McNally 1999 for the latter). Finally, it should be acknowledged that the idea of using degrees to analyze verbs of gradual change in a formal semantics goes back at least to Ballweg and Frosch (1979). Interestingly, Ballweg and Frosch were shy about having degrees represented in their logical language, yet they had them in their model, albeit qua equivalence classes of individuals.

8.2 Two previous accounts: Kennedy and Levin (2002) and Caudal and Nicolas (2005a)

8.2.1 *Kennedy and Levin (2002)*

In presenting Kennedy and Levin's account,[10] I make use of a four-sorted type-logical language, with sorts for *ordinary individuals* (x, x'), *events* (e, e'), *times* (t, t'), and *degrees* (d, d'). Degrees for Kennedy and Levin are positive or negative intervals on a scale, where a scale is modeled as the set of real numbers

---

[9] In Piñón (2000, 2005), my strategy was to show how degrees could be introduced in a Krifka-style analysis without assuming that verbs with an incremental theme have a degree argument to begin with. Although I still think that there is merit in this strategy, the approach that I propose in section 8.3 takes such verbs to have a degree argument from the outset, in agreement with Kennedy and Levin in this respect (though the details differ).

[10] My presentation is largely based on Kennedy and Levin (2002), which has its roots in Hay et al. (1999), Kennedy and McNally (1999), and Kennedy (2001). Note that I do not always recite Kennedy and Levin's formulations verbatim and often take the liberty of reformulating certain points. Kennedy and Levin (this volume) update their account of degree achievements. Although, for reasons of timing, I do not discuss their updated account here, I believe that the essence of my evaluation largely applies to their updated account as well, given that my points concern more the adequacy of their analysis as an approach to aspectual composition and less the details of how to treat degree achievements per se.

between 0 and 1. More precisely, a scale S may be closed, open, closed at 0 (and open at 1), or closed at 1 (and open at 0):

(10)   a. $S_{[]} \overset{\text{def}}{=} [0, 1]$ $\triangleright$ S is closed

       b. $S_{()} \overset{\text{def}}{=} (0, 1)$ $\triangleright$ S is open

       c. $S_{[)} \overset{\text{def}}{=} [0, 1)$ $\triangleright$ S is closed at 0 and open at 1

       d. $S_{(]} \overset{\text{def}}{=} (0, 1]$ $\triangleright$ S is closed at 1 and open at 0

Kennedy and Levin speak explicitly only of closed and open scales, that is, of the cases in (10a) and (10b). However, it seems that half-closed scales play a more important role in their analyses than open scales (e.g., the scale of length is closed at 0 and open at 1). Indeed, it is unclear whether open scales or scales closed at 1 and open at 0 are ever really needed in their framework. Accordingly, I will restrict my attention to closed scales and scales closed at 0 and open at 1 in the following discussion.

Positive and negative degrees for closed scales and scales closed at 0 and open at 1 are defined as follows, where p is a chosen point on the scale in question:

(11)   a.   If S is closed or closed at 0 and open at 1: $\triangleright$ positive degrees of S
            $\mathbf{pos}(S) \overset{\text{def}}{=} \{[0, p] \subseteq S \mid 0 \leq p\}$

       b.   If S is closed: $\triangleright$ negative degrees of S
            $\mathbf{neg}(S) \overset{\text{def}}{=} \{[p, 1] \subseteq S \mid p \leq 1\}$
            and if S is closed at 0 and open at 1:
            $\mathbf{neg}(S) \overset{\text{def}}{=} \{[p, 1) \subseteq S \mid p < 1\}$

According to the definition in (11a), the minimal positive degree is $[0, 0]$ (i.e., 0) if S is closed or closed at 0 and open at 1, the maximal positive degree is $[0, 1]$ if S is closed, and there is no maximal positive degree if S is closed at 0 and open at 1, because S does not include 1 in this case. In contrast, the definition in (11b) states that the minimal negative degree is $[1, 1]$ (i.e., 1) if S is closed, but there is no minimal negative degree if S is closed at 0 and open at 1. Finally, the maximal negative degree is $[0, 1]$ if S is closed, but there is no maximal negative degree if S is closed at 0 and open at 1. Observe that negative degrees have nothing to do with negative numbers – the essential difference between positive and negative degrees depends on whether the degrees (as intervals) begin at the bottom of the scale and go upwards (positive degrees) or begin at the end of the scale and go downwards (negative degrees).

As long as S is closed or closed at 0 and open at 1, positive degrees are closed at the right and negative degrees are closed at the left by definition. Accordingly, we can say that the maximal point of a positive degree is its rightmost point, whereas the maximal point of a negative degree is its leftmost point:

(12)   If d is positive: ▷ maximal point of d

$$\mathbf{max}(d) \stackrel{\text{def}}{=} \iota p(p \in d \land \neg \exists p'(p' \in d \land p < p'))$$

and if d is negative:

$$\mathbf{max}(d) \stackrel{\text{def}}{=} \iota p(p \in d \land \neg \exists p'(p' \in d \land p' < p))$$

As Kennedy and Levin point out, this model of degrees allows for the 'addition' ($+'$) of degrees to be expressed. In the case of two positive degrees, the idea is that the lengths of the two degrees are added together to yield a greater positive degree. Note that $+$ in (13) stands for arithmetic addition.[11]

(13)   For all $d, d' \in \mathbf{pos}(S)$:   ▷ addition of two positive degrees
if S is closed and $\mathbf{max}(d) + \mathbf{max}(d') \leq 1$:

$$d +' d' \stackrel{\text{def}}{=} \iota d''(d'' = [0, \mathbf{max}(d) + \mathbf{max}(d')])$$

and if S is closed at 0 and open at 1 and $\mathbf{max}(d) + \mathbf{max}(d') < 1$:

$$d +' d' \stackrel{\text{def}}{=} \iota d''(d'' = [0, \mathbf{max}(d) + \mathbf{max}(d')])$$

For example, if S is closed at 0 and open at 1, d is $[0, .4]$, and d' is $[0, .2]$, then $d +' d'$ is $[0, .6]$, given that $.6 = .4 + .2$ and the condition that $.6$ is less than 1 is fulfilled.

The addition of a negative degree and a positive degree is less straightforward. However, the intuitive strategy is to increase the length of the negative degree by the length of the positive degree to arrive at a potentially greater negative degree. Formally, this amounts to subtracting the maximal point of the positive degree from the maximal point of the negative degree:[12]

---

[11] This definition differs from Kennedy and Levin's in that it makes explicit the condition that the sum of the two maximal points should not be greater than 1 if S is closed and less than 1 if S is closed at 0 and open at 1, for otherwise the maximal point of the resulting degree would fall "off the scale," so to speak, which should be avoided. This at once brings out an intuitive difficulty with the formal notion of degree addition appealed to by Kennedy and Levin, namely, that it is neither as general nor as innocent as it initially appears.

[12] This definition differs in two respects from Kennedy and Levin's. Firstly, and less importantly, it has two subcases, depending on whether S is closed or closed at 0 and open at 1, whereas Kennedy and Levin's assumes that S is closed (and the definition in Hay et al. 1999 assumes that S is closed at 0 and open at 1). Secondly, and more importantly, it makes explicit the condition that the difference of the maximal point of the negative degree and the maximal point of the positive degree should be

(14)   ▷ addition of a negative and a positive degree
For all $d \in$ **neg**(S) and $d' \in$ **pos**(S) and $0 \leq$ **max**$(d) -$ **max**(d'):
  if S is closed:
  $$d +' d' \stackrel{\text{def}}{=} \iota d''(d'' = [\mathbf{max}(d) - \mathbf{max}(d'), 1])$$
  and if S is closed at 0 and open at 1:
  $$d +' d' \stackrel{\text{def}}{=} \iota d''(d'' = [\mathbf{max}(d) - \mathbf{max}(d'), 1))$$

As an illustration, if S is closed, d is [.5, 1] (a negative degree), and d' is [0, .3] (a positive degree), then $d +' d'$ is [.2, 1], because .2 = .5 − .3 and the condition that 0 is less than or equal to .2 is satisfied.[13]

An attractive feature of Kennedy and Levin's approach is that it offers an insightful analysis of pairs of gradable adjectives such as *long/short*. Kennedy and Levin take such adjectives to denote functions from individuals and times to degrees. For example, *long* is analyzed as the function **long**, where **long**$(x)(t)$ is read as "the degree to which individual x is long at time t". To get things off the ground, it also needs to be postulated both that the scale of length is closed at 0 and open at 1 and that degrees of length are positive:

(15)   a.   ▷ scale of length is closed at 0 and open at 1
      $\forall x \forall t \forall d (\mathbf{long}(x)(t) = d \rightarrow d \subseteq [0, 1))$

      b.   ▷ degrees of length are positive
      $\forall x \forall t \forall d (\mathbf{long}(x)(t) = d \rightarrow \exists p(d = [0, p]))$

The meaning of *short* can then be defined in terms of the meaning of *long*: the degree to which x is short at t is identical to the negative degree d whose maximal point is equal to the maximal point of the (positive) degree d' to which x is long at t, as formalized in (16).

(16)   ▷ degrees of shortness are negative degrees of length

$$\mathbf{short}(x)(t) \stackrel{\text{def}}{=} \iota d(\exists p(d = [p, 1)) \wedge$$
$$\mathbf{max}(d) = \mathbf{max}(\iota d'(\mathbf{long}(x)(t) = d')))$$

at least 0, for if it were not, the maximal point of the resulting negative degree would also fall "off the scale," though this time to the left, similarly to be avoided. Again, this reaffirms the intuitive difficulty mentioned in note 11.

[13] Hay et al. (1999) claim that the addition of two negative degrees is undefined. Although this may be desirable for empirical reasons, the technical apparatus would certainly allow for the addition of two negative degrees to be defined, even if it would have to be restricted in a way similar to how the addition of other degrees has to be (see notes 11 and 12). For example, one could imagine defining the addition of two negative degrees d and d' in terms of the addition of their respective maximal points, analogously to the addition of two positive degrees. In this case, the addition of two negative degrees would generally result in a *lesser* negative degree.

For instance, suppose that the (positive) degree to which x is long at t is $[0, .4]$. Then, according to this definition, the (negative) degree to which x is short at t is $[.4, 1)$, because the maximal point of $[0, .4]$ is $.4$. In general, a hallmark of Kennedy and Levin's approach is to model what appear to be lesser degrees (e.g., "x is shorter than y (at t)") and decreases in degrees (e.g., "x is shortened") with respect to some property (e.g., length) as in fact greater negative degrees and increases in negative degrees, respectively, with respect to that property.

8.2.1.1 *Kennedy and Levin's aspectual account*   Kennedy and Levin propose that verbs of gradual change, that is, degree achievements and verbs with an incremental theme, be analyzed with the help of a certain three-place relation between individuals, degrees, and events that is based on a predicate **increase** and a gradable predicate constant G, as seen in (17a). The definition of **increase**, a four-place relation between gradable predicates, individuals, degrees, and events, is given in (17b).

(17)   a.   ▷ format for verbs of gradual change

$\lambda x \lambda d \lambda e.\mathbf{increase}(G(x))(d)(e)$

b. $\mathbf{increase}(G(x))(d)(e) \overset{\text{def}}{=} G(x)(\mathbf{end}(e)) = G(x)(\mathbf{beg}(e)) +' d$

The gradable predicate constant G denotes a function that takes an individual x and a time t and yields the degree d to which G holds of x at t. This can be made more explicit with the help of the iota operator:[14]

(18) $\lambda x \lambda t. \iota d(G(x)(t) = d)$ ▷ format for gradable predicates G

This, in turn, allows for a more explicit rendition of the formulas in (17):

(19)   a. $\lambda x \lambda d \lambda e.\mathbf{increase}(\lambda t.\iota d'(G(x)(t) = d'))(d)(e)$ ▷ cf. (17a)

b. $\mathbf{increase}(\lambda t.\iota d'(G(x)(t) = d'))(d)(e) \overset{\text{def}}{=}$ ▷ cf. (17b)
$\iota d'(G(x)(\mathbf{end}(e)) = d') = \iota d''(G(x)(\mathbf{beg}(e)) = d'') +' d$

In prose, the definition in (19b) states that the degree to which the gradable predicate constant G holds of the individual x increases by the degree d in the event e just in case the degree to which G holds of x at the end of e is equal to the degree to which G holds of x at the beginning of e plus d. In other words, d, the so-called degree of change, signals the increase in the degree to which G holds of x in e. Note that the degree of change is always a positive degree.

---

[14] Kennedy and Levin do not make use of the iota operator. However, although a syntactic addition, the iota operator does not add anything on the semantic side that they are not already committed to. Once the logical language contains function symbols (e.g., G in 17b), issues of definedness arise, and so it is not the use of the iota operator in combination with function symbols that raises them.

Kennedy and Levin's idea is that the relation in (19a) constitutes the common semantic element between degree achievements and verbs with an incremental theme – what differs is merely how G is instantiated. In each case, the meaning of the verb of gradual change is based on the meaning of a corresponding gradable adjective that instantiates **G**. As an illustration, two VPs containing a degree achievement are analyzed in (20) and (21), and two containing a verb with an incremental theme are represented in (22) and (23).[15]

(20)   a.   long $\rightsquigarrow \lambda x \lambda t. \iota d(\mathbf{long}(x)(t) = d)$ ▷ gradable adjective

     b.   [$_{\mathrm{VP}}$ lengthen x (by d-much)] $\rightsquigarrow$ ▷ degree achievement
        $\lambda e.\mathbf{increase}(\lambda t. \iota d'(\mathbf{long}(x)(t) = d'))(d)(e)$

(21)   a.   short $\rightsquigarrow \lambda x \lambda t. \iota d(\mathbf{short}(x)(t) = d)$ ▷ gradable adjective; cf. (16)

     b.   [$_{\mathrm{VP}}$ shorten x (by d-much)] $\rightsquigarrow$ ▷ degree achievement
        $\lambda e.\mathbf{increase}(\lambda t. \iota d'(\mathbf{short}(x)(t) = d'))(d)(e)$

(22)   a.   written $\rightsquigarrow \lambda x \lambda t. \iota d(\mathbf{written}(x)(t) = d)$ ▷ gradable adjective

     b.   [$_{\mathrm{VP}}$ write (d-much) of x] $\rightsquigarrow$ ▷ verb of creation
        $\lambda e.\mathbf{increase}(\lambda t. \iota d'(\mathbf{written}(x)(t) = d'))(d)(e)$

(23)   a.   eaten $\rightsquigarrow \lambda x \lambda t. \iota d(\mathbf{eaten}(x)(t) = d)$ ▷ gradable adjective

     b.   [$_{\mathrm{VP}}$ eat (d-much) of x] $\rightsquigarrow$ ▷ verb of destruction
        $\lambda e.\mathbf{increase}(\lambda t. \iota d'(\mathbf{eaten}(x)(t) = d'))(d)(e)$

Notice that just as the meaning of *shorten* is based on the meaning of *short*, which denotes a function from individuals and times to (negative) degrees ($\mathbf{short}(x)(t)$ "the degree to which x is short at t" – recall 15), the meaning of *eat* is based on the meaning of *eaten*, which likewise denotes a function from individuals and times to (negative) degrees ($\mathbf{eaten}(x)(t)$ "the degree to which x is eaten at t"). Furthermore, given the definition in (19b), the formulas in (20b), (21b), (22b), and (23b) reduce to the following:

(24)   a. $\lambda e. \iota d'(\mathbf{long}(x)(\mathbf{end}(e)) = d') =$ ▷ reduction of (20b)
        $\iota d''(\mathbf{long}(x)(\mathbf{beg}(e)) = d'') +' d$

     b. $\lambda e. \iota d'(\mathbf{short}(x)(\mathbf{end}(e)) = d') =$ ▷ reduction of (21b)
        $\iota d''(\mathbf{short}(x)(\mathbf{beg}(e)) = d'') +' d$

---

[15] Technically, the meaning of *lengthen* could be derived via the functional application of **increase** (see 17b) to **long** in (20a):

(i) $[\lambda G \lambda x \lambda d \lambda e.\mathbf{increase}(G(x))(d)(e)](\mathbf{long}) =$ ▷ by functional conversion
     $\lambda x \lambda d \lambda e.\mathbf{increase}(\lambda t. \iota d'(\mathbf{long}(x)(t) = d'))(d)(e)$

The meanings of the verbs in (21b), (22b), and (23b) could be derived in a similar fashion.

c. $\lambda e.\iota d'(\mathbf{written}(x)(\mathbf{end}(e)) = d') =$ $\rhd$ reduction of (22b)
     $\iota d''(\mathbf{written}(x)(\mathbf{beg}(e))) = d'') +' d$

d. $\lambda e.\iota d'(\mathbf{eaten}(x)(\mathbf{end}(e)) = d') =$ $\rhd$ reduction of (23b)
     $\iota d''(\mathbf{eaten}(x)(\mathbf{beg}(e))) = d'') +' d$

As Kennedy and Levin observe, the degree of change is not always syntactically expressed. In the case of degree achievements, it may be expressed by an explicit measure expression, as in (25a)[16] and (26a), but it may also remain implicit, as in (25b) and (26b), where it is existentially bound inside the VP.[17]

(25) a. [$_{\text{VP}}$ lengthen the rope (by) ten centimeters] $\rightsquigarrow$
          $\lambda e.\mathbf{increase}(\lambda t.\iota d'(\mathbf{long}(\text{the-rope})(t) = d'))(\text{10-cm})(e)$

      b. [$_{\text{VP}}$ lengthen the rope]^{atel} $\rightsquigarrow$
          $\lambda e.\exists d(\mathbf{increase}(\lambda t.\iota d'(\mathbf{long}(\text{the-rope})(t) = d'))(d)(e))$

(26) a. [$_{\text{VP}}$ eat half of the apple] $\rightsquigarrow$
          $\lambda e.\mathbf{increase}(\lambda t.\iota d'(\mathbf{eaten}(\text{the-apple})(t) = d'))(.5)(e)$

      b. [$_{\text{VP}}$ eat the apple]^{atel} $\rightsquigarrow$
          $\lambda e.\exists d(\mathbf{increase}(\lambda t.\iota d'(\mathbf{eaten}(\text{the-apple})(t) = d'))(d)(e))$

Kennedy and Levin also allow for the degree argument to remain free inside the VP (and possibly existentially bound from outside it), in contrast to the setup in (25b) and (26b), where it is existentially bound inside the VP. The degree argument remains free within the VP in the following variations on (25b) and (26b):

(27) a. [$_{\text{VP}}$ lengthen the rope]^{tel} $\rightsquigarrow$
          $\lambda e.\mathbf{increase}(\lambda t.\iota d'(\mathbf{long}(\text{the-rope})(t) = d'))(d)(e)$

      b. [$_{\text{VP}}$ eat the apple]^{tel} $\rightsquigarrow$
          $\lambda e.\mathbf{increase}(\lambda t.\iota d'(\mathbf{eaten}(\text{the-apple})(t) = d'))(d)(e)$

Observe that the event predicate representing the VP is quantized if the value of the degree argument is fixed within the VP:

---

[16] A lingering worry is how the meaning of the term 10-cm for *(by) ten centimeters* in (25a) relates to the scale of length, which is closed at 0 and open at 1. Strictly speaking, positive degrees in this case should be intervals in $[0, 1)$ (see (11a) and (15)) and not lengths measured in terms of centimeters. For this to be intelligible, the length of ten centimeters should correspond to a positive degree in $[0, 1)$, yet it is not evident which degree this should be. Although there may be a straightforward reply to this worry, it is at the same time easy to suspect that degrees in Kennedy and Levin's account actually play a double role, as (i) indicators of degree of realization and (ii) measurements of particular extents. The question of degree addition (see notes 11 and 12) is less problematic if the latter is the intended role for degrees. The resolution of this worry in the approach that I propose in section 8.3 consists in sharply distinguishing these two roles.

[17] The superscript "*atel*" in (25b) and (26b) simply serves to mark the atelic interpretation of the VPs in question, thereby distinguishing them from those in (27a) and (27b) below, which are telic (and marked with "*tel*").

(28) a.   ▷ cf. (25a)

$$\mathbf{qua}(\lambda e.\mathbf{increase}(\lambda t.\iota d'(\mathbf{long(the\text{-}rope)}(t) = d'))(\mathbf{10\text{-}cm})(e))$$

▷ cf. (27a)

$$\mathbf{qua}(\lambda e.\mathbf{increase}(\lambda t.\iota d'(\mathbf{long(the\text{-}rope)}(t) = d'))(d)(e))$$

   b.   ▷ cf. (25b)

$$\mathbf{nuniq}(\lambda e.\exists d(\mathbf{increase}(\lambda t.\iota d'(\mathbf{long(the\text{-}rope)}(t) = d'))(d)(e))) \rightarrow$$
$$\mathbf{cum}(\lambda e.\exists d(\mathbf{increase}(\lambda t.\iota d'(\mathbf{long(the\text{-}rope)}(t) = d'))(d)(e)))$$

(29) a.   ▷ cf. (26a)

$$\mathbf{qua}(\lambda e.\mathbf{increase}(\lambda t.\iota d'(\mathbf{eaten(the\text{-}apple)}(t) = d'))(.5)(e))$$

▷ cf. (27b)

$$\mathbf{qua}(\lambda e.\mathbf{increase}(\lambda t.\iota d'(\mathbf{eaten(the\text{-}apple)}(t) = d'))(d)(e))$$

   b.   ▷ cf. (26b)

$$\mathbf{nuniq}(\lambda e.\exists d(\mathbf{increase}(\lambda t.\iota d'(\mathbf{eaten(the\text{-}apple)}(t) = d'))(d)(e))) \rightarrow$$
$$\mathbf{cum}(\lambda e.\exists d(\mathbf{increase}(\lambda t.\iota d'(\mathbf{eaten(the\text{-}apple)}(t) = d'))(d)(e)))$$

For instance, consider the statements in (28). The event predicate in (25a) is quantized because any event in which the rope is lengthened by ten centimeters lacks a proper subevent in which it is lengthened by ten centimeters – in any proper subevent, it is at most lengthened by less than ten centimeters. Similarly, the event predicate in (27a) is quantized because any event in which the rope is lengthened by d-much lacks a proper subevent in which it is lengthened by d-much, where the value of d is implicit but fixed for the VP. In contrast, the event predicate in (25b) is cumulative – provided that it is non-unique – because the sum of any two events in which the rope is lengthened by some amount d is also an event in which the rope is lengthened by some (greater) amount d, where the value of d may vary with each event chosen. The reasoning behind the statements in (29) is analogous.

8.2.1.2 *Evaluation*   From the present perspective, the central question is to what extent Kennedy and Levin's account includes an analysis of aspectual composition in terms of gradability. Alternatively, to recall their claim cited in section 8.1, to what extent does quantization/telicity follow completely from the structure of the degree of change argument? At first glance, their account seems to fare well, because the characterizations in (28) and (29) appear unobjectionable. However, as mentioned in section 8.1, it is also desirable for an aspectual theory to derive these results, and here their account leaves something to be desired.

Consider how the following two telic VPs (ignoring the *in*-PPs) might be derived in Kennedy and Levin's framework:

(30) a. [$_{VP}$ eat the apple]^{tel} (in five minutes)

      b. [$_{VP}$ write a letter]^{tel} (in twenty minutes)

Beginning with (30a), since the definite object NP *the apple* may be treated as a term, the meaning of *eat* can be applied to the meaning of *the apple*:[18]

(31) a. eat $\rightsquigarrow \lambda x \lambda d \lambda e . \iota d'(\mathbf{eaten}(x)(\mathbf{end}(e))) = d') = $
          $\iota d''(\mathbf{eaten}(x)(\mathbf{beg}(e))) = d'') +' d$

      b. the apple $\rightsquigarrow$ **the-apple**

      c. [$_{VP}$ eat the apple] $\rightsquigarrow$
          $\lambda d \lambda e . \iota d'(\mathbf{eaten}(\mathbf{the\text{-}apple})(\mathbf{end}(e))) = d') = $
          $\iota d''(\mathbf{eaten}(\mathbf{the\text{-}apple})(\mathbf{beg}(e))) = d'') +' d$

A technical issue with the result in (31c) is that the degree argument has not yet been discharged. Allowing for a default mechanism of existential binding of the degree argument at the VP level (as Kennedy and Levin in fact do), we obtain the following event predicate:

(32) [$_{VP}$ eat the apple]^{atel} $\rightsquigarrow$ $\triangleright$ atelic reading (cf. 1b, 3b)
      $\lambda e . \exists d (\iota d'(\mathbf{eaten}(\mathbf{the\text{-}apple})(\mathbf{end}(e))) = d') = $
      $\iota d''(\mathbf{eaten}(\mathbf{the\text{-}apple})(\mathbf{beg}(e))) = d'') +' d$

Observe that this event predicate is cumulative as long as it is non-unique (cf. 29b): the events in its denotation are events in which some amount d of the apple is eaten, and the sum of any two of these is also an event in which some (larger) amount d of the apple is eaten. This corresponds to the atelic reading of the VP, which is also the reading characteristic of (1b) and (3b) in section 8.1.

  Even so, the issue is still how to derive the telic interpretion of (30a), for which there appear to be two potential strategies. The first would be to have the degree of change argument remain free within the VP, because this would yield a quantized event predicate (cf. 29a):

(33) [$_{VP}$ eat the apple]^{tel} $\rightsquigarrow$ $\triangleright$ telic reading, first version (cf. 27b)
      $\lambda e . \iota d'(\mathbf{eaten}(\mathbf{the\text{-}apple})(\mathbf{end}(e))) = d') = $
      $\iota d''(\mathbf{eaten}(\mathbf{the\text{-}apple})(\mathbf{beg}(e))) = d'') +' d$

Although this event predicate is indeed quantized, it does not capture the intuitive meaning of the VP, because the events denoted in (33) are those in which d-much of the apple is eaten, for a fixed value of d, but nothing

---

[18] For present purposes, nothing depends on whether *the apple* is analyzed as a term, a predicate (namely, $\lambda x . x = $ **the-apple**), or even a generalized quantifier. Accordingly, nothing requires the verb to be treated as a functor for the object NP – cf. (35) below.

forces the value of d to be maximal (or nearly maximal, allowing for a certain vagueness). Yet, intuitively, the meaning of the VP applies to events in which the apple is wholly eaten. Consequently, the first potential strategy, according to which the degree argument is free and implicitly specified, as in (33), would be in general too weak.[19]

The second strategy would be to set the value of the degree of change to be maximal, which would yield the interpretation on which all of the apple is eaten. Technically, Kennedy and Levin treat **eaten** as a "negative property," which means that its possible values are negative degrees. Furthermore, although Kennedy and Levin do not state this explicitly, the scale defined by **eaten** is evidently closed. Consequently, degrees of "being eaten" have the form $[p, 1]$, for a choice of p (recall 11b), and the maximal negative degree is $[0, 1]$. In order to get this as the result, the value of the degree of change (which is always a positive degree) should also be set to $[0, 1]$:[20]

(34) $[_{VP}$ eat the apple$]^{tel} \rightsquigarrow$ ▷ telic reading, final version
$\lambda e . \iota d'(\textbf{eaten}(\textbf{the-apple})(\textbf{end}(e)) = d') =$
$\iota d''(\textbf{eaten}(\textbf{the-apple})(\textbf{beg}(e)) = d'') +' [0, 1]$

Since the degree of change in (34) is specified as $[0, 1]$, it follows that the degree to which the apple is eaten at the beginning of an event in the denotation of this predicate is $[1, 1]$ (or 1), which is the minimal negative degree. In other words, none of the apple is eaten at the beginning of such an event, and it is fully eaten by the end.

Although the second strategy would yield the desired result, it is a bit unclear how to obtain it in Kennedy and Levin's framework. More precisely, how does d, which is an argument of the verb, get specified as $[0, 1]$? More generally, if the value of d is not explicitly specified, Kennedy and Levin suggest that it may be inferred on the basis of the lexical semantics of the verb or its arguments, or even on the basis of extralinguistic knowledge. In the case of (31c), then, the idea seems to be that since *the apple* is quantized, it is natural to infer that the value of d is maximal. However, unless more is said about how this inference mechanism works in conjunction with representations like that in (31c), the account is lacking something.

---

[19] Note that this is not a problem in the case of degree achievements. For example, the meaning of *lengthen the rope* (cf. 27a) does not require the degree of change d to be maximal – indeed, given that the scale of length is closed at 0 and open at 1 (cf. 15), d could not have a maximal value anyway.

[20] Then the first clause in (14) would apply, where d is $[1, 1]$ (the minimal negative degree) and d' is $[0, 1]$ (the maximal positive degree of change), therefore $d +' d' = [1, 1] +' [0, 1] = [0, 1]$ (the maximal negative degree).

The telic VP in (30b) poses the same problem, though here the object NP is indefinite. If *a letter* is analyzed as a generalized quantifier, as in (35b), it can apply to the meaning of *write* in (35a) to yield the relation between events and degrees in (35c).

(35)　a.　write $\leadsto \lambda x \lambda d \lambda e. \iota d'(\textbf{written}(x)(\textbf{end}(e)) = d') = \iota d''(\textbf{written}(x)(\textbf{beg}(e)) = d'') +' d$

　　　b.　a letter $\leadsto \lambda R \lambda d \lambda e. \exists x (R(x)(d)(e) \wedge \textbf{letter}(x))$

　　　c.　[$_{\text{VP}}$ write a letter] $\leadsto \lambda d \lambda e. \exists x (\iota d'(\textbf{written}(x)(\textbf{end}(e)) = d') = \iota d''(\textbf{written}(x)(\textbf{beg}(e)) = d'') +' d \wedge \textbf{letter}(x))$

As before, the problem is how to discharge d and to restrict its value to be maximal in the absence of an explicit degree expression. Moreover, as seen earlier in connection with (32), it would not suffice simply to existentially bind d at the VP level, because this would yield an atelic VP.

Suppose that we have a mechanism for setting the degree of change to be maximal. Then nothing would restrain it from applying in the case of atelic VPs, illustrated in (36).

(36)　a.　[$_{\text{VP}}$ eat applesauce]　　(for five minutes)

　　　b.　[$_{\text{VP}}$ write letters]　　(for two hours)

Consider how the VP in (36a) might be derived, treating the object NP *applesauce* as a generalized quantifier (cf. 35b):

(37)　a.　eat $\leadsto \lambda x \lambda d \lambda e. \iota d'(\textbf{eaten}(x)(\textbf{end}(e)) = d') = \iota d''(\textbf{eaten}(x)(\textbf{beg}(e)) = d'') +' d$

　　　b.　applesauce $\leadsto \lambda R \lambda d \lambda e. \exists x (R(x)(d)(e) \wedge \textbf{applesauce}(x))$

　　　c.　[$_{\text{VP}}$ eat applesauce] $\leadsto \lambda d \lambda e. \exists x (\iota d'(\textbf{eaten}(x)(\textbf{end}(e)) = d') = \iota d''(\textbf{eaten}(x)(\textbf{beg}(e)) = d'') +' d \wedge \textbf{applesauce}(x))$

Given the relation between events e and degrees d in (37c), one possibility would be to existentially bind d at the VP level:

(38)　[$_{\text{VP}}$ eat applesauce] $\leadsto$　　　　　　　　　　　　▷ first version
　　　$\lambda e. \exists d \exists x (\iota d'(\textbf{eaten}(x)(\textbf{end}(e)) = d') = \iota d''(\textbf{eaten}(x)(\textbf{beg}(e)) = d'') +' d \wedge \textbf{applesauce}(x))$

This event predicate is cumulative (provided that it is non-unique), hence this analysis would successfully capture the fact that the VP *eat applesauce* is atelic. In prose, this predicate denotes events in which some amount d of some applesauce is eaten, and the sum of any two such events is also an event in which some (greater) amount d of some (greater quantity of) applesauce is eaten. However, once a mechanism for fixing the value of d to be $[0, 1]$ is available, it could apply to the relation in (37c) to yield the following event predicate (cf. 34):

(39) [$_{VP}$ eat applesauce] $\rightsquigarrow$ ▷ second version
$$\lambda e.\exists x(\iota d'(\text{eaten}(x)(\text{end}(e)) = d') =$$
$$\iota d''(\text{eaten}(x)(\text{beg}(e)) = d'') +' [0, 1] \wedge \text{applesauce}(x))$$

Perhaps somewhat surprisingly, this event predicate is also cumulative (provided that it is non-unique): it denotes events in which some applesauce is maximally eaten, but the sum of any two events in which some applesauce is maximally eaten is also an event in which some (greater quantity of) applesauce is maximally eaten. Of course, the quantity of applesauce is not held constant here, but nor does it have to be, given that x is existentially bound in (39).

The contrast between the event predicate in (34), which is quantized (telic) and specifies a maximal degree of change, on the one hand, and the event predicate in (39), which is cumulative (atelic) and specifies a maximal degree of change, on the other, sharply demonstrates that quantization/telicity does *not* follow completely from the structure of the degree of change argument, contrary to Kennedy and Levin's initial claim. Clearly, the choice of object NP is a crucial factor here.[21] In the case of *the apple*, which is quantized, the way in which the degree of change is specified *does* matter, as seen in the contrast between (32) (cumulative, atelic) and (34) (quantized, telic). However, in the case of *applesauce*, which is cumulative, the way in which the degree of change is specified does *not* matter, as witnessed in the *lack* of contrast between (38) and (39) (both cumulative, atelic).

The same issue arises for the atelic VP in (36b), which contains the cumulative object NP *letters*. No matter how the degree of change is specified, the corresponding event predicate is cumulative, which differs from the VP in (35c) with the quantized object NP *a letter*, for here the way in which the degree of change is specified does determine whether the VP is telic or atelic.

In sum, Kennedy and Levin's account does not quite succeed in offering an analysis of aspectual composition in terms of gradability, contrary to initial claims and appearances, because it does not relate the value of the degree of change argument to the quantized/cumulative character of the object NP.

[21] Rothstein (2004: 118) makes a similar point in a critique of Kennedy and Levin (2002) based on examples such as *The tailor lengthened skirts five centimeters for three months*, claiming that Kennedy and Levin's account is not a theory of telicity. Although I basically agree with Rothstein on this point (though it is perhaps arguable whether Kennedy and Levin really promised a "theory of telicity"), it is also evident that she has little sympathy for a degree-based account to begin with, given her own non-degree-based approach to promote. Furthermore, as far as I can tell, she does not actually show how degree achievements would be treated in her framework.

Related to this is the point that their analysis also does not allow character-izations such as those in (28) and (29) to be strictly deduced. Naturally, this conclusion does not entail that their account is on the wrong track, but it does mean that as presently formulated it is incomplete in an important respect.

8.2.2 *Caudal and Nicolas (2005)*

Caudal and Nicolas propose a degree-based aspectual alternative to the approaches by Kennedy and Levin, Krifka, and Verkuyl, hence it is relevant to the present discussion. Although they make a number of useful observations and aim to account for a wide range of facts, their proposed alternative is prob-lematic in terms of its conceptual and formal development. My comments will be comparatively brief, and I will focus on their analysis of *John eat an apple* (again, ignoring tense), because the treatment of this kind of example brings their discussion closest to the present one:

(40) John eat an apple $\rightsquigarrow$ $\triangleright$ based on Caudal and Nicolas' (55)
       $\exists x \exists e \exists d (\mathbf{eat}(e)(d) \wedge \mathbf{become}(\mathbf{eat}) \wedge \mathbf{quantity}(x)(d) \wedge$
       $\mathbf{agent}(\mathbf{john})(e) \wedge \mathbf{patient}(x)(e) \wedge \mathbf{apple}(x))$

This formula states that there is an individual x, an event e, and a degree d such that e is an eating to degree d, the event type "eat" is a becoming, the quantity of x is d, the agent of e is John, and the patient of e is x, which is an apple. Setting aside the two thematic relations **agent** and **patient**,[22] the crux of the matter comes down to the interpretation of **eat**, **become**, and **quantity** in order to understand the formula in (40). In this connection, it is also vital to ask about Caudal and Nicolas' conception of telicity and how the formula in (40) captures the telic reading of the sentence in question.

Beginning with **eat**, how does this predicate relate events to degrees? For Caudal and Nicolas (p. 287), in the case of non-atomic predicates such as **eat**, degrees are taken from the set of positive real numbers. However, Caudal and Nicolas do not say what the maximal degree is in this case, and even more cru-cially they do not indicate how degrees are supposed to be assigned to eating events.[23] Yet suppose that we have an eating event e: how is it determined what degree is assigned to e? For example, when would the degree assigned to e be 1 and when would it be 2 and when would it be 102? If there is any eating at all, why is the degree not maximal? Unfortunately, since Caudal and Nicolas

---

[22] At the same time, it is unclear what principles Caudal and Nicolas assume for **patient**. Do Krifka-style mapping properties hold for **patient** and, if not, how are parts of the patient argument related to parts of the event? Caudal and Nicolas recite (note 15) two of Krifka's (1998a) mapping properties, but it is unclear to what extent they are committed to them.

[23] Although Caudal and Nicolas do not state explicitly that **eat** is functional with respect to its degree argument, I assume that it is.

do not address such questions, it is unclear what **eat** actually measures in the end.[24] Alternatively, if the degree assigned to e should also depend on what is eaten in e, then it would be more expedient to treat **eat** as a *two-place* function on events and individuals, yet this is not what Caudal and Nicolas do.

The clause **become(eat)** in (40) is unproblematic once **eat** is accepted. In prose, it says that there is a one-to-one mapping between initial subevents of eating events and degrees such that if **eat** yields d for e, then every initial subevent of e is mapped to a unique degree lower than d (but higher than 0), and every degree lower than d (but higher than 0) is mapped to a unique initial subevent of e. In other words, degrees steadily increase in the course of eating events. Although there is something intuitively correct and attractive about this, it is still unclear what exactly **eat** is measuring.

Turning to **quantity**, the problem is similar as for **eat**: it is unclear what is being measured. Does **quantity** count atomic individuals, or does it measure the mass of an individual with respect to some unit of measure? And what is the maximal degree for **quantity**?[25] It is easy to imagine that the clause **quantity**$(x)(d)$ in (40) counts apples, but then why not specify d to be 1 in this case? It is also unclear what the motivation is for identifying the degree argument of **quantity** with that of **eat** in (40).

Caudal and Nicolas do not model telicity in terms of quantization but instead offer a new definition:

(41)   **Caudal and Nicolas' definition of telicity** (based on their 56): A predication is telic iff (i) it has an associated set of degrees with (ii) a specified maximal degree and (iii) its verbal predicate satisfies **become**.

Not immediately obvious is that this notion of telicity applies to relations between degrees and events and *not* to one-place event predicates, as quantization does. Consequently, this definition has to be applied to the relation between degrees and events underlying the formula in (40):

(42) $\lambda d \lambda e. \exists x(\mathbf{eat}(e)(d) \wedge \mathbf{become(eat)} \wedge \mathbf{quantity}(x)(d) \wedge$ ▷ cf. (40)
       $\mathbf{agent(john)}(e) \wedge \mathbf{patient}(x)(e) \wedge \mathbf{apple}(x))$

Firstly, however, it is not evident that this relation specifies a maximal degree, and even if d were specified as 1 (assuming that individual apples are counted), it is unclear why this would be a maximal degree (how about the case of two apples?). But even if it were deemed that d is maximal in this case, it is hard

---

[24] A reasonable but unintended interpretation for **eat** would be that it measures temporal length with respect to some unit of measurement (e.g., seconds), but Caudal and Nicolas clearly do not have this interpretation in mind.

[25] Caudal and Nicolas' axiom for **quantity** in their (56) presupposes a maximal degree.

to see why d should not also be maximal in the following formula (which presumably underlies the analysis of *John eat applesauce*), because presumably the particular quantity x of applesauce at issue also has a maximal value:

(43) $\lambda d \lambda e. \exists x (\mathbf{eat}(e)(d) \wedge \mathbf{become}(\mathbf{eat}) \wedge \mathbf{quantity}(x)(d) \wedge$
        $\mathbf{agent}(\mathrm{john})(e) \wedge \mathbf{patient}(x)(e) \wedge \mathbf{applesauce}(x))$

However, this formula should be atelic, in contrast to the formula in (42), which should be telic.

Secondly, the definition in (41) is global in an uncanny way, because it presupposes that we can tell, given an arbitrary relation between degrees and events, whether the verbal predicate buried inside (if there is one) satisfies **become**. However, on the usual assumptions of a compositional semantics, this information will in general no longer be accessible.[26]

In sum, it is difficult to view Caudal and Nicolas' account in its present state as a serious contender to either Kennedy and Levin's or Krifka's. Although they suggest a number of ideas which are intuitively attractive (e.g., a monotonic increase of degrees as a component of incrementality – even if they do not quite put it this way), their account needs significant work to cohere as it should.

8.3 A new account: degrees and descriptions

If the double aim is to treat verbs with an incremental theme as gradable *and* to provide an analysis of aspectual composition in terms of their gradability, then such verbs will need more than just a supplementary degree argument. But this claim implies that any approach that simply adds a degree argument to verbs with an incremental theme will fall short of being able to provide an analysis of aspectual composition in terms of gradability. However, if a degree argument is not sufficient, what more is needed? What has been lacking thus far is a tighter connection between the degrees and how the incremental theme is *described*. If correct, then the description of the incremental theme has to be integrated more tightly into the gradable property that a verb with an incremental theme denotes. In what follows, I will show how this integration may be envisioned, beginning with a detailed treatment of verbs with an incremental theme in section 8.3.1, and then returning briefly to degree achievements in section 8.3.2.

---

[26] Caudal and Nicolas may have in mind a kind of representational approach, but then they should clarify this up front, and needless to say it would place their analysis in a different ballpark and accordingly make direct comparisons between their account and those by Kennedy and Levin, Krifka, and Verkuyl (not to mention the present account) more difficult to make.

8.3.1 *Grading verbs with an incremental theme*

The basic gradable properties that underlie the semantics of verbs with an incremental theme are measure functions from ordinary individuals x, descriptions O, and events e to degrees, as illustrated in (44).

(44) a. $\text{eat}_\delta(x)(O)(e)$ "the degree to which x qua type O is eaten in e"

b. $\text{write}_\delta(x)(O)(e)$ "the degree to which x qua type O is written in e"

c. $\text{read}_\delta(x)(O)(e)$ "the degree to which x qua type O is read in e"

Note that O is just a one-place predicate of individuals (where "O" is mnemonic for "object" or "ordinary individual"). The subscript δ is merely a discreet reminder that the respective predicate is a function symbol, yielding degrees as values.[27] For convenience, I will call such functions *incremental degree functions*.[28]

Strictly speaking, verbs with an incremental theme are taken to denote four-place relations between individuals x, descriptions O, degrees d, and events e, as illustrated in (45), obtained by abstracting over the output degrees of the respective incremental degree functions.

(45) a. eat $\rightsquigarrow \lambda x \lambda O \lambda d \lambda e . \text{eat}_\delta(x)(O)(e) = d$

b. write $\rightsquigarrow \lambda x \lambda O \lambda d \lambda e . \text{write}_\delta(x)(O)(e) = d$

c. read $\rightsquigarrow \lambda x \lambda O \lambda d \lambda e . \text{read}_\delta(x)(O)(e) = d$

It is vital to emphasize at the outset that what is measured by degree functions is the degree to which x qua type O is affected (or effected) in e with respect to the verbal property in question. Thus, the incremental degree function eat_δ in (45a) does *not* measure the degree to which x as a "bare individual" or quantity gets eaten in e but *instead* measures the degree to which x as an individual of type O gets eaten in e. This is the essential, fundamental difference between the present approach and Kennedy and Levin's – all of the other differences (e.g., whether verbs should be further decomposed or not) are ultimately less basic and more cosmetic.

In the next section, I present an axiomatic treatment of verbs with an incremental theme on the assumption that their meanings are based on incremental degree functions. I use $\mathbf{V}_\delta$ in the axioms as a predicate constant instantiating such functions (namely, eat_δ, write_δ, etc.). In addition, the conception of

[27] Thus, despite appearances, δ here is not the same as the degree function δ employed in Piñón (2000, 2005), which was not a mere subscript.

[28] The general background framework that I have in mind is that of *fuzzy set theory* (Zadeh 1987). In particular, incremental degree functions can be viewed as a sort of *fuzzy relations*. Lack of space prevents me from comparisons, but I remark that ordinary fuzzy sets are much simpler than such fuzzy relations. Moreover, degrees here are not construed as degrees of truth.

degrees adopted here is simpler than Kennedy and Levin's: a degree is simply a rational number (i.e., a point and not an interval) from 0 to 1. Although degrees could be modeled as real numbers from 0 to 1, it seems questionable whether irrational numbers are needed for semantic applications. Moreover, there is no distinction made here between positive and negative degrees, which would also be rather tricky to implement if degrees are just points. At any rate, negative degrees are not essential for present purposes.[29]

8.3.1.1 *An axiomatic treatment*   The first axiom for incremental degree functions simply makes explicit the claim that O holds of x (the incremental theme), for otherwise there would be no sense in speaking of "x qua type O":

(46)   ▷ AXIOM: application of O to x
$$\forall x \forall O \forall d \forall e (V_\delta(x)(O)(e) = d \rightarrow O(x))$$

The second axiom affirms thematic uniqueness with respect to x:

(47)   ▷ AXIOM: thematic uniqueness of x
$$\forall x \forall x' \forall O \forall d \forall e (V_\delta(x)(O)(e) = d \wedge V_\delta(x')(O)(e) = d \rightarrow x = x')$$

For example, if x qua type O and x' qua type O are eaten to degree d in the same event e, then x and x' are identical.[30]

The third axiom states that if x qua type O and x' qua type O are affected in e and e', respectively, with respect to V_δ, where e' is a proper part of e, then x' is a proper part of x:

(48)   ▷ AXIOM: mapping from events to ordinary individuals
$$\forall x \forall x' \forall O \forall d \forall d' \forall e \forall e' (V_\delta(x)(O)(e) = d \wedge V_\delta(x')(O)(e') = d' \wedge e' \sqsubseteq e$$
$$\rightarrow x' \sqsubseteq x)$$

This axiom is similar in spirit to Krifka's "mapping to objects" (see section 8.1), though it is actually weaker because it does not simply require every part of e to correspond to a part of x.[31]

---

[29] This is not intended as a criticism of Kennedy and Levin's conception of degrees – rather, it is simply a practical decision of implementation on my part. Needless to say, the question of negative degrees would be a topic in its own right.

[30] The English paraphrase with "in the same event" is potentially misleading, because x' may be a proper part of x as long as x' is eaten in a *proper subevent* of e.

[31] Although Kennedy and Levin claim to be able to dispense with mappings between argument structure and events for the treatment of verbs with an incremental theme, their claim is not so easy to verify until their account is more fully formalized.

The fourth axiom asserts that incremental degree functions are *summative* with respect to their incremental theme and the event argument, provided that O is cumulative:[32]

(49)   ▷ AXIOM: summativity of V_δ with cumulative O

$$\forall x \forall x' \forall O \forall d \forall d' \forall e \forall e'(V_\delta(x)(O)(e) = d \wedge V_\delta(x')(O)(e') = d' \wedge$$
$$d' \leq d \wedge \text{cum}(O) \rightarrow$$
$$V_\delta(x \oplus x')(O)(e \oplus e') = d)$$

Observe that the degrees in this case are not summed or added together but instead the higher of the two degrees is selected for the value of the summed event. For instance, if an event in which some x qua type "applesauce" is eaten to degree 1 is summed with another event in which x' qua type "applesauce" is eaten to degree 1, then the sum is an event in which some applesauce is eaten to degree 1. It would make no sense to add the two degrees to get 2, because 2 is not a possible degree to begin with.[33]

The fifth axiom affirms that if x qua type O is affected to degree d in e with respect to V_δ, d is positive, and O is cumulative, then d is 1:

(50)   ▷ AXIOM: cumulative O yields $d = 1$ if $d > 0$

$$\forall x \forall O \forall d \forall e(V_\delta(x)(O)(e) = d \wedge d > 0 \wedge \text{cum}(O) \rightarrow d = 1)$$

The idea behind this axiom is that if x qua type O is affected in e and O is cumulative, then x qua type O is fully affected in e – there is no hedging or halfway house in this case. More precisely, incremental degree functions are *defective* in this kind of situation, for they crucially depend on O for distinguishing degrees of change, and yet if O is cumulative, it does not provide the kind of property against which degrees of change can reasonably be distinguished. Another way of putting this is that if O is cumulative, then incremental degree functions are *ungradable*.

As an illustration, consider an event e in which some applesauce x is (possibly partly) eaten. In this case, O is the type "applesauce", which is cumulative, thus the question is to what degree x qua type "applesauce" is eaten in e. Suppose that in fact half of x is eaten in e. Bear in mind, as emphasized earlier, that the incremental degree function **eat**$_\delta$ does *not* measure the degree to which x as a "bare individual" or quantity is eaten in e. Instead, it measures the

---

[32] Krifka employs a notion of summativity for (two-place) thematic relations. However, the matter is more complex in the present case, because the predicate argument O and the degree argument d of V_δ also have to be considered.

[33] In the present framework, there is no addition of degrees in isolation, in contrast to Kennedy and Levin's account (recall notes 11, 12, and 16 in this connection). How degrees are combined or "added" depends on the arguments of the degree functions in question. In this connection, see also (51) below.

degree to which x qua type "applesauce" is eaten in e, and so a sensible answer seems to be that if x qua type "applesauce" is eaten at all in e, then the degree to which x qua type "applesauce" is eaten in e is 1. Although, naturally, eating more of x would mean that a larger quantity of applesauce is eaten, it would not change the degree to which x qua type "applesauce" is eaten. To harp on this point, we are not measuring quantities of applesauce that are eaten – we are measuring the degree to which the event type "eat applesauce" is realized.

The next two axioms play for quantized O a role parallel to those in (49) and (50) for cumulative O. The first of these axioms determines, for a given x and quantized O, whether V_δ applies to the sum of e and e' if it applies to e and e' independently. In (51), $\wr$ stands for the *discreteness* relation (i.e., no overlap), whereas $\oslash$ designates the *proper overlap* relation (i.e., overlap in a proper part only).

(51) $\triangleright$ Axiom: summativity with quantized O and fixed x
$$\forall x \forall O \forall d \forall d' \forall e \forall e'(V_\delta(x)(O)(e) = d \wedge V_\delta(x)(O)(e') = d' \wedge \mathbf{qua}(O) \rightarrow$$
$$e' \wr e \rightarrow$$
$$d + d' \leq 1 \rightarrow V_\delta(x)(O)(e \oplus e') = d + d' \wedge$$
$$d + d' > 1 \rightarrow \neg \exists d''(V_\delta(x)(O)(e \oplus e') = d'') \wedge$$
$$e' \oslash e \rightarrow \neg \exists d''(V_\delta(x)(O)(e \oplus e') = d''))$$

This axiom guarantees that if e and e' are discrete and the arithmetic sum of d and d' is less than or equal to 1, then V_δ applies to the sum of e and e' with the value $d + d'$. However, if $d + d'$ is greater than 1, then V_δ does not yield a degree for $e \oplus e'$ – this is an instance in which V_δ is undefined on its input. Furthermore, if e and e' properly overlap, then V_δ also does not yield a degree for $e \oplus e'$, which is another instance of undefinedness. This axiom does not mention the case in which e' is a part of e (note that the part relation is incompatible with the proper overlap relation), because the result is independently derivable: if $e' \sqsubseteq e$ holds, then $e' \oplus e$ is just e and so the degree is d, as already determined by the premise. Clearly, as seen in (49)–(50), the matter is less complex when O is cumulative, because in this case the degrees are never added together.

The seventh axiom, which parallels the one in (50), states that the value of the degree argument strictly increases in the course of an event if O is quantized, thereby encoding a strict notion of incrementality:

(52) $\triangleright$ Axiom: strict incrementality
$$\forall x \forall O \forall d \forall d' \forall e \forall e'(V_\delta(x)(O)(e) = d \wedge V_\delta(x)(O)(e') = d' \wedge e' \sqsubseteq e \wedge$$
$$\mathbf{qua}(O) \rightarrow$$
$$d' < d)$$

For example, consider an event e in which x qua type "(an) apple" is eaten to degree d. Since "(an) apple" is quantized, this axiom applies and requires the degree to which x qua type "(an) apple" is eaten in any proper subevent of e to be less than d.

The eighth and final axiom determines a kind of initial condition on incremental degree functions, asserting that if x qua type O is affected to degree d in e with respect to $\mathbf{V}_\delta$, then x qua type O is affected to degree 0 in the very beginning of e with respect to $\mathbf{V}_\delta$:

(53)   ▷ Axiom: $d = 0$ in the left boundary of e
$$\forall x \forall O \forall d \forall e (\mathbf{V}_\delta(x)(O)(e) = d \rightarrow \mathbf{V}_\delta(x)(O)(\textbf{left-bound}(e)) = 0)$$

The predicate **left-bound** is a function that yields the instantaneous beginning or *left boundary* of an event. Note that the left boundary of an event is a sort of event (albeit instantaneous) and not a time; as a subtle reminder of this, I write "*in* the left boundary of e" as opposed to "*at* the left boundary of e."[34]

At first glance, the axiom in (53) may appear undesirable in light of the following kind of example. Suppose that x qua type "half an apple" is eaten to degree d in e. This axiom would then require x qua type "half an apple" to be eaten to degree 0 in the left boundary of e. However, it is easy to imagine that the other half of the apple had already been eaten before the beginning of e, hence it would seem wrong to require that no part of the apple be eaten before the beginning of e. This would indeed be wrong, but this is also not what the axiom in (53) enforces, because it leaves completely open what may have happened to the other half of the apple prior to e. It restricts itself to what happens in e, stating that x qua type "half an apple" is eaten to degree 0 in the left boundary of e. Again, we are not measuring the degree to which x is already (statively) eaten by the time that e begins – we are measuring the degree to which x qua type "half an apple" gets eaten in the left boundary of e, which is another matter altogether.

The eight axioms in (46)–(53) specify the core of what it means for $\mathbf{V}_\delta$ to be an incremental degree function. What follows are various facts that are pertinent to the semantic analyses presented in the next section.

At the outset, it is useful to make explicit a notion of *iterativity* for an individual or event a with respect to a one-place predicate P. We say that a is iterative with respect to P just in case P applies to a and to at least two parts of a (where, in the limiting case, one part could be a itself).

---

[34] See Piñón (1997) for a proposal making use of events and boundary events in an analysis of achievements.

(54)   ▷ *a* is iterative with respect to *P*

$$\mathbf{iter}(a)(P) \overset{\text{def}}{=} P(a) \wedge \exists b \exists c (b \sqsubseteq a \wedge c \sqsubseteq a \wedge \neg(b = c) \wedge P(b) \wedge P(c))$$

If *P* is cumulative, then there is always some *a* with respect to which *P* is iterative:

(55)   ▷ FACT: cumulativity implies iterativity for some *a*

$$\forall P(\mathbf{cum}(P) \rightarrow \exists a(\mathbf{iter}(a)(P)))$$

(56)   ▷ FACT: quantization excludes iterativity for any *a*

$$\forall P(\mathbf{qua}(P) \rightarrow \neg \exists a(\mathbf{iter}(a)(P)))$$

The proofs are immediate from the respective definitions.

Turning to incremental degree functions more specifically, if *O* is quantized and the values of *x* and *d* are fixed, then $\mathbf{V}_\delta$ is not iterative for any *e*:

(57)   ▷ FACT: no iterativity with quantized *O*, fixed *x*, and fixed *d*

$$\forall x \forall O \forall d \forall e (\mathbf{V}_\delta(x)(O)(e) = d \wedge \mathbf{qua}(O)) \rightarrow$$
$$\neg\mathbf{iter}(e)(\lambda e'.\mathbf{V}_\delta(x)(O)(e') = d))$$

PROOF. Abbreviating $\lambda e'.\mathbf{V}_\delta(x)(O)(e') = d$ as $\epsilon(x)(O)(d)$, suppose to the contrary that *e* is iterative with respect to $\epsilon(x)(O)(d)$. Then by the definition of iterativity in (54) there is at least one proper subevent *e'* of *e* such that $\epsilon(x)(O)(d)(e')$ holds. But this is ruled out by strict incrementality in (52), which requires a lower value of the degree argument in this case. Consequently, $\epsilon(x)(O)(d)(e')$ does not hold, and neither does $\mathbf{iter}(e)(\epsilon(x)(O)(d))$.

Observe that the value of the degree argument is fixed in (57). If it is allowed to vary, then the corresponding event predicate may be iterative with respect to some event. This is the case whenever the antecedent of the axiom of strict incrementality in (52) is satisfied:

(58)   ▷ FACT: iterativity with quantized *O*, fixed *x*, and existentially bound *d*

$$\forall x \forall O \forall d \forall d' \forall e \forall e' (\mathbf{V}_\delta(x)(O)(e) = d \wedge \mathbf{V}_\delta(x)(O)(e') = d' \wedge e' \sqsubseteq e \wedge$$
$$\mathbf{qua}(O) \rightarrow$$
$$\mathbf{iter}(e)(\lambda e'.\exists d(\mathbf{V}_\delta(x)(O)(e') = d)))$$

The proof is immediate from the definition of iterativity in (54).

A comment is in order about the result in (57), because it may appear unduly restrictive at first. There are verbs with an incremental theme that seem to allow for iterativity even assuming a fixed degree. For example, it is certainly possible to (completely) read a certain letter more than once, though this appears to be excluded by the fact in (57). Note, though, that the fact in (57) does not prohibit the possibility of multiple readings of a certain letter – what it says is that incremental degree functions are not iterative for any event if *O* is quantized and the value of the degree argument is fixed. For concreteness, imagine an event e that is the sum of two discrete events e' and e'' in each of which one and the same letter is read to degree 1. The fact in (57) affirms that the incremental degree function **read**$_\delta$ cannot apply both to e' and e'' and to e. But what this means is that in order to describe e we need something more than just **read**$_\delta$ – we need to form a (new) event predicate based on **read**$_\delta$ that can apply to (iterative) events like e, for example by means of an iterative operator. Although I do not (for lack of space) define such an iterative operator here, the point here is precisely to restrict the intended interpretation of incremental degree functions to exclude iterativity of this kind in the case of a quantized O and a fixed d.

A relaxed notion of incrementality for either a quantized or cumulative O is captured by the following fact, which states that the value of the degree argument does not decrease in the course of an event:

(59)   ▷ FACT: incrementality

$$\forall x \forall O \forall d \forall d' \forall e \forall e' (V_\delta(x)(O)(e) = d \wedge V_\delta(x)(O)(e') = d' \wedge e' \sqsubseteq e \wedge$$
$$(\textbf{qua}(O) \vee \textbf{cum}(O)) \rightarrow$$
$$d' \leq d)$$

PROOF. There are two cases to consider, depending on whether O is quantized or cumulative. If O is quantized, it suffices to point out that strict incrementality in (52) implies incrementality. If O is cumulative, then by the axiom in (50) the only positive value for the degree argument is 1, which trivially satisfies the consequent.

The next result confirms that if an event predicate based on a degree function is non-unique, O is cumulative, and x and d are existentially bound, then the event predicate is cumulative:

(60)   ▷ FACT: cumulativity with cumulative O and existentially
                                                              bound x and d

$$\forall O (\textbf{nuniq}(\lambda e.\exists d \exists x (V_\delta(x)(O)(e) = d)) \wedge \textbf{cum}(O) \rightarrow$$
$$\textbf{cum}(\lambda e.\exists d \exists x (V_\delta(x)(O)(e) = d)))$$

PROOF. Abbreviating $\lambda e.\exists d \exists x (V_\delta(x)(O)(e) = d)$ as $\epsilon(O)$, it has to be shown that for any e, e' such that $\epsilon(O)(e)$ and $\epsilon(O)(e')$ hold, it follows that $\epsilon(O)(e \oplus e')$ also holds. Given the definition of $\epsilon(O)$, there are (possibly identical) x, x' and (possibly identical) d, d' such that $\epsilon(x)(O)(d)(e)$ and $\epsilon(x')(O)(d')(e')$ hold. By summativity in (49), if d' is less than or equal to d, then $\epsilon(x \oplus x')(O)(d)(e \oplus e')$ holds, otherwise $\epsilon(x \oplus x')(O)(d')(e \oplus e')$. In either case it follows that $\epsilon(O)(e \oplus e')$ holds, which is what needed to be shown.

As a variation on the event predicate in (60), if O is cumulative, existentially binding d and restricting its value to be greater than 0 is tantamount to fixing its value to be 1, hence there is no need to consider the case of a fixed d separately:

(61)   ▷ FACT: no difference between $d > 0$ and $d = 1$ with cumulative O
$\forall O(\mathbf{cum}(O) \rightarrow$
$\lambda e.\exists d \exists x(\mathbf{V}_\delta(x)(O)(e) = d \wedge d > 0) \leftrightarrow \lambda e.\exists x(\mathbf{V}_\delta(x)(O)(e) = 1))$

The proof is immediate from the axiom in (50).

If an event predicate based on an incremental degree function takes a quantized O, an existentially bound x, and a fixed d, then it is quantized:

(62)   ▷ FACT: quantization with quantized O, existentially
                                            bound x, and fixed d
$\forall O \forall d(\mathbf{qua}(O) \rightarrow \mathbf{qua}(\lambda e.\exists x(\mathbf{V}_\delta(x)(O)(e) = d)))$

PROOF. Abbreviating $\lambda e.\exists x(\mathbf{V}_\delta(x)(O)(e) = d)$ as $\epsilon(O)(d)$, suppose to the contrary that $\epsilon(O)(d)$ is *not* quantized. Then there are e, e' such that $e' \sqsubset e$, $\epsilon(O)(d)(e)$, and $\epsilon(O)(d)(e')$ hold. But then (by the definition of $\epsilon(O)(d)$) there are also x, x' such that $\epsilon(x)(O)(d)(e)$ and $\epsilon(x')(O)(d)(e')$ hold. By the axiom in (48) it follows that $x' \sqsubseteq x$ holds, which in turn means that either $x' \sqsubset x$ or $x' = x$ holds. Yet the former is ruled out by the quantization of O, and the latter is excluded by strict incrementality in (52) (since d is fixed). Hence there is no such x', and $\epsilon(O)(d)$ is quantized after all.

As a special case of the fact in (62), the resulting event predicate is also quantized if x is fixed:

(63)   ▷ FACT: quantization with quantized O and fixed x and d
$\forall x \forall O \forall d(\mathbf{qua}(O) \rightarrow \mathbf{qua}(\lambda e.\mathbf{V}_\delta(x)(O)(e) = d))$

The proof is similar to the one for (62), only there is no need to appeal to the axiom in (48).

As a variation on the event predicate in (62), if O is quantized and d is existentially bound, the resulting event predicate is quantized as long as the value of the incremental theme varies:

(64)   ▷ FACT: quantization with quantized O and existentially
                                            bound x and d
$\forall O(\mathbf{qua}(O) \rightarrow \forall x \forall x' \forall d \forall d' \forall e \forall e'((\mathbf{V}_\delta(x)(O)(e) = d \wedge$
$\mathbf{V}_\delta(x')(O)(e') = d' \wedge \neg(e = e')) \rightarrow \neg(x = x') \rightarrow$
$\mathbf{qua}(\lambda e''.\exists d'' \exists x''(\mathbf{V}_\delta(x'')(O)(e'') = d''))))$

PROOF. Abbreviating $\lambda e.\exists d \exists x(\mathbf{V}_\delta(x)(O)(e) = d)$ as $\epsilon(O)$, suppose to the contrary that $\epsilon(O)$ is *not* quantized. Then there are e, e' such that $e' \sqsubset e$, $\epsilon(O)(e)$, and $\epsilon(O)(e')$ hold. But then (by the definition of $\epsilon(O)(d)$) there are also d, d' and x, x' such that $\epsilon(x)(O)(d)(e)$ and $\epsilon(x')(O)(d)(e')$ hold. By the axiom in (48) it follows that $x' \sqsubseteq x$ holds, which in turn means that either $x' \sqsubset x$ or $x' = x$ holds. However, the former is ruled out by the quantization of O, and the latter is excluded by the premise that value of the incremental theme varies. Hence there is no such x', and $\epsilon(O)$ is quantized after all.

As a final result, an event predicate based on an incremental degree function that takes a quantized O, a fixed x, and an existentially bound d is cumulative if it is non-unique and is restricted to pairs of events that are discrete and whose degrees added together are less than or equal to 1 or to pairs of events one of which stands in the part relation to the other, as formalized in (65). This fact is crucial in accounting for the possible atelicity of examples such as those in (1b) and (3b).

(65) $\triangleright$ Fact: cumulativity with quantized O, fixed x, and existentially bound d

$$\forall x \forall O (\text{qua}(O) \wedge \text{nuniq}(\lambda e. \exists d (\mathbf{V}_\delta(x)(O)(e) = d)) \wedge$$
$$\forall d \forall d' \forall e \forall e' (\mathbf{V}_\delta(x)(O)(e) = d \wedge \mathbf{V}_\delta(x')(O)(e') = d' \rightarrow$$
$$(e \wr e' \wedge d + d' \leq 1) \vee (e \sqsubseteq e' \vee e' \sqsubseteq e) \rightarrow$$
$$\text{cum}(\lambda e''. \exists d'' (\mathbf{V}_\delta(x)(O)(e'') = d''))))$$

Proof. Abbreviating $\lambda e. \exists d (\mathbf{V}_\delta(x)(O)(e) = d)$ as $\epsilon(x)(O)$, there are two cases to consider. The first case is to show that for any e, e' such that $\epsilon(x)(O)(e)$, $\epsilon(x)(O)(e')$, $e \wr e'$, and $d + d' \leq 1$ hold, it follows that $\epsilon(x)(O)(e \oplus e')$ holds. But this follows by the axiom in (51), with the value of $d + d'$ for the degree argument. The second case is to show the same for any e, e' such that $\epsilon(x)(O)(e)$, $\epsilon(x)(O)(e')$ and $e \sqsubseteq e'$ or $e' \sqsubseteq e$ hold. If $e \sqsubseteq e'$ holds, then $e \oplus e'$ is e' and the degree argument is d', otherwise $e \oplus e'$ is e and the degree argument is d. Hence $\epsilon(x)(O)(e \oplus e')$ holds here as well.

8.3.1.2 *Applications*   The theory of incremental degree functions presented in the previous sections may be a bit hard to digest at first and may even seem somewhat removed from the down-to-earth aspectual issues posed by data such as those in (1)–(4). The task now is to show how to bring the two together.

As previewed in the opening of section 8.3.1, the idea is to treat the meaning of verbs with an incremental theme as based on incremental degree functions. More precisely, such verbs denote four-place relations between individuals x, descriptions O, degrees d, and events e:

(66)   a. $[_{VP} [_V \text{eat}] [_{NP} \alpha]]$ $\triangleright$ cf. (45a)
        eat $\rightsquigarrow \lambda x \lambda O \lambda d \lambda e. \text{eat}_\delta(x)(O)(e) = d$

      b. $[_{VP} [_V \text{write}] [_{NP} \alpha]]$ $\triangleright$ cf. (45b)
        write $\rightsquigarrow \lambda x \lambda O \lambda d \lambda e. \text{write}_\delta(x)(O)(e) = d$

c. $[_{VP} [_V \text{ read}] [_{NP} \alpha]]$ ▷ cf. (45c)
     read $\rightsquigarrow \lambda x \lambda O \lambda d \lambda e.\textbf{read}_\delta(x)(O)(e) = d$

However, if incremental degree functions form the semantic core of verbs with an incremental theme, there is a small price to pay when it comes to treating semantic composition. The technical obstacle is that since these verbs take both an individual argument x and a predicate argument O for what is syntactically a single incremental theme argument, it is hard to see how a type-driven functional application could be employed to combine the verb with the object NP without first resorting to fancy type-shifting maneuvers. The strategy adopted here is to invoke a special rule of semantic composition for VPs headed by verbs with an incremental theme, formulated as follows:

(67)   1:   If γ is of the form $[_{VP} [_V \alpha] [_{NP} \beta]]$,   ▷ VP semantic rule
       2:      where $[\alpha \rightsquigarrow]$ is of the type $\langle e_O, \langle\langle e_O, t\rangle, \langle e_D, \langle e_E, t\rangle\rangle\rangle\rangle$:
       3:         if $[\beta \rightsquigarrow]$ is of the type $\langle e_O, t\rangle$,
       4:            then $\gamma \rightsquigarrow \lambda d \lambda e.\exists x([\alpha \rightsquigarrow](x)([\beta \rightsquigarrow])(d)(e))$
       5:         and if $[\beta \rightsquigarrow]$ is of the type e_O,
       6:            then $\gamma \rightsquigarrow \lambda d \lambda e.[\alpha \rightsquigarrow](x)(\lambda x'.x' = [\beta \rightsquigarrow])(d)(e)$

The types e_O, e_D, and e_E serve to make clear whether the type e is of the sort of ordinary individuals, degrees, or events. Moreover, a bracketed form such as $[\alpha \rightsquigarrow]$ designates the translation of α in the logical representation language.

Although the rule in (67) may appear involved at first, there is in fact nothing mysterious about it. According to lines (3)–(4), if the object NP is analyzed as a one-place nominal predicate, then it is substituted for O and x is existentially bound. According to lines (5)–(6), if the object NP is analyzed as a term, then it is substituted for one argument of the identity relation, the result of which is in turn substituted for O. In this case, x is free, but this does not pose a concern, because the axiom in (46) has the effect of identifying x with the term representing the object NP.[35]

Since a two-place relation between degrees and events is derived in (67) as the meaning of the VP, a means for discharging the degree argument is necessary. I assume that there are at least two covert ways of achieving this. One is to set the value of the degree argument to 1, thereby maximizing it; another is to existentially quantify over the degree argument, restricting its value to be greater than 0:[36]

---

[35] For lack of space, I do not consider the case where the object NP is quantificational, because the treatment of quantifiers in an event semantics raises a number of issues in its own right.

[36] A third way would be to set the value of the degree argument to be greater than or equal to some contextually fixed value. Indeed, the degree maximizing operator in (68a) might be considered a special instance of the third way, yet for simplicity I treat it as a separate case here.

(68)   a. $[_{\rm VP}\,a]^{/1} \rightsquigarrow \lambda R\lambda e.R(1)(e)$ ▷ degree maximizing operator

       b.   ▷ positive degree binding operator
       $[_{\rm VP}\,a]^{/+} \rightsquigarrow \lambda R\lambda e.\exists d(R(d)(e) \wedge d > 0)$

Other things being equal, the use of the degree-maximizing operator seems to be preferred to that of the positive degree-binding operator. Presumably, this is because the use of the former yields a stronger meaning than that of the latter, and so unless there is information to the contrary, the stronger meaning is to be preferred.[37]

The first derivation to consider is that of the telic VP *eat an apple* in (1a). The object NP *an apple* is treated as a quantized nominal predicate, and the degree-maximizing operator is applied to the ensuing relation between degrees and events. The resulting event predicate is then demonstrably quantized.

(69)   1: $[_{\rm NP}$ an apple$] \rightsquigarrow \lambda x.\mathbf{apple}(x)$ ▷ NP meaning
       2:   $\mathbf{qua(apple)}$ ▷ related axiom
       3:                          ▷ by (66a), (67), and functional conversion
            $[_{\rm VP}\,[_{\rm V}$ eat$]\,[_{\rm NP}$ an apple$]] \rightsquigarrow$
       4:       $\lambda d\lambda e.\exists x(\mathbf{eat}_\delta(x)(\mathbf{apple})(d)(e))$
       5:   $[_{\rm VP}\,[_{\rm V}$ eat$]\,[_{\rm NP}$ an apple$]]^{/1} \rightsquigarrow$ ▷ apply degree maximizer
       6:       $\lambda e.\exists x(\mathbf{eat}_\delta(x)(\mathbf{apple})(1)(e))$
       7:   $\mathbf{qua}(\lambda e.\exists x(\mathbf{eat}_\delta(x)(\mathbf{apple})(1)(e)))$ ▷ by fact in (62)

If, instead, on line 5 of (69) the positive degree-binding operator were applied, by the fact in (64) the resulting event predicate would still be quantized, provided that a different apple is involved in each event in the denotation of the predicate. The derivation of the telic VP *eat a bowl of applesauce* is analogous, assuming that the object NP *a bowl of applesauce* is also analyzed as a quantized nominal predicate.

The derivation of the atelic VP *eat apples* in (2b) is shown in (70), where the object NP *apples* is treated as a cumulative nominal predicate. Although the degree-maximizing operator is applied here as well, recall that by the fact in (61) it would make absolutely no difference if the positive degree-binding operator were applied instead: in either case, the resulting event predicate is cumulative, provided that it is non-unique.

(70)   1: $[_{\rm NP}$ apples$] \rightsquigarrow \lambda x.\mathbf{apples}(x)$ ▷ NP meaning
       2:   $\mathbf{cum(apples)}$ ▷ related axiom

---

[37] Kennedy and Levin (this volume) make a similar point in connection with the preferred telicity of certain degree achievements. It is feasible to view this preference as an instance of the pragmatic principle of maximal informativeness.

3:                                  ▷ by (66a), (67), and functional conversion
   $[_{VP} [_V$ eat$] [_{NP}$ apples$]] \rightsquigarrow$
4:     $\lambda d \lambda e. \exists x(\textbf{eat}_\delta(x)(\textbf{apples})(d)(e))$
5:     $[_{VP} [_V$ eat$] [_{NP}$ apples$]]^{/1} \rightsquigarrow$ ▷ apply degree maximizer
6:     $\lambda e. \exists x(\textbf{eat}_\delta(x)(\textbf{apples})(1)(e))$
7:                                  ▷ by facts in (60) and (61)
   $\textbf{nuniq}(\lambda e. \exists x(\textbf{eat}_\delta(x)(\textbf{apples})(1)(e))) \rightarrow$
8:     $\textbf{cum}(\lambda e. \exists x(\textbf{eat}_\delta(x)(\textbf{apples})(1)(e)))$

Evidently, the analysis of the atelic VP *eat applesauce* from (4b) would be
similar. Note, moreover, that since there is no way to derive a telic reading
of such VPs, the examples in (2a) and (4a) are unacceptable.

The derivation of the atelic VP *ate an apple* in (1b) is displayed in (71). Recall
that the atelic interpretation of this VP requires a specific reading of the object
NP *an apple* (see note 1), in contrast to the telic interpretation, which does
not (cf. 69). For present purposes, all that I need to assume is that the specific
reading is individual-denoting, akin to definite NPs (e.g., *the apple*) in this
respect. As a useful approximation, I take the specific reading of *an apple* to
mean "a certain apple", where *certain* remains unanalyzed. Furthermore, it
is also crucial that the positive degree-binding operator and not the degree-
maximizing operator be used, for otherwise by the fact in (63) the resulting
event predicate would be quantized.

(71)   1:   ▷ NP meaning
      $[_{NP}$ a (certain) apple$] \rightsquigarrow$ **a-certain-apple** (type e_O)
      2:   $[_{VP} [_V$ eat$]$ ▷ by (66a), (67), and functional conversion
      3:     $[_{NP}$ a (certain) apple$]] \rightsquigarrow$
      4:   $\lambda d \lambda e. \textbf{eat}_\delta(x)(\lambda x'.x' = \textbf{a-certain-apple})(d)(e)$
      5:                                  ▷ apply positive degree binder
      $[_{VP} [_V$ eat$] [_{NP}$ a (certain) apple$]]^{/+} \rightsquigarrow$
      6:   $\lambda e. \exists d(\textbf{eat}_\delta(x)(\lambda x'.x' = \textbf{a-certain-apple})(d)(e) \wedge d > 0)$
      7: $\textbf{nuniq}(\lambda e. \exists d$ ▷ by fact in (65)
      8:   $(\textbf{eat}_\delta(x)(\lambda x'.x' = \textbf{a-certain-apple})(d)(e) \wedge d > 0)) \wedge$
      9:   $\forall d \forall d' \forall e \forall e'($
      10:   $\textbf{eat}_\delta(x)(\lambda x'.x' = \textbf{a-certain-apple})(e) = d \wedge$
      11:   $\textbf{eat}_\delta(x')(\lambda x'.x' = \textbf{a-certain-apple})(e') = d' \rightarrow$
      12:   $(e \wr e' \wedge (d + d') \leq 1) \vee (e \sqsubseteq e' \vee e' \sqsubseteq e) \rightarrow$
      13:   $\textbf{cum}(\lambda e. \exists d(\textbf{eat}_\delta(x)(\lambda x'.x' = \textbf{a-certain-apple})(d)(e) \wedge d > 0)))$

The ensuing event predicate is cumulative provided that it is non-unique
and that its denotation is restricted to discrete eating events whose combined
degrees are less than or equal to 1 or to eating events that are contained in

one another. Informally, this means that everything is okay as long as we restrict our attention to discrete events in which the apple in question is partly eaten or to "growing events" in which it is partly eaten. Clearly, the derivation of the atelic reading of the VP *ate a bowl of applesauce* in (3b) would be analogous.

It is an advantage of the present approach that it can treat the aspectual difference between pairs of examples such as (1a)/(1b) and (3a)/(3b) without ambiguity at the lexical level. On Krifka's approach, as far as I can tell, the difference would have to be due to a lexical difference between the thematic relations for the internal argument.

As a final application, I briefly point out that the present theory allows for a straightforward analysis of adverbs of completion in combination with verbs with an incremental theme – at any rate, it is more straightforward than the one offered in Piñón (2005). The basic observation is that adverbs of completion such as *completely*, *partly*, and *half* are acceptable with telic VPs but unacceptable with atelic VPs headed by verbs with an incremental theme:

(72) a.   Rebecca completely ate an apple (in five minutes).

b.   *Rebecca completely ate apples (for thirty minutes).

(73) a.   Rebecca partly ate a bowl of applesauce (in five minutes).

b.   *Rebecca partly ate applesauce (for five minutes).

Focusing on *completely*, the idea is to view it as a kind of overt counterpart of the degree-maximizing operator in (68a), but with the difference that it presupposes that the relation which it applies to may yield degrees greater than 0 but less than 1:[38]

(74) [$_\text{VP}$ completely [$_\text{VP}$ a]]   ▷ cf. (68a)
        completely $\rightsquigarrow \lambda R \lambda e . R(1)(e) \wedge \exists e' \exists d' (R(d')(e') \wedge d' > 0 \wedge d' < 1)$

The presupposition is readily satisfied when the relation that the meaning of *completely* applies to allows for a variety of degrees. This is the case in (72a) and (73a), where a quantized nominal predicate instantiates O of the incremental degree function (recall the axiom of strict incrementality

---

[38] Caudal and Nicolas (2005: 287) state a similar intuition about *completely*. Incidentally, it would be more accurate to embed the presupposition in (74) under a possibility operator, but for simplicity I keep matters extensional here. In Piñón (2005) I argue that adverbs of completion are verb modifiers, whereas *completely* in (74) is treated as a VP modifier. Frankly, it was more crucial to treat adverbs of completion as verb modifiers in my earlier approach than it is now, though the present analysis could be revised to accommodate this view if desired.

in 52). In contrast, the presupposition is not satisfied in (72b) or (73b), where the nominal predicate instantiating O of the incremental degree function is cumulative, due to the fact in (61), since the only positive degree is 1. The analysis of the adverbs *partly* and *half* would involve the same presupposition.

8.3.2 *Back to degree achievements*

At this point, it would be nice to be able to simply apply the analysis developed for verbs with an incremental theme to degree achievements. However, degree achievements differ in a significant respect from verbs with an incremental theme, and so a simple application of the theory developed so far to degree achievements is not feasible. The way in which degree achievements differ from verbs with an incremental theme is not that the former have a degree argument which the latter lack (because the latter also have a degree argument), but rather that the former have (what I will call) an *extent argument* that the latter lack. It is this additional argument, the extent argument, that complicates things in the sense that the degree functions underlying degree achievements need to take it into account. Although it would be feasible to systematically extend the axiomatic treatment developed in section 8.3.1.1 to degree achievements, lack of space prevents me from doing so here. Consequently, the aim of this section is merely to sketch the outlines of such an extension (and so the discussion is significantly less formal), taking *lengthen* as a canonical example.

The degree achievement *lengthen* is analyzed as a five-place relation between individuals x, descriptions O, extents n, degrees d, and events e:

(75) $[_{VP} [_V \text{lengthen}] [_{NP} \alpha] ((\text{by}) [_{NP} \beta])]$
    lengthen $\leadsto \lambda x \lambda O \lambda n \lambda d \lambda e.\textbf{lengthen}_\delta(x)(O)(n)(e) = d$

In order to keep the potentially confusing terminology straight, I emphasize that the extent argument n in (75) corresponds to Kennedy and Levin's degree of change argument (cf. 20b, 24a) and that the degree argument d in (75) has no correspondent in Kennedy and Levin's analysis. Naturally, there is nothing sacred about this terminology and so the extent argument n could well called a "degree of change argument", but then it would be much easier to confound the extent argument n with the degree argument d, which is precisely a distinction that should be kept clear (as previewed in note 16). With this said, the degree function underlying the meaning of *lengthen* in (75) is a function that determines the degree d to which x qua type O is lengthened by extent n in e.

Since the meaning of *lengthen* is not lexically decomposed in (75), it needs to be ensured that the extent argument *n* indeed measures the difference in the length of *x*, which Kennedy and Levin guarantee via the definition of **increase** in (19b) (see also 20b and 24a):

(76)   ▷ Axiom: difference in length is *n* if $d = 1$

$\forall x \forall O \forall n \forall e (\mathbf{lengthen}_\delta(x)(O)(n)(e) = 1 \rightarrow$
$\iota n'(\mathbf{long}(x)(n')(\mathbf{end}(e))) = \iota n''(\mathbf{long}(x)(n'')(\mathbf{beg}(e))) + n)$

In prose, if the degree to which *x* qua type *O* is lengthened by *n* in *e* is 1, then the extent to which *x* is long at the end of *e* is equal to the extent to which *x* is long at the beginning of *e* plus *n*. For example, if the degree to which a rope is lengthened by ten centimeters in *e* is 1, then the extent to which the rope is long at the end of *e* is equal to the extent to which the rope is long at the beginning of *e* plus ten centimeters. Note that this axiom does not apply if *d* is less than 1, because in this case *x* is lengthened to an extent less than *n* in *e*.

The contrasts to be treated below are illustrated in (77)–(79).

(77)   a.   Rebecca lengthened the rope for twenty minutes.   ▷ cf. (8a)

       b.   Rebecca lengthened the rope in twenty minutes.   ▷ cf. (9a)

(78)   a.   *Rebecca lengthened the rope (by) ten centimeters for twenty minutes.

       b.   Rebecca lengthened the rope (by) ten centimeters in twenty minutes.

(79)   a.   Rebecca lengthened ropes (by) ten centimeters for twenty minutes.

       b.   *Rebecca lengthened ropes (by) ten centimeters in twenty minutes.

As seen in (77), if the extent argument is not overtly expressed, the VP *lengthen the rope* allows for both an atelic and a telic interpretation. In (78), in contrast, if the extent argument is overtly specified, only a telic reading of the VP is acceptable (excluding an iterative interpretation). Finally, as shown in (79), if the object NP is the bare plural *ropes*, then the VP is atelic even if the extent argument is overtly specified (as expected, it is also atelic if the extent argument is not overtly expressed).

The atelic VP in (77a) is analyzed as follows:

(80)   a.   [$_{\mathrm{VP}}$ lengthen the rope]^{atel} ⤳   ▷ cf. (77a)
            $\lambda e.\exists n(\mathbf{lengthen}_\delta(x)(\lambda x'.x' = \mathbf{the\text{-}rope})(n)(e) = 1)$

b.   ▷ FACT

$\mathbf{nuniq}(\lambda e.\exists n(\mathbf{lengthen}_\delta(x)(\lambda x'.x' = \text{the-rope})(n)(e) = 1)) \rightarrow$
$\forall e'\forall e''($
$\exists n'(\mathbf{lengthen}_\delta(x)(\lambda x'.x' = \text{the-rope})(n')(e') = 1) \wedge$
$\exists n''(\mathbf{lengthen}_\delta(x)(\lambda x'.x' = \text{the-rope})(n'')(e'') = 1) \rightarrow$
$\qquad e' \wr e'' \rightarrow$
$\mathbf{cum}(\lambda e.\exists n(\mathbf{lengthen}_\delta(x)(\lambda x'.x' = \text{the-rope})(n)(e) = 1))$

The event predicate in (80a) denotes the set of events in which the degree to which the rope is lengthened by some extent is 1. Since n is existentially quantified over, its value may vary with the event chosen. This predicate is cumulative as long as it is non-unique and its denotation is restricted to discrete events.[39] Accordingly, the sum of two such events is also an event in which the degree to which the rope is lengthened by some extent is 1.[40]

The analysis of the telic VP in (77b) differs from the previous one in that the value of the extent argument is implicitly fixed:

(81) a. [$_{VP}$ lengthen the rope]^{tel} $\rightsquigarrow$ ▷ cf. (77b)
$\qquad \lambda e.\mathbf{lengthen}_\delta(x)(\lambda x'.x' = \text{the-rope})(n)(e) = 1$

    b. $\mathbf{qua}(\lambda e.\mathbf{lengthen}_\delta(x)(\lambda x'.x' = \text{the-rope})(n)(e) = 1)$ ▷ FACT

The event predicate in (81a) denotes the set of events in which the degree to which the rope is lengthened by a particular extent n is 1. This predicate is quantized because the value of n is implicitly fixed and hence no proper subevent of such events is also an event in which the degree to which the rope is lengthened by n is 1. Rather, in any proper subevent either the extent is less than n or the degree is less than 1 (or both).

The VP in (78b) differs from the one in (77b) in that the extent argument is overtly specified, but this naturally also gives rise to a telic interpretation:

(82) a. [$_{VP}$ lengthen the rope (by) ten centimeters] $\rightsquigarrow$ ▷ cf. (78b)
$\qquad \lambda e.\mathbf{lengthen}_\delta(x)(\lambda x'.x' = \text{the-rope})(\text{10-cm})(e) = 1$

    b. $\mathbf{qua}(\lambda e.\mathbf{lengthen}_\delta(x)(\lambda x'.x' = \text{the-rope})(\text{10-cm})(e) = 1)$ ▷ FACT

The event predicate in (82a) is quantized and denotes the set of events in which the degree to which the rope is lengthened by ten centimeters is 1. This analysis excludes an atelic interpretation of the VP, ruling out the sentence in (78a).

Finally, the VP in (79a) receives the following analysis:

(83) a. [$_{VP}$ lengthen ropes (by) ten centimeters] $\rightsquigarrow$ ▷ cf. (79a)
$\qquad \lambda e.\exists x(\mathbf{lengthen}_\delta(x)(\text{ropes})(\text{10-cm})(e) = 1)$

---

[39] The restriction to discrete events ultimately makes matters easier because the counting of any extent more than once should be avoided.

[40] The proof of this fact and those in (81b) and (82b) requires certain axioms not introduced here. Even so, the hope is that the results are clear enough on intuitive grounds.

b. $\text{nuniq}(\lambda e.\exists x(\text{lengthen}_\delta(x)(\text{ropes})(\text{10-cm})(e) = 1)) \rightarrow$ ▷ FACT
      $\forall x'\forall x''\forall e'\forall e''($
          $\text{lengthen}_\delta(x')(\text{ropes})(\text{10-cm})(e') = 1 \wedge$
          $\text{lengthen}_\delta(x'')(\text{ropes})(\text{10-cm})(e'') = 1 \wedge e' \wr e'' \rightarrow$
          $x' \wr x'' \rightarrow$
          $\text{cum}(\lambda e.\exists x(\text{lengthen}_\delta(x)(\text{ropes})(\text{10-cm})(e) = 1)))$

The event predicate in (83a) denotes the set of events in which the degree to which ropes are lengthened by ten centimeters is 1. Interestingly, this predicate is cumulative as long as it is non-unique and a restriction to discrete events implies that no ropes are lengthened more than once. Since this analysis does not allow for a telic reading of the VP, the sentence in (79b) is excluded.

8.4 Conclusion

With the title "aspectual composition with degrees" I allude to an aspectual approach in which the notion of the degree of realization of an event type plays a central role. In this chapter, I have proposed how such an approach might look in the context of an event semantics, applying it in greater detail to verbs with an incremental theme and in lesser detail to degree achievements. In a nutshell, it is an attempt to take seriously the idea that such verbs are gradable. The present account differs from Krifka's in that the latter lacks degrees altogether and as a result can express the notion of partial realization in only a roundabout way at best. Somewhat ironically, although the present account shares a degree-based spirit with Kennedy and Levin's approach, it mischievously recasts their degrees as extents, hence it also ends up having degrees where the latter lacks them. Even so, the main contrast with Kennedy and Levin's approach is undoubtedly that the present account makes the degree functions underlying the semantics of verbs with an incremental theme and degree achievements sensitive to the *description* of the internal argument as well, whereas the latter lacks this feature.

Acknowledgments

I am grateful to Fabienne Martin for helpful discussions of these and related issues and for her general encouragement over the months and years. I also appreciate Chris Kennedy and Louise McNally's forbearance as editors. This work was supported by the Hungarian Scientific Research Fund (OTKA TS 049873).

9

Manner modification of state verbs

GRAHAM KATZ

9.1 Introduction

The analysis of manner adverbs as event predicates, first proposed by Davidson (1967) and argued for extensively by Parsons (1990), has become a standard part of the received semantic cannon (Kamp and Reyle 1993; Chierchia and McConnell-Ginet 2000). On this now-traditional analysis, a sentence like (1a) is analyzed at some level of representation as in (1b).

(1) a. John kissed Mary passionately.

b. $\exists e[\text{kiss}(e, \textbf{John}, \textbf{Mary}) \wedge \textbf{passionate}(e) \wedge \textbf{past}(e)]$

Manner adverbs are taken to be event predicates in the guise of predicate modifiers (with predicational meaning essentially identical to that of the corresponding adjective). The adverb *passionately*, for example, is typically assigned the denotation in (2).

(2) $\lambda P \lambda e[P(e) \wedge \textbf{passionate}(e)]$

Such an account appealingly explains the scopelessness and conjunctive meaning of manner adverbs, makes available a straightforward treatment of event anaphora, and solves a number of other puzzles for the semantic treatment of modification.

The Davidsonian analysis presents a number of puzzles for researchers concerned with the syntax–semantics interface, however, such as how a reasonable mapping from syntax to semantics can provide for the additional underlying event argument. In her work on voice, Kratzer (1994) proposes that the event variable be associated with a specific functional projection in the syntax. The basic proposal (discussed at some length by Tenny 2000) is that (1a) has a structure like that in (3).

(3) $[\text{John}_1 \ [_{\text{TP}} \ \text{past} \ [_{\text{EventP}} \ t_1 \ [_{\text{Event}} \ e \ [_{\text{VP}} \ \text{kiss Mary}]] \ \text{passionately}]]]$

This proposal has been taken up by much related syntactic work (Travis 1994; Chomsky 1995; Harley 1995; van Hout 1996; van Hout and Roeper 1997).

One of the pleasing features of such an analysis is the reconciliation between restrictive accounts of the syntax of modification, which involve a strict association of syntactic category with modifier class (Alexiadou 1997; Cinque 1999; and others), and semantically well-grounded analyses of the type adopted by Wyner (1998b) and Ernst (1984, 2000), in which the distribution of the modifiers is derived from their semantic properties. On the account illustrated in (4) the various semantic types of modifiers are closely linked to a specific syntactic position.

(4) a. John probably kissed Mary passionately.

    b. [John$_1$ [probably [$_{TP}$ past [$_{EventP}$ t_1 [$_{Event}$ e [$_{VP}$ kiss Mary]] passionately]]]]

Manner adverbials such as *passionately* adjoin to the EventP and are interpreted as event predicates, while modal adverbs such as *probably* adjoin to the TP and are interpreted as propositional operators.

This treatment also provides the basis for an account of one of the most well known – if less well studied – facts about manner adverbs: the fact that they are restricted from modifying state verbs. The incompatibility between manner adverbs and state verbs, illustrated in (5), has long been known (Harris 1968; Jackendoff 1972) and has often been taken to be one of the distinguishing features of this class of verbs (Vendler 1967; Dowty 1979; Hinrichs 1985).

(5) a. *John resembled Sue slowly.

    b. *She desired a raise enthusiastically.

    c. *They hate us revoltingly.

Following suggestions of Davidson (1967), Galton (1984), Löbner (1988), and Sandstrøm (1993), it has been argued by Katz (1995, 1997, 2000, 2003) and more recently by Maienborn (2003, 2005) that this incompatibility follows from a difference in argument structure between state and event verbs, the fundamental difference being that event verbs have an extra semantic argument position – the event argument – that state verbs lack (see Kratzer 1995 for a slightly different formulation). This semantic contrast is projected into the syntax, with consequences for adverbial licensing.

The claim is that syntactic structure of state sentences and event sentences differ slightly. The syntactic analysis of (6a), for example, is taken to be something like (6b), lacking the EventP projection.

(6) a. John loves Mary.

    b. [John$_1$ [$_{TP}$ pres [$_{VP}$ t_1 love Mary]]]

Manner adverbs, then, have no appropriate projection to adjoin to, and this accounts for the restriction on their use with state verbs as well as for the fact that only modifiers that adjoin "above" the EventP – temporal adverbs, modal adverbs, evaluative adverbs, and the like – can combine with state verbs. This syntactic contrast is motivated by a number of distinctions between event sentences and state sentences which have been discussed at length in the above-cited work. It also provides a principled explanation for the fact that the set of adverbs that appear with state verbs is a proper subset of the set of adverbs that appear with event verbs (see Katz 2003 for extensive discussion).

There are, however, a number of cases in which manner modifiers – those taken on the Davidsonian account to be event predicates – do seem to appear with state verbs. A selection of these is given in (7).

(7)   a.   Peter sleeps soundly.

   b.   Steve holds his bag tightly.

   c.   John lies quietly on the floor.

   d.   Peter knew French well.

   e.   Lisa firmly believed that James was innocent.

   f.   Mary loves Max passionately.

Such cases would appear to counterexemplify the account of the state verb/event verb contrast sketched above, raising doubt about the claim that state verbs and event verbs have different argument structures and different syntactic representations and thus about the account of the facts in (5).

In this chapter we will discuss the issues raised by these data. In particular we will address the claims which have been made that state verbs must, like event verbs, be provided with a Davidsonian-style argument (Parsons 1990, 2000; Landman 2000; and Mittwoch 2005). On this kind of "Neo-Davidsonian" analysis, which has been argued for explicitly by Parsons (1990) and Higginbotham (1986), all verbs are taken to have an associated eventuality argument (Bach 1986). So the state sentence (7f) would, on the neo-Davidsonian approach, be given an analysis like that illustrated in (8).

(8) $\exists s\,[\mathbf{love}(s, \mathbf{Mary}, \mathbf{Max}) \wedge \mathbf{passionate}(s) \wedge \mathbf{pres}(s)]$

In what follows we will evaluate the arguments for such an analysis of the manner modifiers of state verbs. The chapter is structured as follows. First we will clarify the frequent confusion about the relevant class of verbs, making clear what is meant by the term "stative verb." Then we will discuss the class of manner modifiers, reviewing the arguments for the Davidsonian event and evaluating the empirical claims that these arguments can be extended to "underlying states." We discuss a very interesting case of subsective modification, which we show to be a case of pure relational modification. We then discuss the lexical selectivity and idiosyncratic meaning of much putative manner modification of state verbs, and speculate that this is indicative of a certain kind of idiomaticity. In the central empirical part of the chapter, we observe that many of the adverbs that appear to be manner modifiers in (7) are not manner modifiers at all, but a kind of degree modifier. Noting that this manner/degree polysemy appears to be quite general, we discuss the semantics of degree modification and the relationship between manner and degree modifiers. We will see that the fine structure of the semantics of degree modification proposed by Kennedy and McNally (2005) is reflected in the semantic properties of these adverbial modifiers. Finally, we sketch an account of event-related modification associated with individual level predicates (in the sense of Carlson 1977) and related to Chierchia's (1995) analysis of inherent genericity.

9.2 Background

9.2.1 *State verbs*

We are concerned with a contrast between the class of event verbs and the class of state verbs, so let us be clear about which verbs we are calling state verbs. Besides the grammatically special *have* and *be*, we can list: *appear, appreciate, believe, belong, concern, consist, contain, depend, desire, equal, hate, hear, imagine, involve, know, like, love, matter, mean, need, own, owe, perceive, possess, prefer, realize, recognize, remember, resemble, see, seem, smell, taste, tend, think, understand, want,* and *wish.*[1] These verbs share a number of syntactic and semantic properties (see Sag 1973, Dowty 1979, and especially Hinrichs 1985 for extensive discussion). To illustrate, we see in (9) that, without additional context, the state verb *appreciate* is acceptable in simple present tense (9a), but not in the progressive (9b) or the *wh*-cleft construction (9c), while in (10) the event verb *kiss* has the complementary distribution:[2]

(9)   a.   John appreciates Mary.

     b.   *John is appreciating Mary.

     c.   *What John does is appreciate Mary.

---

[1] This list adapted from an online learner grammar of English (www.myenglishteacher.net).
[2] It is well known that (10a) can be used felicitously to describe a habit or give an "on the scene" report. These kinds of uses we set aside here (but see Cowper 1998 and Smith 1991).

(10) a. ??John kisses Mary.

  b. John is kissing Mary.

  c. What John did was kiss Mary.

Verbs that behave like *appreciate* in the above environments will be taken to be state verbs and those that behave like *kiss* will be taken to be event verbs. If the claim we made in the introduction about the state verb/event verb contrast is correct, then we expect manner adverbs to appear only with *kiss*-like verbs and not with *appreciate*-like verbs.

It should be pointed out that a number of the verbs listed above (and appearing in 7) have eventive uses as well as stative uses. This can be illustrated with the verb *think*: when used in the progressive (as in 11b) or as part of a *wh*-cleft (as in 11c) it has an eventive reading, while when used in the simple present tense (as in 11a) it has a stative reading.

(11) a. John thinks that the sky is blue.   (stative)

  b. John is thinking about Mary.   (eventive)

  c. What John did was think about Mary.   (eventive)

As expected, on the eventive readings *think* is compatible with manner adverbial modification while on the stative readings it is not:

(12) a. ??John thinks worriedly that the sky is blue.

  b. John was thinking worriedly about Mary.

  c. What John did was think worriedly about Mary.

We will uniformly set aside the non-stative reading of such verbs. What is of interest to us, then, is not the reading of (7f) on which *love* is taken to mean something like "make love to," but rather the true state reading, in which the truth of (7f) depends on their being a certain mental attitude that Mary has toward Max.

We are also uninterested in the frequently miscategorized verbs *sleep*, *hold*, and *wait* (which Maienborn 2005 has confusingly termed "state" verbs). While these may seem to share many semantic features with statives, they do not behave grammatically as such, as indicated in (13):

(13) a. ??He sleeps.

  b. He was sleeping.

  c. What he did was sleep.

These verbs appear naturally with manner adverbs, as we saw in (7a) and (7b), but this is not of interest to us here, as we fully accept that these verbs have a Davidsonian argument. More problematic, and less readily dismissed, is the *sit-stand-lie* class, which Dowty (1979) calls "interval statives." These clearly have both stative and eventive readings (depending, apparently, on the agentivity of the subject):

(14) a. New Orleans lies at the mouth of the Mississippi.

     b. *What New Orleans does is lie at the mouth of the Mississippi.

     c. *New Orleans is lying at the mouth of the Mississippi.

(15) a. ?John lies on the floor.

     b. What John did was lie on the floor.

     c. John is lying on the floor.

In contrast to the eventive/stative contrast of *think*-type verbs, these verbs can be modified by manner adverbials on both the stative and on the eventive readings:

(16) a. John is lying quietly on the floor.

     b. New Orleans lies quietly at the mouth of the Mississippi.

(17) a. John is clinging tenuously to the rock.

     b. The city of Brunate clings tenuously to the hillside.

It is not clear whether this indicates ambiguity, or whether the stative interpretations in (16b) and (17b) are some sort of metaphorical extension of the event usage with concomitant metaphorical shift of the adverb meaning (Schäfer 2002).

Leaving aside modifiers of non-core state verbs and focusing on the class of core state verbs such as *love*, *know*, *own*, and *consist of*, which express psychological, legal, or physical states, we are left with the following cases of manner-modified stative verbs:

(18) a. Peter knew French well.

     b. Lisa firmly believed that James was innocent.

     c. Mary loves Max passionately.

Our central question, then, is whether the cooccurrence of such core state verbs with manner adverbs indicates that these state verbs have a "Davidsonian" argument. To address this, we turn to a brief discussion of manner adverbials and review why a Davidsonian analysis of event verb manner modification is an appealing one.

9.2.2 *Manner adverbials*

The class of manner adverbs is fairly well defined, both syntactically and semantically. Jackendoff (1972) distinguishcd manncr adverbs as a subclass of the verb phrase adverbs, those that appear sentence-finally but not sentence-initially. This distinguishes them from modal and speech act adverbs such as *possibly* or *frankly* and from temporal and locative adverbials such as *yesterday* and *in Rome*. Syntactically, McConnell-Ginet (1982) takes manner adverbs to be not only associated with the VP but to be VP-internal. Clear cases of manner adverbs are such adverbs as *quickly, slowly, carefully, violently, loudly,* and *tightly*. Additionally, such prepositional phrases as *with all his might* and *in a careful manner* as well as instrumentals such as *with a knife* can also be taken to be a sort of manner modifier. We should note that many manner adverbs exhibit a limited type of regular polysemy (Jackendoff 1972), having a factive speaker-oriented meaning when sentence-initial and their more standard manner reading sentence-finally. This as illustrated in (19).

(19)   a.   Disgustingly, Peter cleaned the fish in the sink.

       b.   Peter cleaned the fish in the sink disgustingly.

Although we will be concerned only with the manner reading here, we will discuss another sort of polysemy below, which may be related.

Semantically, manner adverbials are distinguished by a set of entailment properties (Davidson 1967; Parsons 1990). One of these is their scopelessness. As illustrated in (20), the order in which the adverbials appear doesn't bear on the interpretation of the sentence: (20a), (20b), and (20c) are synonymous.

(20)   a.   Brutus stabbed Caesar with a knife violently in the chest.

       b.   Brutus stabbed Caesar in the chest violently with a knife.

       c.   Brutus stabbed Caesar violently in the chest with a knife.

Additionally, manner modifiers have conjunctive interpretations, meaning that they can be dropped from a sentence, preserving its truth. If (20a) is true, so are (21a), (21b), and (21c).

(21)   a.   Brutus stabbed Caesar violently in the chest.

       b.   Brutus stabbed Caesar with a knife.

       c.   Brutus stabbed Caesar.

This might seem to indicate that manner adverbial modification is simple intersective predicate modification (if something is a red book, it is red and it is a book). Crucially, however, the truth of (21a) and (21b) does not guarantee the truth of (20a) as would typically be the case for intersective modifiers (if something is red and it is a book, it is a red book). Intuitively, this is because (21a) and (21b) might refer to two different events: a violent stabbing in the chest (that was not done with a knife) and a stabbing with a knife (that was not violent). These three properties – which Landman dubbed "Permutation," "Drop," and "Non-Entailment" – characterize true Davidsonian manner modification, and show (as Parsons has argued extensively) that they cannot be treated as simply intersective predicate modification.

On the Davidsonian account, adverbial modifiers are taken to be event predicates which combine as co-predicates of the verb. How this modification proceeds, whether via a process of event-identification (Higginbotham 2000) or simple functional application (Parsons 1990) will not concern us here. On any Davidsonian account, the logical representation of (20a) is something like the following:

(22) $\exists e[\textbf{stabbing}(e, \textbf{b}, \textbf{c}) \wedge \textbf{violent}(e) \wedge \textbf{in-the-chest}(e) \wedge$
$\textbf{with-a-knife}(e)]$

One of the central appeals of Davidsonianism is that elementary facts about first order logic appear to describe exactly the semantic behavior of manner adverbial modifiers analyzed in this way. Given the analysis in (22), it is clear that the order of combination does not matter. Furthermore, since (22) entails both (23a) and (23b) – the analyses of (21a) and (21b) respectively – but is not entailed by them, it is clear why Drop and Non-Entailment hold.

(23) a. $\exists e[\textbf{stabbing}(e, \textbf{b}, \textbf{c}) \wedge \textbf{violent}(e) \wedge \textbf{in-the-chest}(e)]$

b. $\exists e[\textbf{stabbing}(e, \textbf{b}, \textbf{c}) \wedge \textbf{with-a-knife}(e)]$

The fact that the properties of Permutation, Drop, and Non-Entailment follow directly from Davidson's assumption that verbs and manner adverbials are event predicates is certainly strong evidence for the account.

Turning this around, Parsons (1990, 2000), Landman (2000), and Mittwoch (2005) have all suggested that if sentences exhibit this trio of Davidsonian properties, then these sentences should be given a Davidsonian analysis. Landman, for example, bases his argument for the Davidsonian analysis of the verb *know* on what he takes to be the entailments associated with example (24).

(24) I know John well by face from the television.

Specifically, Landman claims that (24) entails each of (25a–c) – the "Permutations," and each of (26a–c) – the "Drops," and furthermore that the conjunction of (27b) and (27c) does not entail (27a) – the "Non-Entailment."

(25) a. I know John by face well from television.

b. I know John from television well by face.

c. I know John from television by face well.

(26) a. I know John by face from television.

b. I know John by face.

c. I know John.

(27) a. I know John by face from a party.

b. I know John by face.

c. I know John from a party.

If these claims are correct, the argument is a very strong one for providing this state verb (and perhaps state verbs in general) with an underlying Davidsonian state argument. In the following section, we will evaluate these claims.

9.2.3 *Modifiers of state verbs*

Typically, of course, modifiers of state verbs fail to evidence the Davidsonian entailment patterns. Consider, for example, (28) in which we have a doubly modified *love*.

(28) a. John loves Mary quietly with all his heart.

b. John loves Mary quietly.

c. John loves Mary with all his heart.

Clearly there is Drop, since (28a) entails (28b) and (28c). But since these modifiers fail to exhibit Non-Entailment – (28b) and (28c) together clearly do entail (28a) – they can be treated simply as predicate modifiers. A sketch of the interpretation of *quietly* is given in (29).

(29) $[\![quietly]\!] = \lambda P \lambda x [P(x) \wedge x \text{ is quiet about } {}^{\wedge}P(x)]$

On such an analysis, the modifier restricts the extension of the predicate subsectively: the set of individuals who love Mary quietly is a subset of those who love Mary, as is the set of individuals who love Mary with all their heart. And the set of individuals who love Mary quietly with all their heart is simply the intersection of these two sets, as standard predicate-modificational accounts would predict (Thomason and Stalnaker 1973).

Returning to (24), consider first the permutation facts: of the permutations given in (25) only (25a) seems perfectly natural; (25c) is quite awkward and (25b) is also somewhat degraded. Of course adverbial-ordering restrictions of this sort need not necessarily reflect any deep syntactic or semantic facts, and might reasonably be given a pragmatic or even prosodic account (Costa 1997). The more semantic Drop and Non-Entailment facts are clearly more central to the argument. It should be pointed out, incidentally, that the Drop facts are primary, since Non-Entailment without Drop doesn't tell us much; Non-Entailment is to be expected if there is no Drop.

Unfortunately for Landman, the modifiers in (24) do not appear to genuinely have the Drop property. While it might be the case that (24) entails both (26a) and (26b), it is fairly clear that neither (26a) nor (26b) entails (26c). To know someone by face from television is not to know that person. It would simply be false for me to claim that I know Peter Jennings or David Letterman, although I know them both well by face from TV. If you know somebody, you typically know his or her name and some significant facts about that person. But you may know somebody by face without knowing much of anything about the person. The adverbial *by face*, then, appears to be a type of non-intersective modifier which has particular, lexically-specific entailments. We will have more to say about such modifiers below, suggesting that these readings are, in some sense "collocational." Note that when the modifier *by face* combines with an event verb, it is droppable – the entailment from (30a) to (30b) certainly goes through.

(30) a. John recognized Bill by face.

     b. John recognized Bill.

This indicates that there is a qualitative semantic difference between state verb modification and event verb modification, even for modifiers such as *by face* that appear with both types of predicates.

In contrast to *by face*, the modifiers *well* and *from a party* do seem be droppable in (24). The fact that it is possible to drop *well* in (31) but not *slightly* in (32) shows us that the droppability is tied to the lexical semantics of this adverb.

(31) a. I know John well.

     b. I know John.

(32) a. I know John slightly.

     b. I know John.

It certainly doesn't indicate that *well* is associated with an event predicate but *slightly* is not.[3] As we shall see shortly, standard treatments of degree adverbial

---

[3] An analogy might be drawn with such adjectival modifiers as *current* and *proven* which share the syntactic distribution of the non-intersective *former* and *alleged* (Siegel 1976a), i.e. their inability to

modification, which do not involve Davidsonian predication, make exactly the right predictions for (31) and (32), and for *well* in (24) as well.

Although the modifier *from television* is clearly droppable in (24), the precise semantics of these adverbs makes it quite dubious that it is an event predicate. Such *from*-modifiers have a fairly broad distribution, appearing not only with verbs but also with nouns:

(33) a. I remember you from our dance class.

  b. My coat smells very smoky from the bar last night.

  c. I recognized you from the way you walk.

  d. John owes Bill money from the last time they were out.

  e. We have free tickets from when the game was rained out.

  f. We just got our prize from when we won the competition.

(34) a. The debris from when the bomb exploded is still being picked up.

  b. I tripped over one of the bottles from last night on the way to the john.

In all cases, the *from*-modifier appears to have a general explanatory character. Thus (33a) seems to mean something like that our being at a dance class is causally related to the fact that I remember you. Like other causal clauses, *from*-modifiers are factive, and thus droppable (Kiparsky and Kiparsky 1971).[4] Whether the causal relation is an event relation is, of course, the subject of hot debate (see, for example, Peterson (1997). There is much evidence that at least *because*-clauses relate propositional meanings, not event descriptions (Johnston 1994).

It is not at all clear, then, that (24) indeed provides evidence for the Davidsonian account of the verb *know*. Equally dubious are a number of similar cases in which modifiers of state verbs appear to evidence Davidsonian-like

---

appear in post-copular predicate position, but which are not non-intersective, at least inasmuch as they can be dropped. An alleged murder may not be a murder, but a proven murder is certainly a murder.

  [4] While clearly factive modifiers can be dropped preserving truth, this is quite obviously a somewhat different issue, again tied to lexical semantics. The fact that the adverb *regrettably*, for example, can be dropped is not a fact about speaker-oriented propositional modifiers in general, but about the lexical semantics of the adverb. This can be illustrated by contrasting *regrettably* with *hopefully* – there being entailment from (ia) to (ib) but none from (iia) to (iib).

(i) a. Regrettably, Katrin doesn't like onions.

  b. Katrin doesn't like onions.

(ii) a. Hopefully, Anke will make kale.

  b. Anke will make kale.

entailment patterns. Mittwoch (2005), for example, suggests that (35a) entails (35b) and (35c), but that (35b) and (35c) taken together do not entail (35a).

(35) a. Ann resembles Beth uncannily in facial expression.

      b. Ann resembles Beth uncannily.

      c. Ann resembles Beth in facial expression.

      d. Ann resembles Beth.

While it is certainly true that (35b) and (35c) taken together do not entail (35a) and it might appear that (35a) would entail (35b–d), closer inspection calls this latter fact into question. If the only thing that Ann and Beth have in common is their facial expression – say Ann is tall, Beth short; Ann blonde, and Beth brunette – we would typically take (35a) to be true, but would certainly say that (35b) and (35d) are false.

Next we will examine a case in which adverbial modifiers of a state verb clearly do exhibit the Davidsonian pattern. Mittwoch (2005) points out that the sentences in (36) have all three of the Davidsonian properties: Permutation, Drop, and Non-Entailment. As she notes, (36a) and (36b) are synonymous, each entails both (36c) and (36d), and neither is entailed by the conjunction of (36c) and (36d).

(36) a. Ann is related to Beth by blood on her mother's side.

      b. Ann is related to Beth on her mother's side by blood.

      c. Ann is related to Beth by blood.

      d. Ann is related to Beth on her mother's side.

Beth may, after all, be Ann's mother's sister-in-law and Ann's father's sister. These examples raise interesting and important issues.[5] In particular what they point out is that there is true relation modification (as discussed by

---

[5] Parsons (1990) discussed cases like (i) which are in many ways similar.

(i)   a. The door is connected to the frame at the base with a chain.

      b. The door is connected to the frame with a chain.

      c. The door is connected to the frame at the base.

He notes that such examples typically contain resultative adjectival predicates and suggests the possibility that the modifiers are (covertly) applied to these associated event predicates. Whether this is correct or not, we should note that the argument Mittwoch (2005) raises against it is flawed. While she rightly points out that (ii) doesn't entail an illegal parking event (the actual parking might have been perfectly legal – what was illegal was the leaving the car there so long), what she overlooks is that *illegal* and *in front of my house* themselves have simple intersective meanings.

(ii)   The car is illegally parked in front of my house.

(iii) a. The car is illegally parked.

       b. The car is parked in front of my house.

McConnell-Ginet 1982). There is certainly no question that relations are objects in the domain of semantic interpretation. Transitive verbs and adjectives (and relational nouns) clearly denote relations, and relations can clearly have properties. My suggestion, then, is that the modifiers in (36) are, essentially, modifying a relation.

Let me give a mathematical example. We are familiar with a number of abstract properties that formal relations can have, such as transitivity, symmetry, reflexivity, and so on. These are second-order properties of relations. We are also familiar with the notion of a subrelation. It is, then, easy to define the notion of a relational modifier to be a function that takes a relation to a subrelation that has a given property. In (37) I specify (in set-of-pairs notation) two relations on the domain {a, b, c}. R1 has the property of being symmetric and R2 has the property of being transitive.

(37)   R1: $\{\langle a\ b\rangle, \langle b\ a\rangle, \langle a\ c\rangle, \langle c\ a\rangle\}$
        R2: $\{\langle a\ b\rangle, \langle b\ c\rangle, \langle a\ c\rangle\}$

Note that *a* stands both in a symmetric relation to *b* and in a transitive relation to *b*, but not in a symmetric transitive relation to *b*. We can define the "modifying" operators **sym** and **trans** as follows:

(38)   a.   **trans**(R) = the $R' \subseteq R$ such that R' is transitive and there is no transitive R'' such that $R' \subset R'' \subseteq R$

        b.   **sym**(R) = the $R' \subseteq R$ such that R' is symmetric and there is no symmetric R'' such that $R' \subset R'' \subseteq R$

It is easy to see that these modifiers have the Davidsonian properties Permutation, Drop, and Non-Entailment. If we let $R0 = R1 \cup R2 = \{\langle a\ b\rangle, \langle b\ a\rangle, \langle a\ c\rangle, \langle c\ a\rangle, \langle b\ c\rangle\}$ we see that **trans**$(R0) = \{\langle a\ b\rangle, \langle b\ c\rangle, \langle a\ c\rangle\} = R2$ and **sym**$(R0) = \{\langle a\ b\rangle, \langle b\ a\rangle, \langle a\ c\rangle, \langle c\ a\rangle\} = R1$; so that **trans**$(R0) \cap$ **sym**$(R0) = \{\langle a\ b\rangle, \langle a\ c\rangle\}$ but **trans**(**sym**$(R0)$) = **sym**(**trans**$(R0)$) = {}. Clearly there is no event predication involved, however.

Returning to (36), the suggestion is that here too we have pure relation modification. Whether two individuals are related is determined by the existence of (chains of) two sorts of events – conceptions and marriages.[6] For *x* to be related to *y* is, in general, for there be a chain of conceptions or marriages that relate *x* to *y* – I am related to my cousin Chris because the

---

These adverbs do not exhibit Non-Entailment: (ii) entails (iiia) and (iiib); but (iiia) and (iiib) together also entail (ii). Anything that is illegally parked and is parked in front of my house is illegally parked in front of my house.

[6] Of course this is idealizing slightly – we must speak of conceptions that have led to a birth and of marriages that have not ended in divorce. There are also issues of adoption to consider. As none of this affects the central argument we will ignore these issues.

person who conceived me was conceived by the person who conceived the person who conceived Chris. This relation has certain properties, based on the properties that this chain of events has. I'm related to Chris on my father's side because one of the individuals involved in the relevant conception events was my father, and I'm related to Chris by blood because none of the relevant events is a marriage.

The modifiers *by blood, by marriage, maternally, paternally, on his father's side*, and so on, specify the type of relation explicitly by specifying what properties these relevant events have. In general, if the events in the chains are only conceptions, it is a *blood* relation, if the chain includes *x*'s mother, it is a *maternal* relation, if the chain includes a marriage it is a relation *by marriage*. The modifiers, then, specify a (second-order) property of the personal relation, as indicated in (39).

(39) a. $[\![by\ blood]\!] : \lambda R\lambda y\lambda x[R(x, y)\wedge$ a set of conception events relates x to $y]$

 b. $[\![on\ her\ mother's\ side]\!] : \lambda R\lambda y\lambda x[R(x, y) \wedge \exists z[R(z, y) \wedge \exists z$ is x's mother$]$

This is clearly not Davidsonian modification. In fact, Davidsonian-style modification of the type envisioned by Landman would actually be very little help here. A logical form such as that in (40) leaves open the question of how to determine whether a state is maternal or by blood.

(40) $\exists s[\textbf{related}(s, \textbf{Ann}, \textbf{Beth}) \wedge \textbf{by-blood}(s) \wedge \textbf{maternal}(s)]$

To capture this would mean encoding, in the state domain, semantic information that already exists in the relation domain.

It does not appear, then, that we find compelling evidence for treating manner modifiers of state verbs in a Davidsonian fashion. If we reject such an analysis, the question becomes how to treat these modifiers, if not as Davidsonian-like co-predicates. We take this up in the next section.

9.3 Proposals

Manner-like modifiers of state verbs appear to come in four types:[7] standard intersective modifiers such as *quietly*, which we will not discuss,

---

[7] Note that Mittwoch's (2005) catalog of adverbial modifiers of adjectives contains two more types of modifiers: the complex degree modifiers *unpleasantly dark* and *uncannily similar* (whose attitude-toward-degree interpretation – e.g., it is unpleasant how dark it is – is discussed in Katz 2005), and the sentential modifiers in *charmingly benign* and *ominously silent* (meaning it is charming that such-and-such is benign or it is ominous that such-and-such is silent). It is clear that neither of these is a Davidsonian-type modifier either.

collocational predicate modifiers such as *by face*, degree modifiers such as *well*, and what we will call event-related modifiers, such as *passionately*. We discuss the last three of these in turn below, starting with a brief discussion of collocational modifiers, moving to a more extensive treatment of degree modification and then to some speculation about event-related modification.

9.3.1 *Adverbial collocations*

One thing that is clear about manner adverbial modification of state verbs is that it is highly lexically restricted. The adverbs *passionately* and *well*, for example, combine with practically any agentive event predicate (*eat lunch*, *make bread*, *play chess*, and hundreds if not thousands more), but can only combine with a very few state predicates (*hate*, *want*, *desire*, and maybe a couple more for *passionately* and *know* for *well*). There is no such thing as *knowing passionately*, *depending on passionately*, or *loving well*. In some cases this selectivity might be semantically based (as is likely the case with *passionately*), but in other cases it is pure lexical selection.

Even in cases where the interpretation of the modifier is clearly some sort of degree modification, there is lexical selection. When we talk about a high degree of love, this is expressed as in (41a), whereas a high degree of knowledge is expressed as in (41b).

(41)   a.   He loves her deeply/*well.

      b.   He knows that well/*deeply.

It appears that many manner adverb/state verb combinations exhibit a sort of conventionalized lexical relation, in other words they are collocations (Firth 1957). As with many other collocations, the particular meaning associated with an adverb–verb combination is not entirely predictable from their independent meanings. As we saw above, *to know by face* is something different than *knowing*. This selectivity and non-compositionality leads us to claim that many manner adverb/state verb combinations are, essentially, idiomatic, and not to be treated compositionally.

There are a number of issues that come up in connection with this claim. Chief among these is the apparent category-neutrality of the predicate modifier constructions. The parallel between verb–adverb and noun–adjective meanings evident in (42) has sometimes been raised as an argument for the Davidsonian analysis (Parsons 1990).

(42)   a.   John left quickly.

      b.   John's leaving was quick.

The basic idea is that the parallel between sentences such as (42a) and (42b) is captured by uniform Davidsonian semantic analysis such as that in (43).

(43) $\exists e[\textbf{leave}(e, \textbf{John}) \wedge \textbf{quick}(e) \wedge \textbf{past}(e)]$

This argument has been extended to state verbs, with the parallels in (44) being taken as evidence for a neo-Davidsonian analysis.

(44)   a.   Peter knows Jill by face.

      b.   Peter's by face knowledge of Jill

      c.   John and Mary own the property jointly.

      d.   John and Mary's joint ownership of the property

The parallel is, we suggest, a syntactic illusion. As has long been known, the collocational status of predicate-modifier structures is entirely independent of their actual syntactic category (Halliday 1966). This appears to be a quite general phenomenon, as illustrated by such examples as (45), where the semi-idiomatic meaning of noun–adjective combinations are seen to carry over to their related verb–adverb use.

(45)   a.   It was an ambulant operation.

      b.   The patient was operated upon ambulantly.

      c.   The ultrasonic testing is complete.

      d.   They were ultrasonically tested.

      e.   Our products have global sources.

      f.   We source our products globally.

Likewise, nominalized state verbs evidence the same selectivity in their association with adjectives as the verb root itself shows with adverbial modification.[8] Just as we cannot apply *firmly* to the verb *love*, or *deeply* to *believe*, we cannot apply *firm* to the noun *love*, or *deep* to *belief* (except in the sense of profound).

(46)   a.   John loves Mary deeply/??firmly.

      b.   Peter ??deeply/firmly believes in the supernatural.

      c.   John's love for Mary is deep/??firm.

      d.   Peter's belief in the supernatural is ??deep/firm.

---

[8] Of course even standard idiomatic expressions evidence this category neutrality:

(i)   a.   The pulling of strings that they engaged in brought about their downfall.
      b.   His kicking the bucket caused an uproar.

Associated adjective–noun combinations exhibit selectivity as well:[9]

(47) a. John has a deep/??firm love for Mary.

  b. Peter has a ??deep/firm belief in the supernatural.

Lexical selection, then, is category-neutral, and there appears to be a phenomenon (little studied) of root–root selection. Let us briefly explore what must be involved in providing a formal analysis of this. Rögnvaldsson (1993) suggested treating such collocational elements as these as complex lexical items which are (optionally) inserted together into the derivation. This idea is directly related to much interesting work on the syntax of nominalization in the framework of Distributed Morphology (van Hout and Roeper 1997; Marantz 1997; London 2000), in which lexical items are taken to have a category-independent status.

In essence the idea behind the Distributed Morphology analyses of nominalization is that there is no lexical difference between the roots *kiss* and *love* that appear as nouns and the roots *kiss* and *love* that appear as verbs. Marantz (2001) argues that nominalization is not a lexical process, but rather is the result of introducing a particular kind of root into a nominal environment. In other words, lexical items are introduced into the derivation in a category-neutral way and acquire their syntactic features from their environment. This is illustrated schematically in (48).

(48) a. [pro$_{masc}$[D $\sqrt{}$KNOW [French]]] = 'his knowledge of French'

  b. [pro$_{masc}$[V $\sqrt{}$KNOW [French]]] = 'he knows French'

We can adopt a similar analysis of the apparent category-flexibility of modifiers of these roots as well. There appears to be a modifier which appears with LOVE and has the verbal-environment form "passionately" and a nominal environment form "passionate." Let us assume that this is a single root PASSIONATE which also acquires its syntactic features (and thus its morphology) from its syntactic environment.

---

  [9] Greenbaum (1982) has pointed out that in some cases there are missing elements in the paradigm. The degree reading of the adverbs *well* and *badly* in collocation with the verbs *know* and *need* doesn't appear to extend to the adjectives *good* and *bad* in collocation with the nominalized forms of these verbs:

(i) a. Peter knows Mary intimately/well.

  b. Peter's knowledge of Mary is intimate/*good.

(ii) a. Peter needs a haircut desperately/badly.

  b. Peter's need for a haircut is desperate/*bad.

(49) a. [promasc[D √GOOD [√KNOW [French]]]] = 'his good knowledge of French'

  b. [promasc[v √GOOD [√KNOW [French]]]] = 'he knows French well'

Marantz provides an account of verb–object idioms in a Distributed Morphology framework which is directly related. He suggests that the actual meaning of roots is listed not in a context-independent lexicon, but rather relative to the context of appearance and with respect to a locality domain. This allows us to account for the kind of light-verb lexical idioms given in (50), by essentially listing the different meanings.

(50) a. take a leap

  b. take a leak

  c. take a walk

  d. take cover

Here presumably the root √TAKE gets an appropriate meaning conditional on it occurring in the context of a particular direct object. Returning to our root-modifier case, then, the suggestion is that the root √KNOW selects for a very particular meaning of the modifier √GOOD, that is that √GOOD has a context-dependent meaning listed once in the lexicon, namely its meaning when it occurs with √KNOW, and that this shows up in all environments where these two roots appear together. Of course the modifier √GOOD has a base manner reading, which is that that it has as an event verb modifier; it is just when it appears with √KNOW that it acquires a specialized meaning. This is not dissimilar to the case of √TAKE, which has a straightforward compositional meaning when combined with inanimate concrete object NPs such as *the book*, but an idiomatic reading in constructions of the *take a leak* type (Jackendoff 1996b).

  Marantz argues that there are very fixed locality domains for this kind of conditional meaning – essentially the conditions need to be stated "within the vP." One argument for this is that there are no idioms with a fixed agent piece, in the way we see the idioms in (50) have a fixed theme piece. Interestingly, as we noted in the introduction, it is exactly the class of manner adverbs that have this close syntactic association with the verb. In contrast to temporal and locative adverbs, manner adverbs are closely tied to the verb (McConnell-Ginet 1982; Cinque 1999). It might even be – and this is indeed pure syntactic speculation – that the syntactic difference between state verbs and event verbs interacts with this locality constraint. The structure we have assumed, repeated in (51), is one on which the manner modifiers are vP (EventP-internal) but VP-external.

(51)   [John$_1$ [probably [$_{TP}$ past [$_{EventP}$ t_1 [$_{Event}$ e [$_{VP}$ kiss Mary]] passionately]]]]

For "manner" modification of state verbs, a natural alternative is that the modifiers here are VP-internal elements – in the more restricted sense of Chomsky (1995) and Harley (1995).[10]

(52)   [John$_1$ [probably [$_{TP}$ past [$_{VP}$ t_1 [$_{V'}$ love Mary] passionately]]]]

Assuming a strict syntax–semantics interface, this is the natural syntactic correlate of treating these modifiers as predicate modifiers, and it correlates with Marantz's locality domain.

We have, then, at least the sketch of an account of the difference between manner modification of state verbs and manner modification of event verbs. In brief, manner modifiers cannot play their normal event-predicational role when they modify state verbs, so they must be reinterpreted. The tight syntactic binding between the verb and the adverb is why the typical Davidsonian entailment pattern doesn't emerge – the adverbs are not acting as simple conjunctive predicates but as predicate modifiers. In the next two sections we discuss two kinds of predicate modifier meanings that these adverbs express.

9.3.2 *Degree modifiers*

As we have seen, one of the ways in which manner modifiers of state verbs are interpreted is as degree modifiers. Indeed it is a puzzle that this should be the case: that so many adverbs that are interpreted as manner modifiers when they combine with event verbs should be reinterpreted as degree modifiers when they are combined with state verbs.[10] This is not something we expect on a Davidsonian-style account. On the hypothetical Davidsonian analyses of (53a) and (53b) given in (54), we expect the adverb *well* to have a univocal interpretation.

(53)   a.   John speaks French well.

        b.   John knows French well.

(54)   a. $\exists e [\text{speak}(e, \text{John, French}) \wedge \text{good}(e) \wedge \text{past}(e)]$

        b. $\exists s [\text{know}(s, \text{John, French}) \wedge \text{good}(s) \wedge \text{past}(s)]$

We don't expect *well* in (53a) to indicate the quality of speech, but *well* in (54b) to indicate the degree of knowledge. An important open question, then,

---

[10] Herwig (1998) documents a historical process of manner to degree shift in English.

concerns the source of this regular polysemy. To try to make sense of this question (and to make good on the claim we made above that the droppability of *well* follows from its degree-modifier semantics), we turn now to a discussion of degree modification.

Degree modification is intrinsically tied to the notion of gradability. Traditionally, gradable adjectives, such as *tasty* or *tall*, have been distinguished from non-gradable adjectives, such as *female* and *American* (Bolinger 1972; Kamp 1975), gradable adjectives being those that accept degree modification and can appear in the comparative, and non-gradable adjectives being those that do not and cannot:[11]

(55)   a.   Those tomatoes are very tasty.

     b.   ??Fifi is very female.

(56)   a.   Fresh tomatoes are tastier than day-old coffee.

     b.   ??Fifi is more female than Fido.

Bolinger (1972) noted that, like adjectives, verbs can be classified as gradable and non-gradable. Gradable verbs can combine felicitously with the adverbial phrase *very much* and can be used in the comparative.

(57)   a.   Mary loves John very much.

     b.   John cooled the soup very much.

(58)   a.   Mary loves John more than John loves Sue.

     b.   John cooled the soup more than he heated the bread.

Non-gradable verbs are either degraded or have only a temporal interpretation[12] when combined with *very much* or used in the comparative:

(59)   a.   ??She owns a car very much.

     b.   ?John kissed Mary very much.

(60)   a.   ??John owns the house more than Mary owns the bike.

     b.   John kissed Mary more than Mary kissed John.

---

[11] Non-gradable predicates can often be reinterpreted as such, so while *dead*, *alive*, and *female* don't really admit of degrees, we sometimes use degree modifiers or comparative forms of these metaphorically, as in (i).

(i)   She is very female.
    "She is very feminine."

[12] Temporal readings are those in which the number of times is what is being measured or compared. For reasons that are not clear, for state verbs temporal readings are more remote than for event verbs. Note that for comparative adjectives these readings are clearly distinguished syntactically:

(i)   a.   John is more sick than Mary is. [degree-comparison]
    b.   John is sick more then Mary is. [time-comparison]

Stereotypical stative verbs such as *love, know, want, desire, believe, depend, appreciate,* and *resemble* are all gradable, while stereotypical event verbs such as *kiss, eat, notice,* and *arrive* are all non-gradable. There is a small class of non-gradable state verbs, examples being *own, contain, belong, consist of,* and *cost,* and a small class of event verbs such as *fill, empty, clean, cool, widen,* and *lengthen* (the so-called "degree achievements" of Dowty 1979 and Kennedy and Levin, this volume) are gradable.

Turning now to semantics, degree modifiers are typically taken to be a type of predicate modifier whose interpretation makes reference to the abstract notion of the degree to which a predicate holds (Cresswell 1977; von Stechow 1984; Heim 1985; Kennedy 1999b, 2001; Kennedy and McNally 2005). On Kennedy's (1999b, 2001) account, for example, gradable adjectives are interpreted as relations between individuals and degrees on a scale.[13] The adjective *tall*, for example, relates individuals to their degree of tallness, and degree modification involves predication about or specification of this degree. In (61a), for example, the degree of tallness is specified explicitly, while in (62a) two degrees of tallness are compared, and in (63a) John's degree of tallness is predicated to be high.

(61) a.   John is six feet tall.

      b.   **tallness(John)** = 6 feet

(62) a.   John is taller than Mary.

      b. $\exists d\,[\textbf{tallness}(\textbf{John}) = d \wedge \exists d'\,[\textbf{tallness}(\textbf{Mary}) = d'] \wedge d > d']$

(63) a.   John is very tall.

      b. $\exists d\,[\textbf{tallness}(\textbf{John}) = d \wedge \textbf{high}(d)]$

Formally, these modifiers are treated as functions from relations to relations, with existential closure applying after the application of the modifier. It is also frequently assumed that gradable predicates have a degree argument and that this argument is projected in the syntax (Abney 1987, Kennedy 1999b).

Degrees are, of course, ordered, and ordered sets of degrees are known as scales. The predicate *high* in (63b) and the ordering relation in (62b) are defined on the basis of the tallness scale, for example. Interestingly, Kennedy and McNally (2005) have shown that adjectives can be categorized on the basis of a number of semantic properties of their associated scales. The predicate *tall* is associated with a scale which has no maximal element (there is no maximal

---

[13] Analyses of gradable event verbs are similar. Parsons (1990), explicitly rejecting a Davidsonian account of degree adverbs, takes *partially* to be interpreted as an operator that takes predicates of events and returns predicates of partial events of the same type. More detailed analyses have been given by Hay, Kennedy and Levin (1999) and more recently by Caudal and Nicolas (2005), and Piñón (2005).

degree of tallness), while the predicate *dry* is associated with a scale which does have a maximal element. This contrast between scales with no maximum – "open" scales – and scales with a maximum – "closed" scales – is reflected in the distribution of the degree adverb *completely*, which appears only with closed-scale predicates:

(64) a. The paint is completely dry.

  b. *The man is completely tall.

In addition, gradable adjectives are typically associated with a standard of comparison, which serves to distinguish individuals that are in the extension of the given adjective from those that are not (Klein 1980; von Stechow 1984; Kennedy 2001). This is taken to be a specified degree on the scale, which is lexically specified. Kennedy and McNally distinguish two varieties of standards: contextual standards and absolute standards. The predicate *tall* has a contextual standard – to be tall is to be taller than some contextually specified height.[14] For (65a) to be true, in a given context c it must be the case that John's tallness exceeds a contextually determined standard for tallness d_c (as indicated in 65b).

(65) a. John is tall.

  b. $\exists d[\textbf{tallness}(\textbf{j}) > d \wedge d > d_c]$

In contrast, predicates such as *dry* and *wet* have absolute standards. To be dry is to be maximally dry and to be wet is to be minimally wet. This distinction is evident from the entailments associated with comparative uses of the predicates. In (66a) the towel and the shorts cannot both be dry, in (66b) both of them must be wet, and in (66c) neither Peter nor John need be tall (but one or both might be).

(66) a. The towel is drier than the shorts.

  b. The shorts are wetter than the towel.

  c. Peter is taller than John.

Kennedy and McNally, then, classify gradable adjectives in terms of their associated scales and standards: the scale can be open (no maximum degree: *tall, rich, far*) or closed (there is a maximum degree: *dry, healed, near*) and the standard of comparison can be contextual (*tall, poor, near*), absolute-minimal (*wet, scratched*) or absolute-maximal (*dry, flat*).

---

[14] The well-known context-dependence of such adjectives (Kamp 1975) is thus addressed – *tall* in *tall basketball player* is typically associated with a different standard than *tall* in *tall jockey*.

As one might expect, gradable verbs can similarly be classified on the basis of their associated scales and standards. In contrast to the scales associated with such concrete scalar adjectives as *tall* or *short*, the scales associated with state verbs are often quite abstract (the love scale, the desire scale, the knowledge scale), making it difficult to determine what properties these scales have. Is there a maximal degree of liking? Are the standards for knowing contextual or absolute? Fortunately such tests as the felicitous cooccurrence with the adverb *completely* and the entailments associated with the comparative serve as useful guides. As we see in (67), *depend (on)*, which appears naturally with *completely*, seems to be associated with a closed scale, while *like*, which does not, appears to be associated with an open scale.

(67) a.   Steve depends on Mary completely.

  b.   ??Steve likes Mary completely.

The verb *like* also appears to be associated with a contextually specified standard, contrasting with the verbs *love* and *hate*, which seem to be associated with minimal standards. This follows from the entailments associated with the comparative – (68a) can be true even if Peter doesn't like either Mary or Sue, while (68b) can only be true if Peter hates both of them.

(68) a.   Peter likes Mary more than Sue.

  b.   Peter hates Mary more than Sue.

The verbs *like*, *love*, and *know* appear to be associated with open scales, while *depend (on)* and *understand* are associated with closed scales; *like* and *know* are associated with a contextual standard, while *hate* and *understand* are associated with absolute-minimal and absolute-maximal standards, respectively. We can now account for the fact that the "manner" modifiers *well* and *firmly* are both droppable – with (69a, b) entailing (70a, b).

(69) a.   Peter knew French well.

  b.   Lisa firmly believed that James was innocent.

(70) a.   Peter knew French.

  b.   Lisa believed that James was innocent.

This follows directly from the fact that both *know* and *believe* are associated with contextual standards, and the degree adverbs *well* and *firmly* indicate that the standard of comparison is shifted up the scale. In the case of *well*, for example, to know someone well is to have a high degree of knowledge of that person and to have a high degree of knowledge of that person is typically to have a degree that is above the contextually specified standard associated with *know*. The analyses of (69a) and (70a), given in (71) illustrate this.

(71)   a. $\exists d\,[\mathbf{knowledge}(\text{Peter, French}) = d \wedge \mathbf{high}(d)]$

     b. $\exists d\,[\mathbf{knowledge}(\text{Peter, French}) > d \wedge d > d_c]$

On the assumption that $\mathbf{high}(d) > d_c$ it follows that (71a) entails (71b). Note that a degree adverb such as *slightly* would shift the standard down below the contextual standard, capturing the fact that to know someone slightly is not to know that person, and thus that *slightly* cannot be dropped.

    Let us return to the question of why adverbs such as *firmly* or *well*, which clearly have a manner interpretation when combined with event verbs, have degree interpretations when combined with state verbs. One suggestion is that this is a form of polysemy similar to that with which we are already familiar. If we are correct that *speak* and *know* differ in their syntactic structure, with *speak* having an event argument and *know* having a degree argument, then perhaps the contrast in the interpretation of *well* in (72) is very much like the syntactically determined polysemy of *disgustingly* discussed above.

(72)   a.   John speaks French well.

     b.   John knows French well.

Concretely, we can speculate that *well* is simply associating with different projections in (72a)than it is in (72b), as illustrated in (73).

(73)   a.   [John₁ [TP pres [EventP t_1 [Event e [VP speak French]] well]]]

     b.   [John₁ [TP pres [DegP t_1 [Deg d [VP know French] well]]]]

Of course non-gradable state predicates will lack the degree projection, and (more interestingly) gradable event predicates will have both an event projection and a degree projection, accounting for the ambiguity of such sentences as (74).

(74)   John cooled the soup a little.

On one interpretation the degree modifier *a little* associates with the event and on the other with the degree, as indicated in (75).

(75)   a.   [John₁ [TP past [EventP t_1 [Event e [DegP [Deg d [VP cool the soup]]] a little]]]]

     b.   [John₁ [TP past [EventP t_1 [Event e [DegP [Deg d [VP cool the soup] a little]]]]]]

This account in (73) is, of course, not available if state verbs and event verbs both have Davidsonian arguments and both project the same kind of syntactic superstructure.

It is not the case, however, that all non-idiomatic manner modification of state verbs is simply degree modification. It is certainly clear, for example, that *passionately* – while related to a degree of love – expresses something more in (76), and that this meaning is not obviously collocational.

(76)   John loves Mary passionately.

In the next section, we will argue that in some cases – such as the case of *passionately* – modification of state predicates is to be reduced to properties of events intrinsically related to these predicates. We will then use this idea to attempt to resolve the puzzle of how the meaning of *love passionately* is related to the meaning of *love*.

9.3.3 *Event-related modifiers*

In many contexts the habitual sentence (77a) is synonymous with the generic (77b).

(77)   a.   John plays tennis.

      b.   John is a tennis player.

When modified by the adverb *passionately*, however, a subtle contrast in meaning becomes evident. The habitual has only what we might call the "event-related" reading, made salient in the discourse in (78), while the generic has also what we might call the "state-related" reading, made salient in the discourse in (79).

(78)   John plays tennis passionately. He only plays quite rarely, however. When he is off the court he never thinks of the game at all. But as soon as the game starts he puts his whole soul into it. (He is passionate when playing tennis.)

(79)   John is a passionate tennis player. He subscribes to all the magazines, goes to many tournaments, and talks only about the game. When he plays, however, he plays with a certain calm. (He is passionate about being a tennis player.)

In the one case, then, the adverb appears to specify something about individual tennis-playing events themselves: each tennis game is carried out in a passionate way. If we adopt a quantificational account of habituals, of the sort proposed by Diesing (1992) and Kratzer (1995) on which habitual sentences involve a sort of quantification over underlying events, then we can think of the adverb as taking narrow scope with respect to this quantificational operator. This is indicated in (80b).[15]

(80) a. John plays tennis passionately.

　　　b. $Gen[C(e) \wedge \textbf{play-tennis}(e, \textbf{John})][\textbf{passionate}(e)]$

Essentially this says that every relevant event of tennis-playing by John is a passionate event. We should note that on the Diesing/Kratzer conception, representations such as that in (80b) are not syntactic representation, but rather a post-LF level of interpretation – perhaps the level of Discourse Representation or some other conceptual level.

On the most natural reading of the first sentence of (79), however, it isn't the tennis games that are carried out passionately, but something else: John is passionate about being a tennis player. Let us consider briefly what this might mean. As suggested above, the passion finds its expression in activities that are associated with being a tennis player, but these aren't (necessarily) playing tennis. They can be events of traveling to tournaments, subscribing to magazines, etc. In other words the events that distinguish someone who might be characterized as a tennis player from someone who merely plays tennis. It is these events that are carried out with passion.

Let us explore one way of turning this observation into an analysis. Chierchia (1995) has argued that generic predicates such as *love* and *know* (Carlson's (1977) Individual-level predicates) should be given a quasi-quantificational analysis along the lines of that just sketched for habituals. Both habituals and generic predicates induce a quasi-universal reading of their bare plural subjects – as illustrated in (81) and (82). One of Chierchia's desiderata is to derive this by providing both kinds of sentences with the same kind of semantic structure.

(81) a. Czechs play tennis.

　　　b. $Gen[C(e) \wedge \textbf{Czech}(x) \wedge \textbf{Agent}(e, x)][\textbf{play}(e, x, \textbf{tennis})]$

(82) a. Czechs love tennis.

　　　b. $Gen[C(e) \wedge \textbf{Czech}(x) \wedge \textbf{Agent}(e, x)][\textbf{love+}(e, x, \textbf{tennis})]$

In both (81) and (82), the free variable introduced by the bare plural subject is bound by the quasi-universal **Gen** operator, and this is what gives rise to the quasi-universal reading. The difference between these sentences, of course, is

---

[15] Gen is taken to have something like universal force (see Krifka et al. 1995), and – like a quantificational adverb – is taken to bind the free variables in its scope. The predicate C is a contextual restriction (of the sort argued for by von Fintel 1994) restricting the quantification to a relevant domain.

what is in the nuclear scope. For habitual predicates it is clear that we are talking about events of playing tennis and so the event predicate *play* is what is in the nuclear scope. For generic predicates although the claim is that there is quantification over events, there does not appear to be a lexicalized event predicate which is analogous to *play*. Chierchia's important innovation was to hypothesize a non-lexicalized underlying event predicate (here **love+**), which behaves in the semantic representation analogously to **play** and which appears in the nuclear scope in (82). This hypothesized predicate is intended to be one that holds of events related to the loving of tennis, such as going to watch games, playing tennis, talking about tennis, etc. And the intuition that this proposal attempts to capture is that to claim that someone loves something is to claim something about the kinds of event that they participate in.

Conceptually there is much to be said for this interpretation. Certainly to determine whether someone loves tennis we observe the range of events that they participate in, and it is from this observation that we draw our conclusion. Likewise, if we are told that Peter loves Mary, we expect there to be a range of events that Peter engages in which reflect this.[16] Given such an account of the semantic interpretation of *love*, it is fairly clear how to treat manner modification. It should be treated along the same lines as manner modification of habitual predicates: that is, the predicate is simply interpreted as occurring in the nuclear scope as a conjoined event predicate. This is illustrated in (83).

(83)   a.   Peter loves Mary passionately.

   b. $\text{Gen}[C(e) \wedge \textbf{Agent}(e, \textbf{Peter}) \wedge \textbf{Theme}(e, \textbf{Mary})][\textbf{love+}(e) \wedge$
         $\textbf{passionate}(e)]$

What (83b) means, then, is that the relevant events associated with *love* of which Peter is the Agent and Mary the Theme are passionate. This certainly seems a reasonable interpretation of what it means to love someone passionately.[17]

This, of course, is all highly speculative. In some ways it is a way of making concrete the claim that the use of manner verbs when combined with state verbs is, in a sense, metaphorical. There is no passionate state, but rather there are passionate events that are closely related to certain states, and we can use adverbials to call up these passionate events, even when talking about states.

---

[16] Common-sense folk-psychology is, in a sense, exactly this approach (Lewis 1972).

[17] This analysis bears a number of similarities to the analysis of subsective adjectives (Siegel 1976a) proposed by McNally and Boleda (2004).

9.4 Conclusion

Applying the Davidsonian analysis to state verbs is appealing in its uniformity, as adverbial modification can, in general, be treated as predication over underlying eventualities (in Bach's (1986) terminology). Both Landman (2000) and Mittwoch (2005) attempt to bolster Parson's (1990) argument that the semantics of state sentences must involve quantification over underlying state variables by showing that manner adverbial modification of state verbs has properties that require such an analysis. We have argued that this attempt is ultimately unsuccessful and that, in fact, manner modification of state verbs is a highly constrained phenomenon which receives a better analysis as classical predicate modification.

There was much clearing of the brush to be done in distinguishing the relevant set of verbs and adverbs, thus eliminating a large class of apparently problematic cases. We showed that the few types of adverbs that can be used to modify state verbs typically don't have the semantic characteristics associated with eventuality predication: they don't have the properties Drop, Permutation, and Non-Entailment. For particular examples that have been raised in the literature which appear to exhibit these properties, we have shown that the observations are either mistaken or best otherwise analyzed.

Manner adverbials that modify state verbs appear to be much more closely associated with the verb they modify than are manner adverbials modifying event verbs (far more closely than we might expect on a Davidsonian analysis). We have made some tentative proposals accounting for this, suggesting that many verb–adverb combinations are a sort of idiomatic expression or collocation. In passing we discussed the category-neutrality of collocations, pointing out that adverb/adjective parallels cannot really be taken as evidence for a Davidsonian account. We have seen that many manner adverbials acquire a degree modifier reading when used to modify state verbs, and attempted to suggest why this might be. We also noted that the fine structure of degree modification predicts precisely which degree modifiers can be dropped preserving truth and which not. Finally we have suggested that there are event-related modification meanings associated with state verb modification and showed how the meanings of these might be derived from the conceptual structure of generic predicates.

While we have left many threads untied, we hope to have made clear that the case for treating "manner" modifiers of state verbs as predicates of underlying states and not as classical predicate modifiers is a weak one, based on a superficial similarity. While it may still be the case that such an analysis is defensible, there are a number of issues to be addressed. There is the restriction of manner modification of state verbs to gradable predicates, the fact that manner modifiers of state verbs are so frequently reanalyzed as degree modifiers, and the close lexical selectivity of manner modifiers of state verbs. Each of these needs an explanation, even on a Davidsonian account of state verb modification. We have provided at least preliminary accounts here on a classical account which makes no reference to underlying states. Whether reference to underlying states provides any empirical benefit would remain to be seen.

Acknowledgments

The material in this chapter was presented at Sinn und Bedeuting VII Frankfurt (October 2003), at the Zentrum für Allgemeine Sprachwissenschaft in Berlin (June 2004), at King's College, London (July 2004), as well as, in part, at the Barcelona Workshop on Adjectives and Adverbs (April 2005). The audiences at each of these events were very helpful, as were Ben Shaer, Louise McNally, Carla Umbach, Peter Bosch, Adam Wyner, and Anita Mittwoch.

10

Towards flexible types with constraints for manner and factive adverbs

ADAM ZACHARY WYNER

10.1 Introduction

In this chapter, I discuss the syntax and semantics of so-called factive and manner adverbs such as in (1a) and (2a), with their respective paraphrases in (1b) and (2b).[1]

(1)   a.   Stupidly, Bill kissed Jill.

     b.   The fact that Bill kissed Jill was stupid.

(2)   a.   Bill kissed Jill passionately.

     b.   The manner in which Bill kissed Jill was passionate.

In section 10.2, I provide syntactic and semantic evidence to support the distinction between these two classes. Other factive adverbs are *wisely*, *rudely*, and *appropriately*; other manner adverbs are *gently* and *roughly*. For the moment, let us say that *stupidly* in (1a) is a *sentence* adverb, while *passionately* in (2a) is a *verb phrase* adverb. Some factive adverbs are polysemous between a factive and a manner interpretation (e.g., *rudely*), but I do not address polysemy in this chapter.[2]

   In a recent overview of research on the syntax and semantics of adverbs, Lang, Maienborn and Fabricius-Hansen (2003: 1, 25) present two widely accepted assumptions concerning the syntax and semantics of adverbs:

---

[1] Such paraphrases are found in Reichenbach (1947: 301–307), Quirk, Greenbaum, Leech, and Svartvik (1985: 557, 612–631), Jackendoff (1972: 49, 52), Parsons (1990: 62–64), Asher (1993), and Moore (1993: 136), among others.

[2] There are a range of other approaches to what I call here factive adverbs, in terms of vagueness (Barker 2002), conventional implicatures (Potts 2005), and so-called disjuncts (Espinal 1991), among others. These approaches are tangential to the core facts and issues I discuss here.

Almost any treatment of adverbials starts from a long-established classification of adverbials that is somehow based on semantic intuition.... Normally, syntacticians and semanticists make different choices in selecting a subset of these types, by starting their approach with a division into, say VP- vs. sentential adjuncts or predicates vs. operators, and then concentrate on finding and justifying refined subdivisions below that intuitively assumed level. (Lang et al. 2003: 4)

They assume that one should distinguish classes of adverbials in terms of the syntactic and semantic category they modify; for example, factive adverbs are modifiers syntactically of sentences and semantically of propositions, while manner adverbs are modifiers syntactically of verb phrases and semantically of predicates. Moreover, given the classification, they implicitly assume that these types are fixed; that is, once an adverbial type is ascribed to an adverb, it cannot be changed. These two assumptions are based on syntactic tests and semantic intuitions, some of which I review later. I refer to these two assumptions together as the "fixed types hypothesis" of adverbial modification and a theory which makes use of this hypothesis as a "fixed types theory." In other words, put broadly, if an adverb is a factive adverb, it must apply to the sentence level and not the VP level, while if it is a manner adverb, it must apply to the VP level and not the sentence level. In general, adverbs can only appear adjoined to syntactic and semantic positions associated with their syntactic and semantic category. If they do not, the resulting sentences are ungrammatical. Where adverbs do in fact appear in alternative positions, some other explanation must be given, for example with movement or as exceptions. These basic assumptions appear in a broad spectrum of syntactic and semantic research, as I report later.

Other grammatical and semantic frameworks do not adhere to the fixed types hypothesis, for example allowing an adverb to apply to a range of syntactic positions and correlated semantic expressions. I refer to this as the "flexible types hypothesis," and a theory which makes use of this as a "flexible types theory." For instance, in such an approach, a manner adverb might have both an S- and a VP-level expression, so the adverb could apply in either position. Such an approach could account for a range of alternative positions that are problematic for a fixed types theory. However, it has a reciprocal problem: it must then account for the syntactic tests and semantic intuitions which support the fixed types theory. One way to do so is to provide constraints on the application of the types. Yet, so far as I am aware, this possibility has largely gone unexplored for the problems I examine.

To decide between the two types of theories, I consider cases of discourse anaphora which paraphrase the sentential examples. I observe that the available and unavailable cases of discourse anaphora parallel available and unavailable cases of adverbial modification within the sentence. These observations lead to the most important contribution of this chapter, which is the identification of formal mechanisms from the semantics of discourse which are used to constrain the distribution and interpretation of factive and manner adverbs within the sentence. A fixed types theory cannot account for the discourse cases since it is a theory of sentence grammar. A flexible types theory can accommodate both discourse and sentence facts given the constraints. I then suggest a theory which unifies the interpretations and distributions in both the sentence and discourse cases. The analysis indicates that for the syntax and semantics of factive and manner adverbs, sentence grammar and discourse grammar share some key components.

As I have made this argument in detail previously (Wyner 1994, 1998b), in this chapter, I only briefly present the main lines of the argument again, focusing on the conceptual and empirical issues. In particular, I emphasize what is at stake in the choice between fixed types and flexible types with respect to adverbial syntax and semantics. I leave the interested reader to consult Wyner (1998b) for an explicit formal analysis within the approach of Discourse Representation Theory (Kamp and Reyle 1993 and Asher 1993).

In section 10.2, I discuss fixed types and flexible types analyses and show some of the problems of each. I do not claim any novelty in this section other than in how I frame the problems, and I provide a basis for the discussion of discourse analogies. In section 10.3, I provide comparisons between adverbs in sentences and discourse paraphrases. I argue in support of a flexible types theory with constraints over a fixed types theory.

10.2 Fixed types and flexible types

In this section, I review the differences between *fixed types* and *flexible types* for factive and manner adverbs. For each, I introduce several problems that must be addressed.

10.2.1 *Fixed types*

As Lang, Maienborn and Fabricius-Hansen (2003) observe, there is a long-standing claim that certain adverbs are sentence modifiers, while others are VP modifiers. Semantically, sentence modifiers are functions from propositions to propositions, while VP modifiers are functions from predicates to predicates. In a sketch, we may provide the following phrase structure bracketings of (1a) and (2a), respectively.

(3)   a.   [$_S$ Stupidly, [$_S$ Bill kissed Jill]]

      b.   [$_S$ Bill [$_{VP}$ [$_{VP}$ kissed Jill] passionately]]

The assumption is that factive adverbs can only adjoin to sentences and manner adverbs can only adjoin to verb phrases. Where we find other syntactic
distributions, we must provide some alternative analysis. In the following two
subsections I explore some of the evidence for this assumption and then some
of the problems.

10.2.1.1 *Supporting evidence*   A wide variety of semantic and syntactic evidence is provided in the literature to support the claim that there are two
sorts of adverbials with different syntactic distributions.[3] I assume these observations are relatively well known, so I do not present more details than are
necessary.

Let us consider manner adverbs first. An early and key assumption in formal
grammatical thinking was that since manner adverbs appear to modify the
verb or the event of the sentence, they should appear in close proximity to
that which they modify.[4] Thus, manner adverbs modify the verb, so should
appear in close proximity to the verb. More specific tests include whether the
adverb appears under the semantic scope of a sentence operator (Thomason
and Stalnaker 1973). For instance, consider negation (4a), universal quantifiers
in object position (4b), and the relative interpretation of the adverbs in (4c),
where I take negation, universal quantification, and the factive adverb to be
sentence operators (the latter claim to be supported below).

(4)   a.   Bill didn't kiss Jill passionately.

      b.   Bill kissed every girl passionately.

      c.   Stupidly, Bill kissed Jill passionately.

In each case, we find interpretive restrictions: in (4a), negation has scope over
the manner adverb; in (4b), the universal quantifier in object position has
scope over the manner adverb; and finally, in (4c), the factive adverb has scope
over the manner adverb.

---

[3] The following partial list of references indicates just how deeply rooted and widespread this
conception is in both the syntactic and semantic literature: Ajdukiewicz (1935: 211–216), Lambek (1958),
Bar-Hillel (1960), Chomsky (1965), Keyser (1968), Montague (1974), Parsons (1990: 62–67), Jackendoff
(1972, 1977), Thomason and Stalnaker (1973), Kamp (1975), Dowty, Wall, and Peters (1981: 232–234),
McConnell-Ginet (1982), Cresswell (1985: 13–66), Quirk, Greenbaum, Leech, and Svartvik (1985: 438–
653), Travis (1988), Gamut (1991: 198–201), Ernst (1991), Bowers (1993), Dekker (1993), Larson and Segal
(1995: 465–466), Radford (1997: 142–143), Cinque (1999), Haegeman and Gueron (1999: 80–81, 461–462,
486).

[4] See Keyser (1968) as well as discussions of iconicity in grammar in Newmeyer (1992).

By similar considerations, we might conclude that an adverbial modifier such as *with wet lips*, among others, is also a VP modifier. Furthermore, observe that we can "scramble" certain classes of adverbial modifiers as in (5): the sentences are synonymous. This seems to be further evidence that *with wet lips* is a VP modifier: that is, we can freely scramble modifiers of the same class.

(5) a. Bill kissed Jill passionately with wet lips.

   b. Bill kissed Jill with wet lips passionately.

Contrast these observations with factive adverbs.

(6) a. Stupidly, Bill didn't kiss Jill.

   b. Stupidly, every boy kissed Jill.

   c. Stupidly, Bill kissed Jill passionately.

In (6a), the factive adverb appears outside the scope of negation. In (6b), the factive adverb can appear outside the scope of the universal quantifier in subject position.[5] In (6c), as noted above, the factive adverb applies to expressions which contain manner adverbs, and not vice versa. Such evidence has been taken to indicate that the factive adverb applies to the sentence and has semantic scope over the entire proposition.

In addition, VP-ellipsis data suggest that manner adverbs are "abstractly" within the VP (because it is a VP adjunct), while, as McCawley (1982) and Wyner (1994) show, the factive adverb is not in the VP. We interpret (7a) as (7b); we do not interpret (8a) as (8b), meaning that each kissing itself was stupid. It does have an interpretation where the conjunction of the kissings was stupid.[6] However, this only reinforces the sense that the factive adverb has scope over a sentence as it can apply to a complex sentence.

(7) a. Jill kissed Bill passionately, and Meg did too.

   b. Jill kissed Bill passionately, and Meg kissed Bill passionately.

(8) a. Stupidly, Jill kissed Bill, and Meg did too.

   b. Stupidly, Jill kissed Bill, and stupidly, Meg kissed Bill.

10.2.1.2 *Problems*   There are problems with this strict distinction between sentence and VP adverbs. Let us consider the following examples which are somewhat different from those we target here, but which are raised in the literature. They also show the generality of the issues.

---

[5] A reviewer suggests there is also the wide-scope quantifier interpretation; however, this is not an interpretation other speakers get. In any case, it is tangential to our point.

[6] There is also an interpretation where the adverb applies to the first conjunct only, but this is not relevant to our discussion.

(9) a. Possibly, Bill kissed Jill.

b. It is not the case that Bill kissed Jill.

Here, the adverb *possibly* and negation *It is not the case that* appear to apply syntactically to expressions of the type sentence to yield expressions of type sentence. After all, the expressions appear on the left-periphery of the sentence *Bill kissed Jill*, and the resultant complex expression is a sentence. Our semantic intuition suggests that they apply to the meaning of the sentence *Bill kissed Jill*, namely a proposition, and create propositions as a result. The VP-ellipsis test shows that the elided VP does not copy the adverb or negation. We could say that form and meaning are correlated.

In contrast, we have cases in (10) where form and meaning are *not* correlated but the sentences are nonetheless synonymous (for our purposes) with sentences in (9).

(10) a. Bill, possibly, kissed Jill.

b. Bill didn't kiss Jill.

In these cases, where it superficially appears that the subject is outside the scope of the adverb, the adverb does not apply to a sentence; similarly, negation does not apply to the sentence. Indeed, it would appear that *possibly* and negation apply to VPs syntactically and predicates semantically. Where we systematically have such alternative forms of the same meaning, we want a systematic account. That is, it is not an incidental relationship between *Bill kissed Jill*, *possibly*, and *not*, but rather we find similar relationships between other sentences and expressions which apply to sentences, as I discuss further below.

Of course, whether this is a problem for a syntactic and semantic analysis depends on the basic assumptions. The examples in (10) are problems for grammatical frameworks which associate linear order with structural hierarchy as in the phrase structure rules for Government-Binding theory. These sentences are less problematic given alternative grammatical assumptions such as the rule of Right Wrap in Categorial Grammar (Bach 1979) or theories which make use of discontinuous constituent structure following McCawley (1982). Indeed, I argue for such an alternative view. However, any theory must address not only the distribution and interpretation of adverbs within sentences, but also, I claim, discourse parallels. More fundamentally, at least these two alternate approaches are similar to a transformational approach in that they provide mechanisms whereby alternative sentence forms are yoked into an underlying logical form that is consistent with the assumption that the operator applies to a sentence level expression. Our proposal explicitly argues against this assumption.

We find the same basic issue with factive adverbs, where all of the following are grammatical.

(11)   a.   Stupidly, Bill gave no present to any grandchild.

       b.   Bill, stupidly, gave no present to any grandchild.

       c.   Bill gave no present, stupidly, to any grandchild.

In all of these, the adverb is used with so-called "comma intonation," the function of which appears to be to signal the factive interpretation of *stupidly* (cf. Wyner 1994 and Potts 2005). In none of these examples can we interpret the adverb as a manner. We use an expression with a Negative Polarity licenser *no present* and licensee *any grandchild* which are both within the verb phrase. Thus, in (11), the adverb *must* appear within the VP, even if it has sentential interpretation, at least in Government-Binding frameworks; alternative frameworks previously mentioned provide analyses where the adverb is attached to or functioning on the sentence level.

In a somewhat similar vein, we may look at manner adverbs such as *passionately*. (12a) is the usual English word order for the reading of the sentence where the manner of the kissing is passionate. Yet we can also have (12b), where the adverb has a manner meaning and the overall sentence implies a contrast; that is, we use (12b) to deny some previous assertion. Similarly, we can have (12c), where the adverb appears to be an afterthought (see Geuder 2000).

(12)   a.   Bill kissed Jill passionately.

       b.   Passionately, Bill kissed Jill.

       c.   Bill kissed Jill, and passionately.

It appears that in (12a), the manner adverb syntactically modifies a VP and semantically modifies a predicate. In the other examples, we have to provide some other account, and a range of possibilities have been proposed. One is to abandon a surface-oriented syntax, as mentioned previously. Another is to suggest some sort of movement analysis for the adverbs. Other elements in the sentence might move over the adverb if it is base generated in a position other than as an adjunct (Larson 1988, where manner adverbs are V complements). Issues may be raised about the concept of adjunction (Chametzky 1994). There could be a range of additional functional categories to support adverbs in a range of locations (along the lines of Cinque 1999). Or one could claim that some examples are outside the usual syntactic processes (Shaer 2003). That there are substantive issues with the syntactic and semantic analysis of adverbs in the fixed types analysis is relevant at the moment, not that there are alternative proposals, which must still address this range of observations.

We may associate the syntax–semantics relationship described in relation to the above examples with the fixed types hypothesis (Montague 1974 and Dowty, Wall, and Peters 1981). The following is in Landman (1991: 148):

(13) **Fixed type hypothesis:** The grammar associates with every syntactic category a unique semantic type. All syntactic structures of that syntactic category translate as expressions of the corresponding semantic type.

Thus, we have verb phrase adverbs which adjoin to VPs and semantically are functions from VP denotations to VP denotations. For the moment, let us assume that VP denotations are sets of individuals. We have sentential adverbs which adjoin to sentences and semantically are functions from sentence meanings to sentence meanings. For the moment, let us assume that a sentence meaning is a proposition, which is a set of possible worlds. The examples in (3) are in keeping with this hypothesis.

Any of the alternative forms (10), (11b), (11c), (12b), (12c) must have some alternative analysis that is outside of, makes additions to, or abstractly reconstructs the fixed types assumed for the adverbs. For instance, a theory along the lines of McCawley (1982) would allow crossing branches for structures in (11) such that the factive adverb applies *in situ* to a sentence level expression.

This analysis is just as represented in Lang, Maienborn and Fabricius-Hansen (2003). Indeed, they are correct to claim that the classification of adverbials into sentence and VP modifiers has long been assumed in a particular line of analysis. Indeed, it is hard to find in this body of literature (*pace* comments below on Categorial Grammar) any alternative, nor for that matter, the observations above which would motivate an alternative.

10.2.2 *Flexible types*

Let us consider another line of analysis which does not assume the fixed types hypothesis. I focus the discussion on Categorial Grammar, essentially for expository purposes: it has a long history (particularly with respect to the analysis of adverbs), is widely known, and is easy to use to present the central issues. There are a range of other, relatively recent, grammatical frameworks and semantic theories which also do not assume the fixed types hypothesis; these theories focus on the analysis of ambiguity and underspecification.[7]

---

[7] See Bunt (2003) for an overview. More specifically, we have Cooper stores (Cooper 1983), Lexical Functional Grammar and Glue Semantics (Dalrymple 2001; Lev 2006a, b), underspecified semantics for modifiers (Maienborn 2001), the constraint language for lambda structures (Egg et al. 2001), and others.

However, our topic is neither ambiguity nor underspecification: the sentences, under the intended interpretations, are unambiguous; the adverbs have fixed, specific interpretations. Instead, our inquiry is about how synonymous interpretations arise given a range of alternative forms. In addition, we are concerned with how interactions among elements account for constraints in the interpretation and distribution of adverbs. Other than Categorial Grammar, it is not clear and explicit how these alternative theories handle in a cohesive way the range of examples and issues discussed in the previous section.

In Categorial Grammar, it was observed that it was a problem to account for those elements which appeared in positions other than those stipulated by the categorial rules (Ajdukiewicz 1935: 211–216, Lambek 1958: 165, Bar-Hillel 1960, Geach 1972, Wood 1993: 46, and Humberstone 2005: 281). In fact, example sentences with adverbs such as (9a) and (10a) were central to the discussion. The formal flexibility of sentential adverbial expressions was recognized as early as Lambek (1958: 165) (see Wood 1993: 46 for further discussion). A solution to the variant forms was particularly pressing for Categorial Grammar, as it had no transformational devices for moving elements about within the sentence. Thus, the claim by Lang, Maienborn and Fabricius-Hansen (2003) that adverbial syntax and semantics have been peripheral is false; it has been rather a matter of neglecting an alternative line of analysis. Indeed, Cresswell (1985: 6) places adverbs at the very center of syntactic and semantic analysis when he states that to determine the semantic value of an adverb is to determine the semantic value of the expression to which the adverb applies to. In other words, one of the key ways in which we infer the semantics of verbs, verb phrases, and sentences is from the study of adverbs. The introduction of the event argument in Davidson (1967) is a prime example of this approach.

In order to account for the alternative forms, rules of type change were proposed in Categorial Grammar which were adopted in Montague Grammar (Montague 1974 and developed in other ways by Partee and Rooth 1983, among others). In particular, we have mention of the following, which I refer to as the flexible types hypothesis; it is formally provided by the so-called Geach Rule, which is discussed further below:[8]

A special case of this proposal is that any expression in the category of sentence modifiers also falls within the category of predicate modifiers, thus explaining *inter alia* why negation, primarily an operation which applies to a sentence to yield another sentence, is derivatively an operation which applies to a predicate to yield a predicate. (Humberstone 2005: 281)

---

[8] Humberstone (2005) discusses the rule and its antecedents in detail. I follow convention in referring to it as the Geach Rule.

In this view, the adverb and negation in (9) are in basic positions, while those in (10) are in derived positions. Nonetheless, though the syntactic forms vary, the semantic translations are the same.

Let us investigate flexible types more particularly for our cases with reference to the Geach Rule (Geach 1972, Wood 1993: 46). The version of the rule below is from Gamut (1991: 257–263). In (14) and (15), we have the syntax and semantics of a single, general rule which permits one basic syntactic and semantic type to have a variety of derived forms; this permits an expression to apply to a variety of different syntactic categories, while semantically, the variety of types all reduce to the same expression.

(14)   **The Syntax of the Geach Rule**
       Suppose (a, b), a function from category a to category b.
       If an expression has category (a, b), then it also has category ((c, a), (c, b)), for all categories c.

(15)   **The Semantics of the Geach Rule**
       Where we have an expression a which is a function from a to b,
       then we also have the semantic expression:
       $\lambda y_{(c,a)} \lambda z_{(c)} [a_{(a,b)} (y_{(c,a)} (z_{(c)}))]$,
       where y is an expression that is a function from c to a, and z is an expression of type c.

Notice that when we apply $z_{(c)}$ to an expression $y_{(c,a)}$, the result is an expression of type a; that is, the result of $(y_{(c,a)} (z_{(c)}))$ is of the right type to apply as input to $a_{(a,b)}$. The output is then an expression of type b. As there is a tight correlation between the syntactic functions and their semantic interpretation in the λ-calculus, I focus just on the semantics.

I should emphasize, with this last point, that since I am mainly interested in the semantic claims which are couched in terms of the λ-calculus, whatever criticisms one might want to make of the proposed analysis should concern the semantics and the λ-calculus. That is, this chapter is not an argument for Categorial Grammar per se, which here is essentially a vehicle for discussion. Given that the semantics allows type-shifting, one must argue against the semantics.

We can see how this rule works for our adverbial cases. I first consider factive adverbs and then turn to manner adverbs. I assume the neo-Davidsonian analysis of relations (Parsons 1990), giving a broad indication of how the semantics associates with the syntactic structure.

(16)   a. $\lambda e [\text{kiss}(e) \wedge \text{agent}(e) = \text{bill} \wedge \text{theme}(e) = \text{jill}]$

Sentence Level

b. $\lambda x \lambda e [\mathbf{kiss}(e) \wedge \mathbf{agent}(e) = x \wedge \mathbf{theme}(e) = \mathbf{jill}]$

Verb Phrase Level

c. $\lambda y \lambda x \lambda e [\mathbf{kiss}(e) \wedge \mathbf{agent}(e) = x \wedge \mathbf{theme}(e) = y]$

Verb Level

For two reasons, I focus entirely on the neo-Davidsonian analysis of adverbs rather than also examining the classic analysis in terms of propositional and predicate modifiers (Montague 1974; Parsons 1970, 1990; Thomason and Stalnaker 1973; Kamp 1975; Dowty et al. 1981: 232–234; Gamut 1991: 198–201). First, many of the same issues involving fixed versus flexible types arise on the two types of analysis – the Geach rule applies to the classic version as well as the neo-Davidsonian version. However, the classic view does not give the manner adverbs the sentence type for they do not have the right properties for sentence operators. In and of itself, this restriction to the predicate/relation type accounts for why manner adverbs cannot semantically apply to sentence type expressions or after negation, disjunction, conjunction, or other sentence operators. However, there are well-known problems with the classic view: the classic view seems intuitively implausible, it requires meaning postulates to account for the factivity entailment, transparency of manner adverbs, and permutations of transparent adverbs (see McConnell-Ginet 1982, Parsons 1990, Wyner 1994, Eckardt 1998, and Landman 2000).

The second reason relates to the center of our analysis. In every representation in (16), an event argument appears. As I discuss shortly, if a manner adverb is essentially a predicate of an event argument, then there is no reason in principle why we could not have a manner adverb which applies to any of these representations to yield synonymous results. The distinction between predicate and sentence modification does not necessarily extend to adverbs in the neo-Davidsonian view. I develop the consequences of this below, but let us consider factive adverbs first.

For factive adverbs, I make the following simplifying assumptions; the representation below is for expository purposes and is refined later. First, I shall assume for the time being that factive adverbs are predicates of events as in the neo-Davidsonian theory. The key difference for our purposes is that they include existential closure over the event argument, unlike manner adverbs. We see the impact of this below. Thus, factive adverbs such as *stupidly* are functions from predicates of events to propositions. In the logical form, an adjective *stupid* predicates of an event argument.[9]

(17) $\lambda P \exists e [P(e) \wedge \mathbf{stupid}(e)]$

---

[9] I do not address tense in this chapter. However, we could assume there is a tense argument in relation to the event argument, so existential closure on the event argument would not block tense.

This expression applies *after* all other arguments have been fed into the relation: it corresponds to the form where the factive adverb appears on the left (or right) periphery of the sentence.

Applying the Geach Rule to the semantic expression in (17) results in a family of semantic translations, as pointed out in Wyner (1994).

(18)   a. $\lambda Q\lambda x\exists e[Q(x)(e) \wedge \textbf{stupid}(e)]$

     b. $\lambda R\lambda y\lambda x\exists e[R(y)(x)(e) \wedge \textbf{stupid}(e)]$

     c. $\lambda S\lambda z\lambda y\lambda x\exists e[S(z)(y)(x)(e) \wedge \textbf{stupid}(e)]$

(18a) is a function from predicates to predicates, and thus applies to VPs. (18b) is a function from relations to relations, and thus applies to Vs. It could also apply in direct–indirect object constructions between the direct object and the indirect object.[10] (18c) is a function from ditransitive relations to ditransitive relations.

It might be claimed that this leads to an unwelcome overgeneration. The constructions which are marked as marginal in other analyses (i.e., those based on fixed types) are not intrinsically marked as marginal in this approach. For example, we might say that the unmarked construction is (19a), while the others are marked, especially (19c).

(19)   a.   Stupidly, Jill kissed Bill.

     b.   Jill, stupidly, kissed Bill.

     c.   Jill kissed, stupidly, Bill.

In our view, this is not an unwelcome result. Just as the generalized movement rule *Move-α* required other components of the grammar to control for overgeneration, we might here allow a semantic correlate, the Geach Rule, to be controlled by other syntactic or semantic mechanisms. For example, (19c) could be ruled out, if one wanted, with restrictions on case assignment (though examples with Heavy NP-Shift raise independent issues).

Let us turn to manner adverbs. We have a choice here of what we assume is the basic type. In keeping with the spirit of the analysis, I postulate the highest level type and allow the more specific types to be given by the Geach Rule. Thus, manner adverbs are functions from predicates of events to predicates of events as in the neo-Davidsonian analysis. As with the factive adverb,

---

This representation of the factive adverb allows multiple modification, as I discuss in the body of the chapter.

[10] There are a range of important but tangential issues about the syntax and semantics of direct–indirect object and double object constructions which I neglect here. See Larson (1990) and Carpenter (1997).

the adjective *passionate* predicates of the event argument. I will support this further below.

(20) $\lambda P \lambda e[P(e) \wedge \textbf{passionate}(e)]$

The more specific types are:

(21)   a. $\lambda Q \lambda x \lambda e[Q(x)(e) \wedge \textbf{passionate}(e)]$

     b. $\lambda R \lambda y \lambda x \lambda e[R(y)(x)(e) \wedge \textbf{passionate}(e)]$

(21a) is the most similar to the form in the classic analysis, for the adverb is a function from predicates of individuals and events to predicates of individuals and events. After the application of such an adverb, we have an optional rule of existential closure over the event argument to make an expression which is a proposition.

With these types, we can account for a range of complex expressions. For example, it is well known that there is an ordering restriction between factive and manner adverbs (Jackendoff 1972: 87–93, Travis 1988, Ernst 2002, Bowers 1993, Cinque 1999, Wyner 1994, among others). In the fixed types analysis, this is accounted for by fixing the adverbials to higher and lower positions relative to one another. In the flexible types analysis, a similar observation is accounted for simply because of type compatibility and the availability or unavailability of an event argument.

Reading the order of application of the adverbs off the surface structure, we may assume that the order of application of the adverbs for (22a) is (22b); the manner adverb appears on the surface to apply before the subject combines with the predicate. Where the manner adverb applies before the factive adverb, then it reduces to (22c), which is a well-formed expression. In fact, (22a) is compatible with a variety of alternative syntactic and semantic analyses, all of which reduce to the same expression.[11]

(22)   a.   Stupidly, Bill passionately kissed Jill.

     b. $\lambda Q \exists e[Q(e) \wedge \textbf{stupid}(e)]((\textbf{bill})[\lambda P \lambda y \lambda e[P(y)(e) \wedge \textbf{passionate}(e)]$
        $(\lambda x \lambda e[\textbf{kiss}(e) \wedge \textbf{agent}(e) = x \wedge \textbf{theme}(e) = \textbf{jill}])])$

     c. $\exists e[\textbf{kiss}(e) \wedge \textbf{agent}(e) = \textbf{bill} \wedge \textbf{theme}(e) = \textbf{jill} \wedge \textbf{stupid}(e) \wedge$
        $\textbf{passionate}(e)]$

This analysis straightforwardly accounts for cases which are otherwise highly problematic in the fixed types approach. If (23a) is acceptable, and (23b) were the result of movement to a topic position, then the fixed types approach

---

[11]   I have placed the subject of the sentence *Bill* in its surface linear order and assume that the λ expressions can apply either to the right or the left given an expression of the right type.

cannot explain the ungrammaticality of (23c) without an ad hoc stipulation; in other words, though the individual expressions are grammatical, the combination is not.

(23)   a.   Bill, stupidly, kissed Jill.

       b.   Passionately, Bill kissed Jill.

       c.   *Passionately, Bill, stupidly, kissed Jill.

Our analysis accounts for this ordering restriction straightforwardly as shown in (24). If we apply the factive adverb before the manner adverb, the type of expression which results from the application of the factive adverb is incompatible with the type required by the manner adverb – existential closure blocks application of a manner adverb. The key observation is that application of the factive adverb existentially closes over the event argument, so the event argument is not subsequently available for predication by the manner adverb as is required.

(24) $\lambda Q \lambda e [Q(e) \wedge \mathbf{passionate}(e)]$
       $((\mathbf{bill})[\lambda P \lambda y \exists e [P(y)(e) \wedge \mathbf{stupid}(e)]$
       $(\lambda x \lambda e [\mathbf{kiss}(e) \wedge \mathbf{agent}(e) = x \wedge \mathbf{theme}(e) = \mathbf{jill}])])$

Application of a factive adverb blocks application of a manner adverb, but application of a manner adverb does not block application of a factive adverb. And this is the case no matter where the particular adverbs apply; for example we could get the same result if both adverbs apply after the application of the subject, just so long as the order of application of the adverbs is compatible; similarly, we could apply both adverbs in their relation type. The lexical semantics of the adverbs and their relative order of application accounts for the ordering restriction, not misattachment, restricted types, intonation, or other factors. Notice that the key notion is here less about type compatibility and more about the availability or unavailability of an argument to predicate of. I discuss this further in the presentation of the discourse cases.

   The analysis also addresses a problem for Categorial Grammar noted in Humberstone (2005). If manner and factive adverbs both apply *in the same way* to sentential expressions and are of the same type, then we would expect that we could conjoin them, where only expressions of like syntactic and semantic categories can conjoin. However, this is not the case, where we take *stupidly* to have a factive interpretation and *passionately* to have a manner interpretation.

(25)   *Stupidly and passionately, Bill kissed Jill.

On our analysis, their basic types are different – one a function from predicates of events to propositions and the other a function from predicates of events to predicates of events.

We have seen that if we apply a factive adverb, we cannot then subsequently apply a manner adverb, as the event argument is unavailable. We can provide an analysis of negation which similarly blocks application of a manner adverb. Consider the following examples.

(26)   a.   *Passionately, Bill didn't kiss Jill.

     b.   *Bill didn't kiss Jill, and passionately.

It is unclear how to systematically rule out these cases in a fixed types approach, given that the positive sentences are acceptable.

In our approach, negation and factive adverbs both block the subsequent application of manner adverbs for the same reason: the event argument is unavailable for predication. I assume the following analysis for negation of an eventive sentence, where there is existential close over the event argument and negation is applied to the result (see Wyner 1994).

(27) $\lambda P \neg \exists e [P(e)]$

As with the factive adverb, we can apply the Geach Rule to negation, where (27) is a function from predicates of events to truth values. We use one of the derived forms below:

(28) $\lambda Q \lambda e [Q(e) \wedge \textbf{passionate}(e)]((\textbf{bill})[\lambda P \lambda y \neg \exists e [P(y)(e)]$
     $(\lambda x \lambda e [\textbf{kiss}(e) \wedge \textbf{agent}(e) = x \wedge \textbf{theme}(e) = \textbf{jill}])])$

We cannot reduce this expression so that the manner adverb applies after negation has applied. If the manner adverb applied before the application of negation, then there would be no problem. This accounts for the asymmetrical order of application of manner adverbs and negation without assuming that manner adverbs are only VP operators.

However, the current analysis cannot account for the combination of a factive adverb and negation as in (29) since I have (temporarily) assumed that the factive adverb also takes eventive arguments.

(29)   Stupidly, Jill didn't kiss Bill.

In the next subsection, I refine the analysis.

10.2.3 *Factivity*

Up to this point, I have treated manner adverbs and factive adverbs much alike, the key difference being that factive adverbs deploy existential closure over the event argument. In Wyner (1998b), I argued that factive adverbs should be distinguished from propositional adverbs such as *possibly* or *allegedly*. Among the key points are that factive adverbs do not induce opacity, entail the truth of the expression they apply to (that is, $Adv(P)$ entails P, for Adv a factive adverb), and predicate of a particular semantic entity. On the latter point, factive adverbs make no implications concerning more specific expressions (i.e., 30a does not entail 30b), nor do they make implications concerning more general expressions (i.e., 31a does not entail 31b).

(30)   a.   Wisely, Bill kissed Jill on the cheek.

       b.   Wisely, Bill kissed Jill on the cheek with wet lips.

(31)   a.   Stupidly, Bill kissed Jill on the cheek with wet lips.

       b.   Stupidly, Bill kissed Jill on the cheek.

In addition, I follow Peterson (1997), Asher (1993), and Zucchi (1993), who provide arguments for postulating abstract objects such as events, propositions, and facts. Following this line of analysis, I postulate that factive adverbs predicate of fact arguments (see Geuder 2000 and Bonami and Godard, this volume, for different views). The basic idea is that a fact is a *literal* of predicate logic, that is, a positive or negative expression which is true or false in a world and does not quantify over worlds. Modal propositions are not literals. Thus, lambda-reduced expressions which are existentially closed over the event argument are literals. I assume that facts appear in a structure (see Wyner 1994) such that the fact that Bill kissed Jill on the cheek with wet lips is a distinct fact from Bill kissing Jill on the cheek, even if the first implies the second. While this is an important element of our analysis, it is somewhat tangential at this point. I discuss abstract objects further in the section on discourse anaphora.

I will assume, then, that we have a function *FACT* from literals to fact arguments (see Asher 1993 for how this is done in Situation-theoretic Discourse Representation Theory). The factive adverbs predicate of this fact argument. The Geach Rule applies to the proposition to yield a family of expressions which allow the factive adverb to apply in a range of positions, but reduce to the same semantic interpretation.

(32) $\lambda P \, \exists f \, [FACT(P) = f \wedge stupid(f)]$,
       where P is a literal and f is an individual fact.

The postulation of abstract individuals of fact and event is key to the structure of argument to follow.

10.2.4 *Summary*

At this point, I have introduced two approaches to the syntax and semantics of adverbial modification, fixed types and flexible types. Flexible types with an ontology including events and facts have some advantages, as I have demonstrated. In the next section, I consider discourse analogies which support the importance of what sort of argument the adverb predicates of in the logical form as opposed to where the adverb applies. In addition, the discourse analogies indicate that the same sorts of constraints apply to the distributions of adverbs within the sentence as to correlated discourse anaphora. This supports the argument that the adverbs can appear across a range of types and apply in situ, for the restrictions are not particular to the adverbs' types, but arise as interactions between the adverbs and other components of the grammar rather than as a result of having a fixed position in the syntax.

10.3 Comparison to discourse cases

The analysis here draws heavily from Discourse Representation Theory (DRT) (Kamp and Reyle 1993) and more specifically from Asher (1993). First, I consider some of the basic cases of pronominal reference and extensions to anaphora to abstract objects. Then I consider how these observations extend to adjectival predication and parallels to adverbial modification.

Consider the basic cases which DRT is designed to handle:

(33)   a.   Bill/a man$_i$ kissed Jill. He$_i$ was tall. And he$_i$ was fat.

     b.   Bill kissed Jill$_i$. She$_i$ was thin. And she$_i$ was short.

     c.   Jill didn't kiss a man$_i$. *He$_i$ was tall.

     d.   Jill kissed every man$_i$. *He$_i$ was tall.

     e.   Allegedly, a man kissed Jill. *He$_i$ was tall.

We know that proper names and indefinites can serve as discourse antecedents of pronouns (33a, b); the pronouns depend on, and do not introduce, a discourse referent. Furthermore, as (33a) and (33b) show, we may add intersective adjectives such as *tall* and *fat* in either order; they simply predicate additional properties of the antecedent. These cases also show that whether the antecedent is in a subject position or an object position is irrelevant; in general, we relate the pronouns and antecedent in these cases without resorting to a syntactic relationship between them, for the antecedent is made available semantically. Obviously, the structural relationship between the clauses is irrelevant as well. (33c–d) show well-known restrictions on discourse anaphora: negation, universal quantification, and modal operators make discourse antecedents unavailable for anaphora. In brief, the analysis in DRT for these restrictions is that the discourse referents are too deeply embedded in the DRT structure to be accessible for anaphora.

We also know (Peterson 1997 and Asher 1993) that we can have pronominal anaphora to a variety of abstract objects (propositions, facts, events, and concepts), and we can type verbs and adjectives by the sort of abstract object they predicate of. One antecedent expression, as in (34), can serve as the antecedent of the pronouns in (35), where I indicate the sort of anaphora involved.

(34)   Bill kissed Jill.

(35)   a.   It indicated that Bill liked Jill.   (Fact Anaphora)

      b.   Will believed it.   (Proposition Anaphora)

      c.   It occurred at 10pm.   (Event Anaphora)

We see that (34) can serve as the discourse referent in a range of sorts. Following Ginzburg and Sag (2001), we can understand this as instances of type coercion; that is, the expression in (34) may have a default semantic type, but it can be systematically changed. Exactly how and when it can be coerced must be defined, though I will not do so here.

The adjectival predicates *to be passionate* and *to be stupid* appear to behave in the same way: *to be passionate* predicates of an event and *to be stupid* (under the relevant interpretation) predicates of a fact (to be demonstrated in a moment). The pronoun *it* in (36b) and (36c) is taken to refer to Bill's kissing Jill.

(36)   a.   Bill kissed Jill.

      b.   It was stupid.

      c.   It was passionate.

Moreover, (36a) and (36b) taken together seem to be synonymous with (37a), the adverbial form with the factive interpretation. (36a) and (36c) taken together seem synonymous with (37b) for our purposes.[12]

(37)   a.   Stupidly, Bill kissed Jill.

      b.   Bill kissed Jill passionately.

---

[12]   As an anonymous reviewer points out, there is a difference between the adverbial case and the adjectival case, which is interesting in and of itself, but somewhat tangential to the point of the discussion; in particular, the adjectival cases seem to attribute passionateness equally to both participants, while the adverbial cases seem to attribute passionateness just to Bill. This observation points to issues concerning the relationship between adverbs and arguments. For our purposes, the kissing is attributed passionateness to a greater or lesser extent whether in the intersentential or intrasentential cases.

It would appear that the adjectival and adverbial cases contribute much the same information. In the adjectival case, anaphora and predication of an argument are explicit. In the neo-Davidsonian analysis of the adverbials, there is implicit predication of an argument, which appears in the logical form. There is no explicit anaphora in the adverbial case. However, in both adjectival and adverbial cases we see predication of an available argument of the right sort. For our purposes here, it is not essential that the adjectival and adverbial cases work exactly the same way.

What is highly significant, in our view, is not just that these parallels exist in these simple intersentential (adjectival) and intrasentential (adverbial) cases. Rather, the parallels are extensive and consistent with other aspects of the DRT analysis. More importantly, the fixed types theory does not provide any mechanism to account for the analogy, while the flexible types theory augmented with the DRT analysis does. One way to put the claim is that the constraints on discourse anaphora are at work within the sentence. Consider the evidence which supports this claim.

I build up the intersentential data to parallel the intrasentential data discussed earlier. Just as adverbial phrases which predicate of an event can appear in either order, so too can we have parallel discourse continuations in either order. All the cases in (38a) are synonymous. Adverbs can be contained within expressions which serve as pronominal antecedents; the discourses can be extended, gradually adding more and more information.

(38) a. Bill kissed Jill with wet lips. It was passionate.

  b. Bill kissed Jill passionately. It was with wet lips.

  c. Bill kissed Jill. It was passionate. It was with wet lips.

  d. Bill kissed Jill. It was with wet lips. It was passionate.

  e. Bill kissed Jill passionately with wet lips.

  f. Bill kissed Jill with wet lips passionately.

The examples in (38c) and (38d) are a critical problem for the fixed types approach, for while it might be possible to build a theory in which the pronouns in (38a) and (38b) refer to a VP-like entity which also contains the subject, this possibility is unavailable for (38c) and (38d). The problem is that the second occurrence of the pronoun in these examples refers to the information comprised of the first two sentences; obviously, these don't comprise a VP, yet the adjective still predicates of them; for example, the event described by *Bill kissed Jill* and *It was passionate* is the antecedent for the pronoun in *It was with wet lips*, allowing us to conclude that Bill's kissing Jill was both passionate and with wet lips. We cannot construe that there was one instance of Bill's kissing Jill which was passionate and another instance of Bill's kissing Jill which was with wet lips. The first (unavailable) interpretation could be represented as (39a), where the pronouns (here the variables u and v) are deictically associated with different instantiations of the variable. In the second interpretation, the discourse continuations have variables bound by the existential quantifier over the event argument, just as in the intrasentential representations.

(39) a. $\exists e[\text{kiss}(e) \wedge \text{agent}(e) = x \wedge \text{theme}(e) = \text{jill}] \wedge \text{passionate}(u) \wedge$
         $\text{with-wet-lips}(v)$

     b. $\exists e[\text{kiss}(e) \wedge \text{agent}(e) = x \wedge \text{theme}(e) = \text{jill} \wedge \text{passionate}(e) \wedge$
         $\text{with-wet-lips}(e)]$

I want next to consider more complex discourse cases in order to see whether the adverbial orderings we saw above hold in discourse as well. First, we should observe that it is not entirely clear whether expressions with factive adverbs or adjectives can serve as pronominal antecedents. For example, the discourse in (40a) and the sentence in (40b) are outright infelicitous for some speakers. In (40a), the idea is that the pronoun with the factive predicate *indicates* is to be paraphrased as (40b). However, in both cases, it is not certain that we have a "fact" antecedent, for (40a) and (40b) seem better expressed as (40c), where the *judgment* is the subject. Furthermore, propositional anaphora (40d) does not clearly have as antecedent *Stupidly, Bill kissed Jill*. Certainly event anaphora in (40e) does not have *Stupidly, Bill kissed Jill* as antecedent. We could, in contrast, have a manner adverb in the sentence which, as a whole, serves as antecedent for either fact, proposition, or event anaphora.[13]

(40) a. Stupidly, Bill kissed Jill. It indicates that we no longer tolerate affection in public.

     b. That Bill kissed Jill was stupid indicates that we no longer tolerate affection in public.

     c. The judgment that Bill kissed Jill was stupid indicates that we no longer tolerate affection in public.

     d. Will believed it.

     e. It occurred at 10pm.

---

[13] There appear to be some differences in felicity judgments in some of the cases. The intrasentential case might be better with expressions such as *also*, *yet*, *and*, *but*, and so on. They can improve if we suppose these are dialogues between two parties. *That* as a pronoun or *one of those* works better for some speakers than *it*. I have avoided the use of *did it* or *was done*, for this introduces a verbal element, which unnecessarily detracts from the argument.

We see that, in general, factive adverbs cannot appear in expressions which are antecedents of discourse anaphora. I apply this observation below. It is not clear why this might be the case. However, it does not affect the basic point I make in this chapter, and I do not specifically account for it, though I speculate that it may have something to do with type coercion. If factive adverbs coerce the expression they operate on into a compatible type, and if the other predicates *indicate*, *believe*, and *occur* similarly coerce their antecedents, we might account for the observations in (40) if we assume that coercion is not iterative, but more consideration must be given to these matters. These observations are consistent with the observation that factive adverbs do not appear in the antecedents for VP-ellipsis.

At this point, we see that we can add adverbial information within a sentence or adjectival information across sentences to yield, overall, the same result. In the following, we see that adjectival cases pattern like the adverbial cases with respect to the relative scope of adverbs, negation, and universal quantification. Since we find similar patterns, it would make sense to account for the adverbial cases along the lines of the adjectival cases using the same fundamental mechanisms.

As we saw earlier, the interpretive order of the adverbials in (41a) follows the paraphrase in (41b), not (41c); that is, we may apply a factive adverb to an expression containing a manner adverb, but not vice versa. To this, we can add the observation that pronominal anaphora in (41d) and (41e) follows exactly the same pattern: while the pronoun in (41d) can have as antecedent "Bill's kissing Jill passionately," the pronoun in (41e) cannot have as antecedent "that Bill kissed Jill was stupid." To the extent that the discourse in (41e) is well formed, it must be the manner of the kissing itself which was passionate, although there is something odd about such continuations, for it is not clear what is stupid, the kissing itself or the passionate kissing. To sum up, there is a meaning which is unavailable in the sentence (41a), the paraphrase (41c), and in the discourse (41e).

(41) a. Stupidly, Bill kissed Jill passionately.

   b. That Bill kissed Jill in a manner which was passionate was stupid.

   c. *The manner in which Bill's kissing Jill was stupid was passionate.

   d. Bill kissed Jill passionately. It was stupid.

   e. Stupidly, Bill kissed Jill. *It was passionate.

In an account which uses DRT, the acccount for (41d) and (41e) rests on the availability of a suitable discourse referent. That (41d) is acceptable and (41e) is not suggests that the expression of Bill's kissing Jill passionately is a suitable referent for the pronoun predicated of by *stupid*. In contrast, that Bill's kissing Jill was stupid is not a suitable referent for the pronoun predicated of by *passionate*. What is particularly striking is the parallel between the unavailability of discourse referents under a modal operator in (33e) and (41e). This indicates that a similar mechanism is at work; namely, both *possibly* and *stupidly* make discourse referents unavailable for subsequent discourse anaphora. I claim that just as for the intersentential cases, so for the intrasentential cases. In other words, in principle, a manner adverb can apply to sentential level expression so long as an event argument is available. Such an argument is available *under* the scope of the factive adverb, but not *over* it. Thus, manner adverbs cannot apply after factive adverbs not for syntactic reasons (as in the fixed types approach), but for semantic reasons. However, except for such a restriction, the manner adverb can apply freely in the sentence wherever an event argument is available.

One potentially saving strategy for the fixed types approach must be ruled out; we can show that the facts in (41c) and (41e) are not simply a matter of intrasentential or VP predication. This is indicated by patterns in extended discourse.

(42) a. Bill kissed Jill. It was passionate. It was stupid.

b. Bill kissed Jill. It was stupid. It was passionate.

(42a) and (42b), to the extent that they are well formed, have just the same interpretations as the good cases in (41a), (41b), and (41d). The other interpretation of (41e), as we have seen before, is simply unavailable no matter what the order of the predicates. (42b) is a problem for the fixed types approach. As we have seen earlier, we can use pronominal anaphora in such cases, and the issue of attachment is irrelevant here. We cannot explain the restriction on interpretation which we find here in structural terms. It appears that we must refer to some semantic restriction. But if we need such a semantic restriction on the relative order of application in the intersentential cases, then for simplicity, we can use it for the intrasentential cases as well.

Let us consider quantifier and negation cases, which are said to be evidence for the fixed types approach. I show that they also support the DRT analysis of intrasentential modification. In (43a), the intended antecedent for the pronoun is *Jill kissed every boy*, which fails; in (43b), the intended antecedent is *Jill didn't kiss Bill*, which again fails. In contrast, the cases in (44) with the same intended antecedents work just fine: in (44a), what was stupid was the group of girls kissing Bill; in (44b), what was stupid was Jill's not kissing Bill.[14]

(43) a. Jill kissed every boy. *It was passionate.

b. Jill didn't kiss Bill. *It was passionate.

(44) a. Every girl kissed Bill. It was stupid.

b. Jill didn't kiss Bill. It was stupid.

As before, the issue of attachment is irrelevant here. We must account for why the cases in (43) are ill-formed, but those in (44) are fine.

Consider the cases in (43) in a bit more detail. The problem is why manner adjectives don't work at all in (43), while the analogous adverbial cases are acceptable. A theory which says that the antecedent of the pronoun in (43) is a VP or a verb meaning would fail to account for the data, for the VP or verb meaning are available as an antecedent to the very same extent as they are in the intrasentential case. In principle the intersentential cases should, therefore, provide us with interpretations much like the intrasentential cases, where the adverb appears under the scope of the quantifier and negation. Interestingly, the cases in (43) are parallel to the NP anaphora cases in (33), which suggests a similar account. Just as for the NP anaphora cases, the claim is that at the level at which discourse anaphora is resolved, there are no appropriate discourse referents available as antecedents for the pronouns in (43). Clearly, the universal quantifier and negation determine, in these cases, what discourse referents are available at this level; that is, first we apply the universal quantifier and negation, then provide the domain of discourse referents. If adverbs, as in the intersentential cases, depend on discourse referents, and if the domain of those referents is determined, in part, by application of the universal quantifier and negation, then we can get the effect of the relative scope of adverbs with respect to quantifiers and negation without having to stipulate it in terms of attachment site. In particular, the adverb will apply to any position where the appropriate discourse antecedent is available. As the intrasentential cases in (43) show, the universal quantifier and negation make the relevant discourse referent unavailable; because we are dealing with discourse, the anaphora is determined only after the application of the quantifier and negation. This implies in the adverbial case that a manner adverb cannot apply after negation or have scope over the universal quantifier, for the discourse referent is

[14] A reviewer claims that (43a) with the discourse continuation *That was passionate* can be read as a predication of the sum of events. A paraphrase might be *Jill's kissing every boy was passionate*. However, I find this clearly ungrammatical.

unavailable. But this suggests something rather novel: within the VP, before the application of the quantifier or negation, an appropriate discourse referent is available for the adverb, while after such application it is not. It just so happens that the quantifier and negation apply over VPs as well as over sentences, giving the impression that manner adverbs cannot apply outside of the VP. It should, then, be no surprise that just those cases where a manner adverb cannot appear, that is, where it applies after another sentence operator, are just those cases in which the discourses of the form in (43a) are ill formed.

10.3.1 *Summary*

In this section, I have discussed parallels between intersentential anaphora and intrasentential adverbial modification. I have shown that the intersentential cases not only have parallel interpretations to those in the intrasentential cases, but more importantly, they manifest similar restrictions on these interpretations. It is just these restrictions on interpretations which were key support for the fixed types approach. However, that approach cannot account for the intersentential cases. DRT is explicitly designed to restrict intersentential anaphora in cases of negation, universal, and modal subordination. Thus, there is a straightforward application of DRT to the intersentential cases. The novelty of the analysis is that I have claimed that the intersentential analysis, combined with flexible types, can be then used to explain the distribution and interpretation of adverbs in the intrasentential cases as well. However, for questions of space, I refer the reader to Wyner (1998b) for all of the formal details.

10.4 Conclusions

Adverbs have long been at the center of grammatical and semantic analysis, despite what Lang, Maienborn, and Fabricius-Hansen (2003) have claimed. I have argued against the fixed types approach to adverbial modification, where the distribution and interpretation of two sorts of adverbs are provided in virtue of two different fixed types and the sorts of semantic objects the adverbs apply to; this approach has been held widely for a long time. I have given some of the fundamental evidence in support of this approach as well as some of the problems it encounters. I then contrasted the fixed types approach with the flexible types approach, which allows a freer distribution of adverbs within the sentence. The flexible types approach, given appropriate semantic properties for each class of adverb, provides an account for not just the usually acceptable sentences, but also for additional expressions which have been marginalized in the literature. However, this approach leads to overgeneration, which needs to be constrained. In the section on discourse comparisons, it was shown that there are far-reaching analogies between the interpretation of intersentential examples and their intrasentential counterparts. A DRT analysis can provide for the intersentential analyses, and I have proposed that a DRT analysis can be extended, with flexible types, to the intrasentential cases as well. The key claim has been that the distribution and interpretation of adverbs within the sentence is controlled by the same processes and constraints that apply in discourse, in particular, whether the adverb predicates in the semantics of an available entity of the right sort. Given such constraints, the flexible types theory accounts for more of the data more straightforwardly than the fixed types Theory.

Of course, such an approach raises a range of issues and problems which remain to be explored. We ought to examine what other components of DRT could explain other aspects of the intrasentential grammar of adverbs. More broadly, we must further investigate the similarities and differences between discourse and sentence grammar and see to what extent the analyses of intersentential phenomena can account for intrasentential phenomena.

Acknowledgments

Material related to this chapter appears in Wyner (1994) and Wyner (1998b); talks on this material have been presented at conferences or workshops in Berlin (1997), Tromsø (1999), Oslo (1999), and Barcelona (2005). Thanks to audiences and other individuals along the way for their comments. Errors rest with the author.

11

Lexical semantics and pragmatics of evaluative adverbs

OLIVIER BONAMI AND DANIÈLE GODARD

11.1 Introduction

Evaluative adverbs, such as *unfortunately*, *strangely*, and *curiously*, form a small but interesting class of adverbs. We aim here at proposing a precise account of their lexical semantic and pragmatic properties, using French as our object language. We argue that many peculiar properties of these adverbs follow from their special pragmatic status rather than their semantic type. It is generally recognized that the content of an evaluative is not part of the "main sentential content" (Bartsch 1976; Bellert 1977; Bach 1999; Jayez and Rossari 2004; Potts 2005). We propose that their behavior calls for an explicit modeling of their pragmatic properties in a model of dialogue. In the case of simple assertion, the speaker asserting *p* without an evaluative commits himself to the truth of *p*, at the same time as he asks the addressee(s) to evaluate *p*; when he asserts *evaluative p*, the same conversational moves are present, but, in addition, the speaker commits himself to the proposition associated with the adverb while withdrawing it from the addressee's evaluation.

In section 11.2 we show that attempts to relate the semantic properties of evaluatives to the type of their argument do not lead to satisfactory analyses; we continue in section 11.3 by showing how the semantics of evaluative adverbs relates to that of the corresponding adjectives, and clarify along the way the relation of evaluative adverbs to presuppositions. Section 11.4 contains the core of our proposal. Adopting a version of Ginzburg's (2004) semantics for dialogue, we take evaluatives to provide an *ancillary commitment* of the speaker which is not added to the common ground nor placed under discussion. This proposal accounts directly for the observed semantic properties and further clarifies the special status of evaluatives in dialogue. The final section 11.5 discusses a limited grammar fragment making concrete the analysis set forth in the preceding sections.

11.2 The argument of evaluative adverbs

Evaluative adverbs have a series of three properties which make them distinct from other, better studied adverb classes.[1] First, evaluatives are *veridical*: a simple declarative sentence containing an evaluative systematically entails the corresponding sentence without the evaluative. Second, evaluatives are *non-opaque*: coreferring expressions can be substituted in their scope. Third, evaluatives are *scopal*: they participate in scope ambiguities correlated with their syntactic position.

(1)   a.   *Veridicality*
            Paul est malheureusement déjà parti.
            "Paul is unfortunately already gone."
            ⇒ Paul est déjà parti.
               "Paul is already gone."

      b.   *Non-opacity*
            Marie est la nouvelle directrice. Malheureusement, Paul a critiqué Marie.
            "Marie is the new boss. Unfortunately, Paul criticized Marie."
            ⇒ Malheureusement, Paul a critiqué la nouvelle directrice.
               "Unfortunately, Paul criticized the new boss."

      c.   *Scopal character*
            Heureusement, Paul est venu hier.
            "Fortunately, Paul came yesterday."
            ⇎ Hier, Paul est heureusement venu.
               "Yesterday, Paul fortunately came."

This set of properties distinguishes evaluatives from both *manner adverbs* such as *lentement* 'slowly,' *fortement* 'strongly,' etc., and *modal adverbs* such as *probablement* 'probably,' *forcément* 'necessarily,' etc.: manner adverbs are veridical and do not give rise to opacity, but they are scopeless (2). A well-established tradition stemming from Davidson (1967) accounts for the properties of manner adverbs by taking them to be predicates of events. On the other hand, modal adverbs are scopal, but they are not veridical and do give rise to opacity (3). A well-established tradition stemming from Montague (1970) accounts for this set of properties by taking modal adverbs to be intensional predicates – or, more precisely, predicates of propositions. What is interesting

---

[1] Although he does not address the issue in the same terms as ours, and focuses on an adverb (*appropriately*) with no equivalent in French, Wyner (1994: chapter 2) must be credited for clearly stating how adverbs in this class pose a specific problem for standard theories of the semantics of adverbs.

is that the Davidsonian analysis of manner adverbs and the Montagovian analysis of modal adverbs rely on a single insight to account for the three constrasts between the two classes of adverbs. From this perspective it is quite surprising that a class of adverbs should exhibit a mix of properties that puts them halfway between modal and manner adverbs.

(2) a. Paul est entré lentement.   "Paul entered slowly."
         ⇒ Paul est entré.   "Paul entered."

     b. Marie est la nouvelle directrice. Paul a fortement critiqué Marie.
         "Marie is the new boss. Paul strongly criticized Marie."
         ⇒ Paul a fortement critiqué la nouvelle directrice.
         "Paul strongly criticized the new boss."

     c. Lentement, Paul mangeait dans la cuisine.
         ⇔ Dans la cuisine, Paul mangeait lentement.
         "Paul was slowly eating in the kitchen."

(3) a. Paul est probablement déjà parti.
         "Paul is probably already gone."
         ⇏ Paul est déjà parti.
         "Paul is already gone."

     b. Marie est la nouvelle directrice. Paul a forcément critiqué Marie.
         "Marie is the new boss. Necessarily, Paul criticized Marie."
         ⇏ Paul a forcément critiqué la nouvelle directrice.
         "Necessarily, Paul criticized the new boss."

     c. Forcément, Paul est venu hier.
         "Necessarily, Paul came yesterday."
         ⇎ Hier, Paul est forcément venu.
         "Yesterday, Paul necessarily came."

Previous accounts have tried to assimilate evaluatives to either predicates of events or predicates of propositions. Bellert (1977: 342) postulates that while modals take a proposition argument, evaluatives take "the fact, event, or state of affairs denoted by the sentence in which they occur." A similar move is proposed in Wyner (1994), where evaluatives are treated as a special case of predicates of events.[2]

---

[2] Unlike Bellert's, Wyner's analysis is explicitly cast in a neo-Davidsonian approach to modification (see e.g. Parsons 1990). In Wyner's account, evaluatives are basically predicates of events, which accounts for their veridicality and lack of opacity. They differ from scopeless modifiers such as manner, locative, and temporal adverbials in introducing a minimization operation on the described eventuality: an evaluative predicates over the minimal event verifying the description provided by the rest of the sentence. Wyner's ontology is rich enough to ensure that e.g. (i) and (ii) get different readings,

Events or states of affairs, in contrast with propositions, are parts of the world. Clearly, Bellert's analysis is not adequate, as shown by two observations. First, as noted by Bartsch (1976: 40–43), the analysis of evaluatives as predicates of events or states of affairs does not correspond to the intuitive semantics of a sentence with an evaluative. Sentence (4) does not describe an unfortunate state of affairs, but says that it is unfortunate for this state of affairs to hold. Second, evaluatives can take scope over a disjunction or a conditional (Geuder 2000: 149–152).

(4) a. Malheureusement, soit Paul ne viendra pas, soit il arrivera en retard.
         "Unfortunately, either Paul will not come, or he will arrive late."

     b. Malheureusement, si Paul arrive en retard, tu ne pourras pas le rencontrer.
         "Unfortunately, if Paul is late, you won't be able to meet him."

It is difficult to think of states of affairs or events as being disjunctive or conditional. Rather such properties characterize abstract objects, in contrast with parts of the world (Asher 1993: 40–57).

Turning now to abstract objects, the argument of evaluatives could be either a fact or a proposition. It is tempting to say that it is a fact, given the similarity between veridicality and the factive presupposition associated with the argument of so-called factive predicates such as the verb *regretter* 'regret.' However, there is a great deal of unclarity as to the status of facts in the ontology. First, some authors reduce facts to true propositions. But the argument of an evaluative cannot be a fact in that sense, since evaluative adverbs occur inside the antecedent of a conditional; in that case the argument of the evaluative does not have to be true/factual.

because the minimal event of Paul kissing Marie is distinct from the minimal event of Paul kissing Marie in the park. Adverbs which do not introduce minimization do not give rise to such ambiguities (iii–iv).

(i)   Paul a heureusement embrassé Marie dans le parc.
      "Paul fortunately kissed Marie in the park."
      $\exists e[\textbf{fortunate}(e) \wedge \textbf{MIN}(e, \lambda e.[\textbf{kiss}(e, \textbf{p}, \textbf{m}) \wedge \textbf{in-the-park}(e)])]$

(ii) Dans le parc, Paul a heureusement embrassé Marie.
      "In the park, Paul fortunately kissed Marie."
      $\exists e[\textbf{fortunate}(e) \wedge \textbf{in-the-park}(e) \wedge \textbf{MIN}(e, \lambda e.[\textbf{kiss}(e, \textbf{p}, \textbf{m})])]$

(iii) Paul a embrassé Marie passionnément dans le parc.
      "Paul kissed Marie passionately in the park."
      $\exists e[\textbf{passionate}(e) \wedge \textbf{kiss}(e, \textbf{p}, \textbf{m}) \wedge \textbf{in-the-park}(e)]$

(iv) Dans le parc, Paul a embrassé Marie passionnément.
      "In the park, Paul kissed Marie passionately."
      $\exists e[\textbf{passionate}(e) \wedge \textbf{kiss}(e, \textbf{p}, \textbf{m}) \wedge \textbf{in-the-park}(e)]$

(5)   Tout le monde sera déçu si, malheureusement, Paul est en retard.
      "Everybody will be disappointed if, unfortunately, Paul is late."

A different tradition takes facts to be an ontological category distinct from that of true propositions (Asher 1993; Peterson 1997; Ginzburg and Sag 2001). The motivation for this ontological distinction is distributional: some predicates, such as the adjective *true*, the noun *proposition*, or the verb *believe* take a proposition as their argument, while others, such as the noun *fact* or the verb *regret*, take a fact as their argument. This is taken to account for example for the contrasts in (6).

(6)   a.   That proposition is true.

      b.   John believes that proposition.

      c.   *That fact is true.

      d.   *John regrets that proposition.

Moreover, the distinction can be taken to account for the behavior of *resolutive* predicates, that can embed an interrogative but give rise to the "resolutive" reading corresponding to the paraphrase in (7). Under Ginzburg and Sag's (2001) account, *know* takes a fact as its argument, and interrogative meaning can be type-coerced to fact meaning.

(7)   a.   Paul knows who left.

      b.   Paul knows a correct answer to the question: who left?

While other aspects of Ginzburg and Sag (2001) are convincing, the defense of facts strikes us as ill-supported. First, as Godard and Jayez (1999) and Jayez and Godard (1999) show, the denotation of the noun *fact* does not correspond to the ontological notion of fact, and may vary slightly from language to language. A striking example of this is the fact that the French word *fait* 'fact' cannot serve as a complement to the verb *savoir* 'know.'

(8)   *Paul sait ce fait.
      "Paul knows that fact."

What this and other data show is that one should be wary of any argument resting on the lexical semantics of individual abstract nouns (such as *proposition, fact, situation, possibility*) since the use of these nouns in ordinary usage does not fit their use in ontological discussions.

   Even when restricting the discussion to the analysis of verbs, it turns out that the notion of *fact* does not play any crucial role in Ginzburg and Sag's analysis. To account for the difference between resolutive predicates (such as *know*) and *emotive* predicates such as *regret* (which do not embed interrogatives; see Peterson 1997), Ginzburg and Sag (2001: 353) silently abandon the type coercion analysis in favor of a polysemy analysis: resolutive predicates have two lexical entries, one for their declarative-embedding use, and one for their interrogative-embedding use. But once these predicates have two lexical entries, there is no real sense in which resolutive predicates always take the same type of argument; thus the notion of a fact does not play any role in accounting for the distributional data.

To sum up, the general unclarity of the notion of fact suggests that taking evaluatives to be predicates of facts will raise more questions than it solves. Thus we follow Geuder (2000) in assuming that evaluatives are predicates of propositions. In this respect, they do not differ from modals, which also take a proposition argument. Of course, such a move means that we cannot rely on the semantic type of evaluatives to account for their veridicality (1a) or their non-opacity (1b). We provide below in section 11.4 an explanation of these properties based on the special pragmatic status of evaluative adverbs.

11.3 Evaluative adverbs and adjectives

Another way of approaching the semantics of evaluative adverbs is by comparing them with the base adjective, e.g. *malheureusement* with *malheureux*. Since we assume that evaluative adverbs take a propositional argument, we will compare their use with uses of adjectives where the adjective uncontroversially takes a propositional argument; that is, in French, when the adjective takes a finite clause as its complement.[3] Strikingly, when we look at a root sentence, there is a systematic paraphrase between the sentences with an evaluative adverb and with the corresponding adjective. Moreover, an entailment similar to that noted in (1a) for the adverb is valid with the adjective.

(9)   a.   Paul est bizarrement déjà parti.
           "Oddly, Paul is already gone."

      b.   Il est bizarre que Paul soit déjà parti.
           "It is odd that Paul is already gone."

(10)   Il est bizarre que Paul soit déjà parti.
       "It is odd that Paul is already gone."
       ⇒ Paul est déjà parti.
           "Paul is already gone."

---

[3] Note that many of the relevant adjectives may take other types of arguments, and even give rise to non-evaluative adverbs. For instance the adjective *malencontreux* 'unfortunate' may qualify both propositions and events, and indeed there exist both evaluative and "manner" uses of *malencontreusement*. In the remainder of this chapter we leave aside the problem of adjective and adverb polymorphism, to concentrate on evaluative predications.

It is therefore appropriate to ask whether there is an equivalence (modulo the syntax) between the adverb and the adjective. The answer is clearly negative: first, while the content of the adjective is, as is the usual case, part of the main content of the sentence, this is not so for adverbs; second, while the entailment in (10) is an effect of presupposition, this is not so for the implication in (1a).

Consider the truth conditions of the conditionals in (11). Crucially, they ignore the adverb; that is, the presence of the adverb does not affect what conditional is expressed, and only provides an evaluative comment on the strangeness of one of the related propositions. This is not true with the adjective, which takes part in the semantics of the clause it occurs in, and thus modifies what conditional gets expressed (12).[4]

(11) a. Si Paul, bizarrement, part en vacances, nous serons furieux.
          "If, strangely, Paul goes away on vacation, we will be furious."
          ⇔ Si Paul part en vacances, nous serons furieux.
          "If Paul goes away on vacation, we will be furious."

      b. Si Paul part en vacances, nous ne le saurons bizarrement pas.
          "If Paul goes away on vacation, we will, strangely, not know of it."
          ⇔ Si Paul part en vacances, nous ne le saurons pas.
          "If Paul goes away on vacation, we will not know it."

(12) a. S'il est bizarre que Paul parte en vacances, nous comptons pourtant dessus.
          "If it is strange that Paul goes away on vacation, still we count on it."
          ⇎ ?Si Paul part en vacances, nous comptons pourtant dessus.
          "If Paul goes on vacation, we still count on it."

      b. Si Paul part en vacances, il est bizarre que nous ne le sachions pas.
          "If Paul goes away on vacation, it is strange that we don't know of it."
          ⇎ Si Paul part en vacances, nous ne le savons pas.
          "If Paul goes away on vacation, we don't know of it."

The facts in (11) show that the content of the adverb is not part of the main content: in this instance, it is not asserted as are the other expressions. We come back to this characterization in section 11.4.

The evaluative adverb also differs from the adjective with respect to the status of the proposition argument: the adjective presupposes it while the adverb

---

[4] The difference between evaluative adverbs and adjectives is such that it is difficult to find natural-sounding conditionals where both the adjective and the adverb are appropriate; hence we do not try to give parallel examples. Note that (i) this does not affect our observation on the semantic transparency of adverbs, and on the contrary (ii) it reinforces the observation that the adverb and the adjective do not have the exact same semantics.

does not. Let us first test *presupposition holes* (Karttunen 1974); for instance, the presuppositions included in the antecedent of a conditional are carried over to the whole sentence, as illustrated in (13) with the factive verb *regretter*. The evaluative adjective (14), but not the evaluative adverb (15), patterns with presupposition triggers.

(13)   Si Marie regrette que Paul soit en retard, c'est qu'elle ne le connaît pas bien.
       "If Marie regrets that Paul is late, it is because she does not know him well."
       ⇒ Paul est en retard.   "Paul is late."

(14)   S'il est malheureux que Paul soit en retard, ça l'est encore plus que le patron le soit aussi.
       "If it is unfortunate that Paul is late, it is even worse that the boss is late too."
       ⇒ Paul est en retard.   "Paul is late."

(15)   Si Paul est malencontreusement en retard, le patron sera furieux.
       "If Paul is unfortunately late, the boss will be furious."
       ⇏ Paul est en retard.   "Paul is late."

Modal operators, another class of presupposition holes, confirm this observation.

(16)   Marie regrette probablement que Paul soit en retard.
       "Probably, Marie regrets that Paul is late."
       ⇒ Paul est en retard.   "Paul is late."

(17)   Probablement qu'il est malencontreux que Paul soit en retard.
       "It is probably unfortunate that Paul is late."
       ⇒ Paul est en retard   "Paul is late."

(18)   Probablement, Paul arrivera malencontreusement en retard.
       "Probably, Paul will arrive late, unfortunately."
       ⇏ Paul est en retard.   "Paul is late."

On the other hand, *presupposition filters*, such as the consequent of a conditional, may prevent transmission of the presupposition to a larger context. Here, we observe a different contrast between the adjective and the adverb. While the adjective in (20) behaves as expected (the presupposition is trapped), the evaluative adverb does not seem to be felicitous in such contexts (21).

(19)   Si Paul est en retard, il le regrettera certainement.
       "If Paul is late, he will certainly regret it."
       ⇏ Paul est en retard.   "Paul is late."

(20)   Il est malheureux que Paul ait une femme, s'il en a une.
       "It is unfortunate that Paul has a wife, if he does."
       ⇏ Paul a une femme.   "Paul has a wife."

(21)   # Si Paul est en retard, il est malheureusement en retard.
       "If Paul is late, he is unfortunately late."

If, as suggested above, the adverb does not participate in the main content of the sentence, and has no influence on the truth conditions, one may wonder why (21) is not appropriate while a plain tautology such as (22a) is. It is well-known that tautologies are acceptable insofar as they can be pragmatically reinterpreted in order to play a role in dialogue (e.g., Levinson 1983: 110–111). For instance, (22a) may be uttered in order to convey something like "let us not lament that Paul is late, let us discuss what we can do about the situation." But note that this type of reinterpretation depends on the formal parallelism between the antecedent and the consequent; it is not sufficient that the two clauses be semantically equivalent, as shown by the absence of reinterpretation in (22b–c). Thus it comes as no surprise that the presence of the adverb makes reinterpretation impossible.[5] In fact, (22b–c) may be used to buttress semantic equivalences between expressions, which is not the case, of course, in (22a). It is not the case either in (21) because there is no way of finding an epistemic difference between the antecedent and the consequent, given that the adverb makes no contribution to the main content.

(22)   a.   Si Paul est en retard, Paul est en retard.
            "If Paul is late, Paul is late."

       b.   Si Paul est en retard, Paul n'est ni en avance ni à l'heure.
            "If Paul is late, Paul is neither early nor just on time."

       c.   Si la femme de Paul est en retard, l'épouse de Paul est en retard.
            "If Paul's wife is late, Paul's spouse is late."

We conclude that, although the adverb is associated with the same semantic relation as the adjective, it cannot be considered to be a simple equivalent with a different syntactic category.

---

[5] Of course, if the adverb occurs both in the antecedent and the consequent, as in (i), formal parallelism is met and the expected pragmatic reinterpretation is available.

   (i)   Si Paul est malheureusement en retard, Paul est malheureusement en retard.
         "If Paul is unfortunately late, Paul is unfortunately late."

We account for the semantic behavior of evaluative adverbs with the lexical decomposition schema in (23), where p is a variable over propositions, "$\forall^*$" denotes a universal closure operation (binding all free variables in its scope), and **adjective** is the content of the evaluative adjective corresponding to the adverb. Taking *malheureusement* as our typical evaluative adverb, in the absence of free variables, (23) says that this adverb takes a proposition argument and, if this proposition is true, then it is unfortunate that it is.

(23)   Lexical decomposition content of the evaluative adverb[6]
$$\lambda p.\forall^*[p \rightarrow \textbf{adjective}(p)]$$

The basic lexical relation on which the semantics of the adverb relies is identical to that of the adjective. This does justice to the systematic relation between the adverb and the adjective. However, crucially, schema (23) mentions two differences, the universal closure, and the conditional semantics.

Why the conditional semantics? First, let us note immediately that it solves the problem of the different status of the argument with respect to presupposition, assuming an appropriate partial logic for presupposition. For instance, under Peters' (1979) interpretation of the logical connectives, it is a theorem that if q presupposes p, then $p \rightarrow q$ does not presuppose p;[7] thus (23) accounts directly for the contrast between (20) and (21): although *it is unfortunate that p* presupposes p, *unfortunately p* does not because it means the same as *if p, then it is unfortunate that p*.

Second, the conditional form allows us to get the right truth conditions in the different contexts in which the adverb occurs. Consider an assertion of a simple declarative sentence containing an evaluative, such as (9a). As we have seen and will emphasize in section 11.4, when uttering such a sentence, the speaker commits himself to the truth both of the evaluative comment and of the sentence without the evaluative. Thus here the speaker is committed to the truth of both *Paul is already gone* and *If Paul is already gone, then it is odd that he is*. Assuming that speakers are committed to the truth of obvious entailments of their commitments, this means, by *modus ponens*, that the speaker is committed to the truth of (9b). This

---

[6] Note that we do not assume a definite semantic contribution for the suffix *-ment*, for two reasons. First, the semantic contribution suggested by (23), i.e. $\lambda Q\lambda p.\forall^*[p \rightarrow Q(p)]$, is adequate only for evaluatives, and not, e.g., for modals: modal adverbs do not introduce a conditional or bind free variables. Second, the formation of evaluative adverbs is not productive, and there are only about fifteen items in the lexicon with the relevant properties (Molinier and Levrier 2000 list ten items, to which should be added at least *malencontreusement* 'unfortunately,' *miraculeusement* 'miraculously,' *incroyablement* 'incredibly'), so that there is no interesting morphological generalization to be made.

[7] See Krahmer (1998: chapter 4) for discussion.

accounts for the paraphrase relation between evaluative adverbs and adjectives in simple declarative sentences. Next consider evaluative adverbs occurring in conditionals, as in (11). In such cases, since the argument of the evaluative is not asserted, the conditional semantics in (23) takes its full force. Thus in (11a), the evaluative comment is that if indeed Paul goes away on vacation, it is strange that he does, which conforms to our semantic intuitions.

Finally, consider cases where the evaluative occurs inside a question. Although many authors claim that these are ungrammatical, Bonami et al. (2004) show that this is true only of initial occurrences (24a). If the evaluative is not clause-initial, then it is felicitous (24b).

(24) a.   *Bizarrement, qui est arrivé à l'heure?

      b.   Qui est arrivé à l'heure, bizarrement?
           "Who arrived on time, oddly?"

In (24b), the evaluative is not part of the query: the sentence does not ask for which x it is odd that x arrived on time. Rather, it simply asks who arrived on time, and the evaluative provides a comment to the effect that whoever arrived on time, it is odd that they did. This is as expected, given (23) and a syntax and semantics for questions in the spirit of Ginzburg and Sag (2001). Simplifying somewhat (see section 11.5 for more details), we assume that a *wh*-question such as (25a) denotes the proposition abstract in (25b). The abstraction operation is associated with the *wh*-construction, and thus it has not applied yet when the adverb is combined with the clause's content. Thus we assume that in (24b), the argument of the adverb is the open proposition in (26a); thus the evaluative comment is (26b), which conforms with our initial intuition.[8]

(25) a.   Qui est arrivé à l'heure?
           "Who arrived on time?"

      b. $\lambda x.[\textbf{arrive-on-time}(x)]$

---

[8] One concern with the analysis as stated in (23) is that it does not put enough material in the restrictor to give the right semantics. Thus if the question is (i), we want the universal to quantify over students only, as in (ii), whereas (23) gives (iii). The syntax–semantics interface proposed in section 11.5 solves this issue.

(i)   Quels étudiants sont bizarrement arrivés à l'heure?
      "Which students oddly arrived on time?"

(ii) $\forall x[[\textbf{student}(x) \wedge \textbf{arrive-on-time}(x)] \rightarrow \textbf{odd}(\textbf{arrive-on-time}(x))]$

(iii) $\forall x[\textbf{arrive-on-time}(x) \rightarrow \textbf{odd}(\textbf{arrive-on-time}(x))]$

(26)   a.   **arrive-on-time**(x)

     b. $\forall^*[\textbf{arrive-on-time}(x) \rightarrow \textbf{odd}(\textbf{arrive-on-time}(x))] \equiv$
        $\forall x[\textbf{arrive-on-time}(x) \rightarrow \textbf{odd}(\textbf{arrive-on-time}(x))]$

11.4 Evaluative adverbs and dialogue

11.4.1 *Evaluatives as ancillary commitments*

It has been said in the preceding section that the content of the evaluative adverb is not part of the main content of the sentence in which it occurs. On the other hand, we have also suggested that the speaker is somehow committed to the evaluative comment. We now turn to the special pragmatic status of evaluatives, which accounts for this intriguing double behavior.

As observed by Jayez and Rossari (2004), evaluatives cannot be challenged by the other discourse participants, at least with ordinary means. Compare the dialogues in (27) and (28). On the other hand, evaluatives can be challenged by a speaker who, at the same time, accepts or rejects the main content (Potts 2005: 51). This requires a special form of answer, such as *yes... but* (29).

(27)   *A*:   Paul a malheureusement perdu l'élection.
          "Paul unfortunately lost the election."

      B: Non / C'est faux, ou, en tout cas, ce n'est pas ce que j'ai entendu.
          "No / It's false, or, in any case, it is not what I have heard."

(28)   *A*:   Paul a malheureusement perdu l'élection.
          "Paul unfortunately lost the election."

      B: # C'est faux, je trouve que c'est une très bonne nouvelle.
          "That's not true, I think it is very good news."

(29)   *A*:   Paul a malheureusement perdu l'élection.
          "Paul unfortunately lost the election."

      B$_1$:   C'est vrai, mais moi, je trouve que c'est une très bonne nouvelle!
          "Yes, but I personally think it is great news!"

      B$_2$:   Non, c'est faux, mais, même si c'était vrai, je trouverais que c'est une excellente nouvelle!
          "No, it's false, but, even if it were the case, I would find it an excellent piece of news!"

This data makes sense if the evaluative adverb denotes the judgment of the speaker independently of the other commitments associated with his discourse. We will say that the evaluative conveys an *ancillary commitment* of the speaker.

Assuming that evaluative adverbs convey a commitment of the speaker independent of that effected by the main speech act directly accounts for the two basic semantic properties discussed in section 11.2: veridicality and absence of opacity. Since the adverb does not contribute to the main speech act, this speech act gets effected just as if the adverb were absent. Thus if the utterance is an assertion, the speaker is committed to the truth of the proposition conveyed by the sentence without the adverb. As for non-opacity, since we assume that evaluative adverbs take a propositional argument, nothing in their semantics precludes them from triggering opacity. However their special pragmatic status has the required effect. The crucial observation here is that we are dealing with the beliefs of a single agent. If he says (1b), the speaker (assuming sincerity) indicates he believes that (i) Marie is the new boss, (ii) Paul criticized Marie, and (iii) it is unfortunate that Paul criticized Marie. While it is possible for an agent to have contradictory beliefs, it is not so easy to *knowingly* entertain contradictory beliefs. Thus for a speaker to say (1b) and still deny that Paul unfortunately criticized the new boss would be akin to his asserting (30), which is clearly odd. Thus, just as first person attitude reports are ordinary attitude reports with a special pragmatic status that bars opacity, we assume that evaluative adverbs are proposition modifiers with a special pragmatic status.

(30)   I believe that Marie is the new boss, and I believe that Paul criticized Marie; but I don't believe that Paul criticized the new boss.

This ancillary commitment hypothesis also explains a well-known observation, which nevertheless has resisted syntactic or logical accounts: in contrast with evaluative adjectives, evaluative adverbs cannot be in the scope of negation.

(31)   a.   *Paul n'est pas malheureusement venu.
            "Paul did not unfortunately come."

       b.   Il n'est pas malheureux que Paul soit venu
            "It is not unfortunate that Paul came."

       c.   Paul n'est pas forcément venu.
            "Paul did not necessarily come."

This cannot be due to type mismatch. First, the negation is also an operator taking a proposition argument, so it suffices that the evaluative does not change the type of the expression it combines with (i.e., that it denotes a function from propositions to propositions) for the negation to find the right argument type. Second, some modal adverbs can occur in the scope of the negation (31c). Note that the scope of (prosodically integrated)[9] postverbal adverbs follows order: an adverb has scope over adverbs on its right. Accordingly, the only possible argument of the evaluative in (31a) is **come(p)**. Thus, according to our analysis, (31a) commits the speaker to the two propositions in (32). While these are not contradictory, it is quite odd for a speaker to engage in conditional talk about a proposition which he simultaneously asserts to be false. While this may be done using counterfactuals, it seems that explicit marks of counterfactuality (e.g., the use of tenses in 33) is needed for it to be felicitous.[10]

(32) a. Main assertion of (31a): $\neg$**come(p)**

  b. Ancillary commitment of (31a):
     come(p) $\rightarrow$ unfortunate(come(p))

(33) Si Paul était venu, il serait dommage qu'il l'ait fait.
    "If Paul had come, it would have been unfortunate that he did."

To summarize, evaluatives do not contribute to the main content of the sentence, but they imply a commitment on the part of the speaker. Several analyses have been proposed. The first attempt consisted in associating sentences with evaluatives with two speech acts, one for the main content, and one for the evaluative content (Bartsch 1976; Bellert 1977). Although these analyses delineate the problem, they do not deal with the asymmetric status of the two contents, which do not have the same role in dialogue, as shown above. More recently, Bach (1999) suggested that expressions such as evaluatives constitute ancillary propositions, which are distinct from the main content, but can nevertheless be asserted at the same time as the main content (secondarily). Their occurrence in interrogative sentences noted in (24), where they are not

---

  [9] See section 11.5.2.
  [10] Similarly, unlike adverbs which clearly contribute to the main content (e.g., manner, modal, frequency adverbs), an evaluative cannot be negated by *pas* in an elliptical answer (i). More generally, it appears that an agent cannot commit himself to an evaluative judgment unless he believes at least that the proposition may be true. This explains the contrast between the embedding under the two attitude verbs *croire* 'believe' and *douter* 'doubt' in (ii).

  (i) A Paul est venu. ("Paul came.")

    B *Pas forcément !*   / *Pas souvent !* / * *Pas malheureusement !*
      "Not obligatorily!" / "Not often!" / "Not unfortunately!"

  (ii) a. Je crois que Paul est malheureusement / bizarrement venu.
       "I believe that Paul unfortunately / strangely came."

    b. ?? Je doute que Paul soit malheureusement / bizarrement venu.
       "I doubt that Paul unfortunately / strangely came."

included in the question content and the query speech act, raises a serious problem for this proposal. It seems that we need an ancillary assertion in addition to the query; it is not clear, then, what the difference is with the two speech act proposal. Finally, in two concomitant analyses (Jayez and Rossari 2004; Potts 2005), evaluatives are seen as a case of conventional implicatures in Grice's (1975) sense: although they are not part of "what is said," their semantic content is encoded in the grammar. Accordingly, they contribute to an independent dimension of content. While we believe these analyses to be on the right track, they fall short of accounting for the special dialogical status of evaluatives observed in (27–29): we still need to work out what the dialogical status of that independent dimension is. We thus propose an analysis of the pragmatics of evaluatives, integrated in a model of dialogue, a slightly modified version of Ginzburg (2004).

11.4.2 *Modeling ancillary commitments*

We adopt the view that speech acts are best seen as (possibly complex) dialogue moves. Ginzburg's framework models dialogue moves as updates to a structure he calls the *dialogue gameboard*. The idea is that each participant keeps a gameboard representing what he assumes to be known to the participants in the current exchange. The gameboard is particular to a participant, although normal conversation usually aims at synchronizing the content of the gameboards. The gameboard contains three parts:

- The questions under discussion (QUD), a partially ordered set of questions.
- The set of FACTS that the dialogue participants are publicly committed to.
- The LATEST-MOVE, a representation of the preceding dialogue move.

The set of FACTS is a close analogue to the *common ground* in the sense of Stalnaker (1978): it contains "a set of facts corresponding to the information taken for granted by the C[onversational] P[articipant]s" (Ginzburg and Cooper 2004: 325). For reasons that will become clear presently, we need to distinguish more directly the participant's view of the common ground, that is, what he believes is shared knowledge, from what he is publicly committed to, that is, the *commitments* of that participant in the dialogue (Hamblin 1970). Thus we replace the set of FACTS by two independent pieces of information:

- The common ground (CG), a set of propositions.
- The participant's commitments (CMT), a distinct set of propositions.

Of course there is a link between the commitments of the dialogue participants and the common ground: once every participant is committed to some proposition, that proposition becomes common ground; but (i) some propositions in the CG correspond to background knowledge that nobody is explicitly committed to, and (ii) a participant may reject a proposition that some other participant is committed to.[11]

With those definitions in mind, we can model the dialogue gameboard as a feature structure, and describe dialogue moves as updates to that feature structure. Let us start with a detailed description of successful assertion. When a speaker A asserts p (34a), he puts p in his commitment set; he also puts the question *whether p* on the top of the QUD, which signals that he considers that the question is open to discussion and that he is waiting for the addressee's uptake. The addressee B may react by just refusing to consider A's assertion. But if he is willing to consider it (34b), this amounts to putting the question *whether p* on the top of his own QUD. B may then either accept A's assertion of p or reject it – the issue then stays under discussion. If the assertion is accepted, this amounts to B putting p in his own set of commitments and removing *whether p* from his QUD (34c);[12] as a side effect, B now believes p to be common ground, since both participants are committed to it. Finally, when A realizes that B has accepted p, he considers the question *whether p* to be settled (and thus removes it from QUD) and the proposition p to be common ground (34d).

(34) Assertion in a dialogue gameboard

   a. Participant A's update when asserting p:

$$\begin{bmatrix} \text{CMT} & \boxed{C} \\ \text{CG} & \boxed{G} \\ \text{QUD} & \boxed{Q} \end{bmatrix} \rightsquigarrow \begin{bmatrix} \text{CMT} & \{p\} \cup \boxed{C} \\ \text{CG} & \boxed{G} \\ \text{QUD} & \langle p? \rangle \oplus \boxed{Q} \end{bmatrix}$$

---

[11] Notice that we do not propose to represent explicitly within the dialogue gameboard a record of the addressee's commitments. While it is clear that discourse participants keep track of what their interlocutors are committed to in order to plan their future utterances, it is not clear that this information is used to constrain linguistic form. See Gunlogson (2001); Beyssade and Marandin (2006) for relevant discussion. Also notice that we treat the common ground as a set of *propositions*, while Ginzburg takes them to be *facts*. See section 11.2 above for a critique of Ginzburg's notion of fact.

[12] Notice that on this view some dialogue gameboard updates may have no linguistic reflex, or even no reflex at all. Thus accepting an assertion may consist in an utterance (e.g. *yes*), a non-linguistic event (e.g. a nod) or no reaction at all. The decomposition of assertion in elementary gameboard updates is taken to reflect the fact that signaling explicitly the acceptance of an assertion is the rule rather than the exception.

b. Participant B's update when considering A's assertion of p:

$$
\begin{bmatrix}
\text{CMT} & \boxed{C'} \\
\text{CG} & \boxed{G'} \\
\text{QUD} & \boxed{Q'}
\end{bmatrix}
\rightsquigarrow
\begin{bmatrix}
\text{CMT} & \boxed{C'} \\
\text{CG} & \boxed{G'} \\
\text{QUD} & \langle p?\rangle \oplus \boxed{Q'}
\end{bmatrix}
$$

c. Participant B's update when accepting A's assertion of p:

$$
\begin{bmatrix}
\text{CMT} & \boxed{C'} \\
\text{CG} & \boxed{G'} \\
\text{QUD} & \langle p?\rangle \oplus \boxed{Q'}
\end{bmatrix}
\rightsquigarrow
\begin{bmatrix}
\text{CMT} & \{p\}\cup\boxed{C'} \\
\text{CG} & \{p\}\cup\boxed{G'} \\
\text{QUD} & \boxed{Q'}
\end{bmatrix}
$$

d. Participant A's update when realizing that B has accepted the assertion:

$$
\begin{bmatrix}
\text{CMT} & \{p\}\cup\boxed{C} \\
\text{CG} & \boxed{G} \\
\text{QUD} & \langle p?\rangle \oplus \boxed{Q}
\end{bmatrix}
\rightsquigarrow
\begin{bmatrix}
\text{CMT} & \{p\}\cup\boxed{C} \\
\text{CG} & \{p\}\cup\boxed{G} \\
\text{QUD} & \boxed{Q}
\end{bmatrix}
$$

Our proposal for the role of evaluatives is as follows. When uttering *eval p*, the speaker puts the evaluative in his own set of commitments without putting it on the QUD list. Accordingly, the evaluative is not under discussion, and cannot be rejected or accepted by the usual means (see 28–29). In addition, the main assertion can be accepted or rejected independently of the evaluative. The addressee is not committed either way, since the evaluative is not part of QUD.

(35)   Participant's gameboard when uttering *eval p*:

$$
\begin{bmatrix}
\text{CMT} & \boxed{C} \\
\text{CG} & \boxed{G} \\
\text{QUD} & \boxed{Q}
\end{bmatrix}
\rightsquigarrow
\begin{bmatrix}
\text{CMT} & \{p, \mathbf{eval}(p)\}\cup\boxed{C} \\
\text{CG} & \boxed{G} \\
\text{QUD} & \langle p?\rangle \oplus \boxed{Q}
\end{bmatrix}
$$

Note that this contrasts with the situation which holds when a participant utters a clause including a presupposition. When asserting a proposition p that presupposes q, the speaker acts as if q were common ground (36). Thus on the one hand there is something in common between evaluatives and presuppositions: neither are put under discussion; on the other hand, there is something in common between evaluatives and assertion: in both cases the speaker makes no claim as to the addressee's information state, whereas a presupposition signals a belief about that information state. This explains why presupposing a proposition that one knows the addressee to believe to be false is uncooperative, while making an evaluative comment with the same content – or asserting that content – is not.

(36) Participant's gameboard when asserting p while presupposing q:

$$\begin{bmatrix} \text{CMT} & \boxed{C} \\ \text{CG} & \boxed{G} \\ \text{QUD} & \boxed{Q} \end{bmatrix} \rightsquigarrow \begin{bmatrix} \text{CMT} & \{p\} \cup \boxed{C} \\ \text{CG} & \{q\} \cup \boxed{G} \\ \text{QUD} & \langle p?\rangle \oplus \boxed{Q} \end{bmatrix}$$

11.4.3 *On embedded evaluatives*

Up to now we have assumed that the speaker was responsible for the judgment associated with the evaluative adverb. This is a simplification: although it is by far the most frequent situation, it is not always the case. Whether or not an agent other than the speaker can take charge of conventional implicatures has been the object of some debate. Whatever is the case for the (other) conventional implicatures, the data for evaluatives is clear. There are contexts where the speaker attributes the judgment to another agent; the clearest case is that of speech reports.

Consider sentence (37). Both (37a) and (37b) are possible continuations. Yet the agent responsible for the evaluative is the speaker in (37a), and Marie in (37b).

(37) Marie expliquait que le prêtre, bizarrement, avait perdu la foi.
      "Marie was saying that, strangely, the priest has lost his faith."

   a. Quand je lui dis ma surprise, elle soutint qu'il n'y avait là rien d'extraordinaire.
       "When I expressed my surprise, she maintained that it was not strange at all."

   b. Moi, je ne vois rien d'extraordinaire à ce qu'un prêtre perde la foi.
       "For my part, I do not find it strange for a priest to lose his faith."

Potts (2005: 116–117) dismisses such examples as hidden cases of direct quotation. While this might be the correct analysis in some cases, this cannot be true for sentences like (38). Note that the evaluative phrase contains the indexical *moi* 'me,' which unambiguously refers to the speaker, and not Marie. Thus the evaluative phrase cannot be part of a direct quotation of Marie's speech.

(38) Marie m'a annoncé que, malheureusement pour moi, je n'avais pas été élu. Je lui ai expliqué que cela m'arrangeait plutôt, vu que je n'avais jamais eu l'intention de prendre le poste.
      "Marie announced that, unfortunately for me, I hadn't been elected. I explained that it was all for the best, given that I never intended to accept the position."

Thus, like most researchers (Bach 1999; Geuder 2000; Jayez and Rossari 2004) but contra Potts (2005), we accept that the agent responsible for the evaluative may be different from the speaker. Accordingly, an adequate analysis must not presuppose that evaluatives are strictly speaker-oriented. Although we do not provide an explicit account of examples like (38) here for lack of space, we note that an appropriate analysis can be provided by assuming that speech report verbs give rise to the same type of semantic representations as full utterances, including a representation of the dialogue gameboard of the agent whose speech is reported, where the evaluative can be scoped appropriately. Bonami and Godard (2007b) makes such an analysis explicit within an HPSG grammar.

11.5 Interface issues

In this section we discuss a number of issues pertaining to the status of evaluative adverbs at the syntax–semantics–phonology interface. We start by providing a grammar fragment within the framework of *Head-driven Phrase Structure Grammar* (Pollard and Sag 1994), which is inspired by the approach to clausal content of Ginzburg and Sag (2001). Semantic composition is done using a Cooper storage mechanism in the tradition of Pollard and Sag (1994). We then discuss the advantages and limitations of that fragment, and point to other relevant work.

11.5.1 *The fragment*

In this section we provide an HPSG grammar fragment accounting for the syntax and semantics of clause-initial evaluatives in declaratives. We adopt the framework of Ginzburg and Sag (2001), which is characterized by three notable features. First, clause types are intimately connected to a (situation-theoretic) abstract object ontology which distinguishes, among other things, states of affairs (*soa*), propositions, and questions. A basic proposition is structurally determined by a situation s and a state of affairs σ, and says that σ holds in s. Propositions serve as the denotation of declarative clauses. Questions are analyzed as n-ary abstractions over propositions, where the abstraction operation applies to sets of parameters; the ontology is set up in such a way that a 0-ary abstract is an object distinct from the proposition it abstracts over, and 0-ary abstracts serve as the denotation of polar interrogatives. In the HPSG grammar, each semantic object type is associated with a feature structure specifying the structural parts of this object, as illustrated by the type hierarchy in Fig. 11.1. An *soa* is structurally determined by an elementary predication, its NUCLEUS, and a list of (scoped) quantifiers; a *proposition* is

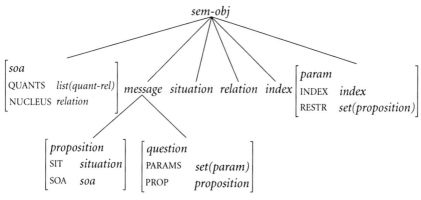

FIGURE 11.1. Part of Ginzburg and Sag's (2001) semantic type hierarchy

determined by a *situation* and an *soa*; and a *question* is determined by a set of parameters (technically, variables associated with a set of restrictions) and a proposition. The types *proposition* and *question* have a common supertype *message*, which encodes the intuition that these semantic objects serve as content for full clauses.

Second, since clause-internal semantic composition relies on *soa*s, some kind of type-shifting is necessary to construct propositions and questions. Here we assume that this is effected by special unary syntactic rules,[13] such as the rule in (39) for declaratives.[14]

(39)
$$
decl\text{-}clause \longrightarrow
\begin{bmatrix}
\text{CONT}
\begin{bmatrix}
proposition \\
\text{SIT} \quad s \\
\text{SOA} \quad \boxed{1}
\end{bmatrix}
\end{bmatrix}
$$
$$
\begin{bmatrix}
\text{CONT} \quad \boxed{1} \, soa
\end{bmatrix}
$$

Finally, speech acts are directly represented in the grammar, at the level of complete utterances. Here we depart slightly from Ginzburg and Sag (2001) by representing directly the effect of the utterance on the dialogue gameboard,

---

[13] Ginzburg and Sag (2001) avoid positing unary rules for declaratives by incorporating type-shifting in head–subject combinations. However this won't do for French, where declarative clauses can consist of a bare VP, when the subject is a pronominal clitic, which we analyze as a prefix on the verb (Miller 1992).

[14] As is usual in HPSG depictions of feature structures as attribute–value matrices, boxed characters such as $\boxed{1}$ are *tags* used to represent reentrancies in the feature structure; thus (39) indicates that the value of the path CONT|SOA on the mother is token-identical to the value of the path CONT on the daughter. Numerical tags ($\boxed{1}$, $\boxed{2}$, etc.) are used for plain objects, while alphabetical tags ($\boxed{A}$, $\boxed{B}$, etc.) are used for lists and sets of objects.

instead of positing an explicit illocutionary relation as the content of the utterance. (40), the constraint on utterances of type *assertion*, reiterates (34) in the format of an HPSG grammar. The feature LMOVE (for LATEST-MOVE) represents the state of the participant's gameboard just before the current move, while unembedded CMT, CG, and QUD features correspond to the state of the gameboard *after* the current move. The propositional content of the clause $\boxed{1}$ gets added to the speaker's commitment, and the corresponding polar question is added to the QUD. In addition, we leave room for extra commitments $\boxed{L}$ of the speaker to be introduced by the clause independently of the main propositional content $\boxed{1}$ and of the commitments inherited from the LMOVE, $\boxed{C}$; this will be crucial to the analysis of evaluatives.[15]

(40)

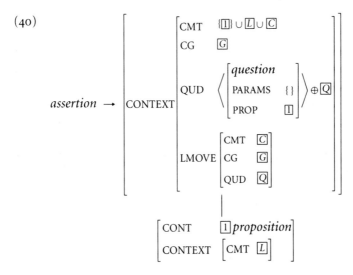

We are now in a position to make explicit the analysis of evaluative adverbs such as *heureusement*. Recall the three main points of our analysis: *heureusement* is a proposition operator; it makes no contribution to the semantic content; and it contributes a proposition to the speaker's commitments. Let us show how these three points are encoded in *heureusement*'s lexical entry, which is shown in Fig. 11.2.

First Fig. 11.2 states that *heureusement* is an adverb, which may modify an expression whose content is of type *proposition*. In the version of HPSG

---

[15] We assume that CMT inheritance inside clauses works as for other contextual features. Ordinary words come with an empty CMT, although there are some exceptions, such as evaluative adverbs. The CMT of a phrase is the union of the CMT of its daughters. It is only at the level of the full utterance that the commitments inherited from the latest move get added to CMT.

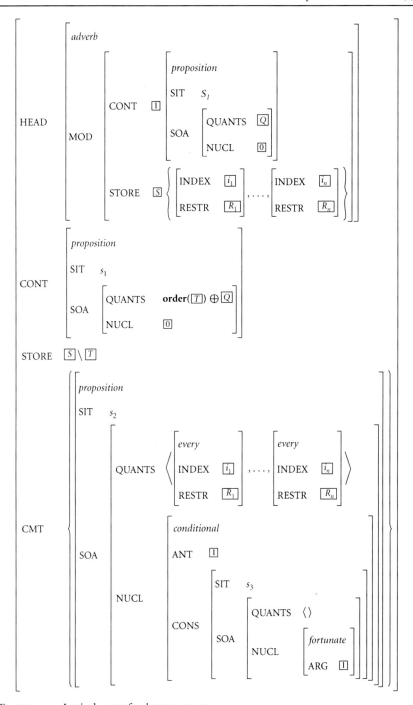

FIGURE 11.2. Lexical entry for *heureusement*

assumed in this chapter, adjuncts get combined with heads via the *hd-adj-ph* phrase type, which states that the adjunct's MOD value is identified with the head's SYNSEM. Thus Fig. 11.2 states that *heureusement* is an adverb which combines with a proposition-denoting phrase. The proposition may be an open proposition, in which case the phrase has binders for free parameters in STORE. In the setup of Ginzburg and Sag (2001), STORE is a Cooper-style storage mechanism that includes both unscoped quantifiers and the parameter associated with *wh*-interrogative phrases.

Second, we want to account for the intuition that the adverb makes no contribution to the main semantic content. Intuitively, this could be encoded by identifying the adverb's CONT with the CONT of the modified head. However, given the way the STORE mechanism works in Ginzburg and Sag's framework, we must leave room for quantifiers to scope at the adverb node, because this might be the only place where they can scope. Thus we only identify the NUCLEUS of the adverb with that of the modified head, and allow for some quantifiers $\boxed{T}$ to be taken out of STORE and scoped (**order**($\boxed{T}$)) at the adverb node.[16] The non-deterministic function **order** outputs an ordered sequence of quantifiers, and thus fixes the relative scope of the members of $\boxed{T}$.

Third, the evaluative adverb makes its semantic contribution as part of the speaker's CMT list. The proposition in CMT is a feature-structural rendering of the semantic analysis in (23). Note that all free variables in the argument of the adverb end up being universally quantified, as needed; the workings of the STORE mechanism ensure that appropriate restrictors are retrieved for the universal quantifiers.

We now illustrate the analysis with a few examples. Let us first assume that the modified phrase's STORE value is empty; the QUANTS list of the speaker's commitment is also empty,[17] and so is $\boxed{T}$, the set of quantifiers scoped at the level of the adverb. As a result, the adverb's CONTENT, which is identified with that of the whole phrase, is identical to that of the head. But a new proposition is put in the set of speaker commitments, corresponding to the meaning of the evaluative. Fig. 11.3 makes explicit the analysis of a simple example. For readability semantic objects have been abbreviated. Note that the evaluative can only combine once the type-shifting *decl-clause* unary phrase has applied, because this is the only way for it to find a proposition argument.

---

[16] "\" denotes set subtraction, i.e. $U = S \setminus T$ iff $S = T \cup U$ and $U \cap T = \emptyset$.

[17] The analysis as presented here is slightly simplified in that it does not allow quantifiers stemming from the evaluative phrase itself, as in *heureusement pour tout le monde* 'fortunately for everybody.' See Bonami and Godard (2007b) for a more complete treatment of the syntax–semantics interface.

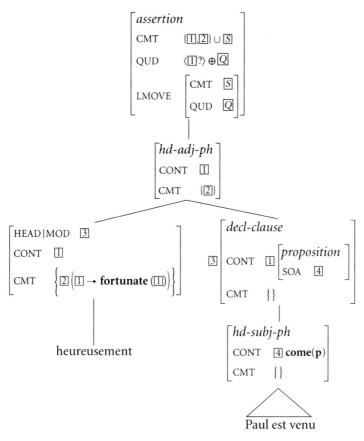

FIGURE 11.3. Analysis for a quantifierless example

We now turn to cases where the STORE value of the modified phrase is not empty. Sentence (41) has two readings, depending on whether *heureusement* takes the quantifier in its scope.[18]

(41) Heureusement, la plupart des étudiants sont venus.
      "Fortunately, most students came."

    a. Most students came, and it is fortunate that most students came (rather than a different proportion).

    b. Most students came, and for those who came, it is fortunate that they did.

---

[18] The second reading is more natural when the adverb is after the verb, and may not be available at all for some speakers, as in many other cases of wide scope proportional quantifiers.

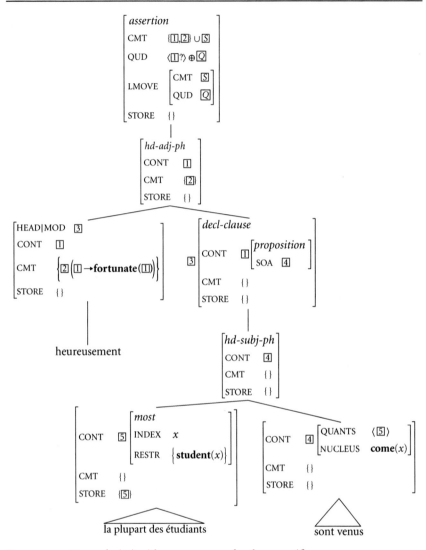

FIGURE 11.4. Example (41) with narrow scope for the quantifier

In Ginzburg and Sag's (2001) setup, quantifiers are scoped at lexical nodes. The first reading is obtained when the quantifier is scoped at the V level. Thus the STORE of the verb is empty, and *heureusement* inherits an empty store. The final analysis is as in Fig. 11.4.

In the other reading, represented in Fig. 11.5, the quantifier is not scoped at the level of the verb. Accordingly, the STORE is non-empty as it reaches the adverb. Let us assume that the quantifier is scoped at the level of the adverb,

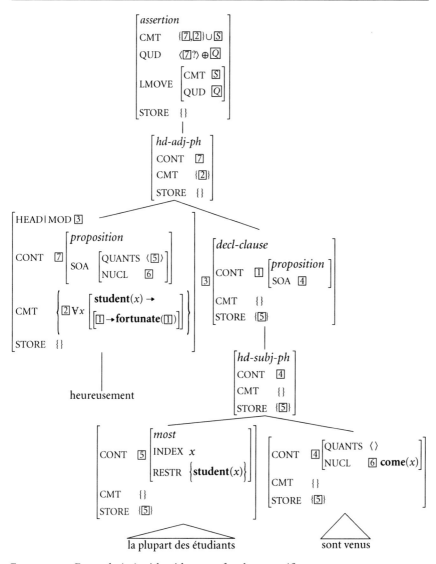

FIGURE 11.5. Example (41) with wide scope for the quantifier

which is the only remaining possibility in this particular example; that is, the STORE of the verb is a singleton containing **most students**, and this singleton ([T] in Fig. 11.2) is scoped at the level of the adverb which thus has an empty STORE. The interesting point here is that since the modified phrase's STORE is non-empty, universal closure comes into play at the level of the ancillary commitment: as stated in Fig. 11.2, a universal quantifier is scoped which takes over the index and restriction of the unscoped quantifier. As a result we get the correct reading corresponding to (41b).[19]

11.5.2 *Prosody, scope, and pragmatic status*

The grammar fragment of the preceding section accounts for the semantics and pragmatics of evaluative adverbs occurring sentence-initially in assertions. What remains to be seen is how this fragment can be extended to the general case. In this section we deal with the issue of non-sentence-initial occurrences of evaluatives. In the next section we discuss the specific problems raised by evaluatives in questions.

At this point, we should stress an important distinction which is not usually made in the literature (Bonami et al. 2004): the distinction between a prosodic property, called here *incidentality*, and a semantico-pragmatic property, called here *parentheticality*. Expressions are incidentals when they are not prosodically integrated in the sentence: they are set apart by a number of prosodic cues that make them akin to independent intonational phrases (Fagyal 2002). This corresponds to what is referred to as "comma intonation" in much of the literature. On the other hand, parentheticals are expressions that do not contribute to the main semantic content, but provide an ancillary commitment. This may correspond to the terms "disjunct" (Greenbaum 1969; Espinal 1991) or "supplement" (Huddleston and Pullum 2002; Potts 2005). The problem is that these two properties are usually conflated. However, this is a mistake: the two properties are independent.

Consider (42), where incidentality is noted by commas, and prosodic integration by an absence of commas. It is clear that an evaluative adverb, which is a parenthetical, can be either incidental (42a) or integrated (42b).

(42) a. Malheureusement, Paul s'est comporté comme un idiot.
         "Unfortunately, Paul behaved like an idiot."

      b. Paul s'est malheureusement comporté comme un idiot.
         "Paul unfortunately behaved like an idiot."

As exemplified in (43), manner adverbs can also be used either with an incidental or an integrated prosody. Note that (44) is an appropriate response

---

[19] Note that the use of the same STORE mechanism for *wh*-phrase content entails that, when extended to interrogatives, the current treatment will solve the problem noted in footnote 8. In the implementation of universal closure encoded in Fig. 11.2, the restrictions on unscoped indexes $\boxed{R_1}, \ldots \boxed{R_n}$ are taken over as restrictions of the universal quantifiers. This is true both for indexes corresponding to unscoped quantifiers and for indexes corresponding to unscoped *wh*-phrases.

to both (43a) and (43b), which shows that manner adverbs contribute to the main content, irrespective of their prosody (compare 28).

(43) a. La rivière amorçait lentement sa décrue.
          "The river was slowly dropping in level."

      b. Lentement, la rivière amorçait sa décrue.
          "Slowly, the river was dropping in level."

(44) C'est faux; la décrue a été très rapide cette année-là !
      "It's false; the level dropped very rapidly that year!"

We conclude that the prosodic property of incidentality and the pragmatic property of parentheticality are independent. Actually this is to be expected, since the two properties have independent sources: being a commentary is a property of lexical items while being incidental is a property of their occurrences. Accordingly, evaluatives are parentheticals while manner adverbs are not, whether or not they are incidentals.

A final quick clarification is in order concerning the interaction of incidentality with interpretation. That incidentality is orthogonal to being a parenthetical does not mean that the prosodic property has no import on interpretation. In fact, it is crucially correlated with scope (Bonami et al. 2004): the correlation between scope and the syntactic property of order (alternatively, c-command in some other approaches)[20] that characterizes integrated adverbs does not hold for incidentals. The findings are summarized in (45).

(45) **Scope–order relations** (Bonami et al. 2004: 156–161)

      a. Non-incidental adverbs scope from left to right.

      b. Incidentals always outscope non-incidentals.

      c. Scope between incidentals is not constrained by order.

Let us take two adverbs whose relative scope is clear and well known: for obvious semantic reasons, modals have scope over manner adverbs, but not the other way around. Compare examples in (46), with one incidental and one integrated adverb, and (47), with two incidentals. Sentence (46b) is not acceptable, because the manner adverb is incidental and thus must have scope over the integrated modal adverb, which is not a licit scoping. Sentence (47a) shows that the incidental manner adverb may very well occur to the

---

[20] In a framework where adverbs are systematically the left daughter in a right-branching structure, the correlation can be reduced to a relation between scope and c-command rather than scope and order.

left of the modal adverb, as in (46b). In fact, in (47), the two orderings are acceptable, because both adverbs are incidental, and the relative scope of incidental adverbs is not constrained by order. Although we cannot dwell on this matter here, the import of incidentality on adverb scoping indicates that the prosodic behavior may be related to syntactic properties (mode of combination).

(46)   a.   Probablement, Paul répondra calmement à la question.
            "Probably, Paul will answer the question calmly."

       b.   *Calmement, Paul répondra probablement à la question.

(47)   a.   Paul, calmement, répondra à la question, probablement.
            "Probably, Paul will answer the question calmly."

       b.   Paul, probablement, répondra à la question, calmement.

These observations mean that a satisfying fragment accounting for the scope of evaluative adverbs cannot be formulated before hard decisions about the syntax of incidentality, and the syntax–semantics interface for modifiers in general, have been made. Bonami and Godard (2007a) proposes a general syntactic treatment of incidental adverbs, relying on a distinction between phrase structure and word order domains (Reape 1994; Kathol 2000): according to this analysis, incidental adverbs are always adjoined to clauses in phrase structure, but can be linearized in different positions via domain union. Bonami and Godard (2007b) provides a syntax–semantics interface for evaluative adverbs which deals in detail with the scopal properties of integrated occurrences, by adopting Bouma et al.'s (2001) syntax for VP-internal modifiers and coupling it with underspecified semantic representations based on Minimal Recursion Semantics (Copestake et al. 2006). Integrating this syntactic and combinatory semantic work with the present work on the lexical semantics and pragmatics of evaluative adverbs would yield a complete analysis of evaluatives in assertive contexts.

11.5.3 *Evaluatives in interrogatives*

In section 11.3 we noted that although evaluatives are not felicitous sentence-initially in questions, they are possible if linearized in other positions. This holds not only for *wh*-questions, but also for polar questions:

(48)   a.   *Bizarrement, qui est arrivé à l'heure?   (=24)

       b.   Qui est arrivé à l'heure, bizarrement ?
            "Who arrived on time, oddly?"

(49) a. *Bizarrement, Paul est-il arrivé en retard?

     b. Paul est-il, bizarrement, arrivé en retard?
       "Did Paul oddly arrive late?"

This observation poses an interesting interface issue. Note that, leaving aside the problems posed by sentence-internal occurrences of adverbs, the fragment presented above can be extended quite easily to questions. All we need are appropriate definitions for a *query* utterance type parallel to (40) and an *interrogative-clause* type parallel to (39). However the ban on initial occurrences is quite surprising. If only *wh*-questions were affected, one could assume that the *head-filler-phrase* turns a proposition into a question, and thus that evaluative adverbs are not possible on the left of the *wh*-phrase because they find no proposition to combine with. But in the case of polar questions no such account is available: since there is no overt marking of the polar interrogative status, we cannot forbid the possibility that the adverb combines with the (proposition-denoting) basic clause before the type-shifting from proposition to question occurs.

Although we presently have no account of the data in (48–49), we note that the phenomenon at hand might shed new light on the status of adverbs occurring in the initial position of questions in general. First, Bonami et al. (2004: 167–170) notes that the class of adverbs occurring sentence-initially in questions is quite odd, and corresponds only loosely to the set of adverbs that occur sentence-initially in assertions. Second, in assertions, it is clear that sentence-initial adverbs may scope lower than some sentence-internal operators, such as tense. As Bonami (2002) emphasizes, the choice of a perfective tense in (50a) can only be justified by the fact that this tense takes the sentence-initial time-span adverbial in its scope. But initial adverbials in questions exhibit no evidence of a similar behavior: note in particular that time-span adverbials are infelicitous in this position (50b).

(50) a. Pendant deux heures, Paul dormit profondément.
       "For two hours, Paul slept.PERF deeply."

     b. *Pendant deux heures, Paul dormit-il profondément ?
       "Did Paul sleep.PERF deeply for two hours?"

This and similar observations suggest that the syntax–semantics interface works quite differently for sentence-initial adverbials in assertions and in questions. A detailed investigation of this issue will have to await future work.

11.6 Conclusion

We have provided an analysis of the semantics and pragmatics of evaluative adverbs relying on two crucial ideas. First, the adverb takes a propositional argument and has a conditional semantics; this accounts for the relation between adverb and adjective semantics while acknowledging their different semantic import. Second, the use of an evaluative adverb constitutes a specific type of dialogue move, which we call an *ancillary commitment*. This move is distinct from both assertion and presupposition. The pragmatic properties of ancillary commitments account for the fact that evaluative adverbs exhibit mixed properties despite their having the same semantic type as intensional operators. Our analysis shows by example how semantic properties, such as robust entailment patterns, are sometimes best analyzed in pragmatic terms.

In the last section, we presented a grammar fragment which accounts for the details of the combinatorics of evaluative adverbs. This fragment has a limited coverage, since our focus in this chapter is on semantics and pragmatics rather than on the syntax–semantics interface; the problems evaluatives raise for the syntax–semantics interface is the topic of a different paper, to which we refer the interested reader (Bonami and Godard 2007b).

Acknowledgments

Aspects of this work have been presented at the Second Journées sémantiques et modélisation (Lyon, 2003), at the GDR2521 workshop on dialogue (March, 2004), and at the workshop on the semantics of adjectives and adverbs (Barcelona, 2005). We thank for their comments and suggestions the audiences at these events, and in particular Claire Beyssade, Francis Corblin, Jonathan Ginzburg, Jacques Jayez, Chris Kennedy, Jean-Marie Marandin, Louise McNally, Adam Wyner, as well as two anonymous reviewers.

12

Discourse adjectives

GINA TARANTO

12.1 Introduction

This chapter introduces and provides a semantic analysis of discourse adjectives, a natural class of predicates whose members include *apparent, evident, clear,* and *obvious* in their use as propositional modifiers in sentences such as those in (1).

(1) a. It is *apparent* that somebody committed a crime.

    b. It is *evident* that the police are on their way.

    c. It is *clear* that Briscoe is a detective.

    d. It is *obvious* that someone watches way too much *Law & Order.*

Discourse adjectives are a predicate type whose meaning is not typical of expressions in natural language. The main claim made is that discourse adjectives provide interlocutors with a way to talk about their conversation rather than their world. To illustrate, compare the sentences in (2).

(2) a. Briscoe is a detective.

    b. It is clear that Briscoe is a detective.

Sentence (2a) is an informative sentence – it provides information about the world. Specifically, (2a) specifies that Briscoe has the property of being a detective. In contrast, sentence (2b) does not provide new information about whether or not Briscoe is a detective. Instead, the new information provided is information about the discourse itself. An utterance of (2b) makes a claim about the interlocutors' beliefs about the proposition expressed by *Briscoe is a detective* – specifically, that in the current discourse situation there is sufficient evidence to conclude that Briscoe is a detective, at least to a minimum, vague standard of clarity.

    The idea presented is that discourse adjectives do not add new information to the common ground in the conventional manner (Stalnaker 1978: 325;

van der Sandt 1992: 367, etc.); they are an example of a predicate whose seman-tics carries no new descriptive content. Their function is to allow speakers to synchronize their common ground. The key elements of this analysis are an understanding of vagueness, factivity, and the interpretation of the sometimes implicit experiencer of a discourse adjective. Additionally, to represent the synchronizing effect of utterances with discourse adjectives, the analysis makes crucial use of a framework that leverages a representation of the speaker's and addressee's distinct information states.

This chapter will provide a complete analysis of the semantics of sentence (2b). It is structured as follows. First, support for the claim that discourse adjectives are a natural class is provided by showing that they share a unique syntactic distribution. The syntactic distribution of discourse adjectives is contrasted with that of two other types of proposition-modifying predicates, raising adjectives and what I call *attitude adjectives*, which correspond in large part to emotive factive predicates (Kiparsky and Kiparsky 1971). The obser-vation is made that discourse adjectives often give the appearance of being factive predicates, even though they ultimately fail standard diagnostics for factivity. The heart of the chapter is a case study of the semantics of *clear* which includes a discussion of experiencers, beliefs, and vagueness. As this case study modifies the framework proposed by Gunlogson (2001), the final section is a brief discussion of the consequences for this model.

12.2 Preliminary observations about discourse adjectives

12.2.1 *Discourse adjectives are a natural syntactic class*

The data in (3)–(8) show that discourse adjectives have a syntactic distri-bution that partially overlaps with, yet is distinct from, that of two other classes of proposition-modifying adjectives. These are the familiar class of raising adjectives, such as *apt, bound, certain,* or *likely*, and the class of atti-tude adjectives such as *absurd, intriguing,* or *ridiculous*. Raising adjectives are a subset of Kiparsky and Kiparsky's non-emotive (not suggestive of an emotional response or reaction), non-factive (not presupposing the truth of their complement) predicates. Attitude adjectives are a subset of Kiparsky and Kiparsky's emotive factive predicates, a label they apply to predicates that express either a speaker's emotional response to a proposition, or a qualitative opinion.

To begin, the only structure that all three classes appear in is the extraposed structure in (3).

(3)   a.   It is clear that the suspect was not advised of her Miranda Rights.

(discourse adjective)

b.   It is absurd that the suspect was not advised of her Miranda Rights.

(attitude adjective)

c.   It is likely that the suspect was not advised of her Miranda Rights.

(raising adjective)

The data in (4) show that raising adjectives is the only one of the three classes to allow so-called *subject-to-subject* raising.

(4)   a.   *The accused is clear to be released on bail.

b.   *The accused is absurd to be released on bail.

c.   The accused is likely to be released on bail.

The data in (5) show that the only class that always licenses an overt experiencer is the class of discourse adjectives. Raising adjectives never do, and attitude adjectives sometimes do.[1]

(5)   a.   It is clear to the D.A. that getting a conviction will be difficult.

b.   It is *absurd/shocking to the D.A. that getting a conviction will be difficult.

c.   *It is likely to the D.A. that getting a conviction will be difficult.

Discourse adjectives are also distinguished as the only class that allows *wh*-complementation. They allow both tensed *wh*-complements, as in (6), and infinitival *wh*-complements as in (7).

(6)   a.   It is usually clear whether or not a jury will buy the Twinkie Defense.

b.   *It is usually absurd/shocking whether or not a jury will buy the Twinkie Defense.

c.   *It is usually likely whether or not a jury will buy the Twinkie Defense.

(7)   a.   It is clear how to prosecute a case like this.

b.   *It is absurd how to prosecute a case like this.

c.   *It is likely how to prosecute a case like this.

Attitude adjectives differ from both discourse and raising adjectives in allowing non-*wh* infinitival complements, as shown in (8).

---

[1] The class of attitude adjectives is admittedly ill-defined in this chapter. Further research is necessary to determine whether and how many subtypes of adjective are captured under this label. What is important for the purposes of this chapter is that there are adjectives in this class that share certain semantic and syntactic properties.

TABLE 12.1. Summary of the syntactic distribution of discourse, raising, and attitude adjectives

	extraposition	subject raising	overt experiencer	*wh*-tensed	*wh*-infinitival	infinitival
Raising	yes	yes	no	no	no	no
Attitude	yes	no	sometimes	no	no	yes
Discourse	yes	no	yes	yes	yes	no

(8) a. *It is clear to address the court in iambic pentameter.

    b. It is absurd/?shocking to address the court in iambic pentameter.

    c. *It is likely to address the court in iambic pentameter.

A summary of the syntactic distribution of discourse, raising, and attitude adjectives is provided in Table 12.1.

12.2.2 *Discourse adjectives are not factive*

Kiparsky and Kiparsky's list of factive predicates is presented in (9), and their list of non-factive predicates is provided in (10).

(9) a. **Factive predicates:** *significant, odd, tragic, exciting, relevant, matter, count, make sense, suffice, amuse, bother.*

    b. **Emotive factives:** *important, crazy, odd, relevant, instructive, sad, suffice, bother, alarm, fascinate, nauseate, exhilarate, defy comment, surpass belief, a tragedy, no laughing matter.*

    c. **Non-emotive factives:** *well known, clear (self-evident), go without saying.*

(10) a. **Non-factive predicates:** *likely, sure, possible, true, false, seem, appear, happen, chance, turn out.*

    b. **Emotive non-factives:** *improbable, unlikely, a pipedream, nonsense, urgent (requires future tense), vital (requires future tense).*

    c. **Non-emotive non-factives:** *probable, likely, turn-out, seem, imminent (requires future tense), in the works (requires future tense).*

Kiparsky and Kiparsky characterize the class of factive predicates as based on presuppositions in the sense of "propositions that the speaker presupposes to be true" (1971: 147). For them, factivity depends on presupposition rather than assertion. Factive predicates presuppose the truth of their complement. That is, a sentence *A* presupposes a sentence *B* if and only if *B* is true whether or not *A* is true or false.

It is noteworthy that Kiparsky and Kiparsky categorize *clear* as a factive predicate. In what follows I show that *clear* is in fact not factive, though I admit that it has a strong flavor of factivity. Consider the pair of sentences in (11).

(11)   a.   It is clear that Briscoe is a detective.

      b.   It is clear that Briscoe is a detective even though he isn't/might not be.

Sentence (11) seems to entail that Briscoe is a detective. That is, an initial assumption an addressee may make after hearing an utterance of (11) is that Briscoe is a detective. A standard cancellation test as applied in (11b) shows that the entailment can be canceled, indicating that *clear* doesn't entail the truth of its complement proposition.

What have now become standard diagnostics for presupposition as it relates to factivity are that the presuppositions remain constant under negation and questioning. The interaction of negation with factive verbs is illustrated in (12).

(12)   a.   It is not odd that the door is closed.

      b.   John doesn't regret that the door is closed.

In (12), only the emotive reaction to the embedded proposition is negated. The sentences still presuppose that the embedded proposition (here, the proposition expressed by the sentence *the door is closed*) is true. As a result, overtly denying that the door is closed leads to a contradiction unless the utterance is meant to challenge the appropriateness of the choice of the word *odd* or *regret* in a metalinguistic use of negation (Horn 1985, 1989). As a result, overt cancellation of this proposition results in a contradiction, as shown in (13).

(13)   a.   #It is not odd that the door is closed because it isn't closed.

      b.   #John doesn't regret that the door is closed, and it isn't closed.

The presuppositions of discourse adjectives, unlike the presuppositions of true factives, do not remain constant under negation. Thus, in contrast to the sentences in (13), the sentences in (14) are not contradictory.

(14)   a.   It is not clear that the door is closed, and it isn't closed.

      b.   It is not evident that the door is closed, because it isn't closed.

With respect to the constancy of presuppositions under questioning, Kiparsky and Kiparsky discuss the example in (15).

(15)   Are you dismayed that our money is gone?

When a speaker utters (15) the conveyed meaning is not an inquiry as to whether or not the money is gone. Rather, it takes for granted that the money is gone, and questions the addressee's reaction to that fact. Discourse adjectives fail to pattern like true factives with respect to this diagnostic as well. Consider (16).

(16)   Is it clear that our money is gone?

While it is possible to interpret a speaker's utterance of (16) as an indication that she believes the money is gone and is inquiring about the addressee's reaction to this fact, this is not the only reading possible. That is, (16) is indeterminate between a reading in which the speaker is questioning whether or not the money is gone, and questioning whether or not this is clear to the addressee.

In summary, in spite of the empirical facts that show *clear* is not factive, it is difficult to deny its strong flavor of factivity. That is, it intuitively feels like (11a) entails that Briscoe is a detective. This intuition will be explained by the analysis in section 12.3.5.

12.2.3 *Interpreting the experiencer of a discourse adjective*

As was noted in section 12.2.1, discourse adjectives and some attitude adjectives are predicates that allow the overt expression of the conceptually necessary experiencer. Consider the data in (17) and (18).

(17)   a.   It is clear that Briscoe is a detective.

     b.   It is clear *to me* that Briscoe is a detective.

     c.   It is clear *to you* that Briscoe is a detective.

(18)   a.   It is shocking that Briscoe is a detective.

     b.   It is shocking *to me* that Briscoe is a detective.

     c.   ?It is shocking *to you* that Briscoe is a detective.

There is a difference in the default interpretation of the experiencer of the discourse adjective *clear* in (17a) and the default interpretation of the experiencer of the attitude adjective *shocking* in (18a). I approximate the meaning of (17a) as the conjunction of (17b) and (17c). If it is clear that Briscoe is a detective, then it is clear to the discourse participants that Briscoe is a detective. The identity of the experiencer is resolved as the discourse participants. A cancellation test shows that trying to cancel this entailment results in the contradictory sentence in (19).

(19)   #It is clear that Briscoe is a detective, even though we don't all agree that he is.

In contrast, the default interpretation of the attitude adjective *shocking* in (18a) is not easily resolved as the discourse participants. I approximate the meaning of (18a) as (18b). That is, if a speaker utters (18b), the most likely interpretation is that this emotional reaction is being attributed to the speaker only. Support for this might be taken from the fact that (18c) is marked. The markedness of this sentence has to do with the fact that the emotivity associated with *shocking* is something that is best discussed from a first or third person perspective. If the second person (*you* in 18c) is participating in a conversation, then she would be in the best position to comment on what she does or does not find shocking.

12.3 A case study of the semantics of *clear*

12.3.1 *The paradox of asserting clarity*

The starting point for a semantic analysis of clear is to review the paradox of asserting clarity, as introduced in Barker and Taranto (2003). The paradox as it is presented here is faithful to the analysis in Barker and Taranto, but the formal semantics that is introduced, which takes as its starting point the model of context update proposed by Gunlogson (2001), is taken from Taranto (2006). The discussion in this chapter takes *clear* to be representative of the entire class of discourse adjectives.

  The paradox of asserting clarity arises from the standard assumption in (20), namely that an assertion is felicitous only if it adds new information to the common ground.

(20)   **Informativeness Constraint on Assertions:** an assertion is felicitous only if it adds new information to the common ground (after Stalnaker 1978: 325; van der Sandt 1992: 367)

After all, what use could it be to claim that a proposition is true if it is already accepted as true? A possible answer is that some sentences can have side-effects besides adding new information about the world to the common ground, and it can be worth asserting a sentence entirely for the sake of these side-effects. To motivate this claim, consider the variation of Partee's famous marble example in (21).

(21)   a.   Exactly two out of three marbles are on the table.

       b.   One marble is not on the table.

       c.   It's under the couch.

Sentence (21b) is entailed by (21a). It adds no new information about the situation under discussion. However, it does cause the creation of a discourse referent for the missing marble, which allows a pronominal reference in (21c). If (21b) were omitted from the discourse, it would be infelicitous to use the pronoun *it* in (21c). Thus, as pointed out in Beaver (2002), it is possible to assert a sentence purely for the sake of its side-effects, in this case, building a discourse referent to facilitate anaphora.

What will emerge in the discussion of the discourse adjective *clear* is that assertions of clarity are useful in establishing which propositions are genuinely in the common ground of a discourse and which are not. With this in mind, consider the core example for this chapter's discussion of *clear*, the sentence in (22).

(22)   It is clear that Briscoe is a detective.

Intuitively, if (22) is true, then before it is uttered, both the speaker and addressee must already believe that Briscoe is a detective. If either is not already convinced that Briscoe is a detective, then it is not clear at all. But if it was already evident that Briscoe is a detective, then asserting (22) adds no new information to the context, contra the assumption in (20). The question to ask, then, is what new information might an utterance of (22) provide?

In order to address this question, it is necessary to distinguish between the different types of beliefs that individuals in a discourse may have. I propose the definitions provided in (23), which assume a conversation with exactly two participants, *A* and *B*.

(23)   a.   A belief p is a **private belief** of a discourse participant *A* iff
        i.   *A* believes p, and
        ii.   *B* does not believe that (i).

    b.   A belief p is a **public belief** of a discourse participant *A* iff
        i.   *A* believes p,
        ii.   *B* believes that (i), and
        iii.   *A* believes that (i) and (ii).

    c.   A belief p is a **shared belief** of discourse participants *A* and *B* iff
        i.   *A* believes p,
        ii.   *B* believes p, and
        iii.   Both *A* and *B* believe that (i) and (ii).

d.   A belief p is a **mutual belief** of discourse participants A and B iff
   i. A believes p,
   ii. B believes p,
   iii. B believes that (i), and
   iv. A believes that (ii).
   ... and so on ...

12.3.2   *The framework – a version of Gunlogson's model of context update*

The starting point for the analysis of discourse adjectives is Gunlogson's 2001 version of a standard Stalnakerian model of context update. The basic idea of Gunlogson's model is outlined in (24).

(24)   **Gunlogson's adaptation of the standard model**

a.   Within the Common Ground a distinction is made between the discourse commitments of the speaker and addressee.

b.   An individual's discourse commitments are identified with that individual's public beliefs.

c.   The Context Set of a discourse with two participants A and B ($CS_{A,B}$) is an ordered pair of sets of the discourse commitments of A and B: the commitment set of A (cs_A) includes the worlds of which A's public beliefs are true; the commitment set of B (cs_B) includes the worlds of which B's public beliefs are true.

The context as defined in (24c) represents a departure from more standard implementations of a Stalnakerian model. Gunlogson takes the distinct discourse commitments of individual participants to be basic, and she uses this to derive a standard Stalnakerian context set. This isn't to say that one cannot derive the individual commitments from the standard Stalnakerian conception of the context of a discourse, but in order to talk about discourse adjectives, access to individual commitments is crucial. Gunlogson's model is a natural choice for the ease of exposition.

An example of the effect an utterance of *Briscoe is a detective* has on the common ground is shown in (26). The model of possible worlds under consideration is given in (25). The context set in (26) separates the commitment sets (the worlds consistent with the public beliefs) of A and B.

(25)   **Model of possible worlds**
   $w_1 =$ Briscoe is a detective.
   $w_2 =$ Briscoe is not a detective.

w_3 = Briscoe is a detective.

w_4 = Briscoe is not a detective.

(26)

		cs_A	cs_B
a.	input Context C	$\{w_1, w_2, w_3, w_4\}$	$\{w_1, w_2, w_3, w_4\}$
b.	C + *Briscoe is a detective*	$\{w_1, w_3\}$	$\{w_1, w_2, w_3, w_4\}$

In (26a) all of the worlds in the model in (25) are included as live options for both A and B. Update with A's assertion of *Briscoe is a detective* removes w_2 and w_4, worlds in which Briscoe is not a detective, from A's individual commitment set. The context in (26b) is *biased* toward the truth of the proposition expressed by *Briscoe is a detective*. *Bias* is a technical term introduced by Gunlogson, to contrast with the notion of contextual neutrality. Definitions of contextual bias and neutrality are provided in (27).

(27)   a.   A context C is **biased** toward p iff p is a public commitment of exactly one discourse participant.

   b.   A context C is **neutral** toward p iff neither discourse participant is committed to either p or $\neg p$.

By these definitions, before A's utterance of *Briscoe is a detective*, the context in (26a) is neutral with respect to the proposition expressed. The effect of the utterance is a context that is biased toward the proposition expressed by *Briscoe is a detective*.

With this terminology established, it is possible to proceed with an analysis of *clear*. The starting point is the convergence of three observations about discourse adjectives: first, that they are not factive; second, that they have experiencers; and third, that there are a number of possibilities for the way the world might be, and that these are ordered in terms of their plausibility. For instance, regarding the proposition that Briscoe is a detective (28), in any given world the possible explanations might include that Briscoe is a detective, as in w_5, that he is not a real detective, but he dressed like one to attend a costume party, as in w_6, or perhaps even the more unlikely alternative in w_8, that Briscoe is not a detective at all, but the CIA wants us to believe that he is.

(28)   Possible explanations for the evidence suggesting that Briscoe is a detective, from most to least likely.

   a. w_5 = Briscoe is a detective.

   b. w_6 = Briscoe is not a detective, he's dressed up for a costume party.

   c. w_7 = Briscoe is a detective, but coincidentally he's holding a gun and badge that belong to his friend.

    d. w_8 = Briscoe is not a detective, but the CIA wants us to believe that he is.

To consider a situation in which an utterance of *It is clear that Briscoe is a detective* might be made, imagine that the propositions expressed by the sentences in (29) are true, and that they have just been uttered by *B*.

(29)   a.   Briscoe works for the NYPD detective division.

          b.   Briscoe's partner is a detective, Detective Logan.

          c.   Briscoe carries a gun and a badge wherever he goes.

          d.   Briscoe is interviewing a witness at the scene of a crime.

Nothing in the sentences in (29) rules out any of the possible worlds given in (28). But because in some of these worlds Briscoe is a detective, update with *It is clear that Briscoe is a detective* will do some work. It will at least eliminate those worlds in which Briscoe is not a detective. This result is immediately suspicious because, as was shown in (25) and (26), simply asserting *Briscoe is a detective* will achieve the same result.

    The question that emerges is the following: Why not just assert that Briscoe is a detective? Why ever assert that it is *clear* that Briscoe is a detective? The answer to this question is clear. A speaker might be reluctant to assert that Briscoe is a detective because Briscoe might not be a detective. There are other live possibilities. Since it is known from Grice that it is uncooperative for a speaker to assert something for which she lacks sufficient evidence, it would be uncooperative to claim that Briscoe is a detective in the absence of absolute certainty.

    If this analysis is on the right track, it points to the conclusion that clarity is asserted only in contexts in which there is some lingering uncertainty about whether the complement is in fact true. Due to the lingering uncertainty about Briscoe's status as a detective, an utterance of *It is clear that Briscoe is a detective* should not be felicitous, but it is. The problem is that discourse participants may not be sure how strong the evidence used to conclude that a proposition is true needs to be in order to support a determination that a proposition is true. This is what Barker and Taranto identified as the paradox of asserting clarity.

    The key to resolving this paradox depends on appreciating how the grammar deals with degrees of probability. In other words, the appropriateness of asserting clarity depends on the degrees of probability of the different explanations of the facts. An assertion of clarity depends on the likelihood of the probability of a proposition *p* as determined by a discourse participant who is evaluating evidence in support of *p*. Situations in which the applicability of a predicate depends on degrees are well known in the literature. This is an example of vagueness (Fine 1975; Williamson 1994, 1999; Kennedy 1999b), or the observation that in a given situation, it's not always clear how clear a proposition needs to be to count as *clear*.

12.3.3 *Vagueness*

Following Barker (2002) and Barker and Taranto (2003), the solution to the paradox of asserting clarity involves adopting a delineation function that takes a situation and an adjective meaning and returns the vague standard for the adjective in the given situation. An introductory example is best used with a vague predicate that is easier to quantify than clarity. One such predicate is *tall*, which operates over a scale of height. Specifically, this predicate is concerned with maximal length on the vertical axis. A delineation function written to capture the meaning of *tall* as used in an utterance of (30a) is written as (30b), and its truth condition is expressed in (30c).

(30) a. Robinette is tall.

     b. $\mathbf{d}(c)(\llbracket tall \rrbracket)$

     c. The maximal degree to which Robinette is tall is at least as great as $\mathbf{d}(c)(\llbracket tall \rrbracket)$.

The truth condition in (30c) guarantees that the applicability of *tall* is evaluated with respect to Robinette's maximal height.

As explained in Barker (2002), sentences like (30a) have both descriptive and metalinguistic uses. In its descriptive use, *tall* provides information about the maximal length of an object with respect to the vertical axis and the conventionally accepted minimum standard for tallness. If in a situation the definition in (30b) returns a value of $6'0''$, an utterance of (30a) provides the information about the lower bound on how tall Robinette is, in this case, $6'0''$.

As an illustration of its metalinguistic use, imagine a situation in which a speaker and addressee know a lot about Robinette, including the maximal degree of his height, which is $6'1''$. In contrast to our scenario to illustrate the descriptive use of *tall*, in this situation the standard for human tallness is more obscure. The discourse participants have their individual ideas about how tall a person needs to be to count as tall, but there is uncertainty about the conventional standard for height. In this case, a discourse like the one in (31) may occur.

(31) a. What counts as tall around here?

     b. Robinette is tall.

c. The maximal degree to which Robinette is tall is at least $\mathbf{d}(c)(\llbracket tall \rrbracket)$.

d. Therefore, $\mathbf{d}(c)(\llbracket tall \rrbracket) \leq 6'1''$.

Here, the addressee of (31b) has learned nothing new about Robinette by the information associated with the truth condition as expressed in (31c). However, the addressee has learned something about the prevailing standard for tallness. Specifically, it must be less than or equal to Robinette's height. The discourse participants have learned something more about the meaning of the word *tall*, but nothing about Robinette's physical properties. In this way, the use of *tall* in (31) is metalinguistic rather than descriptive.

As this analysis of vagueness is employed in the current study of the semantics of *clear*, the main idea is that different possible worlds may differ precisely in the standard they impose on a vague adjective. So in one world the absolute standard may be set higher or lower than it is in another world. One aspect that distinguishes the semantics of *clear* from the semantics of *tall* is that with *clear* the relevant scale is harder to identify. Instead of maximal height on the vertical axis, we're interested in probability of a proposition being true based on an analysis of available evidence. With this in mind, the truth conditions of (32a) can be characterized as (32b).

(32) a. That Briscoe is a detective is clear.

b. The maximal degree to which the proposition expressed by *Briscoe is a detective* is clear based on available evidence is at least $\mathbf{d}(c)(\llbracket clear \rrbracket)$.

12.3.4 *The analysis*

It is easy to model the use of vague predicates in a Stalnakerian model of context update by making the assumption that during a conversation the common ground includes the facts that a conversation is taking place, that the speaker is speaking, the addressee is being addressed, and so on. Incorporating this with the analysis of vague predicates leads to the observation that one way in which the worlds in a context may vary is in the value of the delineation function that is associated with a vague predicate as applied to the version of the conversation in that world.

Bearing these assumptions in mind, a first attempt at an analysis of *clear* is provided in (33).

(33) $cs_x + \llbracket Itisclearthatp \rrbracket = \{w \in cs_x$: the maximal degree to which p is likely to be true based on available evidence that suggests p in cs_x is at least as great as $\mathbf{d}(c)(\llbracket clear \rrbracket)$ in $w\}$. [to be revised in (34)].

The analysis in (33) captures the connection between likelihood and clarity, as mediated through a stage of analysis of available evidence. The idea behind this is the observation that for a determination of probability to occur, an experiencer needs to make an evaluation based on available evidence. In this way, the nature and perceived applicability of the nature of available evidence is hard to separate from a determination of the probability of a proposition.

The analysis in (33) also specifies the respect in which asserting clarity is similar to asserting the applicability of a vague predicate. However, it cannot be right. The problem is that in Gunlogson's model (as well as other Stalnakerian models), propositions don't have probabilities. For any given possible world, either Briscoe is a detective, or he is not. No matter what the standard for clarity is, worlds in which the probability is 1 will survive update according to (33), and worlds in which the probability is 0 will not. Thus, in the absence of acknowledging probability, the meaning of *It is clear that Briscoe is a detective* is identical to the meaning of *Briscoe is a detective*, which has been shown to be incorrect.

This problem can be solved by building on the observation made above that likelihood is a judgment made by some sentient creature who is contemplating *p*. Therefore, if likelihood plays a role in assertions of clarity, it is possible to appeal to the judger of likelihood. As was discussed in respect of example (17) above, in an assertion of simple clarity, the default resolution of the experiencers, or judgers of likelihood, is as the discourse participants.

In a departure from standard Hintikka-style assumptions about using an equivalence relation to model doxastic accessibility between worlds, with the result that individuals effectively have the same beliefs in all accessible worlds, I follow Barker and Taranto and refine the context change potential in (33) as (34), which considers judgments of likelihood at each world. That is, every possible world in w is evaluated in terms of how likely the counterpart of x considers p to be. The definition in (34) recognizes that belief is a gradient attitude, and behaves just like any other vague predicate.

(34) $cs_x + [\![It\,is\,clear\,that\,p]\!] = \{w \in cs_x$: the maximal degree to which the counterpart of x judges that p is likely to be true based on available evidence that suggests p in cs_x is at least as great as $\mathbf{d}(c)([\![clear]\!])$ in $w\}$.

In practical terms, this means that if a speaker asserts (35a) with the semantics in (35b), then only those worlds will survive update at which the speaker believes Briscoe is a detective, based on her determination of likelihood in light of available evidence.

(35) a. It is clear to me that Briscoe is a detective.

  b. $\{w : \mathbf{believe}(w)(\mathbf{d}, \mathbf{speaker}, \mathbf{detective}(\mathbf{Briscoe})) \geq \mathbf{d}(c)(\llbracket clear \rrbracket)\}$

Worlds that are excluded will include worlds in which there is enough uncertainty (or not enough certainty) to reduce the speaker's belief in Briscoe's status as a detective to below that world's specified threshold for clarity. Worlds may survive in which Briscoe is not a detective, as long as the speaker believes that Briscoe is a detective in that world.

   An example is provided in (37), based on the states-of-affairs modeled in (36). The model includes information about Briscoe's being a detective, as well as information about the clarity of this proposition in terms of the discourse participants' beliefs. In (36), *D* abbreviates the proposition expressed by *Briscoe is a detective* and *Bel* is a belief operator used to indicate whether *A* or *B* believes that Briscoe is a detective. In (36), w_5 is a world in which both *A* and *B* believe Briscoe is a detective, and w_6 is a world in which neither *A* nor *B* believes that Briscoe is a detective. In these worlds, the discourse participants' beliefs happen to align with the facts in the world. In w_7, however, only *A*'s beliefs align with truth in the world. *A* believes that Briscoe is a detective, which happens to be true, while *B* does not believe that Briscoe is a detective.

(36) Expanded Model of Possible worlds

  a. $w_5 =$ Briscoe is a detective.   *Bel*(*A*, *D*), *Bel*(*B*, *D*)

  b. $w_6 =$ Briscoe is not a detective (costume party).

                                    ¬*Bel*(*A*, *D*), ¬*Bel*(*B*, *D*)

  c. $w_7 =$ Briscoe is a detective.   *Bel*(*A*, *D*), ¬*Bel*(*B*, *D*)

  d. $w_8 =$ Briscoe is not a detective (CIA plot).

                                    Bel(*A*, *D*), ¬*Bel*(*B*, *D*)

Imagine a situation in which the speaker *A* is unaware of the CIA plot; her utterance of (35a) is modeled in (37). The input context is modeled in (37a), and the result of her utterance eliminates w_6, the world in which *A* does not believe that Briscoe is a detective, from her commitment set. Her commitment set still includes w_8, a world in which Briscoe isn't a detective, but because in this world there is sufficient evidence to persuade our speaker that Briscoe is a detective, this world remains a live possibility.

(37)   *CS_A*   *CS_B*

  a. input Context *C* $\{w_5, w_6, w_7, w_8\}$ $\{w_5, w_6, w_7, w_8\}$

  b. $C + \llbracket (35a) \rrbracket$ $\{w_5, w_7, w_8\}$ $\{w_5, w_6, w_7, w_8\}$

In a departure from Gunlogson (which will be addressed below), the analysis of *clear* presented here adopts Walker's Collaborative Principle.

(38)   **Collaborative Principle** (Walker 1992): Conversants must provide evidence of a discrepancy in belief as soon as possible.

The claim made here about the semantics of *clear* is that in the normal course of events, when A utters *It is clear to me that Briscoe is a detective*, B will have no choice but to accept the fact that it is clear to A – A is the highest authority on A's beliefs. By bringing in Walker's Collaborative Principle, it is possible to formalize what happens if B does not immediately express doubt about the truth or sincerity of A's statement. If B remains silent, then the discourse model will reflect individual public commitments on the part of both A and B to A's belief in Briscoe's being a detective. Thus, the representation of B's commitment set as depicted in (37b) is incomplete. B's commitment set must also reflect her belief (or acquiescence) in A's commitment to the clarity of the proposition expressed by *Briscoe is a detective*, as shown in (39).

(39) | | | cs_A | cs_B |
|---|---|---|---|
| a. | input Context C | $\{w_5, w_6, w_7, w_8\}$ | $\{w_5, w_6, w_7, w_8\}$ |
| b. | $C + [\![(35a)]\!]$ | $\{w_5, w_7, w_8\}$ | $\{w_5, w_6, w_7, w_8\}$ |
| c. | no objection from B | $\{w_5, w_7, w_8\}$ | $\{w_5, w_7, w_8\}$ |

The commitment set of B in (39c) includes two worlds in which it is not clear to B that Briscoe is a detective. Her commitment set includes w_7 and w_8, worlds in which it is clear to A that Briscoe is a detective, even though it is not clear to B that Briscoe is a detective. Comparison of the commitment sets of A and B in (39c) shows that synchronization has happened. While there is not agreement about whether or not Briscoe is a detective, the information states of A and B are the same, and they reflect the mutual understanding that A believes that B is a detective, but B does not.

Example (41) shows the update effect of the assertion of simple clarity expressed in (40).

(40)   It is clear that Briscoe is a detective.

(41) | | | cs_A | cs_B |
|---|---|---|---|
| a. | input Context C | $\{w_5, w_6, w_7, w_8\}$ | $\{w_5, w_6, w_7, w_8\}$ |
| b. | $C + [\![(40)]\!]$ | $\{w_5\}$ | $\{w_5, w_6, w_7, w_8\}$ |
| c. | no objection from B | $\{w_5\}$ | $\{w_5\}$ |

Since the semantics of *clear* specify that the default interpretation of the experiencer is as the discourse participants, the only world that survives update is w_5, the sole world in which it is clear to both A and B that Briscoe is a detective. Since *B* makes no objection, the Collaborative Principle licenses an update to *B*'s commitment set as well, showing that all discourse participants are committed to *p* for the sake of the conversation.[2] From a practical stand-point, *B* may allow this to happen in a situation in which she does not yet believe that Briscoe is a detective, but she does not have evidence suggesting that he is not. By accepting an utterance of *It is clear that Briscoe is a detective*, she allows into the common ground a version of the proposition expressed by *Briscoe is a detective* in a way that suggests the proposition may be subject to reevaluation in terms of its truth.

By the analysis, dialogues involving the denial of simple assertions involve contradiction and repair, while denials of assertions of personal clarity do not. Consider (42).

(42)   A: Briscoe is a detective.

      B: Actually, Briscoe isn't a detective. I just asked him and he proved he's not.

Here, *B*'s statement contradicts *A*'s statement. Presumably, some form of repair must occur before the conversation can proceed. In contrast, the dialogue in (43) includes *A*'s assertion of personal clarity.

(43)   A: It is clear to me that Briscoe is a detective.

      B: Actually, Briscoe's not a detective. I happen to be a CIA operative, and I can tell you that it's all part of a supremely devious charade.

In (43), *B* has not contradicted *A*: it remains true that it was clear to *A* that Briscoe was a detective. Further discussion between *A* and *B* might reveal that they disagree on the minimum standard for clarity, that the speaker and hearer do not have access to the same evidence in support of the proposition that Briscoe is a detective, or that they disagree about what evidence is suggestive of the truth of this proposition. Functionally, an utterance of (43) opens the conversation up to continued discussion that might result in synchronizing the beliefs of *A* and *B*. Whether or not *A* will continue to believe that Briscoe is a detective will depend on her belief in the validity of *B*'s statement and how that relates to the likelihood of Briscoe's being a detective.

12.3.5 *Factivity revisited*

With this analysis of the semantics of *clear* in place, it is possible to explain the intuitive feeling that *clear* is a factive predicate. In the absence of an overt

---

[2]   As an anonymous reviewer has suggested, it may be the case that the discourse participants are committed to more than *p* – they are committed to not considering revising their assumptions about *p* for the foreseeable future.

experiencer, the entities doing the experiencing are by default interpreted as the speaker and addressee. The semantics of simple clarity guarantees that in the absence of an immediate and overt objection by the addressee, every world in the updated context will be a world in which the experiencer believes the truth of the proposition. The result is that, in terms of the model relevant to a particular discourse, the discourse participants believe the proposition is likely to be true in every world in the updated context. Thus, asserting *It is clear that p* doesn't entail *p*, but it guarantees that the discourse participants are justified in behaving as if *p* is true. The key point to note is that asserting clarity is purely about the judgment of the discourse participants, and not about what is the case in any part of the world under discussion. That is, asserting clarity synchronizes the common ground. It forces the speaker and addressee to acknowledge that they are in a position to treat a certain proposition as if it were a fact.

In particular, (44) lists some things that at least one of the discourse participants might learn after an assertion of clarity that they might not have known before the assertion.

(44)   a.   The speaker believes that Briscoe is a detective.

b.   The addressee believes that Briscoe is a detective.

c.   The speaker knows that (b).

d.   The addressee knows that (a).
            ... and so on ...

On this analysis, an utterance with a discourse adjective is analyzed as a move by a speaker to synchronize the common ground by promoting what she believes might be shared private beliefs to the status of mutual public beliefs in the context set of a discourse. This analysis provides an explanation of what Barker and Taranto identified as the paradox of asserting clarity (the observation that *It is clear that p* can be felicitously uttered in situations where it is in fact not clear that *p*). Specifically, asserting clarity does not require asserting perfect clarity. By recognizing the role of vagueness, the analysis shows that asserting clarity means that the proposition is clear enough to proceed as if it were true.

12.4 Consequences of modifying Gunlogson's 2001 model

In the final section of this chapter I discuss a consequence of my interpretation and application of Gunlogson's model. In this analysis I have made two modifications to Gunlogson's proposal. First, I have updated her model and incorporated previous research on vagueness by making the model sensitive to degrees. Second, by appealing to Walker's Collaborative Principle, I make a non-trivial (and somewhat controversial) leap: I allow for the possibility that a speaker's utterance may have a substantive effect on the representation of the addressee's commitment set.[3] Having made these modifications, I point out how a combination of Gunlogson's analysis of rising and falling intonation and the proposed semantics of *clear* make a prediction about a strategy a speaker might use to signal commitment on the part of both the speaker and the addressee with the utterance of a single sentence.

Regarding the incorporation of degrees into the analysis, this modification provides a means of representing degrees of public commitment to a proposition. This is a welcome consequence, since a comparison across the class of discourse adjectives reveals that an individual's degree of public commitment toward a proposition can be more or less strong. Consider the sentences in (45), as possibly uttered by Briscoe upon his arrival and after a brief survey of the scene of a crime.

(45) a. It is apparent that the murderer was left-handed.

   b. It is evident that the murderer was left-handed.

   c. It is clear that the murderer was left-handed.

   d. It is obvious that the murderer was left-handed.

If Briscoe utters (45a) and later finds out that the murderer was in fact right-handed, one might reasonably expect him to be mildly surprised. However, if he had instead uttered (45d), one could reasonably find it odd if he showed only mild surprise if he later learned that the murderer was not left-handed. This suggests that *obvious* has a higher minimum standard for "probability in light of evidence" than does *apparent*. Following Taranto (2006), I posit that *clear* and *obvious* have higher minimum standards for probability in light of evidence than do *apparent* and *evident*. The choice of one discourse adjective over another may indicate a greater or lesser degree of commitment to the truth or likelihood of an embedded proposition.

In order to discuss the effect of modifying Gunlogson's proposed model, it is necessary to introduce the data that led her to isolate the individual commitment sets of the speaker and addressee in a discourse. Gunlogson's concern was the interaction of intonation and sentence form, and the contributions that both rising and falling intonation make as they interact with

---

[3] The analysis of discourse adjectives presented here is not meant to dispute Gunlogson's analysis. The claim made here is merely that more than the notion of contextual bias is needed in order to accurately describe the semantics of these adjectives.

declarative and interrogative sentence forms. In the examples in this section, a question mark (?) indicates rising intonation, while a period (.) indicates falling intonation.

(46)   a.   It's raining.   (declarative form, falling intonation)

     b.   It's raining?   (declarative form, rising intonation)

     c.   Is it raining?   (interrogative form, rising intonation)

Gunlogson's work addressed the ability of a declarative sentence with rising intonation to be used as a question, as in (46b). Her observation was that with falling intonation, an utterance of *It's raining* conventionally implicates a speaker's commitment to the content of the proposition expressed by that sentence, while an utterance of *It's raining?* with rising intonation conventionally implicates commitment on the part of the addressee. She further notes that a condition on the appropriate use of (46b) is that the context must already be biased toward the proposition expressed by *It's raining* by virtue of the addressee's prior public commitment to them. By positing a model that isolates the individual commitments of the discourse participants, she is able to capture this restriction in the form of the Contextual Bias Condition, stated descriptively in (47).

(47)   **Contextual Bias Condition:** Rising declaratives can only be used as questions in contexts where the addressee is already publicly committed to the proposition expressed. (Gunlogson 2001)

Without appealing to vagueness or degrees of commitment, Gunlogson shows that rising declaratives pattern like interrogatives in allowing a reading in which the speaker is understood to be skeptical of the proposition expressed. Falling declaratives cannot cooccur with overt expressions of skepticism. An example she provides to illustrate this fact is given in (48).

(48)   [A and B are looking at a co-worker's much-dented car]
     A: His driving has gotten a lot better.
     B's response:

     a.   Has it? I don't see much evidence of that.

     b.   It has? I don't see much evidence of that.

     c.   It has. #I don't see much evidence of that.

In terms that incorporate vagueness, this can be restated as follows: rising intonation signals a degree of commitment to the truth of a proposition that is less than the minimum standard for absolute commitment, while falling intonation signals a degree of commitment that is at least as great as that standard. While the relationship between the discourse adjectives and discourse adverbs is a question for future research, Gunlogson's diagnostic might be translated into a diagnostic for degrees of commitment involved with derivationally related discourse adverbs, as in (49).

(49) [Office gossip maintains that a co-worker's driving has recently improved. A and B are looking at that co-worker's car. A says to B:]

   a. Apparently, her driving has gotten a lot better, but I'm not so sure it's true.

   b. ?Evidently, her driving has gotten a lot better, but I'm not so sure it's true.

   c. #Clearly, her driving has gotten a lot better, but I'm not so sure it's true.

   d. #Obviously, her driving has gotten a lot better, but I'm not so sure it's true.

Though not all speakers agree that the (a) and (b) sentences are good, for those who find the (a) and (b) sentences better than the (c) and (d) sentences, the difference in acceptability of these utterances is explained through consideration of degrees of probability. Specifically, the adverbs derived from *apparent* and *evident* impose relatively loose standards with respect to the minimum degree of probability they tolerate. This allows the speaker to remain skeptical of the truth of the proposition expressed by *Her driving has gotten a lot better.* Because of this, assertions with *apparently* or *evidently* are more compatible with overt expressions of doubt, as in (49a) and (49b).

In contrast, the sentences with *clearly* and *obviously* impose a higher minimum standard of probability, and do not allow such overt expressions of doubt. Inconsistency results when sentences with adverbs derived from *clear* and *obvious* are uttered with a skeptical follow-up. Thus *clear* and *obvious* pattern like falling declaratives in strongly committing the speaker to the proposition expressed.

These points about degrees of commitment lead to a final observation regarding the notion of commitment. This has to do with the attribution of commitment to individual participants in a discourse. As summarized in (50), Gunlogson shows that a speaker can use falling intonation to signal her own commitment to the propositional content of an utterance, and a speaker can use rising intonation to signal commitment on the part of the addressee.

(50)   **Attribution of Commitment in Gunlogson's Model**

    a. The form of a sentence compositionally contributes commitment:

        DECLARATIVE SENTENCE FORM contributes commitment;

        INTERROGATIVE SENTENCE FORM contributes a lack of commitment.

    b. The intonational contour of a sentence compositionally attributes commitment to a discourse participant:

        FALLING INTONATION attributes commitment to the speaker;

        RISING INTONATION attributes commitment to the addressee.

A natural question to ask is: How does a speaker signal commitment on the part of both herself and the addressee – that is, all of the discourse participants – to the propositional content of an utterance? There appears to be no intonational contour that serves this function in English. But the analysis presented in this chapter shows that discourse adjectives fill this role in the grammar. The use of a discourse adjective in a declarative sentence with falling intonation is a strategy a speaker can adopt to commit both speaker and addressee to the content of a proposition by uttering a single sentence, such as the core example of this chapter, *It is clear that Briscoe is a detective.*

Further, this analysis of discourse adjectives, combined with Gunlogson's compositional analysis of rising intonation, makes a prediction about the meaning of an utterance of a declarative sentence with a discourse adjective and rising intonation, as in (51).

(51)   It's clear that Briscoe is a detective?

The prediction is that an utterance of (51) signals a commitment on the part of the addressee to the belief that the interlocutors agree that Briscoe is a detective. This prediction is borne out. The combination of Gunlogson's Contextual Bias Condition with the semantics provided here for discourse adjectives accurately captures the semantics of (51), as well as the intuition that its utterance can only be felicitously uttered in a situation that is contextually biased toward both discourse participants already being committed to the proposition expressed by *It is clear that Briscoe is a detective.*

12.5 Conclusion

This chapter has introduced discourse adjectives as a natural class of predicates. I have shown that discourse adjectives are not factive, though they have an ability to impersonate factive predicates. The analysis has provided an explanation for this fact. It was shown that the semantics of *clear* entail that when an assertion of simple clarity is accepted into the discourse model, the interlocutors are licensed to proceed as if the designated proposition is true, if only for the sake of the current discussion.

Additionally, discourse adjectives provide empirical support for Stalnaker's claim that the discourse model must contain a representation of the conversation taking place, as well as empirical support for Gunlogson's call for a finely articulated model of the common ground that distinguishes between the public commitments of the speaker and addressee, though the implementation proposed here may go beyond what either of these researchers originally intended.

Finally, as for discourse adjectives themselves, the analysis has shown that they are a unique type of predicate. Their context-update effect is entirely metalinguistic – they provide interlocutors with a means of speaking directly about their conversation, which allows for the synchronization of the common ground in a discourse.

Acknowledgments

This chapter is based on my dissertation research, and I am indebted to the support of many who contributed to my efforts there, including Chris Barker, Mark Gawron, and John Moore. Additionally, I am grateful for discussion and comments provided by the participants at the Workshop on the Semantics of Adjectives and Adverbs, especially Adam Wyner, Chris Kennedy, and Louise McNally, and by two anonymous reviewers. Remaining errors are (clearly) my own.

Bibliography

Abeillé, A., Doetjes, J., de Swart, H., and Molendijk, A. (2004). 'Adverbs and quantity'. In F. Corblin and H. de Swart (eds.), *Handbook of French Semantics*. Stanford: CSLI Publications, 185–210.

Abels, K. and Neeleman, A. (2006). 'Greenberg's Universal 20 without the LCA'. Ms., University of Tromsø and University College London.

Abney, S. (1987). *The English Noun Phrase in its Sentential Aspect*. PhD thesis, MIT, Cambridge, MA.

Aboh, E. O. (2004). *The Morphosyntax of Complement-Head Sequences: Clause Structure and Word Order Patterns in Kwa*. Oxford: Oxford University Press.

Abusch, D. (1986). 'Verbs of change, causation and time'. Report 86-50, CSLI, Stanford University, Stanford, CA.

Adger, D. (2003). *Core Syntax. A Minimalist Approach*. Oxford: Oxford University Press.

Aikhenvald, A. Y. (2000). *Classifiers: A Typology of Noun Categorization Devices*. Oxford: Oxford University Press.

Ajdukiewicz, K. (1935). 'Die syntaktische Konnexität'. *Studia Philosophica*, 1: 1–27.

Alexiadou, A. (1997). *Adverb Placement: A Case Study in Antisymmetric Syntax*. Amsterdam: John Benjamins.

——and Wilder, C. (1998). 'Adjectival modification and multiple determiners'. In A. Alexiadou and C. Wilder (eds.), *Possessors, Predicates and Movement in the Determiner Phrase*. Amsterdam: John Benjamins, 303–332.

Allan, K. (1977). 'Classifiers'. *Language*, 53: 285–311.

Andrews, J. R. (1975). *Introduction to Classical Nahuatl*. Austin: University of Texas Press.

Androutsopoulou, A. (1994). 'The distribution of the definite determiner and the syntax of Greek DPs'. In *Proceedings of the 30th Regional Meeting of the Chicago Linguistic Society*, vol. 30. Chicago: The Chicago Linguistic Society, 16–29.

——(1995). 'The licensing of adjectival modification'. In *Proceedings of WCCFL 14*. Stanford: CSLI Publications, 17–31.

Asher, N. (1993). *Reference to Abstract Objects in Discourse*. Dordrecht: Kluwer.

Babby, L. H. (1987). 'Case, pre-quantifiers, and discontinuous agreement in Russian'. *Natural Language and Linguistic Theory*, 5: 91–138.

Bach, E. (1976). 'An extension of classical transformational grammar'. In R. Saenz (ed.), *Problems of Linguistic Metatheory: Proceedings of the 1976 Conference*. Michigan State University, 183–224.

——(1979). 'Control in Montague Grammar'. *Linguistic Inquiry*, 10: 515–531.

——(1986). 'The algebra of events'. *Linguistics & Philosophy*, 9: 5–16.

Bach, E. and Cooper, R. (1978). 'The NP-S analysis of relative clauses and compositional semantics'. *Linguistics & Philosophy,* 2: 145–150.

Bach, K. (1999). 'The myth of conventional implicature'. *Linguistics & Philosophy,* 22: 327–366.

Baker, M. C. (1988). *Incorporation: A Theory of Grammatical Function Changing.* Chicago: University of Chicago Press.

——(2003). *Verbs, Nouns, and Adjectives: Their Universal Grammar.* Cambridge: Cambridge University Press.

Ballweg, J. and Frosch, H. (1979). 'Comparison and gradual change'. In R. Bäuerle, U. Egli, and A. von Stechow (eds.), *Semantics from Different Points of View.* Berlin: Springer Verlag, 75–89.

Bar-Hillel, Y. (1960). 'Some linguistic obstacles to machine translation'. In F. L. Alt (ed.), *Advances in Computers.* New York/London: Academic Press, 146–157.

Barker, C. (2002). 'The dynamics of vagueness'. *Linguistics & Philosophy,* 25: 1–36.

——and Taranto, G. (2003). 'The paradox of asserting clarity.' In P. Koskinen (ed.), *Proceedings of the Western Conference on Linguistics (WECOL) 2002,* vol. 14. Department of Linguistics, California State University, 10–21.

Bartsch, R. (1976). *The Grammar of Adverbials.* Amsterdam: North Holland.

——and Vennemann, T. (1972). 'The grammar of relative adjectives and comparison'. In T. Storer and D. J. Winter (eds.), *Formal Aspects of Cognitive Processes,* vol. 22 of *Lecture Notes in Computer Science.* Berlin: Springer Verlag, 168–185.

————(1973). *Semantic Structures: A Study in the Relation between Semantics and Syntax.* Frankfurt: Athenäum Verlag.

Barwise, J. and Cooper, R. (1981). 'Generalized quantifiers and natural language'. *Linguistics & Philosophy,* 4: 159–219.

Beaver, D. (2002). 'Presupposition in DRT'. In D. Beaver, L. Casillas, B. Clark, and S. Kaufmann (eds.), *The Construction of Meaning.* Stanford: CSLI Publications, 23–43.

Bellert, I. (1977). 'On semantic and distributional properties of sentential adverbs'. *Linguistic Inquiry,* 8: 337–351.

Bennett, M. R. and Partee, B. H. (1982). *Toward the Logic of Tense and Aspect in English.* Bloomington, IN: Indiana University Linguistics Club.

Bernstein, J. (1991). 'DP in French and Walloon: Evidence for parametric variation in nominal head movement'. *Probus,* 3: 101–126.

——(1993). *Topics in the Syntax of Nominal Structure across Romance.* PhD thesis, CUNY, New York.

——(2001). 'Focusing the right way in Romance determiner phrases'. *Probus,* 13: 1–29.

Bertinetto, P. M. and Squartini, M. S. (1995). 'An attempt at defining the class of "gradual completion" verbs'. In P. M. Bertinetto, V. Bianchi, J. Higginbotham, and M. Squartini (eds.), *Temporal Reference, Aspect, and Actionality, 1: Semantic and Syntactic Perspectives.* Torino: Rosenberg and Sellier, 11–26.

Beyssade, C. and Marandin, J.-M. (2006). 'The speech act assignment problem revisited: Disentangling speaker's commitment from speaker's call on addressee'. In

O. Bonami and P. Cabredo-Hofherr (eds.), *Empirical Issues in Syntax and Semantics,* vol. 6. CNRS, 37–68.

Bhatt, R. and Pancheva, R. (2004). 'Late merger of degree clauses'. *Linguistic Inquiry,* 35: 1–46.

Bierwisch, M. (1989). 'The semantics of gradation'. In M. Bierwisch and E. Lang (eds.), *Dimensional Adjectives: Grammatical Structure and Conceptual Interpretation.* Berlin: Springer Verlag, 71–262.

Bobaljik, J. D. (2006). 'Comparative suppletion: Generalizations and implications'. Handout of a talk presented at the University of Tromsø, May 18, 2006.

Bogusławski, A. (1975). 'Measures are measures: In defence of the diversity of comparatives and positives'. *Linguistische Berichte,* 36: 1–9.

Bolinger, D. (1967). 'Adjectives in English: Attribution and predication'. *Lingua,* 18: 1–34.

——(1972). *Degree Words.* The Hague: Mouton.

Bonami, O. (2002). 'A syntax–semantics interface for tense and aspect in French'. In L. Hellan and F. Van Eynde (eds.), *The Proceedings of the HPSG '01 Conference.* Stanford: CSLI Publications, 31–50.

——and Godard, D. (2007a). 'Integrating linguistic dimensions: The scope of Adverbs'. In S. Müller (ed.), *Proceedings of the 14th International Conference on Head-Driven Phrase Structure Grammar.* Stanford: CSLI Publications, 25–45.

————(2007b). 'Parentheticals in underspecified semantics: the case of evaluative adverbs'. *Research on Language and Computation,* 5: 391–413.

————and Kampers-Manhe, B. (2004). 'Adverb classification'. In F. Corblin and H. de Swart (eds.), *Handbook of French Semantics.* Stanford: CSLI Publications, 143–184.

Borer, H. (2005a). *In Name Only* (*Structuring Sense,* vol. I). Oxford: Oxford University Press.

——(2005b). *The Normal Course of Events* (*Structuring Sense,* vol. II). Oxford: Oxford University Press.

Bosque, I. (1996). 'Por qué determinados sustantivos no son sustantivos determinados'. In I. Bosque (ed.), *El sustantivo sin determinación.* Madrid: Taurus, 13–65.

Bouchard, D. (1998). 'The distribution and interpretation of adjectives in French: A consequence of bare phrase structure'. *Probus,* 10: 139–184.

——(2002). *Adjectives, Numbers and Interfaces.* Amsterdam: North Holland.

——(2005). 'Sériation des adjectifs dans le SN et formation de concepts'. *Recherches Linguistiques de Vincennes,* 34: 125–142.

Bouma, G., Malouf, R., and Sag, I. A. (2001). 'Satisfying constraints on extraction and adjunction'. *Natural Language and Linguistic Theory,* 19: 1–65.

Bowers, J. (1993). 'The syntax of predication'. *Linguistic Inquiry,* 24: 591–656.

Bresnan, J. (1973). 'Syntax of the comparative construction in English'. *Linguistic Inquiry,* 4: 275–345.

Brugè, L. (2002). 'The positions of demonstratives in the extended nominal projection'. In G. Cinque (ed.), *Functional Structure in DP and IP: The Cartography of Syntactic Structures*. New York: Oxford University Press, 15–53.

Bunt, H. (2003). 'Underspecification in semantic representations: Which technique for what purpose?' In *Proceedings of the 5th Workshop on Computational Semantics (IWCS-5)*. Tilburg, Netherlands, 37–54.

Campos, H. and Stavrou, M. (2003). 'Articles and clitics'. Ms., Georgetown University and Thessaloniki University.

Carlier, A. (2002). 'Les propriétés aspectuelles du passif'. *Cahiers Chronos*, 10: 41–63.

Carlson, G. N. (1977). *Reference to Kinds in English*. PhD thesis, University of Massachusetts, Amherst.

Carpenter, B. (1997). *Type-logical Semantics*. Cambridge, MA: MIT Press.

Carstens, V. (2000). 'Concord in minimalist theory'. *Linguistic Inquiry*, 31: 319–355.

Caudal, P. and Nicolas, D. (2005). 'Types of degrees and types of event structures'. In C. Maienborn and A. Wöllstein (eds.), *Event Arguments: Foundations and Arguments*. Tübingen: Max Niemeyer Verlag, 277–299.

Chametzky, R. (1994). 'Chomsky-adjunction'. *Lingua*, 93: 245–264.

Cheng, L. and Sybesma, R. (1999). 'Bare and not-so-bare nouns and the structure of NP'. *Linguistic Inquiry*, 30: 509–542.

Chierchia, G. (1984). *Topics in the Syntax and Semantics of Infinitives and Gerunds*. PhD thesis, University of Massachusetts at Amherst.

—— (1995). 'Individual-level predicates as inherent generics'. In G. Carlson and F. J. Pelletier (eds.), *The Generic Book*. Chicago: Chicago University Press, 176–223.

—— (2001). 'Scalar implicatures, polarity phenomena, and the syntax/pragmatics interface'. Ms., University of Milan.

—— and McConnell-Ginet, S. (2000). *Meaning and Grammar: An Introduction to Semantics*. Cambridge, MA: MIT Press, 2nd edn.

Chomsky, N. (1965). *Aspects of the Theory of Syntax*. Cambridge, MA: MIT Press.

—— (1995). *The Minimalist Program*. Cambridge, MA: MIT Press.

—— (1998). 'Minimalist inquiries. The framework'. *MIT Occasional Papers in Linguistics* 15. Cambridge, MA: MIT, Department of Linguistics and Philosophy. [Also in R. Martin et al. (eds.) (2000), *Step by Step. Essays in Honor of H. Lasnik*. Cambridge, MA: MIT Press.]

—— (2001a). 'Derivation by phase'. In M. Kenstowicz (ed), *Ken Hale: A Life in Language*. Cambridge, MA: MIT Press, 1–52.

—— (2001b). 'Beyond explanatory adequacy'. *MIT Occasional Papers in Linguistics* 20. Cambridge, MA: MIT, Department of Linguistics and Philosophy. [Also in A. Belletti (ed.) (2004), *The Cartography of Syntactic Structures*, Vol. 3: *Structures and Beyond*. Oxford: Oxford University Press, 106–131.]

Chung, S. and Ladusaw, W. A. (2004). *Restriction and Saturation*. Cambridge, MA: MIT Press.

Cinque, G. (1994). 'On the evidence for partial N-movement in the Romance DP'. In G. Cinque, J. Koster, J.-Y. Pollock, L. Rizzi, and R. Zanuttini (eds.), *Paths towards Universal Grammar: Studies in Honor of Richard S. Kayne*. Washington, DC: Georgetown University Press, 85–110.

—— (1999). *Adverbs and Functional Heads: A Cross-Linguistic Perspective*. New York: Oxford University Press.

—— (2003). 'The dual source of adjectives and XP- vs. N-raising in the Romance DP'. Handout, North Eastern Linguistic Society (NELS) 35.

—— (2005). 'Deriving Greenberg's Universal 20 and its exceptions'. *Linguistic Inquiry*, 36: 315–332.

Cooper, R. (1983). *Quantification and Syntactic Theory*. Reidel.

Copestake, A., Flickinger, D., Pollard, C., and Sag, I. A. (2006). 'Minimal recursion semantics: an introduction'. *Research on Language and Computation*, 3: 281–332.

Corbett, G. G. (1991). *Gender*. Cambridge: Cambridge University Press.

Corver, N. (1990). *The Syntax of Left Branch Extractions*. PhD thesis, Tilburg University.

—— (1997). 'The internal syntax of the Dutch extended adjectival projection'. *Natural Language and Linguistic Theory*, 15: 289–368.

Costa, J. (1997). 'On the behaviour of adverbs in sentence-final context'. *The Linguistic Review*, 14: 43–68.

Cowper, E. (1998). 'The simple present tense in English: A unified treatment'. *Studia Linguistica*, 52: 1–18.

Craig, C. G. (1986). 'Jacaltec noun classifiers: A study in language and culture'. In C. G. Craig (ed.), *Noun Classes and Categorization*. Amsterdam: John Benjamins, 263–293.

Creissels, D. (2000). 'L'emploi résultatif de *être* + participe passé en français'. *Cahiers Chronos*, 6: 133–142.

Cresswell, M. J. (1977). 'The semantics of degree'. In B. H. Partee (ed.), *Montague Grammar*. New York: Academic Press, 261–292.

—— (1985). *Adverbial Modification*. Dordrecht: Reidel.

Dalrymple, M. (2001). *Lexical Functional Grammar*. Academic Press.

—— Kanazawa, M., Kim, Y., Mchombo, S., and Peters, S. (1998). 'Reciprocal expressions and the concept of reciprocity'. *Linguistics & Philosophy*, 21: 159–210.

Davidson, D. (1967). 'The logical form of action sentences'. In N. Rescher (ed.), *The Logic of Decision and Action*. The University of Pittsburgh Press, 81–95.

Declerck, R. (1979). 'Aspect and the bounded/unbounded (telic/atelic) distinction'. *Linguistics*, 17: 761–794.

Dekker, P. (1993). 'Existential disclosure'. *Linguistics & Philosophy*, 16: 561–587.

Delfitto, D. and Schroten, J. (1991). 'Bare plurals and the number affix in DP'. *Probus*, 3: 155–185.

Demonte, V. (1999). 'El adjetivo: Clases y usos. La posición del adjetivo en el sintagma nominal'. In I. Bosque and V. Demonte (eds.), *Gramática descriptiva de la lengua española*. Madrid: Espasa Calpe, 129–215.

—— (2005). 'Meaning–form correlations and the order of adjectives in Spanish'. Ms., Universidad Autónoma de Madrid.

Di Sciullo, A. and Williams, E. (1987). *On the Definition of Word*. Cambridge, MA: MIT Press.

Diesing, M. (1992). *Indefinites*. Cambridge, MA: MIT Press.

Dikken, M. D. (1998). 'Predicate inversion in DP'. In A. Alexiadou and C. Wilder (eds.), *Possessors, Predicates and Movement in the Determiner Phrase*. Amsterdam: John Benjamins, 177–214.

Dixon, R. M. W. (1977). 'Where have all the adjectives gone?' *Studies in Language*, 1: 19–80.

—— (1982). *Where Have All the Adjectives Gone? and Other Essays on Semantics and Syntax*. Berlin: Mouton.

—— (1986). 'Noun classes and noun classification in typological perspective'. In C. G. Craig (ed.), *Noun Classes and Categorization*. Amsterdam: John Benjamins, 105–112.

—— (2004a). 'Adjective classes in typological perspective'. In R. M. W. Dixon and A. Y. Aikhenvald (eds.), *Adjective Classes: A Cross-Linguistic Typology*. Oxford: Oxford University Press, 1–49.

—— (2004b). *The Jarawara Language of Southern Amazonia*. Oxford: Oxford University Press.

—— and Aikhenvald, A. (2004). *Adjective Classes: A Cross-Linguistic Typological Study*. Oxford: Oxford University Press.

Doetjes, J. (1997). *Quantifiers and Selection*. PhD thesis, Rijksuniversiteit Leiden.

—— and Rooryck, J. (2003). 'Generalizing over quantitative and qualitative constructions'. In M. Coene and Y. D'hulst (eds.), *From NP to DP*, vol. I. Amsterdam: John Benjamins, 277–296.

Dowty, D. R. (1979). *Word Meaning and Montague Grammar*. Dordrecht: Reidel.

—— (1991). 'Thematic proto-roles and argument selection'. *Language*, 67: 547–619.

—— Wall, R., and Peters, S. (1981). *Introduction to Montague Semantics*. Dordrecht: Reidel.

Dryer, M. (1989a). 'Plural words'. *Linguistics*, 27: 865–895.

—— (1989b). 'Article–noun order'. *Papers from the Regional Meeting, Chicago Linguistic Society*, 25: 83–97.

—— (1992). 'The Greenbergian word order correlations'. *Language*, 68: 81–138.

Eckardt, R. (1998). *Adverbs, Events, and Other Things. Issues in the Semantics of Manner Adverbs*. Tübingen: Niemeyer.

Egg, M., Koller, A., and Niehren, J. (2001). 'The constraint language for lambda structures'. *Journal of Logic, Language and Information*, 10: 457–485.

Ernst, T. (1984). *Toward an Integrated Theory of Adverb Position in English*. PhD thesis, Indiana University, Bloomington.

—— (1991). 'A phrase structure theory for tertiaries'. In S. Rothstein (ed.), *Perspectives on Phrase Structure: Heads and Licensing* (*Syntax and Semantics*, Vol. 25). San Diego, CA: Academic Press.

—— (2000). 'Manners and events'. In C. Tenny and J. Pustejovsky (eds.), *Events as Grammatical Objects*. Stanford, CA: CSLI Publications, 335–358.

—— (2002). *The Syntax of Adjuncts*. Cambridge: Cambridge University Press.

Espinal, M. T. (1991). 'The representation of disjunct constituents'. *Language*, 67: 726–762.

Fagyal, Z. (2002). 'Prosodic boundaries in the vicinity of utterance-medial parentheticals in French'. *Probus*, 14: 93–111.

Faller, M. (2000). 'Dimensional adjectives and measure phrases in vector space semantics'. In M. Faller, S. Kaufmann, and M. Pauly (eds.), *Formalizing the Dynamics of Information*. Stanford, CA: CSLI Publications, 151–170.

Fara, D. G. (2000). 'Shifting sands: An interest-relative theory of vagueness'. *Philosophical Topics*, 20: 45–81. (Originally published under the name 'Delia Graff'.)

Farkas, D. and de Swart, H. (2003). *The Semantics of Incorporation*. Stanford, CA: CSLI Publications.

Filip, H. (1999). *Aspect, Eventuality Types, and Nominal Reference*. New York: Garland.

Fine, K. (1975). 'Vagueness, truth, and logic'. *Synthese*, 30: 265–300.

von Fintel, K. (1994). *Restrictions on Quantifier Domains*. PhD thesis, University of Massachusetts, Amherst.

Firth, J. R. (1957). *Papers in Linguistics 1934–1951*. London: Oxford University Press.

Fodor, J. and Sag, I. (1982). 'Referential and quantificational indefinites'. *Linguistics & Philosophy*, 5: 355–398.

Franks, S. (1994). 'Parametric properties of numeral phrases in Slavic'. *Natural Language and Linguistic Theory*, 12: 597–674.

Gaatone, D. (1981). 'Observations sur l'opposition *très–beaucoup*'. *Revue de linguistique romane*, 45: 74–95.

Galton, A. (1984). *The Logic of Aspect*. Oxford: Clarendon Press.

Gamut, L. (1991). *Logic, Language, and Meaning*, Vol. 2: *Intensional Logic and Logical Grammar*. Chicago University Press.

Geach, P. (1972). 'A program for syntax'. In D. Davidson and G. Harman (eds.), *Semantics of Natural Language*. Dordrecht: Reidel.

Geuder, W. (2000). *Oriented Adverbs: Issues in the Lexical Semantics of Event Adverbs*. PhD thesis, Universität Tübingen.

Ghomeshi, J. (1997). 'Non-projecting nouns and the Ezafe construction in Persian'. *Natural Language and Linguistic Theory*, 15: 729–788.

Ghozati, S. (2000). 'On the structure of the Persian noun phrase'. Unpublished Senior Honors Thesis, Stony Brook University, Stony Brook, NY.

Ginzburg, J. (2004). 'A working dialogian's grammar'. Ms., King's College, London.

—— and Cooper, R. (2004). 'Clarification, ellipsis, and the nature of contextual updates in dialogue'. *Linguistics & Philosophy*, 27: 297–365.

—— and Sag, I. A. (2001). *Interrogative Investigations. The Form, Meaning, and Use of English Interrogatives*. Stanford: CSLI Publications.

Giusti, G. (2002). 'The functional structure of noun phrases: A bare phrase structure approach'. In G. Cinque (ed.), *Functional Structure in DP and IP: The Cartography of Syntactic Structures*. New York: Oxford University Press, 54–90.

Göbbel, E. (2004). 'Focus and marked positions for VP adverbs'. Ms., University of Tübingen.

Godard, D. and Jayez, J. (1999). 'Quels sont les faits?' In M. Plénat, M. Aurnague, A. Condamines, J.-P. Maurel, C. Molinier, and C. Muller (eds.), *L'emprise du sens: structures linguistiques et interprétation. Mélanges de syntaxe et de sémantique offerts à Andrée Borillo par un groupe d'amis, de collègues et de disciples.* Amsterdam: Rodopi, 117–136.

Greenbaum, S. (1969). *Studies in English Adverbial Usage.* London: Longman.

—— (1982). 'Some verb-intensifier collocations in American and British English'. In H. B. Allen and M. D. Linn (eds.), *Readings in Applied English Linguistics.* New York: Alfred A. Knopf, 329–337.

Greenberg, J. H. (1963). 'Some universals of grammar with particular reference to the order of meaningful elements'. In J. H. Greenberg (ed.), *Universals of Language. Report of a Conference Held at Dobbs Ferry, NY, April 13–15, 1961.* Cambridge, MA: MIT Press, 73–113.

—— (1978). 'How does a language acquire gender markers?' In J. H. Greenberg, C. A. Ferguson, and E. A. Moravcsik (eds.), *Universals of Human Language,* vol. III, *Word Structure.* Stanford, CA: Stanford University Press, 47–82.

Grice, H. (1975). 'Logic and conversation'. In P. Cole and J. Morgan (eds.), *Syntax and Semantics 3: Speech Acts.* New York: Academic Press, 41–58.

Grimshaw, J. (1991). 'Extended projections'. Ms., Brandeis University.

Grinevald, C. (2000). 'A morphosyntactic typology of classifiers'. In G. Senft (ed.), *Systems of Nominal Classification.* Cambridge: Cambridge University Press, 50–92.

Gunlogson, C. (2001). *True to Form: Rising and Falling Declaratives in English.* PhD thesis, University of California, Santa Cruz.

Gutiérrez-Rexach, J. and Mallen, E. (2002). 'Toward a unified minimalist analysis of prenominal adjectives'. In C. Clements (ed.), *Structure Meaning and Acquisition in Spanish. Papers from the 4th Hispanic Linguistics Symposium.* Somerville, MA: Cascadilla, 178–192.

Hackl, M. (2000). *Comparative Quantifiers.* PhD thesis, MIT.

Haegeman, L. and Gueron, J. (1999). *English Grammar: A Generative Perspective.* Oxford: Blackwell.

Halliday, M. (1966). 'Lexis as a linguistic level'. In C. Bazell, J. Catford, M. Halliday, and R. Robins (eds.), *In Memory of J. R. Firth.* London: Longman, 148–162.

Hamblin, C. L. (1970). *Fallacies.* London: Methuen.

Harley, H. (1995). *Subjects, Events and Licensing.* PhD thesis, MIT.

—— and Noyer, R. (2000). 'Formal versus encyclopedic properties of vocabulary: Evidence from nominalisations'. In B. Peeters (ed.), *The Lexicon-Encyclopedia Interface.* London: Elsevier Press, 349–374.

Harris, Z. (1968). *The Mathematical Structure of Language.* Chicago: University of Chicago Press.

Haspelmath, M. (1997). *Indefinite Pronouns.* Oxford: Oxford University Press.

——Dryer, M. S., Gil, D., and Comrie, B. (eds.) (2005). *The World Atlas of Language Structures*. Oxford: Oxford University Press.

Hawkins, J. A. (1983). *Word Order Universals*. New York: Academic Press.

Hay, J., Kennedy, C., and Levin, B. (1999). 'Scalar structure underlies telicity in "degree achievements"'. In T. Matthews and D. Strolovitch (eds.), *Proceedings of SALT 9*. Ithaca, NY: CLC Publications, 127–144.

Heim, I. (1985). 'Notes on comparatives and related matters'. Ms., University of Texas, Austin.

——(1990). 'E-type pronouns and donkey anaphora'. *Linguistics & Philosophy*, 13: 137–178.

——(2000). 'Degree operators and scope'. In B. Jackson and T. Matthews (eds.), *Semantics and Linguistic Theory 10*. Ithaca, NY: CLC Publications, 40–64.

Heine, B. (1982). 'African noun class systems'. In H. Seiler and C. Lehmann (eds.), *Apprehension: Das sprachliche Erfassen von Gegenständen. I: Bereich und Ordnung der Phänomene*. Tübingen: Narr, 189–216.

Hellan, L. (1981). *Towards an Integrated Analysis of Comparatives*. Tübingen: Narr.

Herwig, R. (1998). 'The interrelation between adverbs of manner and adverbs of degree'. *Erford Electronic Studies in English*, 4.

Hetzron, R. (1978). 'On the relative order of adjectives'. In H. Seiler (ed.), *Language Universals*. Tübingen: Narr, 165–184.

Higginbotham, J. (1985). 'On semantics'. *Linguistic Inquiry*, 16: 547–593.

——(1986). 'Linguistic theory and Davidson's program in semantics'. In E. LePore (ed.), *Truth and Interpretation: Perspectives on the Philosophy of Donald Davidson*. Oxford: Blackwell, 29–48.

——(2000). 'On events in linguistic semantics'. In J. Higginbotham, J. Pianesi, and A. Varsi (eds.), *Speaking of Events*. Oxford: Oxford University Press, 49–79.

Hinrichs, E. (1985). *A Compositional Semantics for Aktionsarten and NP Reference in English*. PhD thesis, The Ohio State University.

Hoekstra, T. (2004). 'Small clauses everywhere'. In R. Sybesma, S. Barbiers, M. den Dikken, J. Doetjes, G. Postma, and G. Vanden Wyngaerd (eds.), *Arguments and Structure: Studies on the Architecture of the Sentence*. Berlin: Mouton, 319–389.

Holmberg, A. and Odden, D. (2005). 'The Izafe and NP structure in Hawrami'. *Durham Working Papers in Linguistics*, 10: 77–94.

Horn, L. (1985). 'Metalinguistic negation and pragmatic ambiguity'. *Language*, 61: 121–174.

——(1989). *A Natural History of Negation*. Chicago: University of Chicago Press.

van Hout, A. (1996). *Event Semantics of Verb-frame Alternations*. PhD thesis, Tilburg University.

——and Roeper, T. (1997). 'Events and aspectual structure in derivational morphology'. In H. Harley (ed.), *Papers from the UPenn/MIT Roundtable on Argument Structure and Aspect, MITWPL 32*. Cambridge, MA: MIT.

Hualde, J. I. and Ortiz de Urbina, J. (2003). *A Grammar of Basque*. Berlin: Mouton de Gruyter.

Huddleston, R. and Pullum, G. K. (2002). *The Cambridge Grammar of the English Language*. Cambridge: Cambridge University Press.

Humberstone, L. (2005). 'Geach's categorial grammar'. *Linguistics & Philosophy*, 28: 281–317.

Ionin, T. and Matushansky, O. (2005). '1001 Nights: The syntax and semantics of complex numerals'. Ms., USC and CNRS/Université Paris 8.

Jackendoff, R. (1972). *Semantic Interpretation in Generative Grammar*. Cambridge, MA: MIT Press.

—— (1977). *X'-Syntax: A Study of Phrase Structure*. Cambridge, MA: MIT Press.

—— (1996a). 'The proper treatment of measuring out, telicity, and perhaps even quantification in English'. *Natural Language and Linguistic Theory*, 14: 305–354.

—— (1996b). 'Semantics and cognition'. In S. Lappin (ed.), *The Handbook of Contemporary Semantic Theory*. Oxford: Blackwell Publishers, 539–559.

Jayez, J. and Godard, D. (1999). 'True to fact'. In P. Dekker (ed.), *Proceedings of the 12th Amsterdam Colloquium*. ILLC/Department of Philosphy, University of Amsterdam, 151–156.

—— and Rossari, C. (2004). 'Parentheticals as conventional implicatures'. In F. Corblin and H. de Swart (eds.), *Handbook of French Semantics*. Stanford, CA: CSLI Publications, 211–229.

Johnson, K. (1991). 'Object positions'. *Natural Language and Linguistic Theory*, 9: 577–636.

Johnston, M. (1994). *The Syntax and Semantics of Adverbial Adjuncts*. PhD thesis, UCSC.

Julien, M. (2002). 'Determiners and word order in Scandinavian DPs'. *Studia Linguistica*, 56: 265–315.

—— (2005). *Nominal Phrases from a Scandinavian Perspective*. Amsterdam: John Benjamins.

Kahnemuyipour, A. (2000). 'Persian Ezafe construction revisited: Evidence for modifier phrase'. In J. T. Jensen and G. van Herk (eds.), *Cahiers Linguistique d'Ottawa, Proceedings of the 2000 Annual Conference of the Canadian Linguistic Association*, 173–185.

Kamp, H. (1975). 'Two theories about adjectives'. In E. L. Keenan (ed.), *Formal Semantics of Natural Language*. Cambridge: Cambridge University Press, 123–155.

—— and Reyle, U. (1993). *From Discourse to Logic*. Dordrecht: Kluwer.

Karttunen, L. (1974). 'Presupposition and linguistic context'. *Theoretical linguistics*, 1: 181–194.

—— and Peters, S. (1975). 'Conventional implicature in Montague Grammar'. In *Proceedings of the First Annual Meeting of the Berkeley Linguistics Society*. Berkeley, CA: Berkeley Linguistics Society, 266–278.

Kathol, A. (2000). *Linear Syntax*. Oxford: Oxford University Press.

Katz, G. (1995). *Stativity, Genericity and Temporal Reference*. PhD thesis, University of Rochester.

—— (1997). 'Against underlying states'. In *Proceedings from the Twelfth Meeting of the Israeli Association of Theoretical Linguistics, Hebrew University, Jerusalem*. Jerusalem: Israeli Association of Theoretical Linguistics, 120–140.

—— (2000). 'Anti neo-Davidsonianism'. In C. Tenny and J. Pustejovsky (eds.), *Events as Grammatical Objects*. Stanford, CA: CSLI Publications, 393–416.

—— (2003). 'Event arguments, adverb selection, and the stative adverb gap'. In E. Lang, C. Maienborn, and C. Fabricius-Hansen (eds.), *Modifying Adjuncts*. Berlin: Mouton de Gruyter, 455–474.

—— (2005). 'Attitudes towards degrees'. In E. Maier, C. Bary, and J. Huitink (eds.), *Proceedings of Sinn und Bedeutung 9*. Nijmegen, 183–196.

Kayne, R. S. (1994). *The Antisymmetry of Syntax*, Cambridge, MA: MIT Press.

Kearns, K. (2007). 'Telic senses of deadjectival verbs'. *Lingua*, 117: 26–66.

Keenan, E. and Stavi, J. (1994). 'A semantic characterization of natural language determiners'. *Linguistics & Philosophy*, 9: 253–326.

Kennedy, C. (1999a). 'Gradable adjectives denote measure functions, not partial functions'. *Studies in the Linguistic Sciences*, 29: 65–80.

—— (1999b). *Projecting the Adjective: The Syntax and Semantics of Gradability and Comparison*. New York: Garland.

—— (2001). 'Polar opposition and the ontology of degrees'. *Linguistics & Philosophy*, 24: 33–70.

—— (2007). 'Vagueness and grammar: The semantics of relative and absolute gradable predicates'. *Linguistics & Philosophy*, 30: 1–45.

—— and Levin, B. (2002). 'Telicity corresponds to degree of change'. Handout, Topics in the grammar of scalar expressions, UCLA. <http://semantics.uchicago.edu/kennedy/docs/telicity.pdf>

—— and McNally, L. (1999). 'From event structure to scalar structure: degree modification in deverbal adjectives'. In T. Matthews and D. Strolovitch (eds.), *Proceedings of SALT 9*. Ithaca, NY: CLC Publications, 163–180.

—— —— (2005). 'Scale structure and the semantic typology of gradable predicates'. *Language*, 81: 345–381.

Keyser, S. (1968). 'Review of Sven Jacobsen, "Adverbial positions in English"'. *Language*, 44: 357–374.

Kiparsky, P. (2005). 'Absolutely a matter of degree: the semantics of structural case in Finnish'. Handout, 41st regional meeting of the Chicago Linguistic Society. <http://www.stanford.edu/~kiparsky/Papers/partitive.ho.pdf>

—— and Kiparsky, C. (1971). 'Fact'. In M. Bierwisch and K. Heidolph (eds.), *Progress in Linguistics: A Collection of Papers*. The Hague: Mouton, 143–173.

Kishimoto, H. (2000). 'Indefinite pronouns and overt N-raising'. *Linguistic Inquiry*, 31: 557–566.

Klein, E. (1980). 'A semantics for positive and comparative adjectives'. *Linguistics & Philosophy*, 4: 1–45.

Klein, E. (1991). 'Comparatives'. In A. von Stechow and D. Wunderlich (eds.), *Semantik: Ein internationales Handbuch der zeitgenössischen Forschung*. Berlin: Walter de Gruyter, 673–691.

——and Sag, I. A. (1985). 'Type-driven translation'. *Linguistics & Philosophy*, 8: 163–201.

Knittel, M. (2005). 'Some remarks on adjective placement in the French NP'. *Probus*, 17: 185–226.

Kolliakou, D. (1998). 'Linkhood and multiple definite marking'. In G. Webelhuth, J. Koenig, and A. Kathol (eds.), *Proceedings of the 1998 Conference on Formal Grammar, Head-Driven Phrase Structure Grammar, and Categorial Grammar (FHCG 98)*, 14–22.

Koontz-Garboden, A. (2007). *States, Changes of States, and the Monotonicity Hypothesis*. PhD thesis, Stanford University, Stanford, CA.

Koopman, H. and Szabolcsi, A. (2000). *Verbal Complexes*. Cambridge, MA: MIT Press.

Krahmer, E. (1998). *Presupposition and Anaphora*. Stanford, CA: CSLI Publications.

Kratzer, A. (1994). 'The event argument and the semantics of voice'. Ms., University of Massachusetts, Amherst.

——(1995). 'Stage-level and individual-level predicates'. In G. Carlson and F. Pelletier (eds.), *The Generic Book*. Chicago, IL: University of Chicago Press, 125–175.

——(1999). 'Beyond *Ouch* and *Oops:* How descriptive and expressive meaning interact'. Ms., University of Massachusetts, Amherst; presented at the Cornell Conference on Theories of Context Dependency.

Krause, C. (2001). *On Reduced Relatives with Genitive Subjects*. PhD thesis, MIT.

Krifka, M. (1986). *Nominalreferenz und Zeitkonstitution. Zur Semantik von Massentermen, Pluraltermen und Aspektklassen*. PhD thesis, Ludwig-Maximilians-Universität München.

——(1989) 'Nominal reference, temporal constitution and quantification in event semantics'. In R. Bartsch, J. van Benthem, and P. van Emde-Boas (eds.), *Semantics and Contextual Expressions*. Dordrecht: Foris, 75–115.

——(1992). 'Thematic relations as links between nominal reference and temporal constitution'. In I. A. Sag and A. Szabolcsi (eds.), *Lexical Matters*. Stanford, CA: CSLI Publications, 29–53.

——(1998a). 'The origins of telicity'. In S. Rothstein (ed.), *Events and Grammar*. Dordrecht: Kluwer, 197–235.

——(1998b). 'Scope-inversion under the rise-fall contour in German'. *Linguistic Inquiry*, 29: 75–112.

—— Pelletier, F. J., Carlson, G., ter Meulen, A., Chierchia, G., and Link, G. (1995). 'Genericity: An introduction'. In G. Carlson and F. J. Pelletier (eds.), *The Generic Book*. Chicago, IL: University of Chicago Press, 1–124.

Kuroda, S. (1969). 'English relativization and certain other related problems'. In *Modern Studies in English: Readings in Transformational Grammar*. Englewood Cliffs, NJ: Prentice-Hall, 55–104.

Laenzlinger, C. (2000). 'French adjective ordering: Perspectives on DP-internal movement types'. In *Generative Grammar in Geneva*, vol. 1: 55–104.

——(2005). 'French adjective ordering: Perspectives on DP-internal movement types'. *Lingua*, 115: 645–689.

Laka, I. (1990). *Negation in Syntax: On the Nature of Functional Categories and Projections*. PhD thesis, MIT.

Lambek, J. (1958). 'The mathematics of sentence structure'. *American Mathematical Monthly*, 65: 154–170.

Landman, F. (1989). 'Groups, I'. *Linguistics & Philosophy*, 12: 559–605.

——(1991). *Structures for Semantics*. Dordrecht: Kluwer.

——(2000). *Events and Plurality: The Jerusalem Lectures*. Dordrecht: Kluwer.

Landman, M. (2001). 'Adjectival modification restricted'. Ms., University of Massachussetts, Amherst.

Lang, E., Maienborn, C., and Fabricius-Hansen, C. (2003). 'Modifying (the grammar of) adjuncts: An introduction'. In E. Lang, C. Maienborn, and C. Fabricius-Hansen (eds.), *Modifying Adjuncts*. Berlin: Mouton de Gruyter, 1–29.

Larson, R. (1988). 'On the double object construction'. *Linguistic Inquiry*, 19: 589–632.

——(1990). 'Double objects revisited: Reply to Jackendoff'. *Linguistic Inquiry*, 21: 589–632.

——(1998). 'Events and modification in nominals'. In D. Strolovitch and A. Lawson (eds.), *Proceedings of SALT XII*. Ithaca, NY: CLC Publications, 145–168.

——(1999). 'Semantics of adjectival modification'. Lecture notes, LOT Winter School, Amsterdam.

——(2000a). 'ACD in AP?' Paper presented at the 19th West Coast Conference of Formal Linguistics (WCCFL 19), Los Angeles, CA, February 15, 2000.

——(2000b). 'ACD in AP?' Handout of paper presented at the International Round Table "The Syntax of Tense and Aspect," Paris, France, November 15–18, 2000.

——(2000c). 'The projection of DP (and DegP)'. To appear in Larson (forthcoming).

——(2006). 'Form and position of nominal modifiers in Indo-Iranian'. Paper presented at the Western Conference of Linguistics (WECOL 06), Cal State Fresno, October 29, 2006.

——(forthcoming). *Essays on Shell Structure*. London: Routledge.

——and Marušič, F. (2004). 'On indefinite pronoun structures with APs: Reply to Kishimoto'. *Linguistic Inquiry*, 35: 268–287.

——and Segal, G. (1995). *Knowledge of Meaning: An Introduction to Semantic Theory*. Cambridge, MA: MIT Press.

——and Takahashi, N. (2007). 'Order and interpretation in prenominal relative clauses'. In M. Kelepir and B. Öztürk (eds.), *Proceedings of the Workshop in Altaic Formal Linguistics (WAFL) 2*. MITWPL, 54, 101–120.

Larson, R. and Yamakido, H. (2005). 'Ezafe and the position of nominal modifiers'. Ms., Stony Brook University.

Lasersohn, P. (1995). *Plurality, Conjunction and Events*. Dordrecht: Kluwer.

Lev, I. (2006a). 'Events in glue semantics'. <http://www.stanford.edu/~iddolev/pulc/gmemos/gmemo-events.pdf>

——(2006b). 'Introduction to the syntax–semantics interface using glue semantics'. <http://www.stanford.edu/~iddolev/pulc/gmemos/gmemo-intro.pdf>

Levin, B. and Rappaport Hovav, M. (1995). *Unaccusativity: At the Syntax–Lexical Semantics Interface*. Cambridge, MA: MIT Press.

Levinson, S. C. (1983). *Pragmatics*. Cambridge: Cambridge University Press.

Lewis, D. (1972). 'Psychophysical and theoretical identifications'. *Australasian Journal of Philosophy*, 50: 249–258.

Liberman, M. and Sproat, R. (1992). 'The stress and structure of modified noun phrases in English'. In I. A. Sag and A. Szabolcsi (eds.), *Lexical Matters*. Stanford, CA: CSLI Publications, 131–182.

Link, G. (1983). 'The logical analysis of plurals and mass terms'. In R. Bäuerle, C. Schwarze, and A. von Stechow (eds.), *Meaning, Use and Interpretation of Language*. Berlin: Walter de Gruyter, 302–323.

Löbner, S. (1988). 'Ansätze zu einer integralen semantischen Theorie von Tempus, Aspekt und Aktionsarten'. In V. Ehrich and H. Vater (eds.), *Temporalsemantik: Beiträge zur Linguistik der Zeitreferenz*. Tübingen: Niemeyer, 163–191.

Longobardi, G. (1994). 'Reference and proper names: A theory of N-movement in syntax and logical form'. *Linguistic Inquiry*, 25: 609–665.

Macià, J. (2002). 'Presuposición y significado expresivo'. *Theoria: Revista de Teoria, Historia y Fundamentos de la Ciencia*, 17: 499–513.

MacKay, C. J. (1999). *A Grammar of Misantla Totonac*. Salt Lake City: University of Utah Press.

Mackenzie, I. (2004). 'Topics in Spanish syntax'. Lecture notes, University of Newcastle Upon Tyne. <http://www.staff.ncl.ac.uk/i.e.mackenzie/syntax.htm.>

Maienborn, C. (2001). 'On the position and interpretation of locative modifiers'. *Natural Language Semantics*, 9: 191–240.

——(2003). *Die logische Form von Kopula-Sätzen*. Berlin: Akademie-Verlag.

——(2005). 'On the limits of the Davidsonian approach: The case of copula sentences'. *Theoretical Linguistics*, 31: 275–316.

Marantz, A. (1997). 'No escape from syntax: Don't try morphological analysis in the privacy of your own lexicon'. In A. Dimitriadis, L. Siegel, C. Surek-Clark, and A. Williams (eds.), *Proceedings of the 21st Annual Penn Linguistics Colloquium*. Philadelphia: University of Pennsylvania, 201–225.

——(2001). 'Words'. Ms., MIT.

Marchello-Nizia, C. (2006). *Grammaticalisation et changement linguistique*. Brussels: De Boeck.

Marinis, T. and Panagiotidis, P. (2004). 'Determiner spreading as referential predication'. Ms., Cyprus College.

Martin, F. (2006). *Prédicats statifs, causatifs et résultatifs en discours: sémantique des adjectifs évaluatifs et des verbes psyhologiques*. PhD thesis, Université Libre de Bruxelles.

McCawley, J. (1982). 'Parentheticals and discontinuous constituent structure'. *Linguistic Inquiry*, 13: 91–106.

McConnell-Ginet, S. (1973). *Comparative Constructions in English: A Syntactic and Semantic Analysis*. PhD thesis, University of Rochester.

—— (1982). 'Adverbs and logical form'. *Language*, 58: 144–184.

McLaughlin, F. (2004). 'Is there an adjective class in Wolof?' In R. M. W. Dixon and A. Y. Aikhenvald (eds.), *Adjective Classes: A Cross-Linguistic Typology*. Oxford: Oxford University Press, 242–262.

McNally, L. and Boleda, G. (2004). 'Relational adjectives as properties of kinds'. In O. Bonami and P. C. Hofherr (eds.), *Empirical Issues in Syntax and Semantics*, vol. 5, 179–196.

Miller, P. (1992). *Clitics and Constituents in Phrase Structure Grammar*. New York: Garland.

Mittwoch, A. (2005). 'Do states have Davidsonian arguments? Some empirical considerations'. In C. M. A. Wöllstein (ed.), *Event Arguments: Foundations and Applications*. Tübingen: Niemeyer, 69–88.

Molinier, C. and Levrier, F. (2000). *Grammaire des adverbes*. Genève: Droz.

Montague, R. (1970). 'English as a formal language'. In B. Visentini et al. (eds.), *Linguagi Nella Società e Nella Tecnica*. Milan.

—— (1974). *Formal Philosophy: Selected Papers of Richard Montague*. Yale University Press.

Moore, R. (1993). 'Events, situations, and adverbs'. In M. Bates and R. M. Weischedel (eds.), *Challenges in Natural Language Processing*. Cambridge: Cambridge University Press, 135–145.

Morzycki, M. (2005). *Mediated Modification: Functional Structure and the Interpretation of Modifier Position*. PhD thesis, University of Massachusetts, Amherst.

Mourelatos, A. P. D. (1978). 'Events, processes and states'. *Linguistics & Philosophy*, 2: 415–434.

Muromatsu, K. (2001). 'Adjective ordering as the reflection of a hierarchy in the noun system'. *Linguistic Variation Yearbook*, 1: 181–207.

Neeleman, A., Van de Koot, H., and Doetjes, J. (2004). 'Degree expressions'. *The Linguistic Review*, 21: 1–66.

Newmeyer, F. J. (1992). 'Iconicity and generative grammar'. *Language*, 68: 756–796.

Norde, M. (forthcoming). 'Van suffix tot telwoord tot bijwoord: degrammaticalisering en (re)grammaticalisering van *tig*'. *TABU*, 35: 33–60.

Nunberg, G., Sag, I. A., and Wasow, T. (1994). 'Idioms'. *Language*, 70: 491–538.

Obenauer, H. (1984). 'On the identification of empty categories'. *The Linguistic Review*, 4: 153–202.

Parsons, T. (1970). 'Some problems concerning the logic of grammatical modifiers'. *Synthese*, 21: 320–324.

—— (1990). *Events in the Semantics of English*. Cambridge, MA: MIT Press.

—— (2000). 'Underlying states and time travel'. In J. Higginbotham, F. Pianesi, and A. Varzi (eds.), *Speaking of Events*. Oxford: Oxford University Press, 81–93.

Partee, B. and Rooth, M. (1983). 'Generalized conjunction and type ambiguity'. In R. Bauerle, C. Schwarze, and A. von Stechow (eds.), *Meaning, Use, and Interpretation of Language*. Berlin: De Gruyter, 361–383.

Paul, W. (2005). 'Adjectival modification in Mandarin Chinese and related issues'. *Linguistics*, 43: 757–793.

Peters, S. (1979). 'A truth-conditional formulation of Karttunen's account of presupposition'. *Synthese*. 40: 301–316.

Peterson, P. (1997). *Fact, Proposition, Event*. Dordrecht: Kluwer.

Picallo, C. (1994). 'A mark of specificity in indefinite numerals'. *Catalan Working Papers in Linguistics*, 4: 143–167.

Piñón, C. (1997). 'Achievements in an event semantics'. In A. Lawson and E. Cho (eds.), *Proceedings of SALT 7*: 273–296.

—— (2000). 'Happening gradually'. In L. J. Conathan, J. Good, D. Kavitskaya, A. B. Wulf, and A. C. L. Yu (eds.), *Proceedings of the Twenty-sixth Annual Meeting of the Berkeley Linguistics Society*. Berkeley, CA: Berkeley Linguistics Society, 445–456.

—— (2005). 'Adverbs of completion in an event semantics'. In H. J. Verkuyl, H. de Swart, and A. van Hout (eds.), *Perspectives on Aspect*. Frankfurt am Main: Springer, 149–166.

Pollard, C. and Sag, I. A. (1994). *Head-driven Phrase Structure Grammar*. Stanford, CA: CSLI Publications.

Potts, C. (2005). *The Logic of Conventional Implicatures*. Oxford: Oxford University Press.

Pullum, G. and Huddleston, R. (2002). 'Adjectives and adverbs'. In R. Huddleston and G. Pullum (eds.), *The Cambridge Grammar of the English Language*. Cambridge: Cambridge University Press, 525–595.

Pustejovsky, J. (1995). *The Generative Lexicon*. Cambridge, MA: MIT Press.

Quirk, R., Greenbaum, S., Leech, G., and Svartvik, J. (1978). *A Comprehensive Grammar of the English Language*. London: Longman.

———— (1985). *A Comprehensive Grammar of the English Language*. London: Longman.

Radford, A. (1997). *Syntactic Theory and the Structure of English*. Cambridge: Cambridge University Press.

Ramchand, G. (1997). *Aspect and Predication: The Semantics of Argument Structure*. Oxford: Oxford University Press.

Rappaport Hovav, M. (to appear). 'Lexicalized meaning and the internal temporal structure of events'. In S. Rothstein (ed.), *Crosslinguistic and Theoretical Approaches to the Semantics of Aspect*. Amsterdam: John Benjamins.

—— and Levin, B. (2005). 'Change of state verbs: Implications for theories of argument projection'. In N. Erteschik-Shir and T. Rapoport (eds.), *The Syntax of Aspect*. Oxford: Oxford University Press, 274–286.

Rawlins, K. (2003). 'A study in some adverb denotations'. B.A. honors thesis, University of Massachusetts, Amherst.

Reape, M. (1994). 'Domain union and word-order variation in German'. In J. Nerbonne, K. Netter, and C. Pollard (eds.), *German in HPSG*. Stanford, CA: CSLI Publications, 151–197.

Reichenbach, H. (1947). *Elements of Symbolic Logic*. London: Macmillan.

Rijkhoff, J. (2002). *The Noun Phrase*. Oxford: Oxford University Press.

Ritter, E. (1993). 'Where's gender?' *Linguistic Inquiry*, 24: 795–803.

Rögnvaldsson, E. (1993). 'Collocations in the minimalist framework'. *Lambda*, 18: 107–118.

Rooth, M. (1985). *Association with Focus*, PhD thesis, University of Massachusetts, Amherst.

Rothstein, S. (2004). *Structuring Events: A Study in the Semantics of Lexical Aspect*. Oxford: Blackwell.

Rotstein, C. and Winter, Y. (2004). 'Total adjectives vs. partial adjectives: Scale structure and higher-order modifiers'. *Natural Language Semantics*, 12: 259–288.

Rullmann, H. (1995). *Maximality in the Semantics of Wh-Constructions*, PhD thesis, University of Massachusetts, Amherst.

Sadler, L. and Arnold, D. J. (1994). 'Prenominal adjectives and the phrasal/lexical distinction'. *Journal of Linguistics*, 30: 187–226.

Sag, I. (1973). 'On the state of progress on progressives and statives'. In C.-J. N. Bailey and R. W. Shuy (eds.), *New Ways of Analyzing Variations in English*. Washington, DC: Georgetown University Press, 83–95.

Samiian, V. (1994). 'The Ezafe construction: Some implications for the theory of X-bar syntax'. In M. Marashi (ed.), *Persian Studies in North America*. Bethesda, MD: Iranbooks, 17–41.

Sandstrøm, G. (1993). *When-Clauses and the Temporal Interpretation of Narrative Discourse*. PhD thesis, University of Umeå.

van der Sandt, R. (1992). 'Presupposition projection as anaphora resolution'. *Journal of Semantics*, 9: 333–377.

Schäfer, M. (2002). 'Pure manner adverbs revisited'. In G. Katz, S. Reinhard, and P. Reuter (eds.), *Proceedings of Sinn und Bedeutung VI*. Osnabrück: Institute of Cognitive Science, University of Osnabrück, 311–323.

Schlenker, P. (2007). 'Expressive presuppositions'. To appear in a special issue of *Theoretical Linguistics*.

Schwarzschild, R. (2005). 'Measure phrases as modifiers of adjectives'. *Recherches Linguistiques de Vincennes*, 35: 207–228.

Schwarzschild, R. (2006). 'The role of dimensions in the syntax of noun phrases'. *Syntax*, 9: 67–110.

Scott, G. (2002). 'Stacked adjectival modification and the structure of nominal phrases'. In G. Cinque (ed.), *Functional Structure in DP and IP: The Cartography of Syntactic Structures*. New York: Oxford University Press, 91–120.

Seuren, P. (1973). 'The comparative'. In F. Kiefer and N. Ruwet (eds.), *Generative Grammar in Europe*. Dordrecht: Reidel, 528–564.

—— (1978). 'The structure and selection of positive and negative gradable adjectives'. In D. Farkas, W. M. Jacobsen, and K. W. Todrys (eds.), *Papers from the Parasession on the Lexicon, Chicago Linguistics Society*. Chicago: Chicago Linguistics Society, 336–346.

Shaer, B. (2000). 'Syntactic position and the readings of "manner" adverbs'. *ZAS Papers in Linguistics*, 17: 265–286.

—— (2003). ' "Manner" adverbs and the association theory: Some problems and solutions'. In E. Lang, C. Maienborn, and C. Fabricius-Hansen (eds.), *Modifying Adjuncts*. Berlin: Mouton de Gruyter, 211–259.

Shlonsky, U. (2004). 'The form of Semitic noun phrases'. *Lingua*, 114: 1465–1526.

Siegel, M. (1976a). *Capturing the Adjective*. PhD thesis, University of Massachusetts, Amherst.

—— (1976b). 'Capturing the Russian adjective'. In B. H. Partee (ed.), *Montague Grammar*. New York: Academic Press, 293–309.

Sigurðsson, H. Á. (1992). 'Aspects of the DP analysis of the Icelandic NP'. In A. Holmberg (ed.), *Papers from the Workshop on the Scandinavian Noun Phrase*. Department of General Linguistics, University of Umeå, Report 32. Umeå: Department of General Linguistics, University of Umeå, 119–144.

Simpson, A. (2005). 'Classifiers and DP structure in Southeast Asia'. In G. Cinque and R. S. Kayne (eds.), *The Oxford Handbook of Comparative Syntax*. New York: Oxford, 806–838.

Smith, C. (1964). 'Determiners and relative clauses in generative grammar'. *Language*, 40: 37–52.

—— —— (1991). *The Parameter of Aspect*. Dordrecht: Kluwer.

Smollett, R. (2005). 'Quantized direct objects don't delimit after all'. In H. J. Verkuyl, H. de Swart, and A. van Hout (eds.), *Perspectives on Aspect*. Dordrecht: Springer, 41–59.

Sproat, R. and Shih, C. (1988). 'Prenominal adjectival ordering in English and Mandarin'. In J. Blevins and J. Carter (eds.), *Proceedings of NELS 18*, Amherst: University of Massachusetts GLSA, 465–489.

—— —— (1991). 'The cross-linguistic distribution of adjective ordering restrictions'. In C. Georgopoulos and R. Ishihara (eds.), *Interdisciplinary Approaches to Language*. Dordrecht: Kluwer, 565–593.

Stalnaker, R. C. (1978). 'Assertion'. In P. Cole (ed.), *Syntax and Semantics 9: Pragmatics*. New York: Academic Press, 315–322.

—— (1998) 'On the representation of context'. *Journal of Logic, Language, and Information*, 7: 3–19.

Starke, M. (2004). 'On the inexistence of specifiers and the nature of heads'. In A. Belletti (ed.), *Structures and Beyond: The Cartography of Syntactic Structures*, vol. 3. New York: Oxford University Press, 252–268.

von Stechow, A. (1984). 'Comparing semantic theories of comparison'. *Journal of Semantics*, 3: 1–77.

Stump, G. T. (1981). 'The interpretation of frequency adjectives'. *Linguistics & Philosophy*, 4: 221–257.

Svenonius, P. (1994). 'The structural location of the attributive adjective'. In E. Duncan, D. Farkas, and P. Spaelti (eds.), *The Proceedings of the Twelfth West Coast Conference on Formal Linguistics*. Stanford, CA: CSLI Publications, 439–454.

—— (2005). 'Extending the extension condition to discontinuous idioms'. *Linguistic Variation Yearbook*, 5: 227–263.

—— (2007). '1 . . . 3–2'. In G. Ramchand and C. Reiss (eds.), *Oxford Handbook of Linguistic Interfaces*. Oxford: Oxford University Press, 239–288.

—— and Kennedy, C. (2006). 'Northern Norwegian degree questions and the syntax of measurement'. In M. Frascarelli (ed.), *Phases of Interpretation*. Berlin: Mouton de Gruyter, 133–161.

Szabolcsi, A. (1994). 'The noun phrase'. In F. Kiefer and K. É. Kiss (eds.), *Syntax and Semantics 27: The Syntactic Structure of Hungarian*. San Diego: Academic Press, 179–274.

Tamm, A. (2004). *Relations between Estonian Verbs, Aspect, and Case*. PhD thesis, Eötvös Loránd University, Budapest.

Taranto, G. (2006). *Discourse Adjectives*. New York: Routledge.

Tenny, C. (1994). *Aspectual Roles and the Syntax–Semantics Interface*. Dordrecht: Kluwer.

—— (2000). 'Core events and adverbial modification'. In C. Tenny and J. Pustejovsky (eds.), *Events as Grammatical Objects*. Stanford, CA: CSLI Publications, 285–334.

Thomason, R. and Stalnaker, R. (1973). 'A semantic theory of adverbs'. *Linguistic Inquiry*, 4: 195–220.

Todd, T. (1985). *A Grammar of Dimili (Also Known as Zaza)*. PhD thesis, University of Michigan, Ann Arbor.

Travis, L. (1988). 'The syntax of adverbs'. *Working Papers in Linguistics. Special Issue on Comparative Germanic Syntax*. Department of Linguistics, McGill University.

—— (1994). 'Event phrase and a theory of functional categories'. In P. Koskinen (ed.), *Proceedings of the 1994 Annual Conference of the Canadian Linguistics Association*. Toronto: Department of Linguistics, University of Toronto.

Trombetta, A. (2002). *Las predicaciones no verbales independientes: El caso de los refranes*. Master's thesis, Instituto Universitario Ortega y Gasset, Madrid.

Truswell, R. (2004). *Attributive Adjectives and the Nominals they Modify*. Master's thesis, Oxford University.

Valois, D. (1991). *The Internal Syntax of DP.* PhD thesis, UCLA.

Vanden Wyngaerd , G. (2001). 'Measuring events'. *Language, 77*: 61–90.

Vangsnes, Ø. A. (1999). *The Identification of Functional Architecture.* PhD thesis, University of Bergen.

—— (2001). 'On noun phrase architecture, referentiality, and article systems'. *Studia Linguistica, 55*: 249–299.

Vendler, Z. (1957). 'Verbs and times'. *Philosophical Review, 46*: 143–160.

—— (1967). *Linguistics and Philosophy.* Ithaca, NY: Cornell University Press.

Verkuyl, H. J. (1972). *On the Compositional Nature of the Aspects.* Dordrecht: Reidel.

—— (1993). *A Theory of Aspectuality: The Interaction between Temporal and Atemporal Structure.* Cambridge: Cambridge University Press.

Walker, M. (1992). 'Redundancy in Collaborative Dialogue'. In *The Proceedings of COLING 1992*, 345–351.

Waugh, I. (1977). *A Semantic Analysis of Word Order.* Leiden: E. J. Brill.

Westerstahl, D. (1985). 'Determiners and context sets'. In J. van Bentham and A. ter Meulen (eds.), *Generalized Quantifiers in Natural Language.* Dordrecht: Foris.

Wetzer, H. (1996). *The Typology of Adjectival Predication.* Berlin: Mouton de Gruyter.

Whorf, B. L. (1945). 'Grammatical categories'. *Language, 21*: 1–11.

Williams, E. (1980). 'Predication'. *Linguistic Inquiry, 11*: 203–238.

Williamson, T. (1992). 'Vagueness and ignorance'. *Proceedings of the Aristotelian Society, Supplementary Series, 66*: 14–162.

—— (1994). *Vagueness.* London/New York: Routledge.

—— (1999). 'On the structure of higher-order vagueness'. *Mind, 108*: 127–143.

Winter, Y. (2006). 'Closure and telicity across categories'. In *Proceedings of SALT 16.* Ithaca, New York: CLC Publications. <http://research.nii.ac.jp/salt16/proceedings.html>

Wood, M. (1993). *Categorial Grammars.* London: Routledge.

Wyner, A. (1994). *Boolean Event Lattices and Thematic Roles in the Syntax and Semantics of Adverbial Modification.* PhD thesis, Cornell University.

—— (1998a). 'Subject-oriented adverbs are thematically dependent'. In S. Rothstein (ed.), *Events in Grammar.* Dordrecht: Kluwer, 333–348.

—— (1998b). 'A discourse theory of manner and factive adverbial modification'. In J. Hulstijn and A. Nijholt (eds.), *The Proceedings of Twendial '98: The Formal Semantics and Pragmatics of Dialogue.* Enschede, The Netherlands: University of Twente, 249–267.

Yamakido, H. (2000). 'Japanese attributive adjectives are not (all) relative clauses'. In R. Billerey and B. D. Lillehaugen (eds.), *Proceedings of WCCFL 19.* Somerville, MA: Cascadilla Press, 588–602.

—— (2005). *The Nature of Adjectival Inflection in Japanese.* PhD thesis, Stony Brook University, Stony Brook, NY.

—— (2007). 'The nature of adjectival inflection in Japanese'. In M. Kelepir and B. Öztürk (eds.), *Proceedings of the Workshop in Altaic Formal Linguistics (WAFL) 2. MITWPL, 54*, 365–377.

Yoon, Y. (1996). 'Total and partial predicates and the weak and strong interpretations'. *Natural Language Semantics*, 4: 217–236.

Zadeh, L. A. (1987). 'Fuzzy sets'. In R. R. Yager, S. Ovchinnikov, R. M. Tong, and H. T. Nguyen (eds.), *Fuzzy Sets and Applications: Selected Papers by L. A. Zadeh*. New York: John Wiley & Sons, 29–44.

Zamparelli, R. (2000). *Layers in the Determiner Phrase*. New York: Garland.

Zanuttini, R. (1996). 'On the relevance of tense for sentential negation'. In A. Belletti and L. Rizzi (eds.), *Parameters and Functional Heads. Essays in Comparative Syntax*. New York: Oxford University Press, 181–207.

—— (1997). *Negation and Clausal Structure: A Comparative Study of Romance Languages*. New York: Oxford University Press.

Zavala, R. (2000). 'Multiple classifier systems in Akatek (Mayan)'. In G. Senft (ed.), *Systems of Nominal Classification*. Cambridge: Cambridge University Press, 114–146.

Zhang, N. N. (2004). 'Representing specificity by the internal order of indefinites'. Ms., National Chung Cheng University, Taiwan.

Zimmerman, M. (2000). 'Pluractional quantifiers: The *occasional* construction in English and German'. In B. Jackson and T. Matthews (eds.), *Proceedings of SALT X*. Ithaca, New York: CLC Publications, 290–306.

Zucchi, A. (1993). *The Language of Propositions and Events*. Dordrecht: Kluwer.

Zwarts, J. (1992). *X-Syntax X-Semantics*. PhD thesis, Universiteit Utrecht.

—— (2004). 'Competition between word meanings: The polysemy of (a)round'. In C. Meier and M. Weisgerber (eds.), *Proceedings of SuB8*. Konstanz: University of Konstanz Linguistics Working Papers, 349–360.

Zwicky, A. M. and Sadock, J. M. (1975). 'Ambiguity tests and how to fail them'. In J. Kimball (ed.), *Syntax and Semantics 4*. New York: Academic Press, 1–36.

Index

OXFORD STUDIES IN THEORETICAL LINGUISTICS